Computer network architectures

**ELECTRICAL ENGINEERING COMMUNICATIONS
AND SIGNAL PROCESSING SERIES**

Series Editor   Raymond Pickholtz
                      The George Washington University

Computer Network Architectures
Anton Meijer and Paul Peeters

Challenges in Telecommunications
and Information Handling for the
New Administration
Conference Proceedings

Another Work of Interest

IEEE Communications Society's
TUTORIALS IN MODERN COMMUNICATIONS
*Victor B. Lawrence, Joseph L. LoCicero,
and Laurence B. Milstein*

Computer network architectures

Anton Meijer
and **Paul Peeters**

COMPUTER SCIENCE PRESS

Text set in 10/12 pt Linotron 202 Times, printed and bound in Great Britain at The Pitman Press, Bath

First published in Great Britain 1982 by Pitman Books, Ltd. First published in the U.S.A. 1983 by Computer Science Press, Inc.

Computer Science Press, Inc.   Pitman Books Ltd.
11 Taft Ct.   128 Long Acre
Rockville, Maryland 20850 U.S.A.   London WC2E 9 AN
ISBN 0-914894-41-2   Great Britain

2 3 4 5 6   88 87 86 85 84

Library of Congress Cataloging in Publication Data

Meijer, Anton, 1941–
    Computer network architectures.

    Includes index.
    1. Computer networks.   2. Computer architecture.
I. Peeters, Paul, 1941–   . II. Title.
TK5105.5.M44   1983   001.64 ′404   82-22165
ISBN 0-914894-41-2

Contents

Introduction

This book is about computer network architectures. It is, however, not a text on architecture in general, or on the functions required for and techniques used in computer networks. Other books have been written on these subjects and they give excellent coverage.

What is missing, however, for many data processing professionals and students is a combination of the 'theoretical' and 'abstract' world with their daily life and concerns with respect to computer communications. It is a fact that most of them do not deal with private, experimental systems but are confronted with a wide variety of product offerings from many manufacturers, from which they have to select or which they have to interconnect. It is the purpose of this book to bring those two worlds more closely together.

The book is organized in three parts. Part 1 introduces the conceptual framework for the description of other architectures. In Chapter 1, an intuitive introduction is given to the functions required of a network and the architectural structure in which they can be placed. Chapter 2 builds on this 'intuitive model' by introducing a more formal model, the ISO Reference Model of Open Systems Interconnection. Although this model is not yet final at the time of writing—it is now a Draft International Standard—it has already gained such wide acceptance that it can be used to advantage to map various proprietary architectures. The remaining chapters of Part 1 illustrate the Reference Model in more detail through a discussion of various standards that have been defined with respect to the model.

In Part 2, a number of proprietary architectures is discussed. From the ever increasing number of architectures that have been or are being defined, we had to select a few that we considered a reasonable cross-section of what exists. The selection should, however, not be taken as any sort of value judgement on the architectures not mentioned here. One criterion was that the architectures selected must cover all layers of the Reference Model. For that reason, the reader will not find in this part of the book any mention of Local Area Networks. Although a very important class of network, they usually cover only the lower layers of the Reference Model and as such are outside the intended scope of this book. Another selection criterion was the 'age' of the architectures involved. Some of the architectures described were—at least initially—defined well before the work on the Reference Model started, others developed more or less in parallel.

In textbooks on computer networks that focus on the network functions and protocols only, references are sometimes made to existing experimental or commercially operated networks or to proprietary architectures. Although useful as illustrations, such references do not give an adequate overall view of such an architecture. It is our purpose to give that overall view, in relation to the Reference Model. Part 2 is therefore divided into one chapter for each architecture, instead of one chapter for each layer of the model. In each description, we have adhered as much as possible to the terminology used by the particular manufacturer. At the end of each chapter, the architecture is mapped against the Reference Model, to put it in perspective for further comparison. This mapping, it must be emphasized, is only to be used as a tool in comparing architectures. It cannot be used to judge the relative merits of one architecture over another or to decide on questions of connectability. For those questions, more detailed analysis of the various protocols is needed in view of the intended purpose. We have not given any such judgements at all; they are left to the reader where and when necessary.

The last part of the book, Part 3, is devoted to a description of Public Data Network offerings that are coming into existence everywhere in the world. In addition, the problem of the interconnection of proprietary networks is discussed in this part. After a general discussion of the problem, a specific example is described. Since there is not much experience at hand about the interconnection of various proprietary architectures directly, we have chosen an example in which one of us was involved, the interconnection of various architectures *through* a public network based on recommendation X.25.

The appendices to the book contain a summary comparison (*at the layer level*) of the architectures discussed.

Most of the material used for this book was prepared for lectures while we were faculty members at IBM's European Systems Research Institute in La Hulpe, Belgium. The information was gathered from various sources in the public domain, including manufacturers' brochures. We are indebted to these companies for making these brochures available. Some of the manufacturers also responded to our request to read the chapter on their particular architecture. They made available comments to improve the quality and the accuracy of the description. We are particularly indebted to Mr Stuart Wecker of Digital Equipment Corporation, Mr Robert F. Lakin of Burroughs' Corporation, Mr Roger Reynolds of International Computers Ltd, and Messrs Philippe DeBacker, Marc Levilion and Bob Niewold of IBM for their cooperation.

We also would like to acknowledge the help of our management and our colleagues at the Systems Research Institute at La Hulpe, both for providing an environment in which the courses on which the book is based could be developed and for providing assistance while we were writing it.

We also would like to thank ISO, the International Organization for Standardization, for granting us permission to reproduce, as an appendix, ISO/DIS 7498 established by the ISO technical committee 97. In our technical area of data processing, ISO has published a very large number of International Standards which has been recently grouped into three handbooks representing an extremely valuable source of information.

Finally, although we are employed by IBM, any opinions expressed in this book are solely our own responsibility and are in no way meant to suggest that these are or are not official IBM positions.

Anton Meijer
Paul Peeters
February 1982

Part 1   The Reference Model and related standards

1 Computer network architecture: an intuitive model

1.1 Introduction

When we talk about computer networks, we can start with the more limited notion of a terminal access network. In such a network, the operator at a terminal is given access to the facilities available in the network. She may access a computer to execute a particular program, access a remote database, communicate with another operator, etc. In an ideal network environment, however, all these facilities should appear to the operator *as if* they were located in her terminal (Fig. 1.1a). More specifically, the operator should not be aware of the fact that actually the resources she is dealing with are physically located somewhere else. This means that there must be 'something', preferably transparent to the operator, that maps the actual resource into what she thinks it is (Fig. 1.1b). Of course, the 'something' has to use some trick to move data from one place to another. This will be a more or less complicated network, consisting of telecommunications lines and 'nodes' that are interconnected by these lines (Fig. 1.1c).

Once we have such a 'something', we assume that it will also perform those functions for other operators, since they may also want to use the resources. Otherwise, it would not make sense to have the resources remote! So, another job for our 'something' is to hide from the operator the fact that other people also use the resources and the 'something' itself (Fig. 1.1d).

The total of this (physical) network and the functions required from the 'something' is what we will call a *communication system*, or also the 'network', but now from a logical point of view.

So, our communication system performs all the functions outlined above on behalf of terminal operators. It is, however, a relatively small step to abstract from the 'human' operator and let the communication system provide the functions on behalf of any form of intelligent process, for example, program-to-program communication. In the following discussion, we will therefore no longer talk about operators, but about *end-users*,

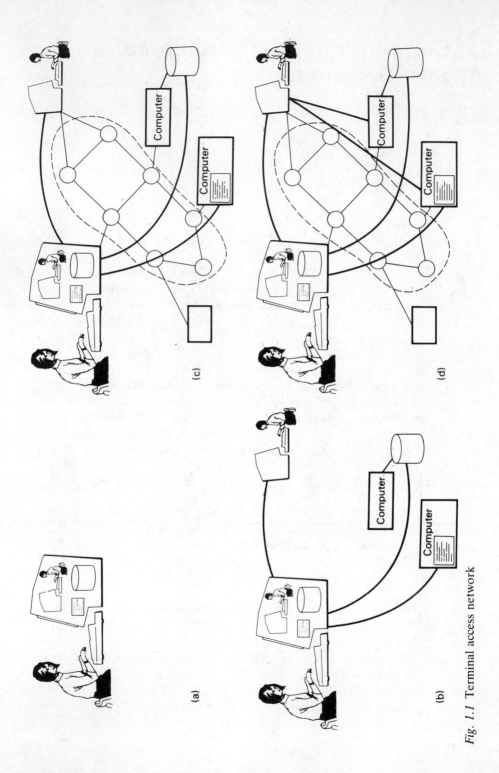

Fig. 1.1 Terminal access network

which can be any operators, but generally will be some programmed processes.

In this chapter, we will look at the structuring of the functions that are required in such a communication system. We will do it from a conceptual point of view and try to find out what the relationships between these functions are.

A good example of the functions involved when two parties engage in a dialog is the conversation between human beings in general. In this communication between people, three levels can be distinguished [1]: cognitive, language and transmission.

At the cognitive level, we find concepts such as understanding and knowledge. For a conversation to be meaningful, it is mandatory that both parties have at least some understanding of what it is all about. The reading of this book, which is one form of human communication, though one-way only, can be taken as an example: it would be useless to read it without at least some basic understanding of data processing.

At the second level, the language level, we are no longer concerned with the subject (or the content) of the conversation. At this level, the problem is how to put the concepts that are being communicated into words. If someone in, say, the United States makes a telephone call to a hotel in Japan and the receptionist answering the call only speaks Japanese, it is rather doubtful that the reservation he wants gets booked. Even though the receptionist will know perfectly well the concept 'reservation', there is no way to let him know that that is what the call is all about.

At the third level, the transmission level, neither the concept nor the language has any relevance. The only problem is how the appropriate physical means can be used to get the information transferred. Here, a useful transmission technique must be selected, based on the circumstances and the capabilities of both parties. It is, for example, not very useful to select letter writing as a means of communicating with a blind person.

Two aspects of this layered structure should be taken into account here:

a All the layers are mutually independent. Although they use the functions of lower layers, it is not important how that function is performed.
b Two communicating parties will agree in advance about the aspects of the conversation at *each* layer. This results in *protocols* being established at each layer. Examples of such protocols in human communications are:

i When somebody speaks, we do not usually interrupt him. We wait until he is finished, then we can speak; depending on the protocol, we either reply to what he said, or we just continue our own thoughts.
ii When we answer a letter, we usually put in some phrase such as 'In response to your letter dated . . .', in order to identify clearly to which original message (i.e. letter) the response is related.

1.2 Structure of a computer network

Using a similar layered approach, we will now discuss a conceptual architecture for computer networks. The terminology used is the same as for the Reference Model of Open Systems Interconnection, defined by the International Standards Organization [2]. The Reference Model itself will be dealt with in more detail in the next chapter. In the 'intuitive' approach used here, we will arrive at a layering of functions, which is somewhat different from the current 'interpretation' of the Reference Model. This should not distract the reader too much: the emphasis is here on the introduction of the concept, not so much on actual correspondence with the model. (The model itself, as it has evolved over the years, has changed in some areas from what we consider a more natural ordering.)

We define the basic function of the network as: to provide a reliable transportation of data between end-users of the network and to support meaningful communication between them. As explained above, these end-users need not be human operators using a terminal—they can also be application programs and so on. For the purpose of generality in the following discussion, we will consider the end-users as being 'processes' without further defining them. These processes reside in the top-most layer of our architectural model, the *Application Layer* (Fig. 1.2), where they 'process' the information that is being exchanged.

Level	Layer
7	Application layer
6	Presentation layer
5	Session layer
4	Transport layer
3	Network layer
2	Data link layer
1	Physical layer

Fig. 1.2 The layered structure

As the task of the network is to transport data between end-users, we do not want these end-users to be aware of the actual mechanism. It should make no difference whether they are communicating directly or via a more or less complex network. This transparency requirement can be made even stronger by requiring that both end-users should also be transparent to each other for those characteristics that are not really relevant to the conversation itself. In the above example of human communication, the language was used as an example. The last requirement states that both end-users should not be bothered by each other's language: a function (i.e. translation) should be provided that performs this shielding.

To achieve this shielding, we define a functional layer as in Fig. 1.2, called the *Presentation Layer*. It contains all those functions that are similar to the translator in the above example. Some more specific functions in the case of a network are

a Presentation of the data in a message: code conversion, compression/expansion of redundant data, use of standard lay-outs for display terminals and/or printers.
b Remote file access, either at the record level or at the total file transfer level.
c The *Virtual Terminal* concept. In this, *standard* terminals are defined with specific characteristics. One end-user can generate data for one of these standard terminals, and the presentation service at the other end will translate it to the specific device control and configuration of its end-user. (Note that the particular standard terminal to be used is selected via a protocol agreement when the communication is established.)

With this Presentation Layer, we have made the end-users as independent of each other's characteristics as possible, such that they can concentrate on the conversation itself.

Next, we introduce a layer that is responsible for the relation between the two end-users, the *Session Layer*. This layer establishes the relation between the two end-users, maintains the integrity of it and controls the data exchange between the two partners.

When a relation or session is established, both session partners are only aware of the 'other' partner in the session. The Session Layer and the lower layers should shield them from the presence of other end-users and conversations between these other end-users. The Session Layer must translate the notion of the 'other' into the identification of a particular end-user in the network. An important aspect of an architecture is, at this level, the specification of how sessions and individual end-users are being identified, i.e. naming conventions and/or addressing schemes.

Another important task of the Session Layer is to make sure that the session is orderly. It should

a check the sequence of the messages in case lower layers do not guarantee delivery and sequence;
b relate messages and the responses to them, using mechanisms such as sequence numbers;
c control the way in which the conversation is carried out, i.e. control the rules for the dialog.

Although the Session Layer is aware of the identity of the partner in the conversation and coordinates the message flow between both partners, it does not know *where* the partner is situated in the network. It is the job of the next layer, the *Transport Layer*, to create a 'transport pipe' between both end-users using the physical transport mechanisms in the network. Such a transport pipe has the same effect as the plumbing in a house: when we throw water in the sink, we know it will go to the sewage (i.e. *where*), but not precisely *how* it will get there. The exact path of the plumbing is not relevant for the function.

Two important functions that can be located in the Transport Layer are

a breaking messages up into 'packets' and reassembling the messages at the destination;
b applying flow control to the packet stream on the transport connection.

This is not the place to elaborate on the principles of packet switching itself. Suffice it to state that, when the communication system is based on the principle of packet switching, the mapping of messages onto packets and the reassembly could take place in the Transport Layer. The next higher layer (Session) should not be aware of the particular technique used in the transport system: it relates end-users to each other and they exchange complete messages. The length of these messages should be an agreement between the end-users and not be affected by considerations about the mechanisms used in between. As we will discuss below, the next lower layer, network control, is a layer that routes individual messages through the actual topology of the network. No relation between individual messages is apparent there, but the limitations on the length of each message posed by the mechanisms used must be taken into account. We therefore call the messages at this level *packets*. Messages are mapped by the Transport Layer into one or more of these packets and vice versa.

At the Session Level, we discussed synchronization of the dialog. It allows for an orderly exchange between the session partners. At the Transport Level, we need another form of synchronization, called *flow control*. Although all sessions using the system may behave properly in terms of their dialogs, the aggregate traffic from all these sessions may be more than the total system can accommodate. For that reason, there must also be a flow control mechanism across the transport connection that will accept a certain number of packets into the transport connection and only accept more if they can be handled properly at the destination side. Later, we will see that a requirement may exist for strong interaction between the Transport Layer and the next layer, the *Network Layer*, to avoid congestion (build-up of packets) along the physical route that is used for a transport connection.

For the creation and maintenance of the logical path used by the Transport Layer, a route has to be found through the network based on its configuration (connectivity) and possibly on other factors as well. This is the main function of the next layer, called the *Network Layer*. In order to make the choice for the best route, the Network Layer can use several techniques. The architecture can either exclude some of these, make them optional or specify them as mandatory. Some examples of these techniques are

a Fixed routing, where each route is determined once and for all when the network is generated. The elements in the Network Layer need to use only fixed tables to find the route to a certain destination.
b Alternate path routing, where routes are established as in fixed routing, but alternate routes, to be used when the normal route fails, are also given.
c Dynamic or adaptive routing, where the route is established dynamically at each moment, so as to find the best use of the available resources and on the other hand to minimize the delay of a message through the network. In this case, of course, a lot more 'intelligence' is needed in the network nodes, because information has to be collected and exchanged between nodes about the state of affairs.

Independent of the routing technique chosen, the result will be that each message (or packet) follows a path through the network that consists of a sequence of transmission links and network nodes. The task of the Network Layer is then to select in each node the proper outgoing link to reach the next node along the path. Since many paths may be routed through the same node, resource (buffer allocation) problems may arise in this node. This constraint on resources is usually called '(*local*) congestion'. A simple example of a network, where local congestion may occur in spite of proper flow control, is a star network. This is a network in which all nodes are directly connected to one central node. The central node can easily become congested since all traffic flows through it.

If local congestion spreads through the network, it may lead to *global* congestion. This may eventually completely lock the network, i.e. no traffic can flow any more. It is a task of the Network Layer to prevent local congestion and to take adequate measures if a problem still arises. When adaptive routing schemes are used, these measures are an inherent part of the scheme itself since congested nodes will automatically be avoided. But even in this case, and certainly in the case of fixed-routing schemes, interaction with the Transport Layer may be required to prevent additional traffic from entering the network until the congestion is eased away.

The actual path through the network is a sequence of nodes and transmission links. These links can be 'normal' telephone lines, but also satellite or microwave connections, etc. The next layer, the *Data Link Layer*, must make sure that messages that are presented to it for transmission do indeed reach the other end of that link without corruption and independently of the actual physical transmission technology used.

This function is required because the physical processes used for the transmission may damage or destroy a message. Some examples are

a The transmission is subject to more or less serious disturbances, such as signal distortion, noise or switching impulses, that may corrupt one or more bits in the message. The sender should therefore add some redundancy to the message (usually a cyclic test code), based on which the receiving side can check whether an error has occurred or not.

b After a message has been received, the sender must be notified in some way about the result of the transmission, i.e. whether an error occurred or not, etc. Since the transmission capacity of the links is finite (e.g. 2400, 4800 or even 48k bits/s) it takes some time before the message is completely transmitted. In addition, it takes time for the message to pass through the link, because of the finite velocity with which the signals are propagated on the link. This velocity is less than or equal to the speed of light, which results, for example, in a propagation delay of approximately 250 ms on a satellite link. This means that the sender must wait a certain time before he can reasonably expect an acknowledgement of the message. If this acknowledgement does not arrive before such a *time-out* expires, the sender must assume that either the message or its acknowledgement was lost on the link. In that case, he must resend the message and the receiver should be able to detect the duplication if the acknowledgement but not the message had been lost.

For efficiency reasons, it is often possible that more than one station use the same link. In such a 'multipoint' or 'multidrop' configuration, link management must make sure that stations do not send at the same time and thus destroy each other's signal. Alternatively, link management has to be able to recover in a situation were stations do send simultaneously. One technique is to divide the available capacity among the stations as needed: one of the stations is responsible for this division, the 'master' or 'primary'. This station *polls* the others, the 'slaves' or 'secondaries', one after the other, in order to give them permission to send.

The last layer is the *Physical Layer*. This layer contains functions to perform the direct translation of the logical information that must be transmitted (bits) into the physical phenomena that make the transmission possible: electric pulses, etc. It is at this level that we find, for example, a modem (modulator/demodulator) that modulates a carrier wave with the bit pattern to be transmitted.

In the preceding discussion, we have introduced step by step the functional layers from which a network architecture can be built. We placed the end-users in this structure in the Application Layer, just above the Presentation Layer. Here, the processing functions of the end-users are localized. Although most of this layer is not defined in an architecture, as far as the application is concerned, some network functions can also be placed in this layer. An example is Network Management. Such a network

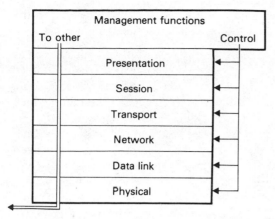

Fig. 1.3 Interaction of management functions with the layers

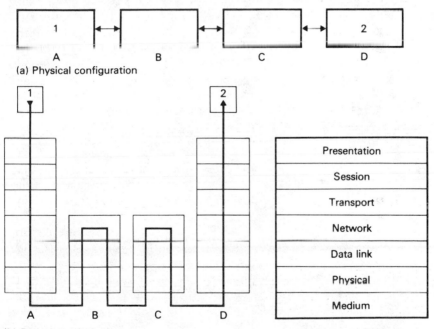

(a) Physical configuration

(b) Path through the layers

Fig. 1.4 Use of intermediate nodes

management function controls all the resources in the network. It may activate new links or bring links down, it may indicate new routes, it may enable or prevent session establishment, etc. The 'decision power' may be distributed among nodes or be centralized in one node. In either case, there must be a 'local representative' in every node to perform the locally required actions. These local functions belong logically to the Application Layer and they use, like any other end-user, the normal communication facilities of the network for their mutual conversation. In each of the nodes, these management functions will have internal interactions with *all* layers to exercise their control function (Fig. 1.3).

Usually, we will find all layers that we have defined, in all nodes of a network. For a particular session, however, for which the transport connection includes several 'intermediate' nodes, a message will not be handled by all layers in all nodes. In the intermediate nodes, the Network Layer will be the highest layer that is used (as shown in Fig. 1.4).

1.3 Communication inside the network

The main reason for the existence of a network is to make the communication between end-users possible, while at the same time allowing the sharing of available resources and providing better availability, etc. For the proper operation of the network, it is also necessary to provide communication between equivalent layers of the architecture in different nodes. For some functions, this can be done in the form of separate messages that are transmitted through the network; for example, the messages to create a new session. For other functions, the information is always related to a particular message and should therefore accompany it, like the address of the receiver. For this reason, every layer in the network adds its own information to a message in the form of a *header* and a *trailer*, although either one may be 'null' (Fig. 1.5).

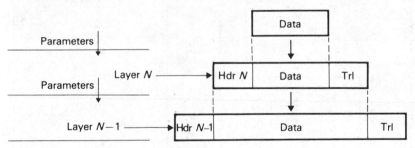

Fig. 1.5 Use of headers and trailers

The combination header+message+trailer is interpreted by the next layer as a message in its own right. This layer envelopes it with another header/trailer pair. In this way, the structure of the system is reflected in the message with its envelopes. Each receiving layer removes the envelope that relates to it and passes the remainder up to the next layer or takes whatever other action is necessary. In this context, any layer may take more than one message that it receives from the higher layer and put them together inside the same envelope. Or it may do the opposite: split one message into several pieces, each of which is wrapped in a separate envelope.

Any architecture must define these envelopes very precisely, in order that different implementations of the same architecture can be included in one network. However, the communication between adjacent layers, which is the mechanism to achieve communication between equivalent layers, should be specified only partly by an architecture. The type of information passed between the layers is the only relevant part and not *how* that information is passed. That remains the responsibility of the product designer, who has to include a vertical cross-section of the architecture in his particular product.

Another important aspect of the architecture is to specify the *protocols* in addition to the message types and the formats of messages and envelopes. This means that agreements about the sequence in which certain messages may occur and the actions which must be taken when errors are detected must be defined. In a complex architecture, it is very difficult to make sure that the protocols perform correctly and achieve what they are intended for. An important field of research is therefore the formal description and verification of these protocols. Description tools are available, such as Finite State Machines, formal grammars, etc., that can also be used to investigate the correctness of the protocols [3].

In this chapter, we have given a brief introduction to the concept of layering for a network architecture. We have used more or less intuitive notions to arrive at the functions that are required in various layers:

a What does the partner *look like*?   Presentation
b *Who* is the partner?   Session
c *Where* is the partner?   Transport
d Along which route do we *get there*?   Network
e How do we make *each step* in that route?   Link
f How do we use the *medium* for that step?   Physical

These notions, although good enough for a general introduction, are not adequate for a precise definition. In the following chapter, we will discuss the Reference Model of Open Systems Interconnection that was defined by the International Standards Organization using more precise rules than we have used so far.

References

1 Cypser, R. J., *Communications architecture for distributed systems*, Addison-Wesley, 1978
2 International Standards Organization, ISO/TC97: *Information processing systems. Open Systems Interconnection—Basic Reference Model*, Draft International Standard ISO/DIS 7498, Apr. 1982. [Reproduced in Appendix A]
3 Bochmann, G. V. and Sunshine, C., Formal methods in communication protocol design, *IEEE Trans. Comm.*, vol. Com-28, no. 4, Apr. 1980, pp. 624–631

2 The Reference Model of Open Systems Interconnection

2.1 Introduction

In Chapter 1 we introduced the intuitive need for a network architecture based on a layered approach. Of course, there is nothing new about this. For several years, the layering concept has been recognized in computer science, most notably after Dijkstra's work on the THE operating system [1]. In recent years, fundamental research has been done in this area with respect to the communications environment and a prominent example of this is Visser's thesis on interfaces [2], in which he formulates the communications problem.

In the International Standards Organization, a number of working groups have been involved in the definition of a *Reference Model of Open Systems Interconnection* [3]. At the time of writing, the Reference Model has obtained the status of Draft International Standard. Because of its importance, the full text of the draft is included in this book as Appendix A. The ISO defines with this model a generalized view of a layered architecture, such that it can be used as a model for the interconnection of systems.

Some clarification of the word 'system' is in place here. One is tempted to regard as a system something big, complex, etc., etc. . . . In the Reference Model, however, a system can be anything from a simple terminal to a total complex network. It follows, then, that the Reference Model can be used to tackle different problems: both the interconnection of two pieces of equipment and the interconnection of two networks can be described using the Reference Model. Moreover, the Reference Model itself can then be used as a model for a network architecture (although that is not what it was defined for).

In this chapter, we discuss the Model, as it is described by the ISO working groups, only in its generality. In addition, we will describe, at some of the layers, standards that may be applied to those layers. Some of these have already been defined, others are still in the process of being defined. For both cases, the reader should, however, get a better feeling of what is and can be achieved by standardizing such important concepts.

2.2 General overview

As explained above, the term 'system' in Open Systems Architecture is very wide. Open Systems Interconnection (OSI) refers to standardized procedures for the exchange of information among terminal devices, computers, people, networks, processes, etc., that are 'open' to one another for this purpose by virtue of their mutual use of these procedures.

'Openness' does not imply any particular systems implementation, technology or interconnection means, but rather refers to the mutual recognition and support of the standardized information exchange procedures. OSI is thus concerned only with the exchange of information between systems and not with the internal workings of those systems.

The layers that are defined in OSI have already been used in Chapter 1 (Fig. 1.2). It is important to realize that this definition is somewhat arbitrary. In Chapter 1, we have 'intuitively' introduced these layers and the division at which we arrived does appeal to common sense. The ISO working groups used somewhat more formal techniques, with a set of 13 criteria to decide on which layers must be defined and what functions must be allocated to each of those layers. They do, however, make the comment [3 (Section 6.2)] that 'It may be difficult to prove that any particular layering selected is the best possible solution'. The most important aspect is, indeed, the ordering of the functions in the respective layers to achieve the total hierarchy and not the specific grouping into the layers, as long as there is a consensus based on the criteria mentioned that the grouping is adequate.

All layers in OSI have a defined theoretical structure that is the same for all of them, except for the highest and the lowest (as boundary problems). In the next section, we briefly introduce this theoretical structure. For more detail, the reader is referred to Appendix A.

In each of the following sections, we review the specific functions of one layer in the Reference Model, starting with the lowest layer, the Physical Layer. In Appendix B, a list of services and functions is given for each layer of the Reference Model. For ease of reference, this list is directly compiled from the text of the Draft Standard. It is used in the same format in later chapters, when specific architectures are discussed.

2.3 The theoretical model

In this section, we introduce briefly a number of terms that are used in the official documentation of the Reference Model. We do, however, keep this to the minimum that is required to understand the comparison made in later chapters between proprietary architectures and the Reference Model.

The Reference Model is concerned with the interconnection of Open Systems. For the purpose of the description of this interconnection, these systems are considered to be composed of an ordered structure of subsystems (Fig. 2.1).

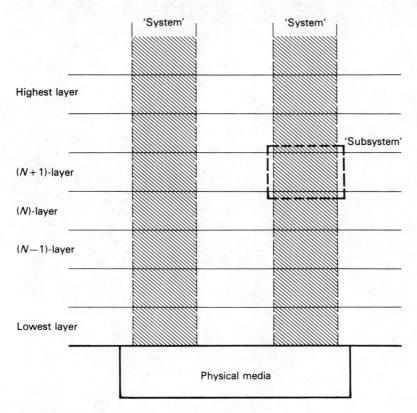

Fig. 2.1 The layering in cooperating open systems

Each subsystem provides certain services to a subsystem of higher rank. In fact, these services are provided by *entities* in the subsystem, if necessary in cooperation with entities in subsystems of the same rank. All subsystems of the same rank, or, equivalently, all entities in these subsystems together form a *layer* of that rank. In the following description, we focus on an arbitrary layer, the (N)-layer. The entities in this layer are called the (N)-entities (Fig. 2.2).

The (N)-layer provides services to the next higher layer, the $(N+1)$-layer. In order to provide the services, the (N)-entities perform certain functions. Sometimes, an (N)-entity needs the cooperation of another (N)-entity which does not reside in the same system. It must then communicate with such an entity, using the services of the next lower layer, the $(N-1)$-layer.

In order to allow for meaningful communication between entities, rules are defined to which the entities must adhere. These rules are called *protocols*. For example, when the (N)-entities communicate, they obey the (N)-protocols.

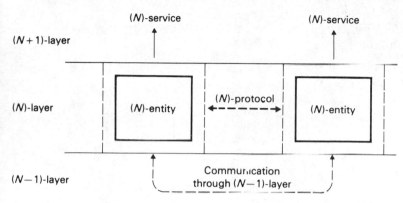

Fig. 2.2 Entities in a layer

Protocols are defined for *peer*-entity communication. It is also necessary to specify precisely how an (N)-entity can communicate with an $(N-1)$-entity in order to request an $(N-1)$-service. For that purpose, *service-access-points* are defined in each layer, which can be used by a next higher layer according to a defined interface. An $(N-1)$-service-access-point is identified by an $(N-1)$-address (or $(N-1)$-service-access-point-address in full). Quite a level of detail is specified in the Reference Model on how (N)-entities and $(N-1)$-entities can connect to $(N-1)$-service-access-points and how they exchange information across the interface. Here, we discuss only the basic exchange. The reader is referred to Appendix A for more detail.

Remember that an $(N+1)$-entity requests a service of an (N)-entity through an (N)-service-access-point. This (N)-entity may need to communicate with a peer (N)-entity, using an $(N-1)$-connection. The unit of information exchanged in this communication consists of two parts:

a The (N)-service-data-unit, the data that the (N)-entities need in order to *perform* the functions for the service requested by the $(N+1)$-entity.

b (N)-protocol-control-information, which is the information exchanged between the (N)-entities to *coordinate* their operation.

The combination of (N)-service-data-unit and (N)-protocol-control-information is called an (N)-protocol-data-unit. Actually, the (N)-service-data-unit need not always be present, since sometimes the (N)-entities may only need to coordinate.

In order to get the data-units to the correspondent entity, the (N)-entities must request the service of an $(N-1)$-*connection* between them. For that purpose, communication across the layer boundary is achieved via an $(N-1)$-service-access-point, to which the (N)-entity attaches. The information passed across the boundary is called

a the $(N-1)$-interface-control-information, used to coordinate the (N)- and $(N-1)$-entities, and
b the $(N-1)$-interface-data, which normally contains the (N)-protocol-data-unit (see above).

The combination of the two, i.e. all information passed between the two layers is called the $(N-1)$-interface-data-unit.

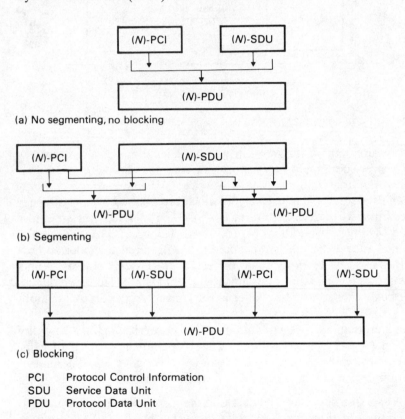

(a) No segmenting, no blocking

(b) Segmenting

(c) Blocking

PCI	Protocol Control Information
SDU	Service Data Unit
PDU	Protocol Data Unit

Fig. 2.3 Segmenting and blocking

In this context, we should also mention the concepts of *blocking* and *segmenting*. Blocking is defined in the (N)-layer as the combination of several (N)-service-data-units and their associated (N)-protocol-control-information into one (N)-protocol-data-unit. Segmenting is more or less the reverse of this. It is defined as the mapping of one (N)-service-data-unit into several (N)-protocol-data-units, each with its own (N)-protocol-control-information (refer to Fig. 2.3).

This process of exchanging data-units, etc., between layers is repeated for every layer, with the exception of the highest layer, where there is no (N+1)-entity to be served as such, and the lowest layer, where there is no formal (N−1)-entity but the actual physical medium.

An important concept in the Reference Model is also the *connection*, which we have mentioned already several times. An (N)-connection is an association between the (N)-addresses of the (N)-service-access-points that serve the (N+1)-entities. Only one (N+1)-entity at a time can be associated with an (N)-service-access-point. However, the service-access-point may be associated with several other (N)-service-access-points. An (N+1)-entity can distinguish all the (N)-connections that terminate in its (N)-service-access-point through a unique (N)-connection-endpoint-identifier for each connection.

In each layer, two types of service-data-unit are defined: a (normal) (N)-service-data-unit and an *expedited* (N)-service-data-unit. Expedited (N)-service-data-units *may* be delivered across the connection before normal ones, even when the latter were submitted earlier; they will *not* be delivered *after* normal data-units that were submitted later.

Now that we have introduced some of the main concepts of the structuring of the Reference Model, we can discuss each of the layers, stating its main functions, as we did in the intuitive model in Chapter 1. We start the description at the bottom of the structure, with the Physical Layer, and then build each successive layer on top.

2.4 Physical Layer

The Physical Layer is responsible for the transparent transmission of bit streams across the physical interconnection of systems. The layer therefore contains all those functions that are required for this connection. Two configurations are defined for the physical-connection on which the transmission takes place: it can be point-to-point or it can be multipoint. Particularly in the latter case, when there are multiple endpoints of the physical-connection, the Physical Layer must provide the using data-link-entities with a means to identify the endpoint where a correspondent data-link-entity is attached.

The physical-connection can be operated in the Full-Duplex mode or in the Half-Duplex mode. The transmission can be either bit-serial or 'n'-bit parallel. Whichever form is used, the Physical Layer must deliver bits in the same order in which they were offered for transmission by the data-link-entity.

The physical-connection may be a concatenation of various data circuits, as is the case in circuit switching. Once such a switched circuit is established, it behaves as one physical-connection. This means that the switching points in the intermediate systems are no longer visible above the Physical Layer, once the 'switches' have been set.

A summary list of the services offered by and the functions performed in the Physical Layer is given in Appendix B. It is used in later chapters to compare specific architectures with the Reference Model. The specifications in the Physical Layer can be divided into four areas:

a Mechanical—such as the dimensions of plugs, allocations of pins, etc.
b Electrical—such as the voltage levels on wires, etc.
c Functional—for instance, what is the meaning of the defined voltage levels on certain wires?
d Procedural—the rules that apply to the various functions, sequences in which events may occur, etc.

Examples of standards (or recommendations) in these areas are:

Mechanical   ISO/DP 4902: *37 pin and 9 pin DTE–DCE interface connector pin assignments* (1980).

Electrical   CCITT Recommendation V.28: *Electrical characteristics for unbalanced double-current interchange circuits.*

Functional   CCITT Recommendation X.24: *List of definitions for interchange of circuits between Data Terminal Equipment (DTE) and Data Circuit-Terminating equipment (DCE) on Public Data Networks* (1976).

Procedural   CCITT Recommendation X.21: *General-purpose interface between DTE and DCE for synchronous operation on Public Data Networks.*

In Chapter 3, we give a detailed discussion of CCITT Recommendation X.21, since it will most likely turn out to be the most important standard at this level.

2.5 Data Link Layer

As we explained in Chapter 1, the main task of a link layer is to shield higher layers from the characteristics of the physical transmission medium. It should provide these higher layers with a reliable transmission which is basically error-free, although errors may occur in the transmission on the physical-connection. The Data Link Layer should therefore provide for error detection and, if possible, error correction. On the other hand, the service should be provided in a way that is independent of the data being transmitted.

The Data Link Layer connects two network-entities in adjacent systems. This connection is called the data-link-connection, which is built on top of one or more physical-connections (splitting). The Data Link Layer does not provide either segmenting or blocking. Each service-data-unit (received from the using network-entity) is mapped on a one-to-one basis into a data-link-protocol-data-unit, together with the data-link-protocol-information. In the remainder of this section, we will for obvious reasons call the data-link-protocol-data-unit a *frame*.

The Data Link Layer must take care of the 'delimiting' of frames, i.e. enforce a structure that allows for the recognition of the beginning and the ending of a frame. This is necessary since to the Physical Layer a bit is a bit is a bit . . . (transparency!). Based on the frame as a unit of transmission, the Data Link Layer must provide error detection and possibly correction capabilities. The error correction can be achieved through retransmission of those frames in which errors were detected. The Data Link Layer must make sure that the frames that are received across the data-link are handed over to the network-entity in the same sequence in which they were offered for transmission. This implies that resequencing must be provided when retransmission is necessary because of detected errors.

Flow control mechanisms can be defined for the data-link-connection, i.e. a data-link-entity can request a correspondent data-link-entity to temporarily stop the transmission of frames.

A summary list of Data Link Layer services and functions defined in the Reference Model is given in Appendix B. We use this list in later chapters to compare the Data Link Layer or its equivalent in other architectures with the Reference Model.

As an example of a standard developed for the Data Link Layer, we discuss in Chapter 4 the ISO standard High-level Data Link Control (HDLC), which is the most important data link standard at the moment. It is an example of a bit-oriented protocol. An overview of character oriented protocols, such as the ANSI standard X3.28 or IBM's Binary Synchronous Communication protocol, in relation to the Reference Model is given in, for example, [4]. These protocols have had a profound effect on the data communications business. Because of their inherent deficiencies, they are being replaced with newer protocols such as HDLC.

Actually, HDLC consists of a number of separate standards:

a ISO 3309: *Data communication. High-level Data Link Control procedures—Frame structure.*
b ISO/DIS 4335: *Data communication. High-level Data Link Control procedures—Elements of procedures.*
c ISO/DIS 6159: *Data communication. HDLC unbalanced classes of procedures.*
d ISO/DIS 6256: *Data communication. HDLC balanced class of procedures.*

2.6 Network Layer

The basic service of the Network Layer is to provide the transparent transfer of all data submitted by the Transport Layer to any transport-entity anywhere in the Open Systems environment. It completely relieves the Transport Layer from any concerns about the way in which the communicating systems are interconnected. The network-connection may therefore be between only two Open Systems (point-to-point) or many Open Systems may be involved.

In the latter situation, the end-systems, i.e. the systems where the communicating transport-entities are located, need not be adjacent. The Network Layer must perform the necessary *routing* functions. Each intermediate system (or *node*) performs a *relay* function along that route. Note that, based on the definition of an Open System, each of these intermediate systems may be a network in itself. The Reference Model does indeed allow that a network-connection spans several (sub-)net-works. A practical example is the concatenation of public and private networks.

Transport-entities are identified to the Network Layer through *network-addresses*. *Network-connections* are provided by the Network Layer between pairs of network-addresses, i.e. there is no possibility for multipoint network-connections. However, between a pair of network-addresses more than one network-connection may exist. This can be used by the Transport Layer to optimize the use of the communication resources (see below).

The actual routing strategies are not defined in the Reference Model. What is defined is that the Network Layer may *or may not* maintain the sequence of the data handled for the Transport Layer. This has to do with the fact that certain routing schemes inherently maintain the sequence, while others cannot guarantee it. This was discussed in Chapter 1.

In any case, the Transport Layer must be made aware of the service provided when the network-connection is established. If necessary, it can then augment that service to the level that is required by the session-entities.

A summary list of Network Layer services and functions defined in the Reference Model is given in Appendix B. We use this list in later chapters to compare the Network Layer or its equivalent in other architectures with the Reference Model.

In Chapter 5, Level 3 of CCITT Recommendation X.25 is described. The full Recommendation X.25 is concerned with the Physical, Data Link and Network Layers, respectively called Levels 1, 2 and 3.

Level 1, for which Recommendation X.21 was defined, is discussed in Chapter 3 as an example of a standard for the Physical Layer. For Level 2, the Recommendation specifies High-level Data Link Control, HDLC, which is discussed in Chapter 4. Level 3, sometimes also called the *Packet Level*, is an example of a standard for the Network Layer. It has already gained wide acceptance and it is also the basis for the various Public Data Networks. These are discussed in their own context in Part 3.

2.7 Transport Layer

The Transport Layer is responsible for the transparent data transfer between two *session-entities*. For this transfer, a *transport-connection* is provided to the session-entities, independent of their location. An important aspect of the Transport Layer is the requirement that it optimizes the use of the underlying resources, i.e. the communication resources that connect the systems together, while maintaining a guaranteed quality of the service. A session-entity may therefore request a certain quality of service and once the Transport Layer provides a transport-connection with that quality, it must maintain it. In situations where the Transport Layer can no longer maintain the quality, it must explicitly notify the session-entities of the fact.

Since the Transport Layer is only concerned with the transfer of data between session-entities, all its transport-protocols have end-to-end significance. The layer is not aware of the structure of the underlying layers, most notably the topology of the network (or networks) that provide the actual physical transfer. For its functioning, it will call on the Network Layer to get a network-connection from the location of one transport-entity to the location of the other one. Depending on the quality of that network-connection, the Transport Layer has to perform additional functions to offer the agreed quality of the service.

Users of the transport service are uniquely identified by *transport-addresses*. The Transport Layer provides these users with *transport-connections* between transport-addresses. Such a connection is a Two-Way Simultaneous (also called Full-Duplex) data path between a pair of addresses. Multipoint transport-connections are not defined in the current Reference Model.

It is possible to have more than one transport-connection between the same pair of transport-addresses. The transport users can distinguish these through a *transport-connection-endpoint-identifier* which is unique for each transport-connection-endpoint.

The Transport Layer is required to optimize the use of the underlying resources, given several constraints (such as the availability of the resources, their cost, etc.) and, on the other hand, to provide the quality of the service required by the session-entities.

When a transport-connection is established, the transport-user can request a certain *Class of Service*, i.e. a predefined set of service parameters. The Transport Layer can allocate resources based on the Class of

Service requirements, e.g. use a network-connection with wide-band links for a batch-type Class of Service.

In order to achieve optimization, the Transport Layer may map several transport-connections onto one network-connection (multiplexing) or it may map one transport-connection onto several network-connections (splitting).

The Transport Layer must perform flow control to avoid session-entities overrunning each other and as a result congesting the network resources. Optionally, the Transport Layer may use segmenting and blocking to accommodate the characteristics of the network-connections or to make a more efficient use of them.

A summary list of Transport Layer services and functions defined in the Reference Model is given in Appendix B. We use this list in later chapters to compare the Transport Layer or its equivalent in other architectures with the Reference Model.

At the moment there is not yet an accepted standard for the Transport Layer, although there are several candidates. One is in preparation in the ISO. Another is the one that we describe in Chapter 6, the *Einheitliche Höhere Kommunikations Protokolle Ebene 4* (EHKP4)—Unified Higher-level Communications Protocol for Level 4. This standard—although still in a development stage—was indicated by the West German Government [7] as the interim standard for West Germany, as long as no other standards exist.

2.8 Session Layer

In the preceding section we have seen the services provided by the Transport Layer as being the transparent transfer of data-units between session-entities. These session-entities can thus behave completely independent of any concern about their location relative to each other. In other words, they can behave *as if* they are communicating face-to-face. To this transport service, the Session Layer now adds the coordination of the dialog between the communicating presentation-entities. That is, the Session Layer will establish a *session-connection* when the presentation-entities request one through a *session-services-access-point*.

The main services that the Session Layer must provide are the establishment of that session-connection and the management of the dialog on that connection. An interesting aspect of the establishment of the session-connection is its mapping onto the transport-connection. The current Reference Model defines that this mapping is one-to-one. Thus, no multiplexing is allowed in the Session Layer (this is left for future extension). The model does allow, however, for a different mapping in time: several session-connections may use the same transport-connection, one after the other. That is, after a session-connection is terminated, another may be established, using the same transport-connection.

More interesting perhaps is the fact that the Reference Model also allows the opposite to happen, i.e. a transport-connection is terminated and another established to serve the same session-connection, without that being noticed by the using presentation-entities. This could be used, for example, when a transport-connection must be terminated because of problems in the underlying network service. A new transport-connection can then be established without the session partners being aware of it. Resynchronization of the conversation must be completely handled in the Session Layer.

The Session Layer is also responsible for managing the interaction between the presentation-entities. Rules must be agreed when a session-connection is established that will be adhered to by the session partners. The Session Layer will watch (and, if necessary, enforce) this adherence. Three forms of interaction have been defined in the Reference Model:

a Both session-partners may send and receive at the same time (TWS—Two-Way-Simultaneous).
b The session partners take turns in which only one may send at a time, while the other receives (TWA—Two-Way-Alternate).
c For the duration of the session-connection, only one presentation-entity sends, the other receives (One-Way).

The Session Layer must further provide a number of services that can help an orderly exchange of data. Several of these services have not yet been defined in the Reference Model—they are left for future extensions. Two services that have been defined are:

a Synchronization of the dialog, which means that the session entities must be able to reset to a certain state in the dialog which they have mutually acknowledged at an earlier point in the dialog.
b Quarantining data-units, which means that a session entity may send data-units to its correspondent but the data-units are not released to the receiving presentation-entity until the sender explicitly releases them. That is, a number of data-units can be 'grouped' together. Such a quarantine unit can also be purged at the request of the sender instead of being delivered to the receiver.

In Appendix B, the services and functions as they are defined in the Reference Model are listed. Since a number of architectures that we compare in later chapters do provide several of the services that are indicated as 'future extensions', we have included them in this checklist.

Currently, no specific standard is available for the Session Layer nor is there consensus as to potential candidates for standardization. There is, therefore, no specific chapter dedicated to the Session Layer. The interested reader can get an impression of what the protocols can involve in the chapters where the proprietary architectures are discussed. One should bear in mind, however, that there is not always a clear separation of layers that corresponds one-to-one with the Session Layer. This is further indicated in the mapping sections at the end of each chapter.

2.9 Presentation Layer

The Presentation Layer provides the Application Layer with services related to the presentation of information in a form that is meaningful to the application-entities. The Reference Model defines three *syntactic* versions of the data that is transferred between the application-entities. One is the syntax used by the originator, another is the syntax used by the receiver and the last is the syntax used in the transfer process. When a presentation-connection is established, the mapping between these syntaxes is selected and agreed to by the parties. To clarify this concept of syntax-mapping, the following example from human communications is useful.

When somebody who speaks only French communicates with somebody who speaks only German, the 'syntax' on the originating and receiving sides is respectively French and German. The 'transfer syntax' in this case can be either German or French, or even English, Dutch or whatever language is understood by the presentation-entities (the translator) on both sides.

The services provided by the Presentation Layer are related mainly to this mapping of different syntax:

a Data transformation, i.e. the presentation-entities may convert codes and/or character sets for the application-entities.
b Data formatting, e.g. the formatting of output data for a specific type of device.
c Selection of the (transfer-) syntax to be used. This selection can be negotiated when the presentation-connection is established. The Reference Model states clearly, however, that this selection may be renegotiated during the existence of the connection.

In Appendix B, the services and the functions of the Presentation Layer as they are defined in the Reference Model are listed. This checklist will be used in the chapters in which proprietary architectures are compared with the Model.

No specific chapter is devoted to standards for the Presentation Layer, since there is not yet such a standard. Many protocols have been defined in this area, most notably Virtual Terminal Protocols and File Transfer Protocols, but none of them is yet standardized. Their description and a general discussion of such protocols is outside the scope of this book.

The CCITT Recommendations X.3, X.28 and X.29 (Section 12.5.9) are also related to the support of terminal communication and data presentation. They are concerned with the support of character oriented terminals across a Packet-Switched Public Network. Since they do not fit completely in the Reference Model (e.g. no end-to-end transport service is assumed) they are not described in this part of the book, but in Chapter 12.

2.10 Application Layer

The highest layer in OSI is the Application Layer. This layer is composed of 'application-entities' that represent those aspects of 'application processes' that are relevant to OSI. These application-entities communicate with each other, in order to perform their specific tasks, using Application Layer Protocols.

Although this is no longer defined in the Reference Model, three specific categories of application processes can be distinguished:

a *System management application processes* that execute the system functions necessary to control and supervise the operation of the participating systems.
b *Application management application processes* that control and supervise the operation of the application processes.
c *User application processes* that perform the actual information processing for the end-user.

The Application Layer Protocols that govern the communication between application processes can be classified in five groups, to get some structure in the wide variety of protocols that may exist between systems and applications. The groups are

Group 1 System management protocols

Group 2 Application management protocols

Group 3 System protocols

Group 4 Industry specific protocols

Group 5 Enterprise specific protocols

These groups are based on the 'span of significance' of the subject protocols, from the point of view of the interconnection. The group with the largest span of significance consists of the systems management protocols, for which the open systems have to participate. An example of this kind of protocol is the activity required to activate a communication between two application processes in different systems. Clearly, standardization is required for this type of protocols. The smallest span of significance is found in the group with the enterprise-specific protocols. Although these protocols may apply to some systems in the total interconnection, it is not appropriate to standardize them at an international level. Rather they would be standardized at the enterprise level. Examples of these protocols are Payroll and Order Entry applications within one enterprise (which may utilize multiple 'systems' to perform the applications).

2.11 Conclusion

In this chapter, we have briefly introduced the terminology of the Reference Model of Open Systems Interconnection. We have also given an overview of the main services and functions of the layers in this model. Purposely, this overview was not complete, since the Draft International Standard which defines the Reference Model is included in Appendix A. Having read the present chapter, the reader should have sufficient background information to appreciate the following chapters in which a number of standards that relate to various layers in the Reference Model are described. This applies equally well to the comparison that is made in Part 2 of a number of proprietary architectures with the Reference Model.

Whenever the reader needs more specific information (or more formal definition) in a specific situation, the full text in Appendix A should be of help.

References

1 Dijkstra, E. W., The structure of THE multiprogramming system, *Commun. ACM*, vol. 11, no. 5, 1963, pp. 341–346
2 Vissers, C. A., *Interface—definition, design and description of the relation of digital system parts*, Thesis, Twente University of Technology, Netherlands, 1977
3 International Standards Organization, ISO/TC97: *Information processing systems. Open Systems Interconnection—Basic Reference Model*, Draft International Standard ISO/DIS 7498, Apr. 1982. [Reproduced in Appendix A]
4 Conard, J. W., Character-oriented data link control protocols, *IEEE Trans. Commun.*, vol. Com-28, no. 4, Apr. 1980, pp. 445–454
5 International Standards Organization, ISO/TC97: *Draft connection-oriented transport service definition*, Document N697, June 1981
6 International Standards Organization, ISO/TC97: *Draft connection-oriented transport protocol specification*, Document N698, June 1981
7 Ministry of the Interior, Bekanntmachung einer Neufassung der Grundsätze für die Gestaltung der automatisierten Datenübermittlung, *Bundesanzeiger*, vol. 33, no. 25a, Feb. 1981

3 Recommendation X.21

3.1 Introduction

The International Standards Organization suggests certain standards that can be used on the Physical Layer of the Reference Model. This chapter gives an overview of one of these standards. We choose Recommendation X.21 of the International Consultative Committee for Telephony and Telegraphy (CCITT). It is rather recent and a part of the X-series of recommendations on *Public Data Networks* (PDN). The chapter should give the reader the necessary background information for further study of the recommendation itself [1].

Recommendation X.21 describes an interface to operate a terminal in a synchronous mode over a Public Data Network (PDN). The PDN is in this case a digital circuit-switched network. The recommendation describes how a terminal can work with this new digital network, commonly called the X.21 network. The services are basically equivalent to today's telephone network services in the way that they provide a communication channel, or connection between terminals, for data transmission.

3.2 The recommendation

This recommendation is concerned with the General Purpose Interface between DTE and DCE for synchronous operation on Public Data Networks (PDN) [1].

The user equipment or terminal that connects to the PDN is called *Data Terminal Equipment* (DTE) in CCITT terminology. The entry point of the network is called *Data Circuit-Terminating Equipment* (DCE).

The new X.21 interface facilitates full automatic call establishment and clearance with a repertoire of call progress and malfunction signals.

3.2.1 X.24 interchange circuitry

The physical connection of the DTE to the DCE is shown in Fig. 3.2. It allows the implementation of the above described facilities.

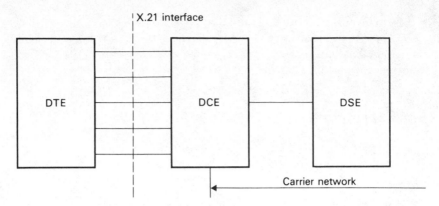

Fig. 3.1 X.21 physical interface

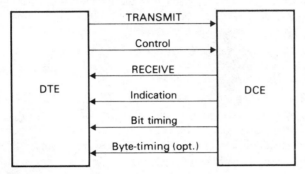

Fig. 3.2 X.24 interchange circuit (level 1976)

The interchange circuits are defined in Recommendation X.24, which gives the functions of the different circuits.

As the figure shows, there are six circuits in the interchange circuitry between the DTE and the DCE. This set-up gives a standard Full-Duplex bit transfer facility through the *Transmit* and *Receive* circuitry. The terminal attached to the network transmits bits over the Transmit circuit to and receives bits over the Receive circuit from its partner in communication.

Two other circuits control the status of the connection, connected or not connected, of the two DTEs. They are the *Control circuit* and the *Indication circuit*. The Control circuit is driven by the DTE and its activation signals the circuit-switched network that it is *off hook*, i.e. connected to the network and willing to participate in a communication. The Indication circuit is controlled by the network and indicates to the DTE that a connection exists with another DTE.

The last two circuits are concerned with timing and provide timing signals from the network to the DTE. The *Bit timing circuit* enables the

DTE to synchronize the transmission and reception of data at the correct bit rate. The other circuit gives a *Byte timing signal*, i.e. a signal every 8 bits, and is normally used by the DTE to interpret or transmit the control information during the Control Phase.

3.3 The X.21 interface

The interface is transparent and allows full-duplex data transmission between DTEs. Recommendation X.21 specifies two types of operation phase:

a Call establishment and other call control phases.
b Data phase.

The DTE makes known its availability by continuously sending one-bits over the Transmit circuit. The network is available when the DTE continuously receives one-bits over the Receive circuit.

	Indication ON	Indication OFF
Control ON	Data Phase	Control Phase
Control OFF	Control Phase	Control Phase

Fig. 3.3 Circuitry control

Figure 3.3 shows the status of the connection between the DTEs as a function of the control circuits setting. When both the Indication and the Control circuits are on, the connection is said to be in the *Data Phase*. In this phase, all the bit combinations travelling over the circuits are transparent.

In the other cases, the connection is in the *Control Phase*. In this phase, bits received over the Receive circuit, assuming the DTE is willing to participate, should be interpreted as control information. Here, the transmitted and received information will have a specific meaning for the network, such as Call Control characters, and/or should be interpreted by the DTE as control information from the network. This control information could be progress information during Call set-up or information concerning the reason why a connection could not be established.

After one DTE has been connected to another DTE, through a leased or switched protocol, and the Data Phase has been entered, the facility is equivalent to, for example, a telephone line, but without voice capability.

Figure 3.4 shows such a connection through a circuit-switched carrier-owned network. The communication from DTE to DTE can be controlled by HDLC, SDLC, BSC or any other synchronous data-link control.

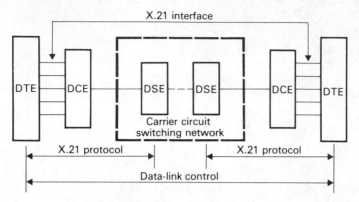

Fig. 3.4 DTE to DTE data-link control in a synchronous network

X.21 protocols are involved only at the connection set-up phase, after which the higher level, data-link control, takes over. When the higher level decides to break the link, X.21 protocols will be used to break the physical connection.

3.4 Call and Clear for a circuit-switched service

The following is given as an example of such an X.21 protocol to be implemented by a DTE. Figure 3.5 represents a typical call-and-clear sequence for a circuit-switched service. At the initial stage, both DTEs will have the Control and Indication circuits off. They are both sending one-bits to the network over the Transmit circuits and are receiving one-bits over the Receive circuits. These one-bits are transmitted by the network to show its availability. One DTE, in this case the left-hand side DTE, indicates it wants a connection by raising its Control circuit to 'ON' and by stopping the transmission of one-bits. The network then transmits to the DTE a SYN bit configuration followed by a series of '+' characters, indicating that the DTE can proceed with the transmission of the selection signals. The DTE transmits a SYN character and the Dial information, i.e. the DTE network number together with optional parameters such as reverse charging, etc. After this, the DTE will go into a wait state.

In the meantime, nothing has happened on the other side. The network now selects the DTE and transmits a SYN and a BELL bit configuration to the called DTE. The latter accepts the call by raising its Control circuit. The network sends, at the same time, information on the progress of the Call

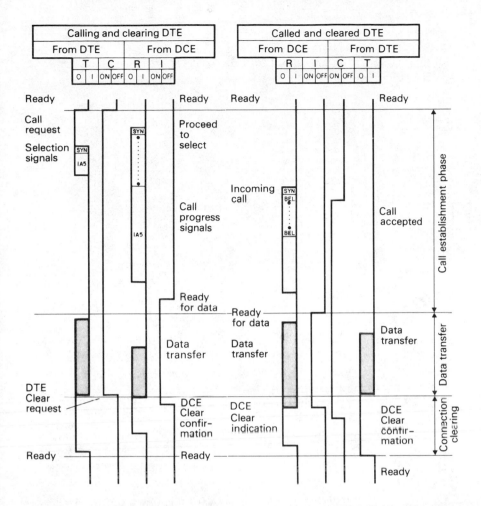

Calling and clearing DTE					Called and cleared DTE			
From DTE		From DCE			From DCE		From DTE	
T	C	R	I		R	I	C	T
O | I	ON|OFF	O | I	ON|OFF		O | I	ON|OFF	ON|OFF	O | I

Ready — Ready | Ready — Ready

Call request — Proceed to select

Selection signals [SYN] [IA5]

[SYN] ......

Call progress signals [IA5]

Incoming call [SYN][BEL] ...... [BEL] — Call accepted

Call establishment phase

Ready for data — Ready for data

Data transfer — Data transfer — Data transfer

Data transfer

DTE Clear request — DCE Clear confirmation — DCE Clear indication — DCE Clear confirmation

Connection clearing

Ready — Ready — Ready — Ready

Fig. 3.5 Successful Call and Clear for circuit-switched service

set-up, to the calling DTE. In the next step, the connection is completed while the network gives Line identification information to both the Calling and Called DTEs. Finally, the network raises the Indication circuits of both DTEs and the connection is now available, i.e. the connection is set up and it is in the Data-Phase State.

During the Control Phase, it is possible that the network uses the Byte timing signal in addition to the required SYN patterns before the control information is exchanged. This is optional in the recommendation, but it can be found in certain implementations.

The two DTEs have a Full-Duplex communication facility available between them. This is shown in Fig. 3.5 by the simultaneous transfer of data over the Transmit circuits. The figure also shows the clearing of the circuit-switched service. The set-up of the connection can be very fast in these networks. The range is from 1 s to 100 ms. Several timings are defined in the recommendation for time-outs for responses from the DTE or from the network.

3.5 Recommendation X.21bis

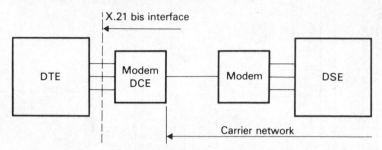

Fig. 3.6 X.21bis physical interface

The implementation of X.21-based circuit-switching networks requires new technology. Most countries do not have the technology installed and it will take time to renew their existing installations. Also, in those countries that have the new-technology networks, the user still will have old V.24-based equipment which should be changed to comply with the X.21 interface. This will be an expensive undertaking.

To ease the conversion from the old-technology installations to the new X.21 interface, Recommendation X.21bis was formulated (Fig. 3.6): the use on Public Data Networks of DTEs which are designed for interfacing to synchronous V-series modems [2].

The V-series recommendations describe data transmission over telephone and telex networks. For example, Recommendation V.24 describes the interface between a terminal and the telephone network, i.e. the way the modem is controlled from the terminal.

The services described in Recommendation X.21bis are (a) leased circuit service, (b) direct call, and (c) address call facility. Direct call is a facility that avoids the use of address selection signals normally provided by the DTE. The network interprets the call request signal as an instruction to establish a connection with a single destination address requested by the user at subscription time.

Recommendation X.25, which is described in Chapter 5, allows the use of X.21bis instead of X.21 for the Physical Layer.

3.6 Comparison with the Reference Model

Recommendation X.21 is one of the possible interfaces that can be used on the Physical Layer of the OSI model. Below we list the services and functions defined in the X.21 recommendation in the format of the list defined for the Physical Layer of the Reference Model (Appendix B). If specific services and/or functions are not explicitly commented on, this indicates that we did not find an explicit equivalent in X.21.

Services provided by the Physical Layer
- Physical-connections. X.21 provides for physical-connections between two users, called DTEs. There can be one and only one connection between one pair of DTEs.
- Physical-service-data-units. These are bits that are transmitted over the physical connection.
- Physical-connection-endpoints. The address of the DTE is the identification of the physical-connection-endpoint.
- Data circuit identification. A data circuit is identified by the pair of DTE addresses that it connects.
- Sequencing.
- Fault condition notification. If at all possible, X.21 provides for fault condition feedback when there is malfunction.
- Quality of service parameters.

Functions in the Physical Layer
- Physical-connection activation and deactivation. Physical connections are activated and deactivated through manipulation of the control and information leads of the X.24 circuitry and the exchange of physical-service-data-units between the DTEs and the X.21 network.
- Physical-service-data-unit transmission. Bits are transmitted over the data circuit.
- Physical Layer Management.

References

1 CCITT, *Data communication networks. Services and facilities. Terminal equipment and interfaces. Recommendations X.1–X.29*, Yellow Book, Vol VII—Facicle VIII.2, CCITT VIIth Plenary Assembly, Geneva, 10–21 Nov. 1980, ITU, Geneva, 1981
2 CCITT, *Data transmission over the telephone network*, Orange Book Volume VIII.1. ITU, Geneva, 1977.

4 High-level Data Link Control

4.1 Introduction

High-level Data Link Control (HDLC) has been defined by the International Standards Organization [1, 2] to replace the existing and widely used character-oriented protocols and to make better use of the improving technology, such as higher-speed lines, more intelligence in the link-station, etc. In this chapter, we explain HDLC in a fair amount of detail, to show what is required for a reliable, error-free exchange across a medium that is not necessarily reliable.

In HDLC, any control information that must be exchanged between two stations is placed in specific fields in the transmission frame. These fields are in a fixed position relative to the boundaries of the frame, as is indicated in Section 4.3.

HDLC may be thought of as consisting of three sub-layers:

a The first (lowest) sub-layer is concerned with the transparency of the bit stream to be transmitted (see Section 4.2).
b The second sub-layer is concerned with the format of the transmission, i.e. the imbedding of the data in a header and a trailer containing the protocol information (see Section 4.3).
c The third sub-layer is responsible for the cooperation between the stations on a link such that orderly exchange is obtained (see Section 4.4).

4.2 Transparency

Since HDLC must be completely independent of the data transmitted, it will view that data as a transparent bit stream. Protocol information that is added by the other sub-layers is also regarded as just part of the bit stream. This means that the only requirement is to have some means to indicate the beginning and ending of a transmission. This is accomplished by the concept of a *frame*. A special bit sequence, the *Flag* sequence, has been defined that is used to indicate both begin-of-frame and end-of-frame. The flag is the unique bit sequence

0 1 1 1 1 1 1 0

In order to ensure the uniqueness of this flag, a sending station will always monitor the bit stream that is being transmitted and whenever five consecutive ones are transmitted, an additional zero is inserted (bit stuffing). The receiving station will similarly monitor the incoming bit stream and after five consecutive ones the sixth bit is dropped if it is a zero. However, if this sixth bit is a one, either the Flag (the next bit must then be zero) or the sequence for abortive termination of the frame (at least seven ones) was received:

0 1 1 1 1 1 1 1 . . .

4.3 HDLC frame format

Flag (F)	Address (A)	Control (C)	Data	Frame Check Sequence (FCS)	Flag (F)

Fig. 4.1 The basic HDLC frame

All transmissions in HDLC are in the form that is given in Fig. 4.1. This basic format is called a *frame*, which begins and ends with a flag, as explained above. The information field in the frame is optional.

The Address Field (A) and the Control Field (C) are in the basic format both 8 bits wide. With extended addressing, the Address Field can be any multiple of 8 bits (see below). In the Extended Control format (see below) the Control Field is 16 bits long. The Frame Check Sequence (FCS) has always a length of 16 bits.

Note that when two frames are sent immediately following each other, the end flag of one frame can also be the begin flag of the next frame. However, more flags in between two frames are allowed.

4.3.1 Address Field

The first field in an HDLC frame is the Address Field. Whether the field contains the address of the sending or the receiving station depends on the particular class of procedure that is used (Section 4.4).

In unbalanced configurations, there are a *primary* and one or more *secondary* stations (see Section 4.4). Every secondary station is assigned a unique address. In addition, certain addresses may be assigned to more than one station. These addresses are called *group addresses*. Frames transmitted using a group address will be received by all stations in the group. The 'all ones' address is reserved to address all stations on the link.

It is called the *broadcast address*. When a secondary station sends a response, it must always use its unique address.

When extended addressing is used, the Address Field can be longer than 8 bits. In that case, the low-order bit of each 8-bit field indicates whether this is the last (bit = 1) or more is to follow (bit = 0).

4.3.2 Control Field

There are three different types of frame in HDLC:

a I-frames (Information frames), used for data transfer.
b Supervisory frames, used to control the *flow* of data. (The frame itself never contains data).
c Unnumbered frames, used to control the link itself. They may sometimes contain data.

The particular type of frame is indicated in the Control Field. The basic format of the Control Field is given in Fig. 4.2, the extended format in Fig. 4.3.

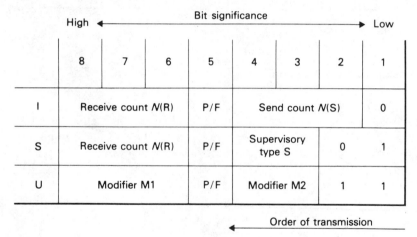

Fig. 4.2 Control Field: layout in the basic format

The letter symbols in the figures have the following meaning:

N (R)   Receive count.
N (S)   Send count.
    All stations maintain counters for the number of I-frames they have sent and received. These counters are transmitted in the Control Field of each I-frame. They are used to synchronize the stations at the frame level, i.e. to check the sequence of received frames and to acknowledge the reception of frames.

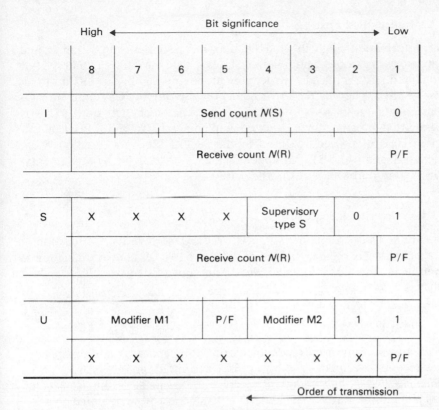

Fig. 4.3 Control Field: layout in the extended format.

In the basic format, the counters are 3 bits wide (refer to Fig. 4.2), thus giving a modulo-8 count. In the extended format (Fig. 4.3), the counters are 7 bits wide, giving a modulo-128 count.

The counters are always used in a wrap-around mode. The effect is that a station may never have more than (modulo − 1) unacknowledged frames outstanding.

P/F   Poll or Final bit. This bit is called the *Poll bit* when used in a command frame. (Refer to Section 4.4.1 for a definition of commands and responses.) It indicates that the receiver must acknowledge this frame through a response frame carrying this bit as the *F*-bit, the *Final* bit.

S   Supervisory frame type indicator. It is used to identify which type of Supervisory frame is sent.

M1, M2 Modifier bits for the Unnumbered frames.

X   These bits are unused and must be set to zero.

4.3.3 Information Field

The Information Field in an HDLC frame is optional in I-frames and mandatory on some unnumbered frames. On all other frames, it is prohibited. If it is present, its length can be any number of bits up to an upper limit implied by the error detection algorithm (FCS). Implementations may limit it to a multiple of the character size used. This is exemplified by some byte-oriented implementations of LAPB (the balanced class of procedures used in the CCITT Recommendation X.25, refer to Section 12.5.3). An upper limit may also be set by implementations, based on buffer sizes in the stations.

4.3.4 Frame Check Sequence

The Frame Check Sequence is a cyclic redundancy check. A discussion of this technique is outside the scope of this book. A good explanation is given in various textbooks and also in an appendix to the ISO Standard 3309 [1, 3, 4].

The generator polynomial for HDLC is:

$$X^{16} + X^{12} + X^5 + 1.$$

When a frame is transmitted, the algorithm to generate the Frame Check Sequence is executed. The result is transmitted in the Frame Check Sequence field. While a frame is received, the same algorithm is executed until the closing flag is detected. The result must now be equal to zero. (Actually, additional procedures are being used, such as presetting the dividend and inverting the result, in order to make the check more robust. The effect will be that the result is not zero but a special value 0001110100001111 [1].) If the Frame Check Sequence is incorrect, the receiver will disregard the frame completely. The loss of the frame will eventually be detected and retransmission initiated, using procedures as described in Section 4.5.

4.4 Classes of Procedure

The operation of an HDLC link is described in terms of the capabilities of the stations and their cooperation. First of all, it may sometimes be required for several reasons to have stations of different capabilities attached to one link. An example can be one intelligent station connected to several very simple stations. In that case, the management of the link, which requires more capabilities, can be localized in the more intelligent station. That station is called a *primary* station, with the others being the *secondary* stations. The configuration of one primary and one or more secondaries is called an *unbalanced* configuration.

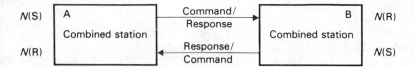

Fig. 4.4 HDLC Asynchronous Balanced Mode

Another characteristic of the HDLC stations is the way in which they cooperate. In the unbalanced configuration, there are two different ways:

a The *normal response mode*, where a secondary station can only transmit after the primary has polled it. In this mode, the *P*-bit in a command frame is indicating permission to transmit. The *F*-bit in a response frame indicates the last frame of a transmission.

b The *asynchronous response mode*, where a station (either primary or secondary) may transmit whenever it finds the link idle.

In other cases, total symmetry between the stations is required. The stations have equal capabilities and are called *combined* stations (Fig. 4.4). Configurations using (two of) these stations are called *balanced* configurations operating in asynchronous mode.

Based on these functional capabilities of the stations, three *Classes of Procedure* have been defined:

1 Unbalanced operation in Asynchronous Response Mode (UAC).
2 Unbalanced operation in Normal Response Mode (UAC).
3 Balanced operation in Asynchronous Response Mode (BAC).

For each of the three classes of procedure, HDLC describes the basic command/response repertoire that must be supported by all implementations, and optional features that may be supported. These sets are shown in Fig. 4.5. In all classes of procedure, the Information frames and the Supervisory frames RR and RNR (see below) must be supported. Most of the Unnumbered frames, however, are optional.

4.4.1 Commands and responses

As indicated before, three types of frame have been defined in HDLC. These are the Information frame, the Supervisory frame and the Unnumbered frame.

A frame of any type is called a *Command* if it is sent by a primary station and a *Response* if it is sent by a secondary station. Combined stations can send both commands and responses. The difference is indicated by the address in the frame. If it is the station's own address, the frame is a response, otherwise a command. The relevant commands and responses for the Supervisory and Unnumbered frames are discussed briefly below.

4.4.2 Supervisory frames

The format for the Supervisory frames allows for four different frames (see the S-field in Fig. 4.2). Two of these, Receive Ready (RR) and Receive Not Ready (RNR) are used on all types of link. The other two, Reject (REJ) and Selective Reject (SREJ) are only useful in Two-Way-Simultaneous communication. The Supervisory frames themselves are not included in the Send and Receive counts.

RR   Receive Ready. This frame is used whenever a station wants to tell its counterpart that it can receive I-frames. Normally, this is implicit when the Poll or Final bit is received in an I-frame. If there is no I-frame to be transmitted or if the other station cannot receive, then this RR frame can be used. Since this frame carries the Receive count of the sender, it can also be used as a separate acknowledgement when no I-frames can be transmitted.

RNR   Receive Not Ready. The Receive Not Ready frame is used by a station to indicate to the other one that it is (temporarily) unable to receive. It depends on the specific procedure class how and when the other station is notified that the station is ready again. The frame carries also the Receive count, to acknowledge the frames correctly received so far.

The next two Supervisory frames are of use in Two-Way-Simultaneous communication only.

REJ   Reject. This frame is used by a station to notify the other station of the fact that otherwise valid frames had to be rejected because of a sequence error. The Receive count in this frame is the counter value expected in the next transmission.

SREJ   Selective Reject. This frame is used to indicate to the other station that a sequence error occurred, but that only the indicated frame needs to be retransmitted (unlike REJ where all the frames following must also be retransmitted).

4.4.3 Unnumbered frames

Unnumbered frames are used to control the link without being included in the send and/or receive sequence counts. This implies that Unnumbered responses cannot be acknowledged via the receive sequence count. Acknowledgement is made via the appropriate response.

Although these commands/responses do not update the sequence counters, they may have an indirect effect on the counters. For example, the mode-setting commands reset the counters to zero.

The various unnumbered frames are

SNRM (E)   Set Normal Response Mode (Extended).

SARM (E) Set Asynchronous Response Mode (Extended).
SABM (E) Set Asynchronous Balanced Mode (Extended).

The mode-setting commands are used to establish link-level contact and bring the stations into the required mode of operation from whatever mode they were in. The Extended version of the commands is used if the extended format of the Control Field is required.

UA Unnumbered Acknowledgement. This frame is used to acknowledge an Unnumbered frame if no other specific Unnumbered frame is defined as a response.

DISC Disconnect. When a primary or a combined station wants to close the link, it sends a Disconnect command. It is acknowledged with an Unnumbered Acknowledgement, after which the receiver goes into Disconnected Mode. In that mode, only the mode-setting commands are valid.

DM Disconnected Mode. This response can be used to report that a station is logically disconnected, for example, after receiving a DISC command. In that mode, the DM response will normally be sent in response to all commands, except the ones for mode setting. It may, however, also be sent in response to a mode-setting command if the station is not able or willing to perform the actions required for the mode setting.

FRMR Frame Reject. A Frame Reject command or response is sent when invalid conditions are detected. These conditions can be

a The Command Field is invalid for the repertoire implemented in the receiver.

b The Receive count is illegal, i.e. a frame is acknowledged that has not yet been sent.

c The Information Field is too long for the receiver's buffers.

d The Information Field is not permitted for the frame type.

All these conditions cause a station to enter the Frame Reject State. In this state, all frames will be discarded until the station can send the FRMR. This exception state can only be reset by one of the mode setting commands.

Note that, in a balanced configuration, the FRMR can be sent by either station. In unbalanced configurations, it can only be sent by a secondary station. It is then also called CMDR—Command Reject.

The Information Field is 20 bits (or 36 bits for the Extended mode) long but can be padded with zeros to obtain a multiple of the character size for a particular implementation. The field contains the following information:

a Eight bits Control Field, containing the Control Field in the frame that caused the FRMR.

b Eight bits containing the Send and Receive counters in the format of the Control Field in an Information frame, with the Poll/Final bit set to zero. This is used to communicate to the receiver what the expected values of the counters are, which is especially important in the case of an illegal receive count.

c Four bits indicating the reasons for the FRMR, as explained above.

The Unnumbered frames discussed above are part of the basic repertoire of HDLC stations (refer to Fig. 4.5). The remaining commands/responses that are discussed below are part of the optional repertoire.

UI   Unnumbered Information. The UI frame can be used to send data to one or more stations, independent of the normal flow of Information frames.

XID   Exchange Identification. The XID command and response is one of the few Unnumbered frames that carry an Information Field. The frame can be used between two stations in order to exchange station identification and the characteristics (capabilities) of the two stations. The actual layout of the I-field is implementation dependent.

SIM   Set Initialization Mode. The SIM command is used when remote initialization of a station is required. The response to the SIM command is the Unnumbered Acknowledgement.

In the Initialization Mode, the required information (e.g. micro-code for the station) can be sent using Unnumbered Information frames. The actual initialization procedure is dependent on the particular implementation. It is usually controlled by the higher layers in the architecture, normally the management functions. The initialization cycle is terminated through the use of one of the mode-setting commands (SNRM, SARM or SABM).

RIM   Request Initialization Mode. The RIM response can be used by a secondary station in response to a mode-setting command if it is not yet capable of performing the required functions. The primary should follow up with a Set Initialization Mode (SIM) command to start the implementation-defined initialization sequence.

RD   Request Disconnect. This response can be used by a secondary station if it wants to terminate operation of the link. The primary should follow up with the DISC command (see above).

RSET   Reset. This command can be used by a station to re-initialize the flow in one direction only. This is unlike the

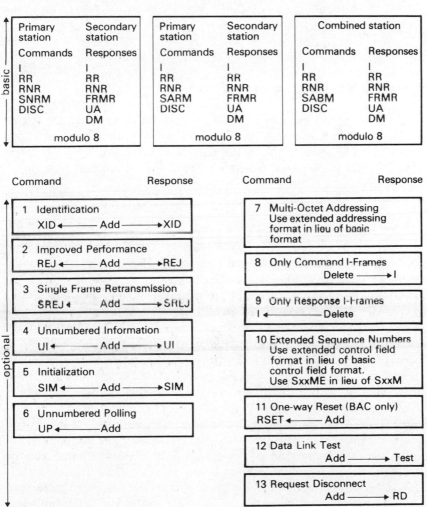

Fig. 4.5 HDLC Classes of Procedure: the three boxes at the top represent the basic repertoire; the numbered boxes are optional functions

mode-setting commands, which reset the flow in both directions. The command is only valid in the repertoire for
balanced configurations.

UP   Unnumbered Poll. This is used to invite one or more
stations on a link to respond. That response is optional,
contrary to when the Poll bit is used. The command is useful
only on unbalanced multidrop configurations, where it is
used in conjunction with broadcast or group addressing.

When a UP is used, special care must be taken to resolve
contention that may result if two or more secondaries
respond simultaneously. For a special procedure using the
Unnumbered Poll, refer to Section 7.3.1, where the SDLC
loop is described.

4.5 Examples of HDLC sequences

In the following, a number of sequences is given to illustrate the use of
HDLC. Most of the examples use the unbalanced, normal response mode
class of procedure. In addition, the transmission facility is Half-Duplex,
unless it is explicitly stated otherwise (Two-Way Alternate communication).

4.5.1 Use of the sequence counters

The sequence counters are used for the acknowledgement protocol. Both
stations maintain a Send and a Receive counter. These counters are copied
into the Control Field when a frame is transmitted. After the sender has
successfully completed transmission, its send counter is updated. When the
receiver has checked that the received frame is OK (i.e. no error in the
Frame Check Sequence) and the value of the $N(S)$ in the frame is equal to
the expected value (which is its receive count $N(R)$), it updates its $N(R)$. In
this way, both sides are kept in synchronism. The $N(R)$ in the frame
indicates how many frames the sender had received at the time the frame
was transmitted. It is therefore an acknowledgement of those frames.

It should be noted that the primary station in an unbalanced configuration must keep copies of the pair of counters for *each* secondary. In Fig.
4.6, an example is given of the use of the Send/Receive counters in the
transmission of I-frames between a primary and a secondary station, with
Two-Way Alternate communication.

Since the sequence counters are 3 bits wide, HDLC makes it mandatory
to wait for a response (i.e. to poll the secondary) after at most seven frames
have been transmitted since the last acknowledgement. Otherwise, ambi-
guity might result when the counter wraps around. Normally, the 3-bit
counter is sufficient. On satellite links, with their high transmission rate but

long propagation delay, it may be a serious limitation. For such cases, the extended format has been defined. In the extended format, the counters are 7 bits wide and the number of unacknowledged frames can therefore be 127.

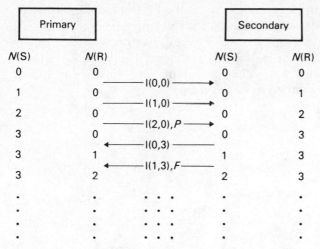

Fig. 4.6 Send and Receive counters in operation

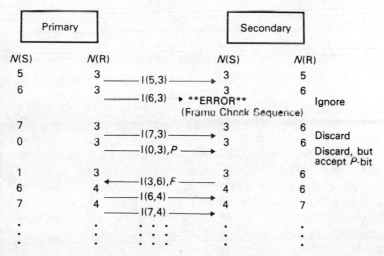

Fig. 4.7 Error signaling

4.5.2 Error signaling

In TWA communication the Receive counters can also be used for error signaling. The basic philosophy is that, whenever a station detects an error in a transmission (FCS error or wrong sequence number), it discards the frame and any frames that follow it until it has an opportunity to send. It then sends its Receive count in an I-frame or in a Supervisory frame (RR or RNR), which tells the sender what the next expected frame is. Figure 4.7 gives an example of error signaling via the sequence numbers.

When the error occurs in a frame that has the Poll bit on, the secondary cannot transmit and both stations wait for the polling time-out to expire at the primary station. After the time-out expires, the primary will normally send $\langle RR, N(R), P \rangle$ in order to find out what happened. After the secondary has responded with either an I-frame or a Supervisory frame, the two stations are again in synchronization.

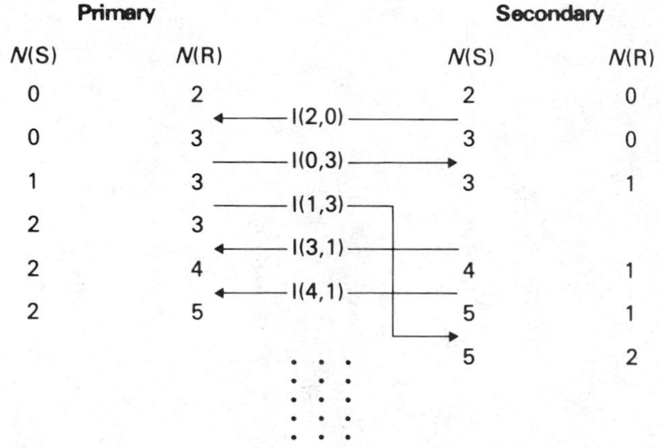

Primary			Secondary	
$N(S)$	$N(R)$		$N(S)$	$N(R)$
0	2		2	0
0	3	← I(2,0)	3	0
1	3	── I(0,3) →	3	1
2	3	── I(1,3)	3	
2	4	← I(3,1)	4	1
2	5	← I(4,1)	5	1
			5	2

Fig. 4.8 Sequence counters in Two-Way Simultaneous communication

In Two-Way-Simultaneous (TWS) communication, it is no longer necessary that *both* counters agree since the transmissions in both directions overlap. The Receive count in a frame may run behind the station's Send count, since the station may have sent frames on the other channel that arrive after the other station sent its frame (Fig. 4.8). The count can therefore be used as an acknowledgement for frames up to and including $N(R) - 1$ and these frames can thus be flushed from the sender's recovery buffers. The constraint of a maximum of modulo $n - 1$ unacknowledged frames outstanding remains applicable. The counters can, however, no longer be used to signal missing frames, and another technique must be used on these links. This is the Supervisory frame *Reject*, discussed in Section 4.5.4.

4.5.3 RR and RNR

An example of the use of Receive Ready (RR) and Receive Not Ready (RNR) is given in Fig. 4.9. Assume that frame $\langle I^{12}, P = 0 \rangle$ filled all the

Primary   **Secondary**

N(S)	N(R)		N(S)	N(R)
2	2	—— I¹²(2,2) ——→	2	2
3	2	—— I¹³(3,2) ——→ *	2	3 (busy)
4	2	—— I¹⁴(4,2),P ——→ *	2	3
5	2	←—— RNR(3),F ——	2	3
3	2	· · ·	2	3
		—— RR(2),P ——→		
		←—— RNR(3),F ——		
		· · ·		
		—— RR(2),P ——→		
		←—— RR(3),F ——		
4	2	—— I¹³(3,2) ——→ · · ·	2	4

Fig. 4.9 Reporting a busy condition

buffers in the secondary and set the Receive count to 3. However, the secondary cannot signal to the primary that its buffers are full, because $P = 0$. Now, when the frame $\langle I^{13},\ P = 0\rangle$ comes in, the secondary will reject it (buffers full). Frame $\langle I^{14},\ P = 1\rangle$ is also rejected, but now the secondary can send (because $P = 1$) a $\langle RNR,\ N(R) = 3,\ F = 1\rangle$. This tells the primary that the secondary accepted frames up to and including I^{12} but no more. The primary will now send $\langle RR,\ P = 1\rangle$ at regular intervals, until the secondary can receive again and thus responds with $\langle RR,\ F = 1\rangle$. The primary will then resend I^{13}.

Primary   **Secondary**

N(S)	N(R)		N(S)	N(R)
0	2	*ERROR* ←— I(2,0) ——	2	0
0	2	←—— I(3,0) ——	3	0
0	2	—— REJ(2) ——	4	0
0	2	←—— I(4,0) ——	5	0
0	3	←—— I(2,0) —— ·	2	0
			3	0
0	4	←—— I(3,0) —— ·	4	0

Fig. 4.10 The use of REJ in Two-Way-Simultaneous communication

4.5.4 Reject

When a station discovers that the Send count in a frame is not equal to its Receive count, it signals this in TWS communication with an REJ frame, ⟨REJ, $N(R)$⟩. The Receive count in the frame indicates to the other end which frames were received correctly. Figure 4.10 illustrates what happens when a link error occurs. Assume that frame ⟨I, $N(S) = 2$, $N(R) = 0$⟩ never reaches the primary because of a link error. When the next frame ⟨I, $N(S) = 3$, $N(R) = 0$⟩ arrives, the primary detects the wrong Send sequence number and sends ⟨REJ, $N(R) = 2$⟩. All incoming I-frames are now discarded, until ⟨I, $N(S) = 2$, . . .⟩ is retransmitted by the secondary and received by the primary. The secondary then continues from there on.

4.6 Comparison with the Reference Model

Now that we have discussed HDLC as a standard applicable to the Data Link Layer, we can examine the list of services and functions defined for this layer in the Reference Model and see whether HDLC matches it. For the mapping, we use the list given in Appendix B. Where no comment is given for a specific service or function, this indicates that we did not identify an explicit definition of it in the HDLC standards documentation.

Services provided by the Data Link Layer
- Data-link-connections. HDLC provides for data-link-connections between its users. In the present definition, one data-link-connection only is built between one pair of physical-connection-endpoints.
- Data-link-service-data-units. HDLC exchanges data-link-service-data-units over the data-link-connection in the Information Field of its frame, the data-link-protocol-data-unit. No maximum length is specified in the standard, although it is implicitly limited by the cycle of the error detection polynomial.
- Data-link-connection-endpoint-identifiers. HDLC allows data-link-connections to be built on multipoint physical-connections. An Address Field is provided in the frame as an endpoint-identifier.
- Sequencing. The acknowledgement scheme used in HDLC guarantees the original sequence of the data-link-service-data units.
- Error notification. The user of the HDLC service will be notified of persistent failures of the data-link-connection.
- Flow control
- Quality of service parameters

Functions in the Data Link Layer
- Data-link-connection establishment and release. Data-link-connections are established with the various mode setting commands (SNRM,

SARM, SABM and their equivalents in the extended format). They are released with the DISC command.

- Data-link-service-data-units mapping
- Data-link-connection splitting
- Delimiting and synchronization. The unique flag is used for delimiting the frames.
- Sequence control. HDLC maintains the sequence of the frames using the Send and Receive counters in its frame for acknowledgement and for retransmission if necessary.
- Error detection. A 16-bit polynomial Frame Check Sequence is used to detect transmission errors in the physical-connection. Operational errors are detected based on the state of the participating stations (i.e. link-entities).
- Error recovery. The Send and Receive sequence counters are used in the recovery from transmission errors, lost or discarded frames. Operational errors may result in discarded frames, which can be retransmitted, or they are reported with the FRMR frames.
- Flow control. Flow control can be exercised on the data-link-connection by using the RR/RNR frames or by using an acknowledgement window smaller than 7 (resp. 127).
- Identification and parameter exchange. Link-stations can exchange and validate their identity and (implementation dependent) parameters via the XID Command and Response.
- Conveying data circuit control to the Network Layer
- Data Link Layer Management

References

1 International Standards Organization, ISO 3309: *Data communication. High-level Data Link Control procedures—Frame structure*
2 International Standards Organization, ISO 4335: *Data communication. High-level Data Link Control procedures—Elements of procedures (independent numbering)*
3 Davies, D. W., Barber, D. L. A., Price, W. L. and Solomonides, C. M., *Computer networks and their protocols*, Wiley, 1979
4 Tanenbaum, A. S., *Computer networks*, Prentice Hall, 1981

5 X.25 Packet Level protocol

5.1 Introduction

Level 3 (also called the Packet Level) of CCITT Recommendation X.25 is an example of a possible standard on the Network Layer. X.25 is an interface description and this chapter is a narrative of its Level 3. As such, it is not a very good example of a possible Layer 3 standard. However, some of the protocols could be found in the Network Layer. Also an OSI-type network can use an X.25 packet-switched network as a Network Machine, containing Layers 1 to 3 under Layer 4. The chapter will give the reader a good background for a more detailed study of the recommendation itself.

5.2 The recommendation

Recommendation X.25 describes how a packet terminal attaches to a Packet-Switched Network (PSN). The recommendation distinguishes three levels. The first is the Physical Level, the same as ISO's Physical Layer, which has already been reviewed. The second level is the Link Level for which a subset of HDLC is defined. The third level is the Packet Level.

The term *Virtual Circuit* can be found in the literature on X.25 [1–4]. This term is used to indicate a logical connection between two terminals or DTEs. The logical connection is a point-to-point Full-Duplex transport mechanism. One of the basic aims of the Packet Level protocol is to multiplex a number of logical connections over one physical connection. Recommendation X.25 does not define a Virtual Circuit, but it defines a *Virtual Call* (VC) and a *Permanent Virtual Circuit* (PVC). The definitions given in the recommendation [5] are as follows.

Permanent Virtual Circuit A user facility in which a permanent association exists between two DTEs which is identical to the data transfer phase of a *Virtual Call*. No call set-up or clearing procedure is possible or necessary.

Virtual Call A user facility in which a call set-up procedure and a Call clearing procedure will determine a period of communication between two DTEs in which user's data will be transferred in the network in the packet mode operation. All the user's data is delivered from the network in the same order in which it is received by the network.

So, in fact, PVC is considered a special case of a VC. Confusing, in the literature, is the use of VC as an abbreviation for Virtual Circuit, whereas it is suggested for Virtual Call in the recommendation. Even though one can argue in favor of the use of the term Virtual Circuit, and we tend to agree with that, we adopt the following terminology throughout the book:

- Permanent Virtual Circuit   PVC
- Virtual Call   VC

Also the *Period of Communication* is called the *Connection*, or *Virtual Circuit Services*, or is indicated through the use of the verb 'connect' as, for example, 'Two DTEs are connected'.

5.3 Logical Channel

The user's DTE will connect with another DTE through a *Logical Channel* in its own DTE. The user's data is transmitted over that channel and is delivered by the network in the same sequence as it was received.

In order to connect a DTE to more than one other DTE at the same time, Logical Channels are defined. A Logical Channel has an identification consisting of a *Logical Channel Group Number*, with a maximum of 4 bits, and a *Logical Channel Number* with a maximum of 8 bits. This gives a possible maximum of 4095 different logical channels.

A Virtual Call (VC) or a Permanent Virtual Circuit (PVC) is mapped onto a particular Logical Channel Number. For a PVC, this channel number is permanently assigned by the administration of the network for each DTE involved. For a VC, the Logical Channel Number assignment is done during the call set-up. The Logical Channel Number becomes available again after the connection is cleared.

Logical Channel Number 1 is recommended for use in single-channel DTEs, such as low-function and low-cost terminals. For multiple channel DTEs, the assignment of Logical Channels starts at 1.

Figure 5.1 shows that PVCs are allocated from Logical Channel Number 1. The rest of the logical channels are used for VCs. The VCs can be divided into three categories: the one-way incoming calls, the two-way incoming and outgoing calls and the one-way outgoing calls. The incoming calls are equivalents of *auto-answer* facilities, also called *ports*, and will be allocated to the lower channel numbers after the PVCs, if there are any. Following is a group which can be used for both incoming and outgoing calls. The highest channel numbers will be allocated to the outgoing calls which are equivalent to *auto-dial* facilities, also called *gates*. The allocation within a group has to be contiguous and is agreed upon with the network

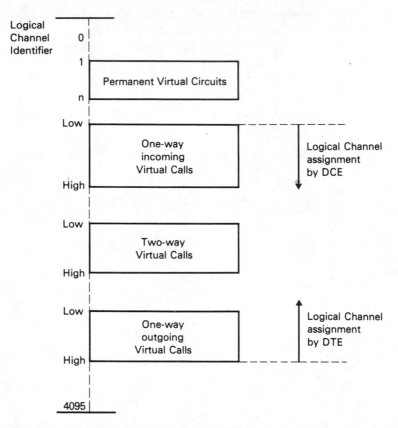

Logical Channel Identifier = Logical Channel Group Number
+ Logical Channel Number

Fig. 5.1 Logical Channel Number assignment

administration. For example, a DTE will subscribe for a network connection with

10 PVCs	15 mixed VCs
20 one-way incoming calls (VC)	20 one-way outgoing calls (VC)

In order to avoid call collisions, search algorithms have to be applied. The network will, in case of an incoming call, allocate to that VC the lowest available channel in the Ready state of the range defined as one-way incoming call channels. If all are busy, then it will try to allocate the lowest available logical channel number in the mixed range. If none is available for the DTE, the network will clear the VC with a diagnostic code indicating the reason.

5.4 The packet format

The user data transmitted through the network has to be in a well-defined format called a *packet*.

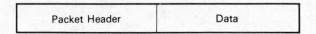

| Packet Header | Data |

Fig. 5.2 A packet

What is a packet? It is a sequence of binary digits, consisting of data and control elements arranged in a special format, which is transmitted as a composite whole. The packet may be of any length up to some fixed maximum, and must include, within its control information, identifying endpoint station addresses or Logical Channel Number. In order to implement the Packet Level, information about the Virtual Circuit service has to be provided to the PSN so that, for example, the packet can be routed to the correct destination. Figure 5.2 shows a packet with its Packet Header where that information is stored. Figure 5.3 shows a Data packet.

The following information can be found in the Packet Header of data packets (as shown in the figure) or of control packets (which are discussed later).

Bytes 1 and 2

General Format Identifier
Consists of 4 bits which describe the general format of the Packet Header. Figure 5.4 gives the various combinations and their significance.

Byte 1
Bit 8, the Q-bit   The Qualifer bit permits a distinction to be made between data packets. It allows, for instance, the transmission of data on two flows: for example, a data flow and a control flow.

Bit 7, the D-bit   The Delivery bit is used for delivery confirmation procedures in Data and Call set-up packets.

Bits 6–5   These indicate whether modulo 8 or 128 sequence numbering is used and whether format extensions are available.

Logical Channel Group Number (bits 4–1)

Byte 2
Logical Channel Number   The Logical Channel Group Number and the Logical Channel Number specify the PVC or VC number.

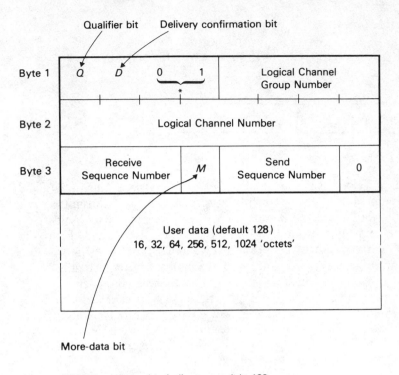

*'10'-bitconfiguration indicates modulo-128
sequence numbers (4-byte Packet Header)

Fig. 5.3 Format of a Data Packet

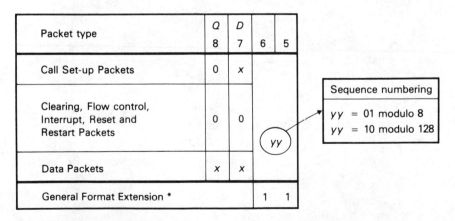

Packet type	Q 8	D 7	6	5
Call Set-up Packets	0	x		
Clearing, Flow control, Interrupt, Reset and Restart Packets	0	0		
Data Packets	x	x		
General Format Extension *			1	1

Sequence numbering
yy = 01 modulo 8
yy = 10 modulo 128

x   May be set to either 0 or 1

*   Extension of General Format Codes (under study)

Fig. 5.4 General Format Identifier options

56 Computer network architectures

Byte 3

If bit $1 = 1$, the packet is a control packet. In this case, byte 3 will indicate the packet type and is called the *Packet Type Identifier*. Figure 5.5 shows the different packet types and their bit configurations.

If bit $1 = 0$, the packet is a Data Packet.

Receive, P(r), and Send, P(s), Sequence Numbers These are used for flow control and for packet identification where delivery confirmation is used (*D*-bit). Only Data Packets have a Send Sequence Number. The sequence numbers are modulo 8 with an option for modulo 128.

Bit 5, M-bit The More-data bit allows the user to put a relationship between packets. For example, since the data can be too long for the network, it has to be cut into pieces compatible with the network subscribed maximum user-data length. The last packet of a series carries the More-data bit set to zero and indicates to the user that it can re-assemble the series of packets into the original data.

User data The default user data area in a packet is 128 bytes. Other data sizes can be available in specific networks with a maximum of 1024 bytes. Packets can have different data sizes in each direction, i.e. DTEs can subscribe to different maximum data-packet sizes.

DCE to DTE	DTE to DCE	Byte 3		
		8 7 6 5	4 3 2 1	
Incoming Call	Call Request	0 0 0 0	1 0 1 1	
Call Connected	Call Accepted	0 0 0 0	1 1 1 1	Call set-up
Clear Indication	Clear Request	0 0 0 1	0 0 1 1	and
DCE Clear Confirmation	DTE Clear Confirmation	0 0 0 1	0 1 1 1	Clearing
DCE Data	DTE Data	$P(r)$ x	$P(s)$ 0	
DCE Interrupt	DTE Interrupt	0 0 1 0	0 0 1 1	Data and
DCE Interrupt Confirmation	DTE Interrupt Confirmation	0 0 1 0	0 1 1 1	Interrupt
DCE RR	DTE RR	$P(r)$ 0	0 0 0 1	
DCE RNR	DTE RNR	$P(r)$ 0	0 1 0 1	
	DTE REJ	$P(r)$ 0	1 0 0 1	Flow control
Reset Indication	Reset Request	0 0 0 1	1 0 1 1	and Reset*
DCE Reset Confirmation	DTE Reset Confirmation	0 0 0 1	1 1 1 1	
Restart Indication	Restart Request	1 1 1 1	1 0 1 1	
DCE Restart Confirmation	DTE Restart Indication	1 1 1 1	1 1 1 1	Restart

* RR, RNR, REJ shown have modulo 8 sequence numbers

x May be set to either 0 or 1

Fig. 5.5 Packet types

5.5 Procedure for Virtual Call service

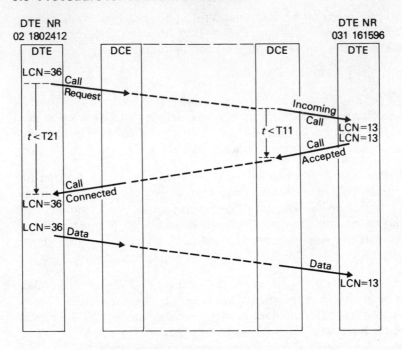

Fig. 5.6 Call Request procedure: T21 = 200s, T11 = 60s

A *Calling DTE* constructs a *Call Request Packet*, which it transmits in the network. It requests the network to establish a connection with a remote DTE based on the information provided in the Call Request Packet. The information put in the packet by the calling DTE is, for example, the Network Address of the *Called DTE*. Figure 5.6 shows such an exchange where a DTE with number 02 1802412 calls another DTE with number 031 161596. The calling DTE chooses, in order to transmit the packet into the network, the Logical Channel with the highest number available in the agreed range. For example, if at subscription time, a logical channel address-range for one-way outgoing calls from addresses 30 to 36 was agreed, and if none of the logical channels is busy, the DTE should have chosen the Logical Channel with address 36. The network or DCE completes the Call Request Packet with the address of the calling DTE. It will then notify the called DTE, by means of an *Incoming Call Packet*, that the calling DTE wants a connection. This packet is identical to the original Call Request Packet. To deliver this packet, the DCE selects a logical channel with the lowest available number. For example, if the one-way incoming call address range spans channel numbers 10 to 15 and channels 10 to 12 are busy, the DCE will select Logical Channel Number 13.

As Fig. 5.7 shows, the Call Request Packet contains also a *Facility Field*, which is discussed in Section 5.9.

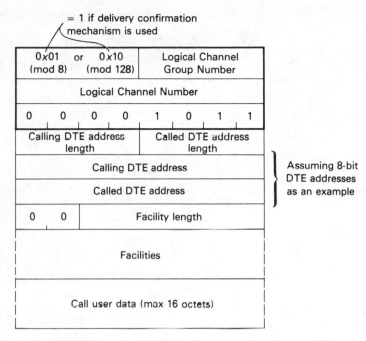

Fig. 5.7 Call Request Packet

The called DTE analyzes the Incoming Call Packet and decides whether it can make a connection or not. Acceptance results in a *Call Accepted Packet* that the DTE sends over the same Logical Channel as the one over which it received the Call Indication Packet. This Logical Channel is now in the Data Transfer State.

The Network delivers a *Call Connected Packet* over the same Logical Channel used by the calling DTE (channel 36 in the example) for the transmission of the Call Request Packet. This Logical Channel goes also into the Data Transfer State and the two DTEs are connected. Now, data packets can be exchanged between both DTEs.

Non-acceptance of the call results in the DTE transmitting a *Clear Request Packet* to the DCE. As a result, the network will clear the Virtual Call and inform the Calling DTE by means of a *Clear Indication Packet*. If a DTE does not answer at all, a Clear Request Packet is sent by the calling DTE after a time-out of 200 s. Calls that are not successful because of Network problems also initiate the transmission of a Clear Indication Packet to the calling DTE by the DCE.

A DTE that wants to break a connection in which it is participating can do that at any time by transmitting a Clear Request Packet into the

network. When the DCE wants to release the Logical Channel, it sends a
Clear Confirmation Packet (see Section 5.8).

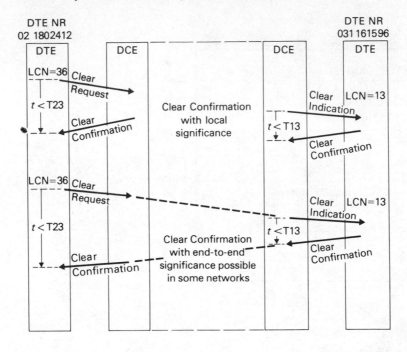

Fig. 5.8 Clearing with local and end-to-end significance: T23 = 180s, T13 = 60s

Figure 5.8 shows that the recommendation assumes only local significance of the Clear Confirmation Packet. Certain network implementations
can give an end-to-end significance to the Clear procedure. The figure also
shows how in that case the Clear Confirmation Packet is only delivered
after the other DTE has accepted to clear the connection through the
transmission of a Clear Confirmation Packet. This control packet is then
delivered to the originating DTE by the DCE. Time-outs are defined for
every exchange of control packets. A DTE or a DCE has to respond to a
control packet before the time-out occurs. All figures with control packet
exchanges show the time-out values.

5.6 Data Transfer Mode

The moment the connection is established, both DTEs will have a
Full-Duplex Facility for exchanging Data Packets. This means that both
ends can start sending packets independently of each other.

The recommendation allows packets to be sent on two flows. The distinction of the flows is made through the setting of the Qualifier bit in the Packet Header (see Fig. 5.3). An example of the use of the Qualifier bit is the implementation of a flow for data transmission and of one for the transmission of control information in Recommendations X.3, X.28 and X.29 (see Section 12.5.9).

Packets that are sent in or out of the network carry *Sequence Numbers* (see Fig. 5.3) in the Packet Header. These sequence numbers are used for local *flow control* and for the sequence check between the DTE and the DCE, and vice versa. There is a *Send Sequence Number*, $P(s)$, and a *Receive Sequence Number*, $P(r)$. These numbers wrap around and they can be modulo 8 or modulo 128. All logical channels of a DTE should use the same modulus.

The maximum length of the user data packet in the network defaults to a size of 128 bytes. Optionally, networks can allow sizes of 16, 32, 64, 256, 512 and 1024 bytes. The user will define at subscription time a particular packet size. It is possible that the network has to divide a packet into packets of smaller length. An example is the case of one DTE being a CPU that, because of its capabilities and throughput requirements, subscribed to use packets of 256 bytes. The other DTE is a simple terminal and can only handle packets with a user data field of 64 bytes. The network will then divide the packets coming from the CPU into a number of packets with a maximum length of 64 bytes. In order to signal the receiving DTE that there is a relationship between the packets, the DCE will use the *More-data bit* to express that relationship.

For example, the CPU sends a packet with a user data field of exactly 256 bytes (Fig. 5.9). The network will split that into four packets with a user data length of 64 bytes. It will put the More-data bit 'on' in the first three data packets and the More-data bit 'off' in the fourth packet. The $P(s)$ and the $P(r)$ delivered to the receiving DTE will be different from the set put in the packet by the originating DTE. The originating DTE transferred one packet into the network and the receiving DTE received four packets. This shows clearly that for recovery purposes, due to the clearing or the restart of a connection, a higher level protocol is required. Some network implementations can have end-to-end significance of the $P(r)$. This happens at the expense, though, of lesser capabilities at the DTE-to-DTE level, such as only one common user data length.

Recommendation X.25 offers also the possibility of having an end-to-end control capability of $P(r)$ by means of the *Delivery Confirmation Bit* in the Packet Header. The sending DTE should set the D-bit to 1 if it wants an end-to-end acknowledgement of the delivery of the data at the remote DTE. This happens through the $P(r)$ returned by the receiving DTE. The $P(r)$ can be in the header of a data or a flow control packet. If both sides have the same packet lengths, the D-bit function is rather straightforward. If the maximum user data size of the sending side is larger than that of the receiving side, the network has to manage the delivery of the correct $P(r)$

to the originator, after the receiving DTE has returned a $P(r)$ equal to the $P(s)+1$ from the packet it received with the D-bit on.

Also the opposite can happen. The receiving DTE has a larger maximum user data length than the originating DTE. Now, the network could combine subsequent packets if the More-data bit is set, the packets are full and the D-bit is off. If the D-bit is set, the network should provide the correct $P(r)$ to the sending DTE. While a D-bit response is pending, the window of the flow control mechanism remains shut.

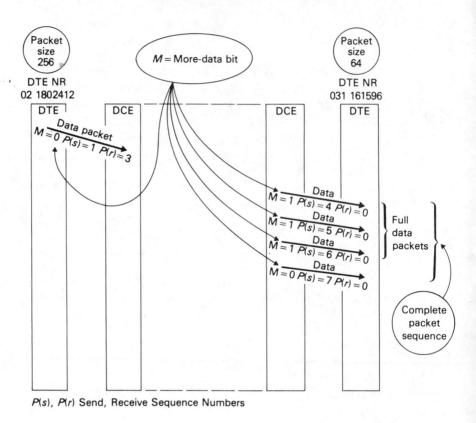

$P(s)$, $P(r)$ Send, Receive Sequence Numbers

Fig. 5.9 Packet splitting by DCE

The recommendation talks in terms of A- and B-type Packets in this context. Figure 5.10 shows the above as a function of M-bits, D-bits and whether the user data field is full. It indicates whether the network should recombine packets (A-type) or not (B-type). The recommendation also defines a *Complete Packet Sequence*, which is composed of a B-type Packet preceded by a number of A-type Packets.

5.7 Flow control procedures

The transmission of data packets is controlled separately for each direction and is based on the authorization of the receiver. This is called *Windowing*.

Type	M-bit	Q-bit	Packet full?	Network combines with subsequent Packet(s) when possible
A	1	0	Yes	Yes
B	0	1	No	
	0	0	No	
	1	0	No	
	1	1	No	No
	0	0	Yes	
	0	1	Yes	
	1	1	Yes	

Fig. 5.10 Data packets categories

The window is a predefined number of packets which the sender may transmit before it has to request authorization, if the window was not opened before, to send more packets. Or, in other words,

A Window (W) is the ordered set of W consecutive packet Send Sequence Numbers $P(s)$ of Data Packets authorized to cross the DTE–DCE interface.

In the reset state, the sequence numbers are set to 0, $P(s) = 0$. At this point, the sender can transmit up to the Send Sequence Number

$$P(s) = P(s)_{min} + W$$

with $P(s)_{min}$ being the lower limit of the window (e.g. $P(s)_{min} = 0$ after reset). The sender cannot transmit the packet carrying the Send Sequence Number

$$P(s) = P(s)_{\min} + W + 1$$

It can only send again when it receives a Data Packet or a flow control *Receive Ready* (RR) Packet, from which it gets a $P(r)$ providing a new lower limit:

$$P(s)_{\min} = P(r)$$

The DTE or DCE can indicate that they cannot handle more packets temporarily. They will transmit a *Receive Not Ready* (RNR) Packet for this purpose. The RNR Packet contains a $P(r)$ which will become the lower window edge. The sender now waits until the receiver wants to resume communication. This is normally done with a Receive Ready Packet.

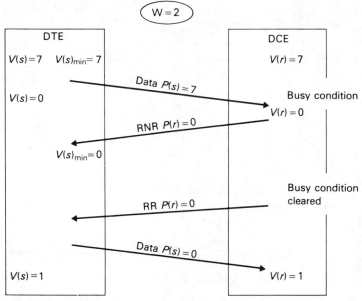

W Window
$V(s)$, $V(r)$ Send, Receive variables
$P(s)$, $P(r)$ Send, Receive Sequence Numbers

Fig. 5.11 Receive Not Ready operation

Figure 5.11 shows such an exchange with a window size of two. It should be emphasized that this flow control is done between DTE and DCE and vice-versa and not from DTE to DTE through the PSN, hence the flow control procedure has only local significance instead of DTE-to-DTE or end-to-end significance. The receiving DTE can, however, influence the sending DTE through its local flow control mechanism [6]. An RR Packet, opening the window, can be withheld or an RNR Packet can be transmitted, keeping the packets from moving into or out of the network. This will cause back-pressure on the source DTE, taking advantage of the limited number of data packets that can reside at the same time in the network. This number is network-dependent.

A DTE can use an *Interrupt procedure* to transmit data to a remote DTE without following the flow control procedure. The *Interrupt Packet* has end-to-end significance. The sending DTE should not send another Interrupt Packet before an *Interrupt Confirmation Packet* is received back from the receiving DTE. As said before, the Interrupt Packet does not follow the flow control procedure nor does it affect the flow of data packets. It will get priority over data packets that are flowing over the VC or PVC. The DCE will pass the Interrupt Packet as soon as possible, even before a data packet that was waiting for transmission to the DTE. Figure 5.12 shows this process.

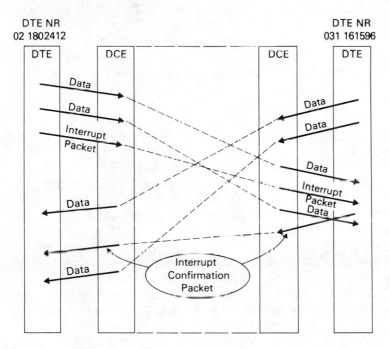

Fig. 5.12 Interrupt procedure

5.8 Restart, Clear and Reset procedures

Once the Link Level is in the Data Transfer Mode, the network node management of the DTE can start the initialization of the Packet Level. It uses the restart procedure for this by sending a *DTE Restart Request Packet* to the DCE. The network responds with a *DCE Restart Confirmation*

Packet. Inherently, all PVCs are reset and all VCs cleared. VCs will now have to be set up through the Virtual Call set-up procedure. For the PVCs, the sequence numbers are reset and the PVCs are immediately in the Data Transfer State.

The restart procedure can also be used to re-initialize the communications in which the DTE was involved. The reason for the restart could be the breakdown of the link between the DTE and the network. It could also be because of network congestion that the DCE decides to release a complete DTE. In both cases, the complete DTE has to be restarted when the failure has recovered. Then, the DCE will send a *Restart Indication Packet*. The DTE has then to respond with a DTE Restart Confirmation Packet.

Recoverable failures can occur on a PVC or VC; examples are sequence errors, loss of packets or, again, network congestion. In this case, the reset procedure will be used to indicate the error. A *Reset Request Packet*, containing a cause field, will be sent by the DTE or DCE over the DTE–DCE interface. The receiver sends back a *Reset Confirmation Packet* and both sides reset, for instance, the sequence numbers of the Packet Headers. Now the Data Packet exchange can resume. A higher level protocol in the DTE is, however, required to determine which packets the communication should restart with.

The Clear procedure is only used for the Virtual Call Services. It will break a Virtual Call connection. Both the DTE, for application reasons, and the DCE, for network errors or on request of the remote DTE, can use the procedure. The procedure has only local significance even though some network implementations could give end-to-end significance, see Fig. 5.8. The DTE sends a *Clear Request Packet* or the DCE sends a *Clear Indication Packet* to indicate that the termination of a VC is required. The receiver responds with a *Clear Confirmation Packet*. To resume communication, the Call set-up procedure should be started by the DTE.

Some networks will use a *Diagnostic Packet*, which conveys information about unrecoverable errors and is sent by the DCE. The network uses this packet when the usual methods of error handling, described above, are inappropriate. The transmission of this Diagnostic Packet does not alter the operational state of the DCE or the DTE. The diagnostics provided concern invalid packet types for a particular state of the service, timer expiration and packets that are not allowed, and explain why. This kind of information can be passed to higher level protocols so that they can take corrective action. This type of diagnostic information together with the diagnostic fields in the Clear Request, Reset Request and Restart Request Packets can be used in the user's network management applications.

5.9 Optional facilities

Recommendation X.25 describes a number of optional user facilities on the packet level. The suggested procedures have special packets defined or parameters that are carried in the facility field of the Call Set-up Packets. Appendix E gives a list of the optional facilities with a short overview of the facility.

5.10 Comparison with the Reference Model

As stated at the beginning of this chapter, Recommendation X.25 describes an interface between a DTE and the network, DCE. Below, we compare the recommendation with the services provided by the Network Layer of the Reference Model as presented in Appendix B. We find that all these services are provided by Level 3 of Recommendation X.25. Most of the functions in the Network Layer are not explicitly defined in Level 3 of X.25. Permanent Virtual Circuits and Virtual Calls could be considered as network-connections that are only defined between the DTE and the network, however. Routing and switching are not defined in the recommendation even though these functions are present in X.25 network implementations. In fact, the recommendation describes only the services that it can provide to a Layer 4.

If there is no comment on a service and/or function in the following summary, it indicates that we did not identify it explicitly.

Services provided by the Network Layer
- Network addresses. The network addresses used are the DTE addresses.
- Network-connections. The connection between the DTE and the DCE in the network, i.e. the Logical Channel, is the network-connection.
- Network-connection-endpoint-identifiers. The Logical Channel Number can be considered as the network-connection-endpoint-identifier.
- Network-service-data-unit transfer. The network-service-data-unit transferred is the packet.
- Quality of service parameters. The user of the service can negotiate Quality of service parameters at call set-up time.
- Error notification. Reason codes in the Clear, Reset and Diagnostic Packets are used to notify the user of the service that errors occurred.
- Sequencing
- Flow control. The Receive Ready and Receive Not Ready Packets are used to achieve flow control across the network-connection.

- Expedited network-service-data-unit transfer. An expedited network-service-data-unit can be transferred as a one-byte field in the Interrupt Packet.
- Reset. Each logical channel can independently be reset.
- Release

Functions in the Network Layer
- Routing and relaying
- Network-connections. Network-connections are established between DTE and DCE.
- Network-connection multiplexing. Multiple network-connections can be multiplexed on one data-link-connection.
- Segmenting and blocking
- Error detection. When an error is detected, the Logical Channel is reset or cleared, or a diagnostic packet is transmitted. In all cases, an error notification is given to the user of the service.
- Error recovery
- Sequencing. Sequencing is provided between the DTE and the DCE and vice versa.
- Flow control. Flow control is achieved using a window technique based on the sequence numbers of the packets transmitted across the network-connection. The RR and RNR packets are used to enforce the flow control.
- Expedited data transfer. Through a one-byte field in the Interrupt Packet.
- Reset. Through the Reset Packet.
- Service selection
- Network Layer Management

References

1 Scantlebury, R., SNA, X.25 and Transpac—can they co-exist?, *Proc. Online Conf. IBM Teleprocessing*, Online Conferences Ltd, Uxbridge, England, 1979
2 Logica Ltd, *Packet switching report*, Sept. 1978
3 Corr, F. P. and Neal, D. H., SNA and emerging international standards, *IBM Syst. J.*, vol. 18, no. 2, 1979, pp. 244–262
4 Drukarch, C. Z., Karp, P. M., Knightson, K. G., Lavandera, L., Rybczynski, A. M. and Sone, N., X.25: the universal packet network, *Proc. 5th Int. Conf. Computer Commun.*, Atlanta, 27–30 Oct. 1980, pp. 649–657
5 CCITT, *Data communication networks. Services and facilities. Terminal equipment and interfaces. Recommendations X.1–X.29*, Yellow Book, Vol VII—Facicle VIII.2, CCITT VIIth Plenary Assembly, Geneva, 10–21 Nov. 1980, ITU, Geneva, 1981
6 Rybczynski, A. M. and Palframan, J. D., A common X.25 interface, *Computer Networks*, vol. 4, no. 3, 1980, pp. 97–110

6 The EHKP4 protocol

6.1 Introduction

As an example of a (potential) standard for the Transport Layer*, we describe a standard defined in West Germany. There, an *ad hoc* Working Group for Higher Communications Protocols was founded in February 1979. This group was commissioned to determine user demand in the public administration sector. It was also supposed to prepare proposals for higher level protocols, keeping in mind the international standardization effort and other existing projects.

The idea was not that the group developed protocols. Rather, the objective was to find a unified solution for all existing and planned projects in this sector. The existing projects were

a DKM, the protocol used in the DVS network (Chapter 14).
b The pilot complex of technical–scientific systems of the University Working Group PIX.
c The subsidized project PAPA—pilot applications of a Public Packet Service for the interconnection of service centers and service center customers.

As a base for EHKP4—*Einheitliche Höhere Kommunikations Protokolle* (Unified Higher-level Control Protocol) for Level 4—the DVS network project [1] was used, supplemented with some functions of the PIX Layer 4/5 protocols. Hence, in describing the government-accepted EHKP4 protocols, we must include the DVS network DKM, which was implemented in 1980. The level of EHKP4 that is described is Version 2.0 [2].

EHKP4 assumes, at the base, the existence of a *Network Machine* from which it can request communications services to another EHKP4. That Network Machine can be an X.25 Public or Private Switched Network. Such a network then takes care of Level 1 through 3 functions, i.e. Physical, Link and Network Layers. The Network Machine provides network-connections. An alternative is the use of a wire or circuit,

---

* In this description, we will use level numbers for the layers of the Reference Model, as is done in the EHKP4 documentation and used to be done in the Reference Model itself. The relation is: Physical Layer, Level 1; Link Layer, Level 2, etc.

telephone line, with HDLC line control. This was seen as a back-up possibility in case the X.25 network should completely fail. It was later extended as a possible part of the Network Machine. EHKP4 itself provides transport services to its users (Level 5 and up) over these connections and also has end-to-end control over its own connection, called a transport-connection—meaning the logical connections of two EHKP4 implementations.

To describe this interim standard for Level 4, we have to look at it from a basic point of view. There is first the protocol between communicating Level 4 entities, or the transport protocol communication rules. Next, there is the communication interface, also called the Service Interface, between Levels 5 and 4. It is the way Level 5 requests functions, such as data transfer, from Level 4. Lastly, there are the functions of the Service Interface between Levels 4 and 3, describing what EHKP4 expects the Network Machine to do. We will describe these three aspects of EHKP4 in this sequence.

6.2 EHKP4 transport protocol

The transport protocol in EHKP4 guarantees by definition an efficient, fast and error-free transmission of user data. The unit of user data on Level 4 is called a *record*. Records consist of the data transmitted for Level 5 complemented with protocol information for Level 4. The protocol information is carried in a header based on the X.25 header layout.

Type	Implied acknowledgment
OPEN	
ACCEPTED	
RESETI	
RESETC	Yes
CLOSE	
ABORT	
END	Yes
Optional	
OPENW	
STATUS	
RR	Yes
RNR	Yes
INTER	
INTERC	Yes

Fig. 6.1 EHKP4: s-records

Before records can be exchanged, the transport-connection must be established. EHKP4 defines a series of control records, the *s-records*, for this purpose. They are listed in Fig. 6.1.

EHKP4 defines a basic set of functions which satisfy the minimum requirements for compatible end-to-end communications. Depending on traffic patterns, additional safety requirements, traffic profiles and so on, the basic set of functions can be expanded with optional functions or services.

The basic set of functions contains the set-up and termination of the transport-connection. In order to set up the connection, a transport-entity sends an s-record, the *OPEN* s-record, to another transport-entity. The OPEN s-record describes the function profile requested for this transport-connection. If the destination transport-entity agrees with the OPEN profile, it sends another s-record, the *ACCEPTED* s-record, to the originator of the OPEN s-record. If it cannot agree, and *END* s-record is sent, explaining why the transport-connection cannot be established. An existing transport-connection is terminated with a *CLOSE* s-record.

The second function in the basic set is the Sending and Receiving of *I-records*. The exchange is sequence-checked by means of a sequence number in the Record Header. If a sequence error or the loss of an I-record is detected, the error is processed through an error protocol. In the basic set, it will result in a notification to the higher layer and the exchange of a RESETI s-record to the sender EHKP4. This one acknowledges the RESETI with a RESETC s-record. Both sides synchronize their sequence numbers by resetting them to zero. No attempt is made to recover lost user data, I-records, in the transport protocol.

The last function in the basic set is called *Fragmentation*. Fragmentation is simply another word for Segmenting. The user of the transport service may transfer messages, the Level 5 unit of data, that can have a length exceeding the maximum length of the I-record. The maximum length of the I-record was agreed at transport-connection set-up time and was defined in the OPEN s-record. A message that does not fit into an I-record will be fragmented and transmitted over the transport-connection in several I-records. The receiving EHKP4 will re-assemble the I-records into the original message before the data is passed to the higher level.

So much for the basic functions. One should notice the absence of an explicit flow control function in the basic set. Level 4 relies on Level 3 flow control through *Data back-pressure* at the Level 3/4 interface at the receiver and the sender side. It works as follows. The receiver on Level 4 will not accept any data as long as it itself cannot free its buffer resources by passing the data to the user, Level 5. Automatically, the receiver's refusal will ripple through the Network Machine into the sending Level 4, which will have to wait before its Level 3 allows it to put in more data.

EHKP4 allows for extensions of the basic set of functions. Decisions, or better agreement concerning the use of any of the options, is negotiated through the OPEN s-record and the ACCEPTED s-record. So, an implementation of EHKP4 could be different from system to system, depending on the additional options it can handle. The options have to do with type of application to be supported, network design or increase of efficiency and quality of service.

A first option is *multiplexing*. This function allows the mapping of several transport-connections onto one network-connection. For example, several users of the Transport Layer would be talking to several users in the same remote node. Between the nodes, a Virtual Circuit service, the network-connection on Level 3, could exist. This Virtual Circuit service will have a specific throughput. If that throughput is not completely taken by a transport service on Level 4, then another transport service, between the other users of the above mentioned collection, could use that Virtual Circuit. The number of transport-connections to be mapped onto a network-connection is limited by the total throughput required and the throughput on Level 3 available. If there is not enough, then a supplementary network-connection is set up. Multiplexing cannot rely on back-pressure flow control because this relies on the Level 3 flow control mechanism. This would stop all transport-connections using the same network-connection. Consequently, explicit flow control is required.

The next option is this explicit flow control. This function controls the data flow within the transport-connection with the windowing technique. The sending EHKP4 can transmit an agreed number of I-records, for example 25. The agreed number is negotiated during set-up time, i.e. in the OPEN s-record, and is called a window. The maximum number of records not acknowledged, and also the maximum window, is 255. When the window size is reached, an acknowledgement is requested in order to open the window again. This is shown in Fig. 6.2.

It is done by setting a bit in the header of an I-record, meaning that an acknowledgement is required. It is also called Poll and has in fact a polling function, but polling for an Acknowledgement (ACK). The receiving EHKP4 can acknowledge by means of the RR or RNR s-record which carries the number of the received I-record up to which acknowledgement is given. In the case of an RR s-record, the window is opened and the transmitting Level 4 can start transmitting again. If it is an RNR s-record, the EHKP4 will have to inquire, on a regular basis and by means of the STATUS s-record, when it can restart transmission.

Another optional function is the recovery by the transport level of I-records lost by the network-connection. In the case of an X.25 network, it is possible that, because of congestion, the Virtual Circuit service becomes reset by the X.25 network. This can result in a loss of packets and thus also in the loss of I-records. This option allows Level 4 to recover by retransmitting the I-records without the higher levels noticing it.

The use of optional parameters in the OPEN s-record is another optional function. In this way, extra security can be imposed through passwords

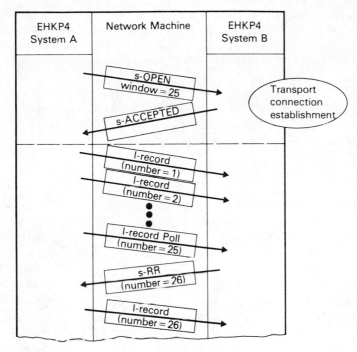

Fig. 6.2 EHKP4: optional flow control

exchanged in the OPEN s-record. Also accounting functions and data could be included.

Re-establishment of a network-connection is an optional function where the Transport Layer attempts to keep a transport-connection going when the network-connection it uses fails. It tries to map the transport connection onto another network-connection without disturbing the users of the transport service.

The users of the transport service are allowed special treatment of their messages through the *interrupt* and *expedited data* functions. It allows the exchange of data over a transport-connection outside the normal data flow control. It uses for that the *INTER s-record*, which is acknowledged by the receiver with an *INTERC s-record*. When several short messages are exchanged by the users of the Transport Layer, an optional *blocking* function can help to improve the efficiency of the transport-connection. It allows several short messages to be blocked in one I-record. In order to permit the receiving EHKP4 to break up the I-record in the original messages, an expansion of the Record Header and a length field are provided for every message.

The final option is called *transaction-oriented service*. This service is comparable with the datagram service in X.25 or its Fast Select service. What is meant is that data is exchanged between users without opening an explicit transport-connection. A special type of record is transmitted, called an *M-record*. An acknowledgement or, rather, an answer can be requested, which the receiver of an M-record will do through an *A-record*, an answer record.

So much for the transport protocols between EHKP4s. It is during the set-up of the transport-connection that all these options and parameters are decided. But where does EHKP4 get them from? Well, it is the user of the Transport Layer that will decide what it expects from transport-connection. It communicates the information through the Level 5 to the Level 4 service interface.

6.3 Level 5 (EHKP5) to EHKP4 service interface

EHKP4 and its underlying Network Machine constitute a transport medium that gives a message transport service to two users at a time. The transport service is described in the previous section. In order to let a user take advantage of this transport service, an interface must be defined between the user and the transport medium. This will have to be an abstract interface that two parties may implement in different real interfaces without restricting the use of the services. What is described in EHKP4 is such an abstract interface between, for example, EHKP5 and EHKP4. The description should be interpreted as services of EHKP4 instead of the implementation of the interface. The services are described as verbs with a number of parameters. The verbs defined are listed in Fig. 6.3. Each verb functions on either side of the interface, from Level 5 to 4 and from 4 to 5.

Verb type	Remarks
LIST	Sign-on to transport layer
IGNORE	Sign-off
CONNECT	Establish network connection
DATA —	REQUEST RESPONSE INDICATION CONFIRMATION
PUSH	Force data transmission
PURGE	Drop all data on transport connection
DISCONNECT	Release transport connection

Fig. 6.3 EHKP4: services provided by Level 4 for Level 5

First, a user of EHKP4 has to be known to EHKP4. This is done through the verb *LIST*, which makes the user known to the transport service. *IGNORE* will sign the user off the service and results in no more access to any other user of the transport medium. Next, a user can request a transport-connection through the *CONNECT* serivce. With the CONNECT, the user provides a series of parameters such as the 'Name of called party', the dcsired throughput class, transport profile, etc. It allows the Transport Layer, EHKP4, to build an OPEN s-record containing the parameters and optional functions of the transport-connection that should be set up. Once the transport connection is made, EHKP4 uses the CONNECT service to acknowledge the establishment to the user. The user can now start to exchange messages with its counterpart. Figure 6.4 shows the set-up of a transport-connection and the verb-dialog requesting it.

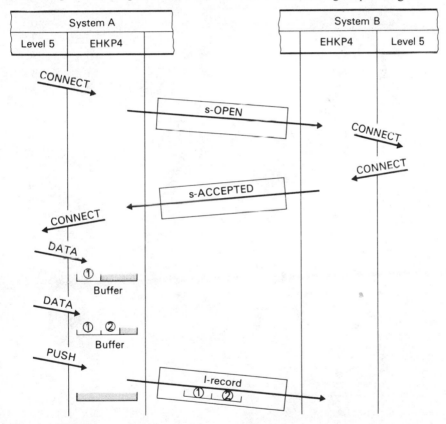

Fig. 6.4 EHKP4: transport connection set-up

The *DATA* service permits the counterpart to send or receive data to and from that user and the *PUSH* service allows that user to force EHKP4 to transmit all pending data. An example is the case where short messages are blocked together. If an I-record is not yet filled completely, EHKP4 will wait to transmit the I-record until it is full. With PUSH, the user can force the transmission of the not completely filled record.

When the user wants to synchronize a reset of the communication with its counterpart, it can use the *PURGE* service. It will drop all I-records on the transport-connection.It will further reset flow control to its original position. The counterpart will be informed through the PURGE service on its side.

When the user decides to terminate the communication, it uses the *DISCONNECT* service. This will result in EHKP4 closing the transport-connection. Since users are considered as peer-to-peer entities, conflict situations are possible. These are resolved by following a priority which will be respected by both layers.

6.4 EHKP4 to Level 3 service interface

The way Level 5 communicates with EHKP4 through an abstract interface is similar to the service interface between Levels 4 and 3. It represents the way EHKP4 communicates what it expects from the Network Machine. Figure 6.5 shows the verbs that are defined at this interface.

Verb type	Remarks	Possible X.25 Level 3 mapping
ALLOCATE	Sign-on to Network Machine	
DEALLOCATE	Sign-off from Network Machine	
INIT	Request network connection	Call Packet
TRANSFER		Complete Packet Sequence
RESET		Reset Packet
TERMINATE	Break network connection	Clear Packet

Fig. 6.5 EHKP4: services requested by EHKP4 from Level 3

Again, the verbs have an up and down meaning. EHKP4 has to sign on to the network service in order to use it. How this actually is implemented is not relevant to this discussion. The function used is the *ALLOCATE* service. To sign off from the Network Machine, EHKP4 uses *DEALLO-CATE*. When EHKP4 has to set up a transport-connection and it cannot multiplex it on an existing network-connection, it has to request one from Level 3. The *INIT* function is used, which requests Level 3 to establish a network-connection. One of the parameters that will be given with INIT is the network address (DTE address in the case of an X.25 Level 3) of the called party. If multiple transport-connections can be multiplexed over an existing network-connection, their records are transferred over that network-connection. Figure 6.6 shows the establishment of a network-connection and the service level dialog.

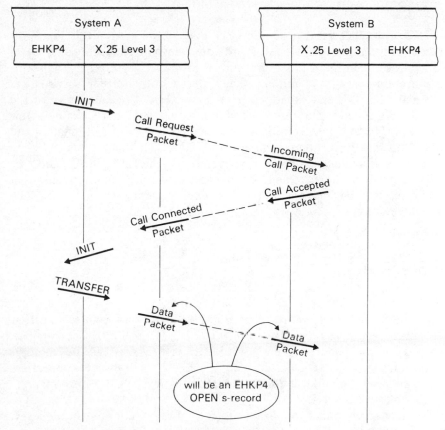

Fig. 6.6 EHKP4: network connection set-up

Records, i.e. s-records, are transferred through the *TRANSFER* service. The TRANSFER service works both ways, up and down, from Level 4 to 3 and vice versa. If EHKP4 detects an error in the record exchange, it may decide to reset the transport-connection. It also can decide to reset Level 3. The *RESET* service will request the reset of the network-connection. The last service is *TERMINATE*, which requests the termination of the network-connection.

The EHKP4 description suggests a mapping of some of the services in terms of X.25 Level 3 packets, if an X.25 Packet-Switched Network is used as the Network Machine. The INIT service is mapped in a Call Packet and the TERMINATE in a Clear Packet. The RESET service is implemented through the Reset Packet. A complete packet sequence is used as the network data unit and no advantage is taken of Q-bits and D-bits.

6.5 Comparison with the Reference Model

EHKP4 provides most of the services that are defined in the Transport Layer of the Reference Model. It provides transport-connections for Level 5. It will identify these connections to Level 5 through transport-connection-endpoint-identifiers. The offered data transfer services are normal data flow and expedited data flow. EHKP4 contains most of the functions defined in the Reference Model. Some of them, for example flow control or blocking, are optional. A missing function is concatenation and the Transport Layer Management is only loosely defined.

Below, a detailed comparison is given, using the list from Appendix B. Where there is no comment on a specific service and/or function, it indicates that we did not identify an explicit definition in the EHKP4 documentation.

Services provided by the Transport Layer
- Identification
  - Transport-addresses.   Each EHKP4 transport entity has a unique network address.
  - Transport-connections.   The transport-connection is the connection between paired EHKP4s.
  - Transport-connection-endpoint-identifiers. There can be multiple transport-connections between EHKP4s. A transport-connection-endpoint-identifier is used to identify the individual connections.
- Establishment services
  - Transport-connection establishment.   Level 5 entities can request a transport-connection through the CONNECT verb.
  - Class of service selection.   A class of service can be selected when the transport-connection is established.
- Data transfer services
  - Transport-service-data-unit.   The transport-service-data-unit is the record.
  - Expedited transport-service-data-unit.   The expedited transport-service-data-unit is limited to 16 bytes.
- Transport-connection release. The transport-connection can be released through the DISCONNECT verb.

Functions in the Transport Layer

- Addressing. The addresses are composed of the EHKP4 unique address together with the user process address that has to be known by the receiving EHKP4.
- Connection multiplexing and splitting. Several transport-connections can be multiplexed over one network connection.
- Phases of operation
  - Establishment phase. In the establishment phase, both EHKP4s will agree on the parameters for the transport-connection as defined in the OPEN s-record.
  - Data transfer phase
    - Sequencing. A sequence number in the Record Header is used to check the sequence of I-records.
    - Blocking. Optionally, information messages can be blocked together in an I-record.
    - Concatenation
    - Segmenting. Segmenting is a basic function which fragments a message in several I-records which are assembled by the receiving EHKP4.
    - Multiplexing and splitting. EHKP4 maps several transport connections on to a network connection depending on the class of service requested in the OPEN s-record.
    - Flow control. At the base, only back-pressure is used. Optionally—but a must for multiplexing—a window technique is used.
    - Error detection. The exchange of transport-service-data-units is controlled through sequence numbers in the Record Header. The sequence is checked by the receiving EHKP4.
    - Error recovery. Optionally, EHKP4 can recover from a lost I-record situation (selected via the OPEN s-record).
    - Expedited data transfer. Expedited data transfer is achieved through the exchange of INTER s-records, which carry 16 bytes of user data.
    - Transport-service-data-unit delimiting. Delimiting is not defined as a basic function. When blocking is used, a length field is added to each message and the Record Header is extended.
    - Transport-connection identification. Transport-connections are identified through the ordered set (sending EHKP4, sending process, receiving EHKP4, receiving process) addresses.
  - Release phase. In this phase, a CLOSE s-record is sent to release the transport connection.
- Transport Layer Management

References

1 *DV-Strom-Prozedur: Realisierung des einheitlichen höheren Kommunikations-protokolls der Transportebene (EHKP4)*, Landesamt für Datenverarbeitung und Statistik, Nordrhein–Westfalen, Düsseldorf. (Status 15 Aug. 1980)
2 *Open Systems Interconnection protocols EHKP4: Version 2*, Ministry of the Interior, Federal German Republic

Part 2 Proprietary architectures

7 IBM's Systems Network Architecture

7.1 SNA history

Systems Network Architecture (SNA) was introduced by IBM in 1974. It is based on the philosophy of the distribution of a particular function to the place where it can best be handled. This distribution is made possible by the increasing use of very large-scale integration (VLSI), which makes it more attractive to put a lot of 'intelligence' in terminal devices. The philosophy of distribution made it also necessary to reconsider the whole concept of computer communication networks: the basic functions that must be performed in such a network and the relationship between them. This was done in a way similar to the reasoning we have followed in the preceding chapters. It is therefore not surprising that there is a similarity between SNA and the Reference Model. This will be discussed in more detail in Section 7.9.

SNA was first made public through the announcement [1] of several products in September 1974. The major products were

a IBM VTAM (Virtual Telecommunications Access Method)—the access method for telecommunications to run in the host system (IBM S/370).
b IBM NCP (Network Control Program)—the control program to run in the network controllers (IBM 3705 Communications Controllers).
c SNA versions of the IBM 3600 (banking applications) and IBM 3650 (retail applications) Cluster Controllers.

They were the first that were designed and manufactured according to the SNA architecture, which was said to be *the* architecture for future communications products. Since, in this book, we are concerned with architecture, we will not refer to specific IBM products in describing SNA. We will refer to the various stages of SNA through the 'generic' SNA release numbers. For an overview of the products included in these releases, the reader is referred to [1].

The first releases of SNA, known as SNA-0 and 1, provided fairly limited function. The main purpose was, however, to set the direction and the concept of an all-encompassing well-structured architecture. In these releases, a network could consist of a host computer, a channel-attached

Communications Controller and attached to it some of the cluster controllers. Neither the channel-attachment of clusters nor remote Communications Controllers were possible. In short, an early SNA network was a very limited tree network, in which the Communications Controller was not much more than a front-end, but it exhibited all the important concepts of SNA.

In the next major release, SNA-2, the most significant enhancements were

a local attachment of Cluster Controllers;
b remote Communications Controllers (but never more than one local and one remote in tandem);
c attachment of Terminal Nodes;
d support of switched communication lines.

These enhancements, however, did not extend the scope of the architecture. That happened with the next release, SNA-3, also known as Advanced Communications Functions (SNA/ACF). Until that time, SNA was often said to be a 'centralized' architecture: a tree network with the network manager (SSCP—System Services Control Point) located in the root. This also implied that there could be only one general purpose computer in the network. The network was more a 'terminal access' network than a 'computer' network. Now, with SNA-3 it became possible to interconnect host computers via their local Communications Controllers. Each of these host computers contains a System Services Control Point (SSCP). These SSCPs are responsible for the control of the set of recources allocated to them, thus constituting so-called 'control domains', or, briefly, *domains*. The domains cooperate on a non-hierarchical basis, while internal to the domain, the centralized management is adopted, as in earlier SNA networks. Another, very important feature of SNA-3 is the fact that, once a terminal is in 'session' with an application in a domain other than its own, the data traffic to that application bypasses the domain host. Domain host involvement is required only to establish the session.

In the last releases of SNA, SNA-4.1 and 4.2 or, in short, SNA-4, first some restrictions were removed that existed in earlier versions. One of the most important was the fact that from now on any number of Communications Controllers could be cascaded from a host. Previously, there could only be one *local* (channel-attached to the host) and one *remote* (attached to the local via a communication line). One could argue, however, that this restriction was more of an implementation nature than an architectural one. An important enhancement from an architectural point of view was the introduction of *parallel sessions*. Formerly, the SNA session entities (Logical Units) could only have one session between them. Especially for communicating transaction-oriented application subsystems, it is now defined how they can have more than one session at the same time.

The most important enhancement, however, was undoubtedly SNA-4.2.

This release, mostly centered around the SNA Path Control Layer, added full networking capabilities to SNA, with inherent ability for future expansion [2, 3]. The backbone of this release is the possibility to use more than one physical path (called an *Explicit Route*) between two network nodes and to have several end-to-end network connections (called *Virtual Routes*) between two network nodes, independent of the network in between. Between adjacent nodes, it is possible to have multiple transmission links that can either behave as separate links or be grouped into *Transmission Groups* in such a way that a Transmission Group behaves as if it were one link.

In the following sections, we will first give a global overview of the SNA architecture and then discuss each of the layers in more detail. The amount of detail presented does not mean that a complete description of SNA is given, but it is used to explain SNA's most important aspects. For an exact and complete definition of SNA, the reader should refer to the appropriate IBM literature, e.g. [4, 5].

7.2 Architecture overview

In an SNA network, all communication between end-users is via a port into the network, called a *Logical Unit*. That means that the end-users themselves are not known to the network. As a matter of fact, even the interface between the end-user and the Logical Unit is not defined in the architecture but it is product, i.e. implementation, specific. The Logical Units perform all those functions for the end-users that are related to the communication between them: in the general terminology, all the session-specific functions. These Logical Units are then interconnected through a Path Control network that performs all those network functions that are not specific for the session but oriented towards the transportation of messages from one Logical Unit to another.

The Logical Unit is only one of a class of communicating entities in the SNA network. In general, these are called *Network Addressable Units*. The others are

a Physical Units. These interface the control functions in a particular physical piece of equipment to the network.
b System Services Control Points. These are used for the management and control of the network.

Communication between Network Addressable Units (NAUs) takes place through messages, which in SNA are called *Request Units*, and the responses to them, called *Response Units*. *Headers* that contain information relevant to a particular layer (or a number of layers) in SNA are added to these Request/Response Units. There are three different headers:

a Request/Response Header. This header contains control information regarding the state of the conversation between two communicating parties.

b Transmission Header. This is a header that contains control information related to the transport of the messages through the Path Control network.

c Link Header. This is a header containing control information regarding the movement of the messages on one particular link (normally SDLC).

Note that actually there is a fourth header, the *Function Management Header*, but this header is *part of* the Request Unit. It can be created by the Function Management Data Services to specify actions to be taken with the data in the RU.

A fundamental rule in SNA is the concept that no communication can take place if there is no *session* between the communicating entities. In addition, these sessions can normally not be set up without the approval of a System Services Control Point. This means that for any Logical Unit to participate in a session, it must first be in session with an SSCP. Using this session, it can then request permission for other sessions. The Logical Unit may therefore be 'standing on several legs', one connecting it to the SSCP and the other(s) to one (or several) other Logical Unit(s). These 'legs' are called *half-sessions*. In Fig. 7.1, this structure of the Logical Unit is given, together with a horizontal structure of three layers.

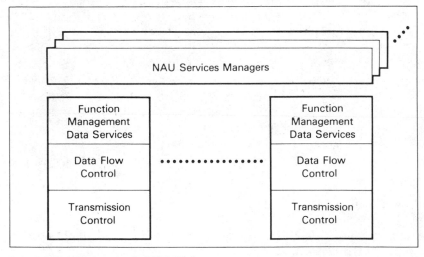

Fig. 7.1 Structure of a Logical Unit

The upmost layer is the Function Management Layer, in which the services that support the end-user are located. The layer contains a number of NAU Services Managers that belong to the NAU itself and a set of *Function Management Data Services* for each half-session. These Function

Management Data Services select the required services from the NAU Services Managers. They are, therefore, session-specific. For a Logical Unit, they define the Presentation Services available to the end-user.

The next layer inside the Network Addressable Unit is the Data Flow Control Layer. This layer is concerned with the management of message exchange protocols. Responses received are correlated to the appropriate Requests that were sent earlier, using a sequence number or some other identification for the Request. If required, Data Flow Control can also manage the dialog between the two session partners by controlling which can send a message and when. In order to perform these functions, information must be exchanged between Data Flow Control elements in each half-session. Normally, that information is related to a particular request and thus contained in the appropriate header, in this case the Request/Response Header. Sometimes, however, it is necessary to exchange information that is not related to a specific Request/ Response. Data Flow Control has its own Requests defined for that case, which implies there is also a Function Interpreter for Data Flow Control.

The bottom layer inside the Network Addressable Units is the Transmission Control Layer, responsible for maintaining the session. It is aware of the identity of the session partners and it makes sure that messages received from the Path Control network are properly routed to the destinations inside the NAU. This routing stems from the philosophy that holds that communication is always between *peer* layers. The destinations can be the Function Management Data Services (via Data Flow Control) and Data Flow Control itself. In addition to these, there are two destinations inside Transmission Control. The most important one is the Function Interpreter for *Session Control*, responsible for session activation, deactivation and recovery. The other is the Function Interpreter for *Network Control*, which helps the Physical Units to manage their particular equipment. This Function Interpreter is therefore only found in Physical Units.

Another important function of the Transmission Control Layer is to build the Request/Response Header for messages that pass through it to the Path Control network, or alternatively, to interpret these headers on messages received from the Path Control network. This function, like the internal routing, is performed by a component of Transmission Control called the *Connection Point Manager*.

The Request/Response Unit (RU), as the message is called in SNA, is combined with the Request/Response Header (RH) to form a *Basic Information Unit* (BIU). This Basic Information Unit is the message that is transported through the *Path Control* network. The half-session passes the BIU to the Path Control network, together with information pertinent to the destination of the message. In addition, some other information is passed, such as the message sequence number. The Path Control network uses this information to route the BIU through the network and deliver it to the destination.

Basically, the Path Control network consists of two layers, Path Control and Data Link Control. Of these two, the Path Control is responsible for the selection of the 'next link' on the path towards the destination, and the Data Link Control Layer for the actual transmission across that link. In recent releases of SNA, mainly the Path Control function has been expanded. The layer can now be looked at as consisting of three sub-layers:

a Virtual Route Control Layer, defining a logical 'pipe' between a source and a destination node.
b Explicit Route Control Layer, defining the actual routing functions, i.e. the path through the network.
c Transmission Group Control Layer, which will make a number of parallel data links appear as one link, i.e. including the guaranteed message sequence.

The Data Link Control Layer is in charge of uncorrupted message transfer across a physical link. In SNA this can be done through Synchronous Data Link Control (SDLC, a subset of HDLC) or the channel interface to the host.

7.2.1 Function subsetting

An important aspect of SNA is the subsetting of functions defined by the architecture. The need for an architectured subsetting stems from the fact that not all functions can be implemented in all products (such as simple terminals), but in order to maintain general connectivity it is necessary to control the subsetting done in the products. Otherwise, a Pandora's box filled with incompatible subsets might be created.

Subsetting is defined in two areas of SNA. First, in the capabilities of the Logical Units, by defining suitable protocol sets in each of the layers of the Logical Unit. These subsets are called *profiles* and they can normally be agreed upon when a session is established. Particular combinations of profiles for each of the layers that can be used in sessions are called *LU–LU session types*. Several LU–LU session types have been defined, all serving specific environments. They are discussed in Section 7.8.

The second form of SNA subsetting is in the Path Control network. Here, the capabilities of the actual boxes are defined as the *Physical Unit Types*. They range from very simple boxes, such as simple typewriter-like terminals (PU type 1), to rather complex nodes, such as Communications Controllers (PU type 4) and Host computers (PU type 5).

The major subsetting at this level, however, is the subsetting between PU types 1 and 2 on the one hand (*peripheral* nodes) and PU types 4 and 5 (*subarea* nodes) on the other hand. Subarea nodes can be interconnected in a mesh-like topology, whereas the peripheral nodes can only be connected to a subarea node in a star-shaped network. This subarea node is then called a *Boundary* node for the peripheral nodes attaching to it.

7.3 Synchronous Data Link Control

The definition of IBM's Synchronous Data Link Control (SDLC) [6] was the result of IBM's participation in the work of the International Standards Organization to define new data link control procedures. For several reasons, IBM could not wait with its product announcements until the definitions were completely settled and it announced a 'starter' definition under the name Synchronous Data Link Control. Later, when HDLC was accepted as a standard, minor changes were made to SDLC to make it a subset of HDLC, with the exception of the loop (see Section 7.3.1). These changes concern mainly terminology and a list of them is published in [6].

SDLC can be classified as a subset of HDLC using the unbalanced, normal response mode class of procedure. This class of procedure was discussed in Chapter 4. A significant extra feature of SDLC is the definition of the *loop*, which has not been defined for HDLC. We will discuss the operation of the loop in the remainder of this section.

7.3.1 The SDLC loop

In SDLC, normally secondary stations are connected to a primary station in a Half-Duplex, multipoint configuration. In such a configuration, it is necessary to send a specific 'poll' (permission to send) to each terminal attached and to wait for a response or a time-out, before the next station can be polled.

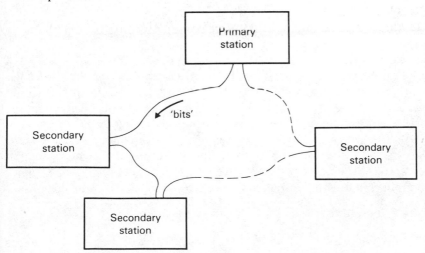

Fig. 7.2 Example of a loop configuration

In a loop configuration (Fig. 7.2), all terminals form a ring in which they repeat incoming bit streams on their outgoing link. Data to be sent by a terminal to the primary can be included in that stream when certain protocol requirements are satisfied.

In the SDLC loop, the primary station manages the loop and it controls the *Poll cycle*. Normally, this cycle is started with frames sent by the primary to the secondary stations. This is followed by the unnumbered command UP (Unnumbered Poll, see Section 4.4.3) with the broadcast address and a special sequence *Go Ahead*, which consists of a 0 and seven 1s:

    0 1 1 1 1 1 1 1 . . .

After that sequence, the primary maintains the idle condition on the outgoing link, by continuously transmitting 1s.

This whole stream is repeated by each station on the loop, but any station that recognizes its address in a frame will also copy that frame for its use. Stations that want to send frames to the primary must wait until they receive the UP command and the Go Ahead. Once they see the Go Ahead sequence, it is the only moment in the cycle that they can transmit. They turn the seventh 1 into a 0, thus creating a Flag and then transmit their own frames instead of repeating the incoming stream of 1s. When the transmission is complete, the station resumes repeating the idle stream. The trailing 0 of the last Flag will form a new Go Ahead sequence with the first seven 1s of the idle stream.

The next station that wants to transmit will also detect the UP, but before it receives the Go Ahead sequence and can transmit, it must repeat all frames that stations 'upstream' have transmitted. The whole Poll cycle is complete when the Go Ahead sequence is received by the primary on its input channel.

In the above description the UP command was sent *after* the primary had completed its output to the secondary stations.

In some cases, it may be required to warn the stations in advance that a new Poll is coming, i.e. first send the UP command and then send the output. It will then be difficult for the primary to distinguish on its input channel what was its own output and what is input from the secondaries. For that reason, another special sequence was defined, the *Turn Around* (TA) sequence. This sequence consists of a flag followed by an all-zero address. It is, therefore, not a valid frame and it will be ignored by the secondaries. The primary interprets it as a signal that all following frames are input frames. The output sequence from the primary is in that case

    UP, output frames, TA, Go Ahead, idle

and the input sequence

    UP, output frames, TA, input frames, Go Ahead, idle

In the description, we have so far assumed that all input was optional and at the discretion of the secondaries. All rules that normally apply to a primary–secondary relation are still valid, however. This means that in any output frame the Poll bit can be set, which means that the secondary *must* respond in that cycle. The rules for transmitting the response are the same as those for optional responses, i.e. the station must wait for the Go Ahead sequence and then immediately react.

The SDLC loop is an example of a *token ring*, a ring in which a station can only transmit when it owns a special token. When it has finished transmitting, it passes the token on to the next station on the ring. On the SDLC loop, the Go Ahead sequence acts as the token.

7.4 Path Control

Path Control is the SNA function that creates a logical channel through the network using the physical connections available. It is therefore the task of Path Control to deliver a message to its destination, given the address of that destination. In an SNA network, the addressing is based on the concept of the Network Addressable Unit (NAU). Each of these Network Addressable Units gets a network address assigned. This Network Address is used by Path Control in establishing connections and routes. Note that these addresses are internal to the SNA network, since in addition each Network Addressable Unit has logical *names* assigned, for use by the end-users of the network. Below, we first discuss the addressing structure that is used by SNA. The remainder of this section discusses the specific Path Control functions.

7.4.1 Addressing in an SNA network

An SNA network consists of two main types of nodes: Subarea Nodes and Peripheral Nodes (Fig. 7.3). The 'backbone' of this network is formed by the interconnected subarea nodes. We will call this network the *major* network in the following text. Peripheral nodes must attach directly to one and only one subarea node. The major network can have a mesh-like topology, while inside the subarea (the *local* access network) the topology is strictly star-shaped.

Based on this view of the SNA network, we will first discuss Path Control as it is defined for the major network. In the local access network, the Path Control function is much more restricted (based on the function-subsetting philosophy). We will discuss this in Section 7.4.3.

Every NAU in an SNA network is assigned a *network address*. It is divided in two parts: a *subarea* address and an *element* address. The

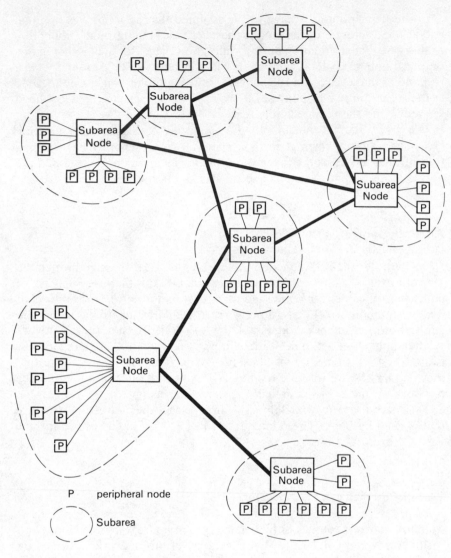

Fig. 7.3 Example of SNA network topology. (By courtesy of IBM Corporation)

element address is unique for each Network Addressable Unit in the subarea. Between subareas, it is sufficient to use the subarea part of the address for the routing.

7.4.2 Path Control functions

The most important function of Path Control is the routing of messages through the major network. This is performed through three sub-layers:

a Virtual Route Control. This layer creates subarea-to-subarea logical pipes on which the traffic from the sessions is multiplexed and on which flow control mechanisms are applied to protect the network.
b Explicit Route Control. In this layer, physical paths through the network, i.e. sequences of subarea nodes and Transmission Groups, are defined.
c Transmission Group Control. This layer makes a number of parallel links behave as if they were one link.

These functions were only included in SNA in later releases (SNA-4.2, refer to [1]). Earlier releases just had a simple routing function that used fixed routing directories without dynamic alternate routing.

In addition to the above functions, there are other functions that are related to the transmission function and therefore located in the Path Control Layer. They were already present in the first release of SNA. These functions are the segmenting of messages and the blocking of messages. Information that is needed to perform the Path Control function is carried in the header that is related to the Path Control Layer, the *Transmission Header* (TH). Four different formats of the Transmission Header are defined. Their usage depends on the type of Physical Unit (i.e. the type of functions it can perform) on each side of the connection (see Section 7.2.1).

a FID1. This format is used between Hosts and Communications Controllers, or, more formally, between (PU.T4 or 5) and (PU.T4), i.e. between subarea nodes. This format uses the full network addressing in the Origin Address Field (OAF) and the Destination Address Field (DAF). In addition, indicators are carried that allow the full Path Control function between these nodes.
b FID2. This format is used inside a subarea, for the traffic between the boundary node and a type-2 peripheral node (PU.T2). It uses local addresses instead of full network addresses (see Section 7.4.3). Since the connected box is simpler than the PU.T4 or 5, less function is supported by the header.
c FID3. This is the simplest form of the TH, and it is used within the subarea for the connection between the boundary node and a type-1 peripheral node (PU.T1). The address carried in this header is an even simpler form of local addressing than that in FID2, called the Local Session Identification, LSID.
d FID4. This format is the replacement for FID1 in networks that support the full Path Control functions, such as Virtual and Explicit Routes and Transmission Groups (i.e. the SNA-4 functions).

Path Control adds the Transmission Header to the Basic Information Unit (BIU) it receives from the half-session. The combination TH.BIU is called a *Path Information Unit* (PIU).

Transmission Group Control

The bottom (sub-)layer in Path Control is Transmission Group Control. It combines one or more parallel links (i.e. SDLC stations in the Link Layer) and makes them appear to the higher layers as one link. The main advantage of this is the increased capacity between two nodes while the first in/first out (FIFO) nature of one link is now guaranteed for the Transmission Group as a whole. In order to achieve this, PIUs are placed in a queue, the *PIU Outbound Queue*, when they must be transmitted. Any SDLC station that is part of the Transmission Group takes PIUs out of this queue when it can transmit. The moment a PIU is taken out of the queue, a sequence number is assigned to it, the *Transmission Group Sequence Number*. The PIU is treated by the SDLC station as a normal message; the SDLC station is not aware that it is part of a multi-link Transmission Group. When the PIU is received at the other side of the link, its sequence number is compared with the expected number. If they are equal, the PIU is passed through, because it was expected. If the sequence number is higher than the expected number, the PIU is apparently ahead of others and should wait until the others arrive. It is therefore placed in the Transmission Group Resequence Queue. Whenever a PIU is passed through, the Resequence Queue is scanned for PIUs that can now also be passed through.

Expect	Receive	Action
2	2	pass through no. 2
3	5	queue
3	3	pass through no. 3
4	6	queue
4	4	pass through no. 4, 5, 6
7	7	pass through no. 7

When a PIU is received with a sequence number lower than expected, it is discarded because it must be a duplicate. Duplicates may be created when it is necessary to retransmit frames due to transmission errors, etc. When such an error occurs, the link should try to recover from it by retransmitting the frame. There is, however, a risk that the error is data-dependent and therefore recurring. That could cause a long build-up in the Resequence Queue if the other links were to continue their transmissions. In order to avoid such a build-up problem, a frame is always scheduled for retransmission on the next link. The dependence on a particular sensitivity of one link is then removed. However, a copy of the frame is retained for retransmission on the original link. This is necessary to obtain information about the behavior of the link. The hand-over process is repeated if the frame also encounters a transmission error on the new link, i.e. the frame is handed over from link to link until it is successfully transmitted *or* it is scheduled for retransmission on all links in the Transmission Group. A *hand-over count* is maintained to detect the latter situation. The result of this procedure will be that, after a frame is successfully received, one or more duplicates may arrive when their re-tries are eventually successful. Because of the low sequence number, they can be discarded as duplicates. A side effect of this procedure is that the Transmission Group Sequence Number cannot be used as a wrap-around counter like the HDLC Send/Receive counters on each link. It would be impossible to decide whether a frame was ahead or delayed. The Transmission Group architecture specifies, therefore, that all links in the Transmission Group must be quiesced when the maximum count is reached. The receiving Transmission Group Control signals, through a special PIU, the Sequence Number Wrap Acknowledgement, that it has delivered in sequence the PIU with sequence number 4095. When this acknowledgement is received and all links are free, one PIU will be sent with Transmission Group Sequence Number 0. Transmission Group Control then waits again until all links are free. Now, no further duplicates of sequence number 0 can be generated and the sending of frames may continue. Note that it is necessary to wait for the links to become free again after the PIU with sequence number 0 is scheduled. If PIUs with sequence numbers 1, 2, etc., were also sent right away, they might arrive before number 0 and then be discarded as duplicates from the previous group. The process of waiting for the links to become available is called the *TG Sweep* action. The sweep action can also be initiated earlier, i.e. before the TG sequence number reaches 4095, for specific control messages that have to do with the control of the Explicit and Virtual Routes and must stay ahead of any messages that are scheduled later. Discussion of these is beyond the scope of this book.

Blocking A special function of Transmission Group Control is the blocking of several PIUs into one BTU, to be transmitted to the next node. Blocking is only defined for Transmission Groups that have only one Data Link. The grouping of several (small) messages into one larger message can be done in order to use the link more efficiently, or to avoid unnecessary interrupts in a host machine. Depending on the channel architecture, each BTU could require the processing of an interrupt. IBM's own S/370 channel architecture allows the use of Channel Control Word (CCW) chaining. This has the same effect as blocking, i.e. only one interrupt for a series of BTUs.

The blocking mechanism itself is very simple: the PIUs are just concatenated to form the BTU. In its Transmission Header, each PIU contains a Data Count Field with the length of the PIU. When a BTU is received, Transmission Group Control compares the count field in the first or only Transmission Header with the total BTU length. If the two are equal, there is only one PIU, i.e. no blocking was performed. Otherwise, there are more PIUs in the BTU and de-blocking must be done using the count fields.

Explicit Route Control

As we explained before, an SNA network can be viewed as an interconnected network of subarea nodes (Physical Units type 4 or 5) and the local
access networks to each subarea node. These local access networks are all
star-shaped networks, terminals and cluster controllers directly attached to
the subarea nodes. This means that the routing function inside the subarea
is a simple process. It is based on the local addresses and consists of
selecting the proper link to the Physical Unit in which the destination NAU
is located. There are no alternatives to select from.

In the major network, things are a little bit different. Since the nodes (in
the following discussion, we will use the word 'node' as a synonym for
'subarea node') can be interconnected in several ways in a mesh-shape
network, procedures must be defined to find a suitable path through the
network for each message. In SNA, the choice has been made for Explicit
Routing, i.e. based on the topology of the network, a number of routes
between a source and a destination node is predefined. All traffic that
originates or terminates in these nodes must use one of these defined paths
[2, 3, 7].

Between any two nodes, SNA defines up to eight Explicit Routes. Each
Explicit Route consists of a *forward path* and a *reverse path*, and is
identified by the quadruple (SA1, SA2, ERN, RERN). SA1 and SA2 are
the endpoint subareas, ERN is the number of the forward path (SA1 to
SA2, Explicit Route Number) and RERN is the number of the reverse
path (SA2 to SA1, Reverse Explicit Route Number). The identification
used suggests that, since the forward path and the reverse path may carry
different numbers, they might also be different otherwise, i.e. be disjoint.
This is, however, not the case. One path is a sequence of (subarea) nodes
and Transmission Groups and the reverse path must contain the same
nodes and Transmission Groups, but traversed in the opposite direction.

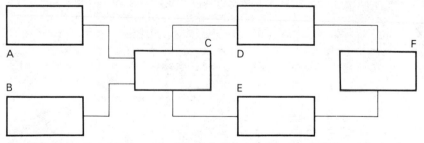

Fig. 7.4 Example of intersecting Explicit Routes. One Explicit Route is A–C–D–F,
the other is A–C–E–F

One reason for still allowing the different numbers is in the routing
algorithms. The routing decisions, i.e. the selection of the next Transmission Group on which to send the PIU, use only the Destination Subarea
Address and the Explicit Route Number, ignoring the Origin Subarea

Address. This places a restriction on the assignment of the Explicit Route Numbers. Two paths that have the same Explicit Route Number and go to the same destination node must, if they intersect somewhere, be the same from there on. This is illustrated in Fig. 7.4.

If both indicated paths with destination F would also have the same Explicit Route Number, node C would be unable to make the decision whether to transmit a PIU next to node D or to node E. This restriction complicates the Explicit Route Number assignment problem considerably. Allowing different numbers alleviates it a little bit. In a complex network, the assignment of Explicit Route Numbers may still be a very complex task, for which assistance is required [8].

Virtual Route Control

The concept of a Virtual Route provides the network with a mechanism for end-to-end control between subarea nodes. This implies, first, the Virtual Route Sequence numbering, to assure the integrity of the flow on the Virtual Route and secondly the Virtual Route Flow Control. This Virtual Route Flow Control is used to dynamically adjust the two sides of the Virtual Route, while all nodes in the Explicit Route that supports the Virtual Route can request a reduction in the PIU flow if circumstances, such as congestion, require it. This mechanism will be discussed below. A Virtual Route is identified by the subarea addresses of the two end-nodes, a *Virtual Route Number* (VRN) and a *Transmission Priority Field* (TPF). There are three Transmission Priorities defined, high, medium and low. These priorities are used by Transmission Group Control in deciding which PIU to de-queue first from the PIU queue.

The combination of Virtual Route Number and Transmission Priority is also called the *Class of Service* (thus giving a maximum of 48 classes of service between any two subarea nodes). It permits the request of a particular 'service class' such as 'interactive', 'batch' or 'secure' by the session partners, without any knowledge of the underlying network. The allocation of a specific Explicit Route that can support the requested service to the Virtual Route is done by the Virtual Route Control, transparent to the session partners.

On the other hand, the same mechanism also relieves the session partners from any responsibilities for the network operation; more specifically, they need not worry about what amount of traffic the network can accept without becoming congested. They may try to communicate at the 'pace' they have agreed during session set-up. Virtual Route Control will make sure that this does not conflict with the network capabilities by reducing the overall rate, if necessary. This reduction will, however, take place for all sessions using the particular Virtual Route.

The scheme defined in SNA for this end-to-end flow control is based on the concept of allowing less traffic into the network at the point of entry, when congestion begins to manifest itself. This manifestation is defined as 'minor' and 'severe' congestion, with further definition of the exact meaning of these terms left to the implementations. A small network node machine with limited storage capabilities may have quite a different view on 'minor' and 'severe' than a large node. They will both, however, use the same mechanism to report the conditions as they experience it. For this purpose, a *pacing* mechanism is used that is similar to the session level pacing that will be described in Section 7.5. The difference is that the mechanism at the session level is fixed when the session is established, but the Virtual Route mechanism is dynamically adjustable within certain limits. These limits are set through a minimum value of the pacing window and a maximum value. The minimum value is set, based on flow control studies [9], to the number of transmission groups that make up the Explicit Route to which the Virtual Route is assigned. This number is therefore reported back to Virtual Route Control during the activation of the route. The maximum size of the window is defined as three times the minimum.

The source node can send a number of PIUs (Path Information Units, the basic message transfer unit at the Path Control level) equal to the current size of the window, but then it must stop and wait for a signal from the destination node that it may continue. This signal is called the *Virtual Route Pacing Response*. The first PIU transmitted in the window carries a Virtual Route Pacing Indicator that invites the destination node to send a VR Pacing Response. The destination may send the response immediately, but it may also delay sending for some time if it is very busy.

If the response arrives at the source node before the window is completed, the sender continues with another window after the current one. If the response arrives after the window has been completed and the sender thus has to *wait* for the response, the window size may be increased by one, unless the maximum has been reached already, or certain other conditions prevent an increase (see below). In that situation, the last PIU in the window would have carried another indicator, the Pacing Count Indicator, telling the destination node that the Pacing Response was not received in time and the sender could not continue at maximum rate. So, would it please try to send the response earlier, if at all possible.

In this way, the window will gradually increase (congestion excluded for the time being) until the maximum is reached, or until the pacing response is received inside the window. It does not make sense to increase the window any further, since the sender can already transmit at its maximum speed.

Now what happens if somewhere along the Explicit Route congestion occurs? Let us first assume that a node is getting into what is called 'minor' congestion. The congested node will turn on an indicator (the *Change Window Indicator*—CWI) in the PIUs that pass through it, telling the destination nodes that there is congestion along the route. Note that all nodes along the Explicit Route may turn on this indicator (but none may turn it off) so the destination cannot tell which node is having problems. It should also be noted that, since the congested node turns on the indicator in all PIUs flowing on Explicit Routes that are affected by the congestion, the following description applies equally to all Virtual Routes that are supported by those Explicit Routes. When Virtual Route Control in a destination node receives the CWI, it knows that at least one node along the route is having problems and it reports this condition back to the origin node the next time a Virtual Route Pacing Response is sent, by setting the *Change Window Reply Indicator* (CWRI). When this indicator is received at the source node, the window size is decremented by one (unless it is already minimum). Each time now a Pacing Response with CWRI on is received, the window is further decremented until the minimum value is reached. When the congestion is eased away, the CWI and, consequently, the CWRI will no longer be set and the window can slowly be increased again as described before, as long as the maximum is not reached and the Pacing Response is arriving after the Pacing Count went to zero.

The described mechanism works fairly slowly, since the notification goes via the destination node. In the case of severe congestion, more direct action must be taken. If the condition occurs in a node, that node may turn on a *Reset Window Indicator* (RWI) in any PIU that passes through it on an affected Explicit Route. When the receiving Virtual Route Control detects this RWI, it resets the window for the flow in the *opposite direction* to the minimum value. In addition, if the Pacing Count exceeds this minimum, it is also reset to this minimum value, and sending continues from there on. This action obviously overrules any other increases or decreases of the window, based on the arrival of the Pacing Response and the CWRI. Normally, however, one would expect that CWRI had been present for some time already, since before severe congestion was detected one would have detected moderate congestion. When the RWI is no longer present in the PIUs received, Virtual Route Control resumes normal operation, i.e. the window will be incremented and decremented as indicated by the Pacing Response arrival and the presence of the CWRI.

Both flow control mechanisms described thus far have end-to-end significance. Let us repeat again that the CWI is set to reduce the flow in the same direction as it is carried—it is reported back to the source through the CWRI. The RWI, which is more immediate, is reducing the flow in the direction opposite to the one on which it is carried. If both methods fail to ease the congestion problem, the node has a final resort—bringing down the traffic on the incoming links through the SDLC command Receive Not Ready. In that case, the node should report this to the SSCP via the *Enter Slowdown* Request Unit, sent on the PU-SSCP session.

Segmenting
It may be necessary sometimes to split a long BIU into smaller parts. There can be several reasons to do so:

a The individual BIU length is large compared to the mean error-free interval on the link. By segmenting the BIU into smaller parts, the retransmission rate can be lower.
b The available buffers on the particular link are too small.
c The overall response time can be improved if transmission never exceeds a certain maximum length. In that case, the transmission of several BIUs can be interleaved.

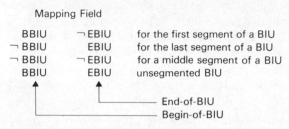

Fig. 7.5 Use of the Mapping Field for segmenting

Segmenting is defined in SNA in the Path Control Layer. It can be applied at different 'places', however. Segmenting can be done by the subarea node, by the Boundary function or by a peripheral node across the Route Extension. Re-assembly can be done in the subarea node or in the peripheral node, but *not* in the Boundary function. This means that the necessary coordination must take place in the Path Control Layer to obtain the proper segmenting and reassembly in such a way that, between the Network Addressable Units, always complete (i.e. unsegmented) BIUs are transported. Whether a BIU was segmented or not is indicated in the Transmission Header, through the use of the *Mapping Field* (MPF). This mapping field has two indicators, the *Begin of BIU* (BBIU) and the *End of BIU* (EBIU) indicators.

When a message is segmented, a Transmission Header is created for each segment. The Transmission Header carries the appropriate setting for the Mapping Field, as indicated in Fig. 7.5.

7.4.3 Boundary functions

Local addressing
Since an NAU is uniquely defined by its element address inside the subarea, routing inside the subarea can be done on the basis of these element addresses. The problem is that it is not known in advance what the size of the element address will be: it is selected at network installation time. The NAUs in the subarea are contained in Physical Units type 1 or 2 and these boxes are relatively simple. In particular, one would like to be able to manufacture them without having to be confronted with the need for logic to recognize different address lengths. It would furthermore be nice if these boxes could get the network addresses assigned to their NAUs

during the manufacturing process. Then, it need not be necessary to include facilities for dynamic address adjustment, which again makes the box simpler and thus cheaper.

For this reason, two forms of *local addressing* are defined in SNA: one for Physical Units type 1 and one for Physical Units type 2.

Physical Units type 1 For Physical Units type 1, the simplest form of addressing has been chosen: *Local Session Identification* (LSID). In fact, this is not just an address, but it is the combination of two addresses: the Origin Address and the Destination Address. The translation of full network addresses to these LSIDs, and vice versa, is performed in the subarea node. The LSID is 8 bits long and has the following layout:

bit 0   Message is coming from or going to the SSCP (bit is on) or the Logical Unit's session partner elsewhere in the network (bit is off).

bit 1   Message is going to or coming from the Physical Unit (bit is off) or a Logical Unit (bit is on) in this box.

bit 2–7 If the message is related to a Logical Unit (bit 1 is on) then these bits identify the particular Logical Unit.

It is interesting to note the architectural limits that are placed on the number of Logical Units in a Physical Unit type 1 and whether they can be shared by this definition of the LSID: there can be only 64 Logical Units in a type 1 Physical Unit. Each of these Logical Units can have its mandatory session with the SSCP and a session with *one* other Logical Unit, i.e. the Logical Units cannot be shared.

Physical Units type 2 For the Physical Units type 2, a form of local addressing is defined, which is 8 bits long. These local addresses are *local to* the Physical Unit type 2, i.e. to the particular box. A Logical Unit in the PU type 2 can now be identified in any one of three ways:

a Through the use of the full network address. This is done outside the subarea. Inside the subarea, the other two ways (*b* and *c*) can be used.
b Through the use of the full network address of the Physical Unit (which identifies the box) and the local address of the Logical Unit (which is unique in that box).
c The (network) address of the link through which the box is connected to the subarea node, and the (link level) station address on that link. This again identifies the box. Inside the box, the LU is identified through its local address.

The definition of this local address also places architectural restrictions on the number of Logical Units in a PU type 2 node. Since the local addresses are eight bits long, a PU type 2 can contain 256 Network

Addressable Units. Address X'00' is reserved for the Physical Unit; the remaining 255 addresses could be used for Logical Units. The network addresses of the NAUs in the network that are in session with the NAUs in the cluster, must also be mapped into an 8-bit address. This mapping is performed in the PU type 4 or 5 to which the cluster attaches, the boundary node. Again, the address X'00' is reserved, now for the SSCP. The remaining addresses can be used for the Logical Units. This implies that each LU in a cluster could have sessions with 255 LUs elsewhere in the network. Current implementations, however, do not allow shared LUs in cluster controllers.

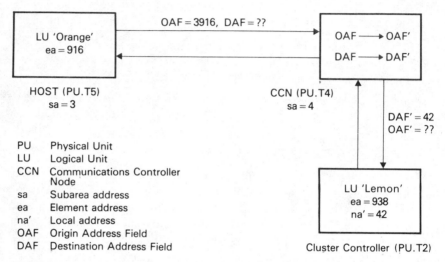

PU   Physical Unit
LU   Logical Unit
CCN   Communications Controller
      Node
sa   Subarea address
ea   Element address
na'   Local address
OAF   Origin Address Field
DAF   Destination Address Field

Fig. 7.6 Local addressing in a PU type 2

The boundary

The use of the local addresses makes peripheral nodes independent of their actual place in a network. This knowledge is kept by the attaching subarea node, the boundary node. Here, we find the tables to translate the full network address into the local address and vice versa. Let us, for example, consider a message that is sent from a Logical Unit *Orange* in a Host node (type 5) to a Logical Unit *Lemon* in a Cluster Controller (type 2). The network address of Orange is '3916', and the address of Lemon is '4938' (see Fig. 7.6). When the message flows from the Host to the Communications Controller, the header carries an Origin Address Field (OAF) '3916'. Since this link is still outside the destination subarea ('4'), the Destination Address Field (DAF) is '4938'. When the message arrives in the Communications Controller, the Boundary function translates the network addresses into the local addresses for the Logical Unit. For the Destination Address, this is no problem: it is the Logical Unit itself, with local address '42'. But what are we going to do for the Origin Address Field? We can fit only an 8-bit address, whereas Orange's address is the full network address, 16-bits long. The solution here is that the Boundary function will *assign* an 8-bit local address to the sending Logical Unit. This is accomplished during session initiation (BIND). It means that, for every Network Addressable Unit (including the SSCP) that has a session with a NAU in a type 2 node, a 'local' address must be assigned. Given the fact that the local addresses are 8 bits long, a Physical Unit type 2 may house up to 64K Network Addressable Units (Logical Units plus one Physical Unit). Since the complementary address is also 8 bits, each NAU may have a session with the SSCP and up to 64K other NAUs. This limit is, of course, the

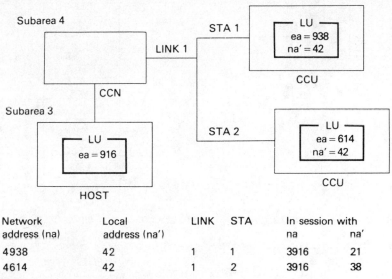

Network address (na)	Local address (na')	LINK	STA	In session with na	na'
4938	42	1	1	3916	21
4614	42	1	2	3916	38

Fig. 7.7 Use of local addresses

architectural limit: no known product yet supports such an amount of sessions. Figure 7.7 demonstrates once more the concept of a local address. The specific emphasis is here on the fact that the addresses are local to their own box: in each box we may have the same local addresses. The Boundary Function can still do the translation since it has, in addition, the identification of each of the nodes individually (through, for example, the link–station combination). As is shown in Fig. 7.7, a local address must also be assigned to the NAU with which the Logical Unit is in session. Although in the case of the figure, both LUs are in session with the same LU in the Host, this LU has been assigned a different local address for each of the sessions. Whether this is actually done or not depends on the implementation.

7.4.4 Formats of the Transmission Header

As mentioned earlier, the Transmission Header is defined in five formats, called FID-types (*Format Identifier*). Their usage depends on the type of node between which the PIU flows. Figure 7.8 shows four formats as far as the logical content is concerned. For the actual layout of the fields the reader is referred to, for example, [5(Appendix D)]. From Fig. 7.8 the effect of the function subsetting for each node-type can be seen. All SNA-4 functions, such as Virtual and Explicit Routes and Transmission Groups,

FID 1	FID 2	FID 3	FID 4
MPF	MPF	MPF	MPF'
EFI	EFI	EFI	EFI
DAF	DAF'	LSID	DEF
OAF	OAF'		OEF
SNF	SNF		SNF
DCF			DCF
			DSAF
			OSAF
			VRN + TPF
			VR Pacing
			VR SEQ
			ERN
			TG SEQ

MPF	Mapping Field	SNF	Sequence Number Field
EFI	Expedited Flow Indicator	LSID	Local Session Indentification
DAF	Destination Address Field	DCF	Data Count Field
OAF	Origin Address Field	VRN	Virtual Route Number
DSAF	Destination Subarea Field	TPF	Transmission Priority Field
OSAF	Origin Subarea Field	VR	Virtual Route
DEF	Destination Element Field	SEQ	Sequence Number
OEF	Origin Element Field	ERN	Explicit Route Number
FID	Format Identifier	TG	Transmission Group

Fig. 7.8 Contents of the Transmission Header

are only defined between subareas through the FID4 Transmission Header. Similarly, the blocking function can architecturally only be used in the inter-subarea traffic. It can be seen, furthermore, that since the FID3 does not carry the sequence number, no correlation between requests and responses is possible. The architecture thus limits the number of messages outstanding between the boundary function and a peripheral node (PU type 1) to one.

7.5 Transmission Control

This section discusses the layer between Path Control and Data Flow Control. We might say that the function of this Transmission Control layer is: to couple the two sides of a session together and to make sure that the transmission within the session is orderly (from a *transmission point of view* and not from a *logical* one). For that reason, Transmission Control has the functions to establish sessions, to operate and monitor them (e.g. checking of the sequence numbers) and to perform error recovery if necessary.

Transmission Control as a layer is composed of a (distributed) set of *Transmission Control Elements* (TCEs), one on each side of a session (they are part of the half-session). In the case of shared Logical Units (i.e. LUs that are in session with several other LUs), one TCE is present in *each* half-session. The TCEs are characterized by the *Session Identifier* (SID), which is the pair of addresses of the two NAUs in the session. In this way, the TCEs assigned to one LU can still be distinguished. This is used, for example by Path Control (Section 7.4.2), in routing messages to an LU: after the LU has been identified through the Destination Address, the appropriate TCE can be selected through the Origin Address Field.

Each Transmission Control Element has basically two components: the Connection Point Manager (CPMGR) and the Session Control (SC). These components will each be discussed in the following sections.

7.5.1 Connection Point Manager

The Connection Point Manager is the 'heart' of the session. It functions as an interface to Path Control for all components that may create Request/Response Units:

Inside Transmission Control:	• Session Control
	• Network Control
In the higher layers:	• Data Flow Control
	• NAU Services Managers

For this function the CPMGR performs a routing function towards these components.

Request/Response Header
The information that must be passed between the two Connection Point Managers is placed in the Request/Response Header (RH). This header is built by the CPMGR when a message is transmitted and it is checked for consistency and correctness when a message is received.

The Request/Response Header is always a 3-byte header, independent of the protocols agreed between the session partners, i.e. the profiles. The first bit indicates whether it is a Request Header or a Response Header; the next two bits the *RU category*, i.e. to which component the RU 'belongs'. As explained above, this can be Function Management, Data Flow Control, Session Control or Network Control. The other bits are used as indicators for the various protocols. Normally, they have the same meaning in both the request and the response. If the information applies to a request only, then the bits in the response are set to a predefined value or they are defined as 'reserved'. This depends on the particular protocol involved. The various indicators are discussed below with the protocols relevant to the CPMGR and in Section 7.6 for those related to Data Flow Control (DFC).

Two indicators are not related to either the CPMGR or DFC, but to Function Management, the *Format Indicator* (FI) and the *Code Selection Indicator* (CSI). The Format Indicator is discussed in Section 7.7.1.

Expedited delivery of messages　For several reasons, it can be necessary to let messages bypass the 'normal' flow of data. This can be the case when session management or recovery messages must be passed: they should not influence the data flow sequence numbering. A typical example is the recovery of the data flow. In that case, the recovery messages cannot use the normal flow because that is the one that must be recovered.

For this purpose, the *Expedited Flow* was introduced in the architecture. An *Expedited Flow Indicator* (EFI) is carried in the Transmission Header. When the EFI is on, the CPMGR will queue the message ahead of messages for which the EFI was off, if queueing is necessary. The reason that the EFI is in the Transmission Header and *not* in the Request/Response Header has probably to do with the fact that initially a kind of priority in the Path Control network was envisaged for the Expedited Flow. The current definition does not use this in Path Control since Expedited messages still flow *in* the session and therefore on the same Virtual Route. Logically, the EFI should now be in the Request Header (refer, however, also to Section 7.9).

Response types　The sender of a Request Unit can specify what type of response he wants to have. The possibilities are

a no response at all (RQN);
b response only in case of an error (Exception Response, RQE);
c always a response (Definite Response, RQD).

The response type requested is indicated in the Request Header, using three indicators (Fig. 7.9): DR1I and DR2I (Definite Response Type 1 and 2 Indicators) and ERI (Exception Response Indicator). In the case of a Response Header, the ERI is called the RTI (Response Type Indicator). If it is on in a response, this indicator means that the response is actually an Exception Response (independent of whether a Definite Response or an

DR1I	DR2I	ERI		
0	0	0	(RQN)	No response required
x	y	0	(RQD)	Definite response
x	y	1	(RQE)	Exception response (x and/or y must be 1)

Fig. 7.9 Types of response that can be requested

Exception Response was requested). The meaning of the DR1I and DR2I indicators is not defined in the architecture: it is left to the sender of the request to attach a special meaning to either one.* When the RTI indicates that a response is an Exception Response, the response cannot merely be the RH, but it must include Sense information and, depending on the type of RU, some bytes of the original RU.

When Sense data is included, a special indicator, the Sense Data Included Indicator (SDI), is set. This is mandatory in Exception Responses, but in some cases it can also be turned on in a request. An example is the case where the Connection Point Manager detects a sequence number error on a received BIU. The CPMGR will then include sense information to indicate the error and turn on the SDI. The request is now called an *Exception Request* (EXR). This Exception Request is not immediately returned to the sender, *but delivered to the addressee*, e.g. Data Flow Control. The reason is that the Request Header may contain protocol information that is still relevant to the addressee. (It is a basic philosophy in SNA that communication is between equivalent layers, if at all possible. It does not apply if, for example, an RU cannot be delivered because the addressee is unknown, but in the case of a CPMGR detected sequence error it still does.) The addressee can then decide what it wants to do with the request. It may send a negative response based on the Exception Request, or another response based on its own information.

A positive response carries only in special cases additional data. An example is the response to the STSN (Set and Test Sequence Numbers) Request from Session Control.

Pacing The pacing mechanism in SNA controls data *flowrate*. (It should not be confused with the Data Flow Control Layer, which is a logical flow protocol.) Pacing has to do with the rate at which requests can flow between the session partners, without them overrunning each other and/or claiming too many network resources.

The basic mechanism is the same as for the Virtual Route, but now it works with a *fixed* window and on a per session basis. One end of the conversation can send an agreed number of requests (say *n*) and must then wait for permission from the other side before the next group of *n* requests

* This applies to the 'end-user generated' requests only. Whenever an architectured component sends an RU, e.g. Session Control, the architecture does specify what type of response must be requested.

can be sent. The first request in the group must have the *Pacing Request Indicator* on in the Request Header. The response uses the same indicator, which is then called *Pacing Response Indicator*. Although the Pacing Request Indicator must always be on in the *first* request of the group, the receiver may use any response that is available to turn on the Pacing Response Indicator when it wants to signal that the next group of requests may be sent. This could cause a problem when there is no such response available when the Pacing Response must be sent, e.g. a long series of requests that ask for Exception Responses only. In that case, the CPMGR will create a special response called the *Isolated Pacing Response* (IPR). This response consists of an RH only, with all bits set to zero, except the ones for Response type, Pacing Response and Chaining.

Pacing is defined in SNA in one or two stages in each (normal) flow direction:

a From the Primary to the Secondary in one stage.
b From the Primary to the Secondary in two stages:
   i from the Primary Logical Unit to the Boundary function and
   ii from the Boundary to the Secondary Logical Unit.
c From the Secondary to the Primary in one stage.
d From the Secondary to the Primary in two stages:
   i from the Secondary Logical Unit to the Boundary and
   ii from the Boundary to the Primary Logical Unit.

When Pacing is used in a session, it can be used for both directions independently. The value of *n* can be different for each of them.

A typical example is a session between a Logical Unit in a Host and a Logical Unit in a Terminal Node. Since the FID3 header to the Terminal Node does not support sequence numbers, the pacing count from boundary to terminal node will be set to 1. The count from the primary LU to the boundary can, however, be higher, e.g. 4 or 5. This ensures that there is always a Request available in the boundary, when the terminal can use the next one, i.e. sends a Pacing Response to the boundary.

Note that the use of pacing may interfere with the use of the Request/Response control modes (discussed in Section 7.6.1). It is the task of the system designer to ensure that all these protocols cooperate harmoniously.

The performance of a particular system may depend heavily on the choice of the pacing parameters. Much research is being done to find what the effects in a particular environment are (see, for example, [9]).

Sequence numbers and IDs When requests are sent in a session and responses are expected, either normal or exception, the sender must correlate the responses to the related request. For that purpose, the requests carry a sequence number or an Identifier (ID). The sequence number is also used by the CPMGR to ensure that the flow is sequential: the received sequence numbers must increase monotonically. On the

Expedited Flow, IDs are always used. These are (more or less) arbitrary numbers, which need not be sequential. This is sufficient since the Expedited Flow uses Immediate Request Mode (see Section 7.6.1) and Definite Responses only, which means that only one Request can be outstanding at any time. For Session Control and Network Control, the IDs are assigned by the CMPGR. For Expedited Data Flow Control and Function Management Requests, the IDs are assigned by Data Flow Control.

On the normal flow, one can use either IDs or sequence numbers (this is selected when the session is started—BIND). When sequence numbers are used, they are assigned by the sending Data Flow Control and checked by the receiving CPMGR. In case the CPMGR finds an error, the Sense Data Included Indicator is set and the RU replaced with sense information that identifies the error. The request is then passed on to the addressee. When a negative response which indicates a sequence number error is received, recovery action is started by Session Control using the *Set and Test Sequence Number RU*.

7.5.2 Session Control

Session Control is the function that can

a activate and deactivate sessions;
b open and close the flow gate for the normal flow in an active session;
c perform session error recovery (particularly sequence number recovery).

These functions will now be discussed in more detail. Since most of these Session Control activities are not directly related to specific RUs in the session, the exchange of information between Session Control in the two half-sessions cannot use the Request/Response Headers. For that reason a number of Session Control Request Units are defined in the architecture.

Session activation
A session is the basic SNA concept to establish a logical relation between Network Addressable Units. Since there are several types of NAU, there are also several types of session possible:

a SSCP–SSCP   These sessions are used for the communication between control domains in a multi-domain network. They must be activated to make any cross-domain activities possible.
b SSCP–PU   These sessions must exist between the SSCP and *all* Physical Units in its Control Domain. They must be activated before any other activity with the nodes controlled by the PUs is possible. The sessions are used to exchange network control information between the SSCP and the PU.

c SSCP–LU These sessions are established between the SSCP and all Logical Units in its Control Domain. They must be activated before the LUs can get involved in any other activity.

d LU–LU These are the sessions that are fulfilling the purpose of the network; through them the actual transfer of data between end-users can take place.

e PU–PU Between Physical Units no specific sessions are defined. There is, however, communication possible between PUs that are adjacent, in order to exchange Network Control information. Request Units that are supported are Network Control (NC) RUs, for the management of the Explicit Routes.

The way in which sessions are established depends on the type of session. The SSCP–SSCP sessions will be discussed in detail in Section 7.7.2. In the remainder of this section, we discuss the start-up of the session that is the most relevant from an end-user's point of view, the LU–LU session. The SSCP–PU and the SSCP–LU sessions are discussed briefly after that, since there is not much difference.

LU–LU session activation A session between two Logical Units is established when Session Control in one LU (the *Primary*) sends the BIND Request Unit to Session Control in the other LU (the *Secondary*) and receives a positive response. Session Control does this at the request of some management function, usually the Logical Unit Services in the LU. This is described in more detail in Section 7.7.2. Session Control needs to know what the characteristics of the other LU are, so it can build the BIND Request Unit with that information. This is usually communicated from the SSCP in a special Request Unit. The most important information that the BIND contains are proposals for the protocols to be used in the new session. These protocols are specified through the *profiles* for Transmission Control, Data Flow Control and Presentation Services. The BIND RU is sent to the destination Session Control, but there a small problem arises. Since the session is not yet established, Path Control cannot deliver the message to the proper half-session. The RU is therefore delivered to a component called *Common Session Control*, which is part of the Physical Unit Services. Common Session Control checks to see whether the destination LU is already in session with the SSCP, since otherwise an LU–LU session would not be allowed, and whether the RU is a BIND. If these conditions are met, a new half session is created and the BIND RU passed to it.

In the preceding discussion, we have simplified the procedure grossly, in order to concentrate on the important aspects of the establishment of a session. Other aspects, such as the involvement of the Boundary function, where the mapping tables for the local addresses must be set up, etc., had to be left out. The reader is referred to the official documentation [5] for these details.

SSCP–PU and SSCP–LU session activation   The sessions between the System Services Control Point and the Physical and Logical Units are established in much the same way as the LU–LU sessions. At the level of Session Control, the only difference is that the Primary (in this case, always the SSCP) does not send a BIND RU, but an *Activate Physical Unit* (ACTPU) for the SSCP–PU session or an *Activate Logical Unit* (ACTLU) for the SSCP–LU session. These Request Units are much simpler than the BIND since the sessions with the SSCP do not require complicated protocol agreements. Usually, very few messages will flow on these sessions, if all goes well.

One special characteristic of the ACTPU is that it can be used to specify an Error Recovery (ERP) activation. This is used when a session with a PU has been broken, e.g. after an SSCP failure. When the SSCP comes back to life, it can do an ERP ACTPU in order not to destroy the active state, tables, etc., of the Physical Unit.

Data Traffic activation
When a session is established through the BIND, it is not necessarily immediately available for message exchange. This depends on the profile chosen for Transmission Control. If the profile specifies that the *Start Data Traffic* (SDT) RU will be used, this (Session Control) RU must be sent after BIND to actually open the data flow. The reason for separating this from the BIND is in the recovery possibilities. If a problem occurs on the Normal Flow, it can be recovered using Session Control RUs such as *Set and Test Sequence Number* (STSN). *CLEAR* is used first to reset the flow and 'clear' it. After CLEAR has been sent, the normal flow can no longer be used, until after the recovery is complete. The SDT RU is used to signal to the secondary LU that the recovery is successful and that the normal flow is open again.

If the profile specifies that SDT will not be used on the session, no recovery is possible, since the flow cannot be reopened after successful recovery.

Session termination
When a session needs to be terminated, the logical relation between two NAUs must be broken. From a Session Control point of view, it means that resources allocated to the two half-sessions can be freed. Session Control assumes that the conversation as such has come to an end already, such that no more messages or responses are underway. This is handled at the next higher level, Data Flow Control (refer to the next section). When Session Control in the primary NAU is requested to terminate the session, it may—depending on the profiles—first send a CLEAR RU to reset the data traffic state such that no more messages can be sent and then it sends UNBIND. This Request Unit tells the Secondary to free all the resources and terminate the relation. How this is actually done depends on the

particular implementation, of course. The positive response to the UN-BIND is the very last message that flows on the session.

The involvement of higher layers, such as Data Flow Control and Session Services, to prepare for an orderly session termination and to inform the SSCP about the end of the session are discussed in later sections.

7.6 Data Flow Control

In this section, we will focus on the functions of the Data Flow Control Layer. Once more, it must be pointed out that this layer should not be confused with the data *flowrate* control function. That particular function is performed by the pacing mechanism in the Connection Point Manager. The discussion of DFC can be split in two parts:

a The protocols that are related to the Request Units directly. These protocols are enforced through the use of indicators in the Request/Response Headers, i.e. they are strictly RU related. The major protocols are: Request/Response Control Mode, Chaining, Send/Receive Mode, and Brackets.
b The DFC functions that are not strictly RU-related, but more with the general control of each of the (normal) data flows. These functions utilize their own set of Request Units.

Sometimes a combination of the two is used: for example, when an RU-related protocol must be initiated via a specific request. An example is the BID RU, used with the bracket protocol.

7.6.1 Flow protocols

The Flow Control protocols that are RU-related provide for a hierarchical set of facilities to relate groups of requests and responses together.

At the lowest level, the Request/Response Control Mode protocol sets rules for the relation between the requests and their responses. At the next level, the Chaining protocol allows one to combine a group of RUs flowing in one direction into a 'chain'. Next, the Send/Receive Mode protocol governs the exchange of chains between the two half-sessions. Finally, a whole series of such bidirectional exchanges may be grouped together into a so-called 'bracket' (or 'transaction') by the bracket protocol.

Request/Response Control Modes
The Request/Response Control Mode protocol sets rules for the relation between a Request and its Response. It is closely related to the Response

types that can be requested through the Request Header (see Section 7.5.1). In summary, they are

- RQN do not send a response
- RQE send a response only in the case of an exception
- RQD always send a response

The following Control Modes exist:

- Request Control Mode
  - Immediate Request Mode
  - Delayed Request Mode
- Response Control Mode
  - Immediate Response Mode
  - Delayed Response Mode

When the *Immediate Request Mode* is used on a flow, the sender may send several Requests that ask for Exception Response (RQE) only. The sender may, however, send only one request that asks for a Definite Response (RQD). After that, no more requests (of any type) may be sent on that flow until the requested response is received. One should realize that this is not synchronized with the Pacing Mechanism at the next lower level (CPMGR): when a series of requests (all RQE) is being sent, the actual transmission may temporarily be halted because of the pacing. In that case, the Isolated Pacing Response can be used to resume the transmission. This is illustrated in a (hypothetical) sequence in Fig. 7.10.

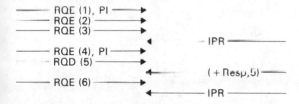

Fig. 7.10 Effect of Pacing and Immediate Request Mode. The flow of data can be temporarily stopped when either an expected Pacing Response or an expected positive response has not yet arrived. The two are not synchronized. (In the example, one-stage pacing with $n = 3$ is used)

When the *Delayed Request Mode* is used on a flow, as many requests (of any type) can be sent on that flow as the sender wants, without waiting for a response. It involves more logic in the sending Logical Unit to correlate a received response to all outstanding requests, particularly when the Delayed Response Mode is used as well (see below).

The *Immediate Response Mode* forces the half-session to return responses (if there are any) in the same sequence as the requests were received in. This can be used to get an acknowledgement for a series of requests for which Exception Response only (RQE) was asked. In such a case, the last request of the series would request a Definite Response (RQD). When that response is finally received, the sender knows that no more Exception Responses to previous requests can come in, since they must have been received before the Definite Response.

In the *Delayed Response Mode*, a half-session may return responses in any order, independent of the order in which the requests were originally received. Obviously, this Response Mode could cause problems when Requests for Exception Response are used in the flow: there would never be any guarantee that an odd negative response might still come in. There is one exception to this rule—the response to the Data Flow Control Request Unit CHASE.

The CHASE Request is used by an NAU to verify that all responses that could be on their way, are received. The RU is sent on the normal flow and must be kept in sequence with other requests, even when the Delayed Response Mode is used. Thus, when an NAU sends a series of requests that specify Exception Response, the CHASE RU can be used to verify that the series was received correctly. When the response to the CHASE is returned, no other (exception) responses can be on their way, independent of the Response Mode.

Chaining

The Chaining protocol is used to group related Request Units as one entity, the *chain*. This chain is then by definition the basic unit of recovery in the session. It is also the basic unit of 'concern ' in some of the other protocols: Send/Receive Mode and Brackets. An example of the use of chains is the printing of output: each line of output is sent as a separate RU, but all RUs for one page belong together, so they are chained. Now, when a problem occurs (e.g. the paper breaks), the whole chain is recovered, that is, after the problem is repaired printing starts at the beginning of the page.

The use of the chaining mechanism is indicated in the Request Header. Similar to the Mapping Field in the Transmission Header, there are two indicators, BC (Begin of Chain) and EC (End of Chain). When both indicators are on, the RU in question is a Single RU Chain.

There are special rules relating to the types of response that may be requested for a chain (Fig. 7.11):

a All requests may be marked *No Response* (RQN). In this case, no response will be generated for any RU in the chain and the chain itself is called a *no-Response Chain*.

b All requests may be marked *Exception Response only* (RQE). In this case, a response will only be generated for an RU in which an error condition exists. The remainder of the chain will then be purged (without further responses being generated). When no error at all is detected, no response will be generated. This type of chain is called the *Exception Response Chain*.

c All requests in the chain, except the last one, may be marked 'Exception Response only' (RQE) and the last one 'Definite Response' (RQD). In this case, an Exception Response is returned when an error is detected in an RU (and the rest of the chain is then purged). When no error is detected, a positive response is generated for the last RU in the chain. This chain is called a *Definite Response Chain*. It is the most common type of chain and normally used in conjunction with the Immediate Request Mode protocol: the response to the last RU is then the acknowledgement of the total chain.

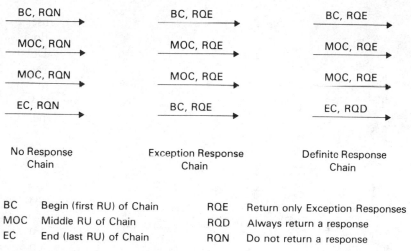

BC	Begin (first RU) of Chain	RQE	Return only Exception Responses
MOC	Middle RU of Chain	RQD	Always return a response
EC	End (last RU) of Chain	RQN	Do not return a response

Fig. 7.11 Three types of chain response

Note that it is not allowed to request a Definite Response for any RU but the last in a chain.

The CANCEL RU is used in the Chaining protocol to terminate a failing chain. When an NAU generates a negative response to a request in a chain, it will enter a 'purge' state and discard all other RUs that come in until the End of Chain indication is received. This EC indicator may be set in a normal Request Header, but it can also be set in the Request Header that accompanies a CANCEL command. The effect of the CANCEL is then that the part of the chain that was received *before* the error occurred is also purged. An example of the use of CANCEL is given in Fig. 7.13.

Send/Receive Modes
Although the session between two Network Addressable Units is basically a Full-Duplex channel, it may be necessary to limit the operation of the session to Half-Duplex. An example can be a Logical Unit serving a

terminal end-user and having only one buffer, which must be used for both send *and* receive operations. If it were involved in a Full-Duplex session, a message might arrive while the terminal operator was keying in a message. Then the message would overlay the contents of the buffer and the operator would have to re-type everything again. (With the risk that it was going to be overlaid again!)

The limited procedure is the Half-Duplex procedure, which can be selected for the session when the session is started (through the BIND Request Unit). SNA provides for two types of Half-Duplex operation: Half-Duplex Flip/Flop and Half-Duplex Contention.

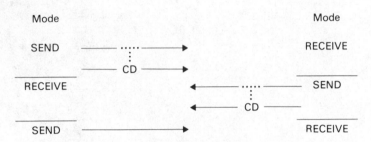

Fig. 7.12 Example of Half-Duplex Flip/Flop

In the Half-Duplex Flip/Flop mode, one of the Logical Units is in the Send state, the other in Receive state. It is the responsibility of the Sender to indicate that the other may go into Send state, while the Sender will then go into Receive state (Fig. 7.12). This indication is given via the Change Direction Indicator in the Request Header. Since it indicates the end of the transmission from the Sender, the End-of-Chain indicator must also be on in the same Request Header, if chains are used.

It is necessary in this protocol to initialize which LU will be the first sender when the session is started. This is done at initialization time, using the Function Management profile in the BIND Request.

The Half-Duplex Contention protocol allows either half-session to start sending. One of the half-sessions is designated the *Contention Winner*, the other the *Contention Loser*. (This specification is also made through the FM profile at session BIND time.)

The Contention Winner may reject any (normal flow) request that it receives while in the Send state (Fig. 7.13). The Loser must queue any request it receives while it is in the Send state. It terminates its current chain, either through End-of-Chain or via the CANCEL Request Unit when it receives the reject response. Next, it de-queues any requests that were queued while it was in the Send state. At the end of the chain, both half-sessions return to the contention state. The winner may avoid this after it has detected the contention by using the Change Direction

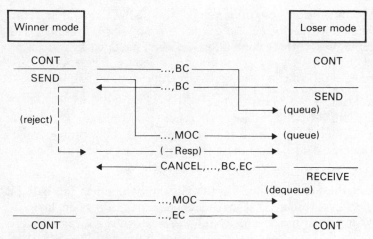

Fig. 7.13 Example of Half-Duplex Contention

Indicator on the last RU in its chain, which allows the Loser to send. This is particularly useful within a bracket (see below).

Brackets

As indicated in the introduction to this chapter, the highest level of ordering normal flow requests in a session is the Bracket protocol. With this protocol, it is possible to group a series of exchanges of RUs (or chains) in both directions. This capability is needed when each half-session may initiate a new transaction. A simple example is the case of a remote station that has both a card reader and an operator keyboard attached to the secondary Logical Unit. If the primary LU would send a request to the secondary to read a card and at the same time the operator would key in some request, the primary would interpret the operator-keyed message as the result of the read operation (Fig. 7.14).

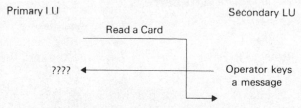

Fig. 7.14 Ships that pass in the night

The Bracket protocol makes it mandatory for each half-session to use the *Begin Bracket Indicator* on the first request of a new 'transaction'. Once a bracket is started, both half-sessions may only send requests and responses that belong to that bracket. If there is contention to start a bracket (as would be the case in Fig. 7.15), this is resolved similar to the

Half-Duplex Contention resolution: at session BIND time, one half-session is defined as the *First Speaker*, the other one as the *Bidder*. The First Speaker always wins the contention, i.e. the First Speaker can always start a bracket (that is to say, if no bracket is active). The Bidder must request permission to start a bracket. This can be done in two ways:

a Using the Data Flow Control Request BID.
b Just sending an RU with the Begin Bracket (BB) Indicator on. This is called an 'implied BID', and it is used mostly when the probability of rejection is low. The Bidder must be prepared, however, to have its request rejected, i.e. that it must resend the chain.

In either case, the First Speaker has the possibility to reject the BID by sending a negative response. The Bidder can then try again later by sending BID at regular times. That could be a waste of resources if it were to get more denials. The First Speaker should, in this case, keep track of the fact that it denied a BID, since it knows when permission could be granted. The architectural vehicle for this is the Ready to Receive RU, together with a special sense code.

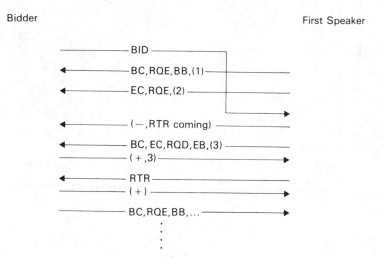

Fig. 7.15 Use of BID and Ready-to-Receive

When the First Speaker sends a negative response to the BID, it can indicate in the sense code that it will send an RTR when it is acceptable to start a bracket (Fig. 7.15). The Bidder will then wait for this READY-TO-RECEIVE. Eventually, the First Speaker sends RTR, whereafter the Bidder may send the Begin Bracket. Note that the Bidder still has the option to send a negative response to the RTR ('I changed my mind').

Since the bracket protocol is the highest level of Data Flow Control, it operates always on the basis of chains. This is reflected in the fact that the

Bracket Indicators in the Request Header can only be turned on in the *first* RU of a chain (the one with BC), but take effect only at the time the last one in the chain is processed. At what moment exactly all the bracket-state changes take place depends on several factors, such as the type of response requested and the Bracket Initiation and/or Termination rule selected.

From the discussion in this and the previous section, it should be clear that, when brackets are used in conjunction with the Half-Duplex Flip/Flop Mode, synchronization between the two half-sessions is required. Refer to Chapter 5 in [5] for more details.

7.6.2 Data Flow Control Request Units

As discussed in the introduction to this chapter, the Data Flow Control functions in the LUs may also communicate through the use of their own Request Units. This is the case when the communication is not directly related to a particular Function Management RU, but to the state of the session. Some of these DFC Request Units will be discussed below. For the others, the reader is referred to the *Format and protocol reference manual* [5].

Quiesce
When one half-session wants the other to temporarily stop sending RUs, it can use the QUIESCE AT END OF CHAIN (QEC) command. The receiving half-session is allowed to complete the current chain and then send the reply QUIESCE COMPLETE. Thereafter, it can no longer *send* on the *normal* flow, although it can still receive on that flow. When the other half-session wants to open the flow again, it sends RELEASE QUIESCE.

Note that all these commands, although they affect the normal flow, are carried in the expedited flow.

Shutdown
The series of SHUTDOWN commands

- SHUTDOWN (SHUTD)
- SHUTDOWN COMPLETE (SHUTC)
- REQUEST SHUTDOWN (RSHUTD)

is used to prepare for session termination. When the primary NAU wants to terminate the session, it can send SHUTD to the secondary NAU (Fig. 7.16). The secondary does the necessary end-of-session processing (e.g. sending CHASE to return any outstanding responses) and then sends SHUTC to notify the primary that the shutdown action was completed. The primary can then complete its end of session processing and end the session (UNBIND—refer to Section 7.5.2).

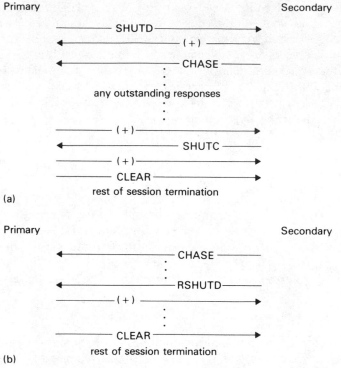

Fig. 7.16 Possible end-of-session sequences: (a) Primary initiated and (b) Secondary initiated

SIGNAL

The SIGNAL RU can be used as a means of transmitting information on the expedited flow (equivalent to the Unnumbered Information at the SDLC level). For this purpose, the RU contains two bytes that have been assigned a specific meaning. Currently, only three possibilities have been defined:

a Request to Send (used in Half-Duplex session to request a Change Direction).
b Intervention required.
c User code (i.e. there are two more bytes that have a user defined meaning).

7.7 NAU Services

The highest layer in SNA is the Function Management or, formally, the Network Addressable Unit (NAU) Services Layer. Actually, this layer consists of two layers: Function Management Data (FMD) Services and NAU Services Managers.

The FMD Services perform a routing for the FMD Request Units to the appropriate NAU Services Manager that can provide the requested function. The FMD Services can be different for each half-session in which a Network Addressable Unit is engaged, whereas the NAU Services Managers are responsible for the operation of the NAU as a whole. In other words, one could say that the NAU Services Managers Layer contains all functions available to an NAU and the FMD Services Layer subsets those for a particular half-session.

The NAU Services can broadly be classified in two areas:

a End-user Services that are used in LU–LU sessions. They interface end-users to each other.
b Session Network Services that are used in sessions between SSCPs and between an SSCP and the PUs and LUs. These Network Services are distributed among the SSCPs and the PUs and LUs. In the Logical Unit, for instance, they interface the end-user to the functions that control the network operation.

7.7.1 End-user Services

In the End-user Services, we find all those functions that are aimed at assisting the end-users in the manipulation of data. This may restrict itself to the presentation or lay-out of the data, which is normally found when application program end-users communicate with terminal-type end-users, e.g. a display station, but also a remote printer, etc. In that case, the End-user Services are called *Session Presentation Services*. In other cases, the role of the End-user Services may be more complicated, allowing communication between different application programs, including the use of committed checkpoints, etc. The End-user Services are then called *Application-to-Application Services*.

The main vehicles with which the presentation of data can be controlled in an SNA network are the *Function Management Header* (FMH) and the *String Control Byte* (SCB).

Function Management Headers

The Function Management Headers can be used to specify the use of special codes for the presentation of the data. They can also be used to select a particular destination for the device, i.e. the particular end-user if the Logical Unit serves more than one end-user.

FM Header-1 is defined to control a multi-device terminal. An example is a workstation for Remote Job Entry Applications, where several devices are served by one Logical Unit, or a station for word processing. The FMH-1 specifies such things as to which medium the data is going, where the medium can be a specific device, a data set on a device or a data stream. When multiple destinations are possible in an NAU, a destination cannot only be selected with FMH-1, but also suspended to allow temporary selection of another destination, resumed and terminated. A destination stacking mechanism is therefore defined in the FMD Services that interpret the FMH-1. It should be noted that it is agreed, via the BIND Presentation Services Profile when the session is established, whether Function Management Headers will be used. But even when it is agreed that they can be used in the session, this does not mean that they will be present in every Request Unit. In a chain, for example, only the first RU may carry an FM Header. The presence of the FMH is indicated with the Format Indicator in the Request Header (refer to Section 7.5.1). An example sequence of the use of FMH-1 for destination selection is

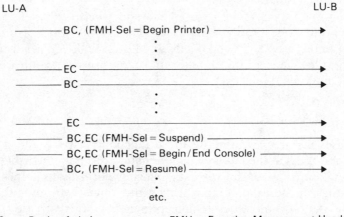

LU-A   LU-B

———— BC, (FMH-Sel = Begin Printer) ————▶

———— EC ————▶
———— BC ————▶

———— EC ————▶
———— BC,EC (FMH-Sel = Suspend) ————▶
———— BC,EC (FMH-Sel = Begin/End Console) ———▶
———— BC, (FMH-Sel = Resume) ————▶

etc.

BC	Begin of chain	FMH	Function Management Header
EC	End of chain	Sel	Select Field in FMH

Fig. 7.17 Usage of Function Management Headers

given in Fig. 7.17. In this sequence, the first RU in the first chain carries a type 1 Function Management Header, which selects a printer. All following RUs in this chain go to the same destination, i.e. the printer. The next chain does not carry an FMH-1, but since the printer is the *active* destination, this chain also goes to the printer. The third chain is a single-RU chain, with an FMH-1 that suspends the selection of the printer. In such an RU, no data is allowed. The next chain is again a single-RU chain, now with an FMH-1 that specifies Begin/End selection of the operator console, i.e. this chain, but only this chain, goes to the console. Finally, the next RU begins a new chain and its FMH-1 specifies that the printer selection must be resumed.

Another aspect of FMH-1 is that it can be used to indicate whether the data in the Request Unit is compressed or compacted. *Compression* means that repetitive characters in the data are recognized by the sender and replaced by a certain code. The receiver must analyze these codes and generate the required number of characters. *Compaction* is a technique in

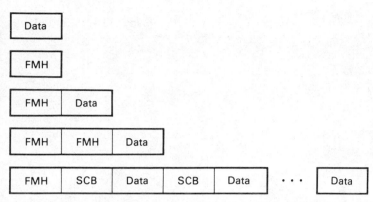

Fig. 7.18 Structure of the Request Unit: use of Function Management Headers and String Control Bytes

which characters that are very frequent are given a new code that is shorter than the normal 8 bits. In the SNA compaction, this new code is always 4 bits, with two of these characters packed in one byte. The control code that is used for both compression and compaction is the *String Control Byte* (SCB). The presence of SCBs in the data is indicated in the FMH-1. If they are present, of course all RUs following that FMH-1 must also be completely described using SCBs (Fig. 7.18). If the sender wants to transmit data without compression or compaction to the same destination, it must insert another FMH-1 and use the Continue option for the destination selection.

Function Management Header-2 is used for operations on the data that are destination dependent. These include Data Management operations like the creation and deletion of data sets (files) and the manipulation of records in these data sets. Another example of the use of FMH-2 is the selection of special forms, number of copies, etc., on printer devices. Translate tables for compaction (see above) can also be sent with FMH-2 if they apply to one destination only. Where they apply to *all* destinations in a Logical Unit, Function Management Header-3 must be used instead.

Other Function Management Headers can be used for the communication between programmed processes that are end-users to the communicating Logical Units, such as two transaction processing subsystems that distribute the processing of a particular transaction. For this purpose, the Headers 4 through 8 have been defined. A detailed discussion of their use is outside the scope of this book.

Another aspect of the presentation of data is the data stream that is used to carry the actual data and to control its presentation on a physical medium such as a printer or a display. In SNA, two data streams have been defined:

a The SNA 3270 Data Stream, which is a version of the one that was already in use for IBM3270 (-like) display devices.

b The SNA Character String, which is designed specifically within the SNA context to cover as wide a variety of devices as possible.

Abbreviation	Code (EBCDIC)	SCS Control Function
BS	16	Backspace
BEL (STP)	2F	Bell (Stop)
CR	0D	Carriage Return
CU1	1B	Customer Use 1
CU3	3B	Customer Use 3
DC1	11	Device Control 1
DC2	12	Device Control 2
DC3	13	Device Control 3
DC4	3C	Device Control 4
ENP	14	Enable Presentation
EBS (NBS)	36	Expanded Backspace (Numeric Backspace)
ESP (NSP)	E1	Expanded Space (Numeric Space)
FF (PE)	0C	Form Feed (Page End)
GE	08...	Graphic Escape
HT	05	Horizontal Tab
IT	39	Indent Tab
IR	33	Index Return
INP	24	Inhibit Presentation
IFS	1C	Interchange File Separator
IGS	1D	Interchange Group Separator
IRS	1E	Interchange Record Separator
IUS	1F	Interchange Unit Separator
LF (INX)	25	Line Feed (Index)
NL (CRE)	15	New line (Carrier Return)
NUL	00	Null
PP	34...	Presentation Position
POC	17...	Program Operator Communication
RPT	0A	Repeat
RFF (RPE)	3A	Required Form Feed (Required Page End)
RNL (RCR)	06	Required New Line (Required Carrier Return)
RSP	41	Required Space
SSR	0450	Secure String ID Reader
SLP	04C1	Select Left Platen
SME	046n	Select Magnetic Encoder
SRP	04C2	Select Right Platen
SA	28...	Set Attribute
SCI	2BD1 Cn	Set Chain Image
SGEA	2BC8	Set Graphic Error Action
SHF	2BC1	Set Horizontal Format
SLD	2BC6	Set Line Density
SPD	2BD2 29	Set Print Density
STT	2BD1 Cn	Set Translation Table
SVF	2BC2	Set Vertical Format
SI	0F	Shift In
SO	0E	Shift Out
SOF	2BC3	Start of Format
SBS	38	Subscript
SUB	3F	Substitute
SPS	09	Superscript
SW	2A	Switch
SHY	CA	Syllable Hyphen
TRN	35...	Transparent
UBS	1A	Unit Backspace
VCS	04...	Vertical Channel Select
VT	0B	Vertical Tab
WUS	23	Word Underscore

Note: Functions with ellipses extending their 1-byte code (i.e. those that have the expression '...' following them) have one or more parameters and are multiple-character code points

Fig. 7.19 SNA Character String Control Codes

The SNA Character String (SCS) is an EBCDIC code, which consists of SCS control codes and data characters. The data characters, or *graphic codes* are represented by the hexadecimal codes in the range X'40'–X'FE'. Their definition depends on the particular alphabet and national character set used. The remaining codes are defined as control codes that are used to achieve certain control functions for the actual presentation. Trivial examples are codes such as 'New Line/Carrier Return', 'Horizontal Tab', etc. Some of the more complicated codes are, for example, Presentation Position, used to specify a new position in the presentation space, and Set Vertical Format, which is used to specify a new layout in the vertical dimension of the presentation space, such as page length, top and bottom margins, etc. They may use more than 1 byte, to allow for parameters. Figure 7.19 gives a summary table of the currently defined control codes for SCS. For a detailed explanation of these codes, the reader is referred to the appropriate IBM literature [10].

7.7.2 Session Network Services

The responsibility for the operation of an SNA network rests with Network Addressable Units called the *System Services Control Points* (SSCPs). In a simple network (such as the ones that were defined in SNA-1 and SNA-2), there is only one SSCP that has total control over all resources in the network. In more advanced networks, such as the ones possible with SNA/ACF (SNA-3 and up), there can be several SSCPs, each residing in a Physical Unit type 5 and responsible for the set of resources that is assigned to them. These resources together form the *Control Domain* of an SSCP. Since an SSCP is responsible for its control domain, it must have a means of communication with the resources it controls, even when they reside in another node.

SNA requires therefore that when an SSCP owns a resource, it must also own the *physical path* towards that resource. For that reason, the Physical Units type 4 (i.e. the normal subarea nodes) and the Transmission Groups can be owned by more than one SSCP—the *shared ownership* concept. It is illustrated in Fig. 7.20, where SSCP1 owns Terminal T1 in Subarea 3, but SSCP2 owns Terminal T2 in the same subarea. The subarea node 3 must thus be shared. Since SSCP2 also owns Terminal T3 in Subarea 4, subarea node 4 is shared *and also* Transmission Group TG1 that connects the two subareas.

In order to be able to control the resources in its domain, the SSCP communicates with 'local' authorities, the *Physical Unit Services* and the *Logical Unit Services*.

Physical Unit Services reside in every node in the network. They form the function that is responsible for the resources in that node. That is, when the SSCP wants action for or from a particular resource in that node (e.g. a link attached to it), it requests the action through a session with Physical Unit Services.

A similar situation applies to the Logical Unit Services: they are present in every Logical Unit, and the SSCP can control the LU through a session

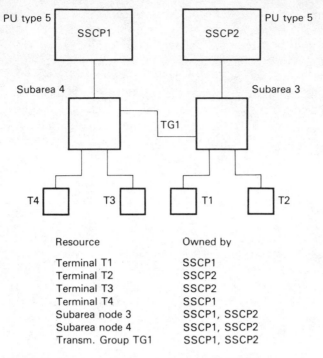

Fig. 7.20 Sharing of resources by several SSCPs

with the LU Services, or, alternatively, the end-user can request services from the SSCP through the Logical Unit Services.

For the control of resources in other domains, the SSCP must rely on the cooperation of other SSCPs (see later). The concept for the control of an SNA Network is one of cooperating SSCPs, which 'distribute' part of their function across Physical Units and Logical Units. This means, in the case of a one-domain network, that the control of network operation is fully centralized. In multi-domain networks, this control is shared among the SSCPs. In these networks, the resources can be assigned to the SSCPs as the network designer sees fit and they are then controlled by that SSCP only. There is no architectural concept of a 'master' SSCP that takes priority over the others. It is however possible during the definition of an SNA network to allocate all resources outside the type 5 PUs to only one SSCP. In such a configuration, the other SSCPs control only the resources in their own node, but no others. Effectively one has then created a network with a 'master' SSCP.

In the following section, we will first discuss the functions of the SSCP from a one-domain viewpoint. Then, in the next section, we look at the SSCP services for multi-domain operation.

System Services Control Point

A System Services Control Point provides Network Services to other Network Addressable Units (NAUs) in its control domain and requests these services from them. For the communication with the other NAUs, a set of Network Services Request Units has been defined.

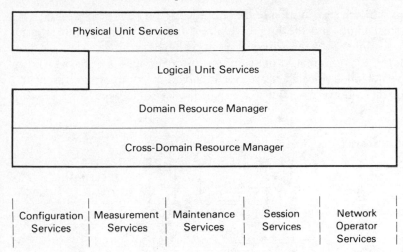

Fig. 7.21 Distribution of Network Services: the SSCP consists of two components, the Domain Resource Manager (DRM) for functions in its own control domain, and the Cross-Domain Resource Manager (CDRM) for communication with other SSCPs

These Requests flow on the sessions between the SSCP and the other NAUs. This means that, before any function can be performed in the domain, the SSCP must establish sessions with all NAUs involved. These sessions (a form of 'control channels') are usually established when the network is activated and they remain active for the 'life' of the network.

The Network Services that the SSCP can provide or request, have been categorized in five classes:

a Configuration Services. These have to do with the physical configuration of the network. The function is used to configure the network and to modify it if required.

b Session Services. These support the activation of sessions between Logical Units.

c Maintenance and Management Services. These support the testing of the facilities in the network, such as a line trace, error statistics, etc.

d Measurement Services. These services will eventually be the focal point for all kinds of measurements that can be performed on the network. Currently, no specific measurement services have been defined, although SNA products do support some implementation-dependent services. These are, however, outside the scope of this book.

e Operator Services. These services provide the network operator with the necessary functions to start the network and further control it as required. Currently, no specific Operator Services have been architectured. All support in this area is implementation defined and thus outside the scope of this book.

In Fig. 7.21 the distribution of these Network Services across the SSCP, the Physical Units and the Logical Units is indicated. Since there are no 'formal' sessions between Physical Units, the Session Services are not found in the PUs. Similarly, the Configuration Services are not present in the Logical Units, since LUs are not involved in configuration management. In the following sections, we will discuss some aspects of Session Services.

Session Services

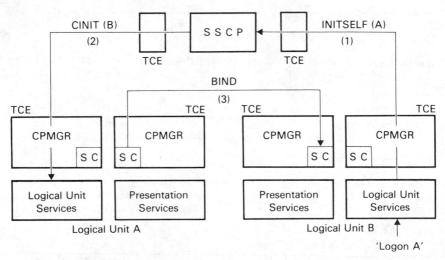

Fig. 7.22 LU–LU session activation

In Fig. 7.22, the activation of a session between two Logical Units is shown. Both Logical Units are already in session with the SSCP. Assume that Logical Unit B represents a typewriter terminal and Logical Unit A some kind of application program. When the terminal end-user types in 'Logon A', this message is interpreted by the Logical Unit Services function in Logical Unit B. These services represent the Services Manager in LU-B for the (SSCP,B) session. A message is created for the SSCP, to request a session with Logical Unit A. The philosophy is that LU-B must ask this from the SSCP since LU-B does not yet know whether LU-A is active or what its address is. The Network Services command that flows on the (SSCP,B) session is INITSELF. The parameters in this message indicate the name of the requested LU (i.e. 'A') and some information about the requesting LU ('B'). The message is interpreted by the SSCP (Network Services) and the necessary checks are made: Is B an acceptable LU? Is A active? And so on.

If all checks are satisfactory, the SSCP sends a message on its (SSCP,A) session to the Logical Unit Services component in A. This message, CINIT (B), indicates that a session is requested by Logical Unit B and that A should start the session. For that purpose, the CINIT request also contains the network address of B, and other information about B that was in the SSCP's tables. That information is used by A to build the BIND request. The BIND request flows on the (not yet existing) session (A,B) and it is sent to the Session Control (SC) component of the newly assigned TCE(A,B). If all the session parameters that are suggested by A via the BIND are acceptable to B, B sends a positive response back to A. The session is now established, and A sends a *notification* RU to the SSCP (SESSION STARTED) to inform the SSCP of the success of the BIND.

In this example, the role of Common Session Control (see Section 7.5.2) is left out, since the purpose is here to emphasize the Session Services requests INITSELF and CINIT.

If the secondary Logical Unit sends a negative response to the BIND, the primary informs the SSCP through the BIND FAILURE (BINDF) RU, which includes a reason code to explain why the BIND failed. To close the triangle, the SSCP informs the secondary through the NET-WORK SERVICES PROCEDURE ERROR (NSPE) RU of the failure. This is necessary, even where the secondary caused the BIND to fail, since the services manager in LU-B has received a positive response to the INITSELF and is thus expecting that the session will be set up. The NSPE tells it, therefore, that the session will not be established.

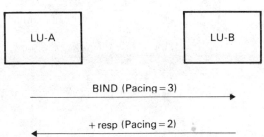

Fig. 7.23 Negotiable BIND. Some of the session parameters may be changed in the response to the BIND. Here, the pacing count that was suggested by the Primary is changed

In some very simple networks, e.g. two terminals that are connected directly, it is allowed not to have an SSCP in the full sense, i.e. both terminals will perform a minimum of SSCP-like function. The session between the two Logical Units can then be initiated by either one via the BIND, without a CINIT from the SSCP. It is then not known, however, what profiles, etc., to use since that information is normally in the SSCP's database. In this particular situation, the BIND is *negotiable*, i.e. the secondary may modify some of the parameters through its response to the BIND (Fig. 7.23). The negotiable BIND can also be used on sessions between LUs that support program-to-program communication (LU type 6, see below). This makes a more dynamic choice of the parameters possible than would be the case if all parameters were held by the SSCP.

Cross-Domain Services

The Logical Units in an SNA network should not be aware of whether they are part of a single-domain or a multi-domain network. They communicate for session services only with the SSCP that owns them. If they engage in a cross-domain session, they should see exactly the same conversation as described above for a single domain. The SSCPs involved will handle everything that has to do with the multi-domain aspects. It is therefore necessary that the SSCPs have sessions established between them, before any cross-domain activity can take place. This session establishment works in much the same way as the session establishment between the SSCPs and other Network Addressable Units. The Session Control component of Transmission Control is here too responsible for the actual session set-up. The Request Unit for this case is the *Activate Cross-Domain Resource Manager* (ACTCDRM).

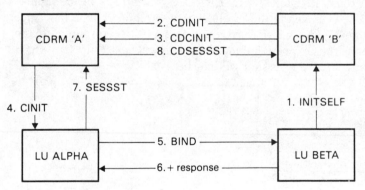

Fig. 7.24 Cross-domain session activation. (All responses, except that to the BIND, have been omitted to simplify the diagram)

Now let us look at the establishment of a session between two LUs that are in different domains. In Fig. 7.24, a Logical Unit *BETA* in the domain of SSCP *B* wants a session with LU *ALPHA* in the domain of SSCP (Cross-Domain Resource Manager) *A*. As in a single-domain network, an INITSELF request is sent to SSCP *B*. This request specifies, among other things, that LU *BETA* cannot play the primary role. *B* analyses the request and finds that *ALPHA* is not in its own domain, but is owned by *A*.

Therefore, a request, the *Cross-Domain Initialize* (CDINIT), is sent to SSCP *A*. This request also indicates that LU *BETA* will be secondary in the session and another RU is sent, the *Cross-Domain Control Initialize* (CDCINIT), which contains the information about *BETA* that *A* must know. *A* then builds the CINIT (that is, if *ALPHA* is capable of being primary) and sends it to *ALPHA*. *ALPHA* sends in the normal way a BIND to *BETA*, whose address was contained in the CDCINIT and CINIT, and *BETA* responds with a positive response if the BIND is acceptable. *ALPHA* tells *A* about the positive result through the *Session Started* RU, and *A* in its turn tells *B* with the *Cross-Domain Session Started* RU.

It is important to realize here that, from the point of view of the two LUs, there is no difference in the procedure compared to the single-domain case which was discussed above. The only difference is the conversation between the two cooperating SSCPs.

SSCP take-over An SSCP may lose its sessions with the PUs and LUs in its domain for several reasons. The SSCP itself may fail or somewhere in the Path Control network a failure may occur that results in the deactivation of the Explicit Routes and Virtual Routes on which the sessions were carried. If such a failure occurs, it does not automatically mean that existing LU–LU sessions are failing as well. As long as the Virtual Routes supporting those sessions remain available, these sessions can go on. A typical example is the case where a host computer with an SSCP goes down. With it also all the Logical Units in that host (application programs) go down. LUs in the domain of this SSCP, but outside the host, that have sessions with LUs in other domains, may continue their sessions. Actually, they are only aware of the loss of their sessions with the SSCP. Physical Units type-4 in the 'failing domain', i.e. the domain controlled by the failing SSCP, that are also controlled by other SSCPs, can signal to those other SSCPs that one SSCP was lost. Implementation and installation-dependent procedures can then be started to establish SSCP sessions with those resources that were exclusively owned by the failing SSCP. The Request Units used for that 'take over' are the same as those for the initial establishment of the sessions with the SSCP, the *Activate Physical Unit* (ACTPU) and the *Activate Logical Unit* (ACTLU), except that the Error Recovery option is used in order not to reset existing sessions. Once the lost SSCP is accessible again, either because the route becomes available or because it has been restarted, similar procedures can be used to regain control over its resources.

7.8 Types of LU–LU session

In Section 7.2.1, we defined the concept of architectured subsets of the SNA functions. At the level of the Logical Units, these subsets are defined in terms of *types of LU–LU session*. All products implemented according to the SNA definitions are classified according to these LU–LU session types, which specify what functions the product can perform when it is in session with other SNA products. In Section 7.2.1, we also introduced the concept of the *profile*, the definition of a particular set of options in one layer of SNA. These profiles are defined for the three layers in the LU that participate in a session, Transmission Control (*TS-profile*), Data Flow Control (*FM-profile*) and Presentation Services (*PS-profile*). Each profile combines a set of functions related to the relevant layer. When a session is established, these functions are selected via a number associated with the appropriate profile. Both session partners must, of course, agree on the same profiles. It is, however, not always sufficient to request just the profile; sometimes more information is needed related to the profile. This is the case, for example, when in the TS-profile it is specified that pacing will be used; the pacing windows will still have to be set. This is done through the *profile usage fields* in the session establishment request (BIND). These usage fields can therefore be considered a further specification of the particular profile.

With each LU–LU session type, a specific set of profiles is defined. The session type is classified through a number, which is the same as the PS-profile number. This stems from an earlier view of the LU–LU session type, when it was called the *Logical Unit Type*, which was defined as a specific PS-profile and the associated FM- and TS- profiles. LU–LU session types are described in detail in [10, 11]. A short summary description is given below of each of the LU–LU session types defined so far.

0 Session type 0 is used to classify sessions that do use SNA-defined protocols for both Transmission Control and Data Flow Control, but not for Function Management Data Services, i.e. for Session Presentation Services. At that level, the protocols are end-user or product defined.

1 Session type 1 is used between application programs and data processing terminals that can have either one or more devices attached to them. In this session type, Function Management Headers can be used to select the appropriate device on which the data is to be presented. The data stream used is the SNA Character String (SCS).

2 Session type 2 is used specifically in sessions between an application program and a single display terminal using the SNA 3270 data stream. It is mainly used for compatibility with existing pre-SNA 3270 application programs.

3 Session type 3 is used similarly to session type 2, but for a single-printer device that uses the SNA 3270 data stream.

4 Session type 4 can be used in two ways:

   a For sessions between two terminals, which may be multiple devices. In this case, no network with a separate SSCP is required, i.e. the two terminals must handle SSCP-like functions themselves. These sessions can be used when two terminals are connected point-to-point, without any further network. The negotiable BIND is required in this case to allow for the selection of certain session parameters like pacing windows, etc.

b For sessions between application processes and terminals that may have multiple devices. In this case, the session type is very similar to session type 1, but more data streams are possible, e.g. for word processing.

5 Session type 5 has not been defined.

6 Session type 6 is defined for communication between application programs that cooperate in a distributed processing environment, for example transaction processing sub-systems. In this session type, various data streams can be selected, such as the SNA Character String, but also specifically defined ones, such as a structured field data stream, a Logical Messages (LMS) data stream or even a user-defined data stream. An important aspect of this session type is the synchronization of resource and update commitments in various parts of the transaction. The architectured vehicles for the exchange are the Function Management Headers FMH-4 through FMH-8 and FMH-10.

7.9 Comparison with the Reference Model

From the description of the SNA layers in the preceding sections it will be clear that the SNA's layers are generally similar to the layers of the Reference Model. In this section we will take a more detailed look at this relationship.

In Fig. 7.25, the layers of both SNA and the Reference Model are shown side by side. The reader should realize that this way of drawing the comparison is subjective and time dependent, also because the Reference Model is not yet fully defined in all its detail. Earlier publications, for example [12], show a mapping that is somewhat different from the one presented here. The differences are mainly in the position of the ISO Transport and Network Layers relative to the SNA Layers. Since the definition of both layers changed while the Reference Model matured, it is not surprising that with today's definition the result of a mapping is different. This emphasizes, once more, that any such mapping is only relevant as an overall indication and can only properly be positioned in time since both the Reference Model and any proprietary architecture, including SNA, continuously evolve.

In the following comparison, we sometimes have to use the same word in two contexts, the Reference Model and SNA, where they may have different meanings. Whenever confusion could arise, we prefix the term in the SNA case with '(SNA)'.

For the mapping, we use the list of services and functions as given in

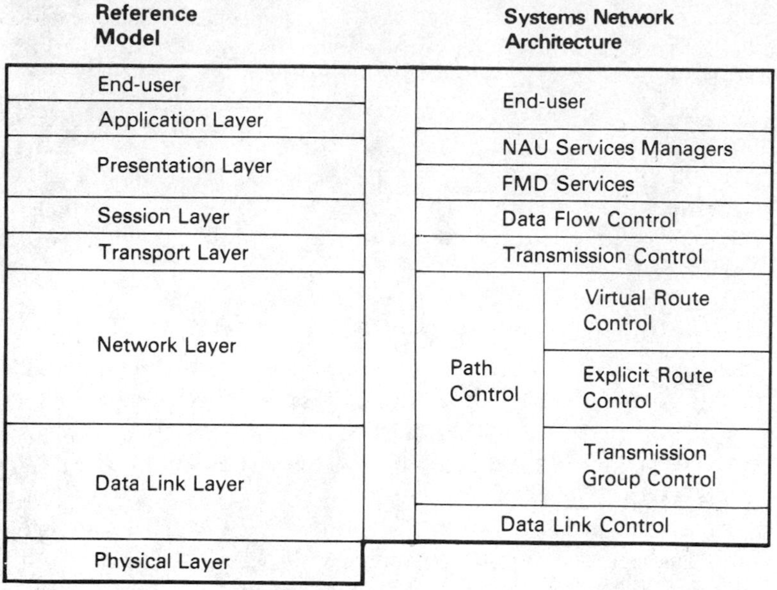

Reference Model	Systems Network Architecture		
End-user	End-user		
Application Layer			
Presentation Layer	NAU Services Managers		
	FMD Services		
Session Layer	Data Flow Control		
Transport Layer	Transmission Control		
Network Layer	Path Control	Virtual Route Control	
		Explicit Route Control	
Data Link Layer		Transmission Group Control	
	Data Link Control		
Physical Layer			

Fig. 7.25 Comparison of the OSI and SNA layers

Appendix B. Where no comment is given for a specific service or function, this indicates that we did not identify such a service or function *in that layer* of SNA.

7.9.1 Application Layer

The Application Layer in the Reference Model is not defined as such in SNA. However, some of the functions defined in the SNA NAU Services Layer, i.e. the Network Services, do in a sense belong to the Application Layer more than to the Presentation Layer.

7.9.2 Presentation Layer

For the SNA Logical Unit to Logical Unit sessions, where the NAU Services are called Session Presentation Services, these services are equivalent to the services defined in the Presentation Layer in the Reference Model. However, some functions are handled by another instance of the NAU Services, the Network Services. These are not connection-specific, but rather Network Addressable Unit specific and therefore do not directly map into the Reference Model. The main functions that were listed in the Reference Model are given below and compared with SNA functions that fulfill the same purpose.

134 Computer network architectures

Services provided by the Presentation Layer
- Data transformation. The data transformations defined in SNA are the compression and compaction facilities using the String Control Byte (SCB) in the FMD Services Layer and the data encryption facility in the Transmission Control Layer. In the FMD Services Layer, the IBM-3270 data stream can be used to select either the EBCDIC or the ASCII code, but no transformation service between the two is available.

  Data encryption is not provided as a presentation service in SNA, but as a session level security service in Transmission Control (see below) or it is performed by the end-user.
- Data formatting. Data formatting is defined in SNA via the IBM 3270 data stream and the SNA Character String data stream.
- Syntax selection. When an SNA session is established, the BIND Request Unit contains information about the transformations (compaction and encryption) that can be used in the sessions. It also specifies the data streams available to the session, depending on the Logical Unit type. The Reference Model also states the requirement for subsequently modifying the selected syntax. For this purpose, SNA uses the Function Management Headers, and the Format Indicator in the Request Header.
- Presentation-connections. In SNA, the presentation-connection is provided via the destination selection mechanism in FMH-1. If Function Management Headers are not used, the presentation-connection is implicitly included in the (SNA) session.

Functions in the Presentation Layer
- General
  - Session establishment request. The request to establish a session (both in the ISO and the SNA sense) is not generated by Session Presentation Services in SNA, but by its management equivalent, Network Services. A session establishment request (INITSELF) is sent to the Network Management function (the System Services Control Point, SSCP) and, after name-to-address mapping, relayed to the Transport Layer equivalent.
  - Presentation image negotiation and renegotiation. During the establishment of the (SNA) session, the presentation image is selected via the agreement of the Logical Unit type. No renegotiation is possible.
  - Data transformation and formatting. Components of Session Presentation Services will perform data transformation and formatting according to the service requested, i.e. the data stream selected (see above).
  - Special-purpose transformations. A service is provided in Function Management Data Services for compression and compaction operations. Encryption is not provided by the NAU Services, but in the Transmission Control Layer. (In SNA, encryption is not considered a

presentation aspect of the data but rather a data-independent security aspect of a session.)

— Session termination request. Session termination can be requested through the Data Flow Control Shutdown service, which terminates the session-connection.

- Addressing and multiplexing. Presentation-service-access-point-addresses are provided in SNA in certain Logical Unit types via the 'Medium selection' and 'device address' in the Function Management Header. If these headers are not used, there is a one-to-one correspondence with the session-connection-endpoint-address.

  In the Reference Model, multiplexing is not permitted for the Presentation Layer. In SNA, some form of multiplexing is defined with the destination selection stacking mechanism.

- Presentation Layer Management

7.9.3 Session Layer

In Fig. 7.25, we have mapped the OSI Session Layer against the Data Flow Control Layer in SNA. In the following list of services and functions of the Session Layer, we indicate the equivalence with the SNA Data Flow Control services and functions.

Services provided by the Session Layer
- Session-connection establishment. The session-connection is implicitly established when the (SNA) session is established as a transport-connection and made available through the Start Data Traffic (SDT) Request Unit. Note that also the SDT Request Unit is sent from Session Control in the next layer (Transmission Control).
- Session-connection release. The Request Shutdown and the Shutdown Request Units release the session-connection.
- Normal data exchange. The Session-service-data-unit transferred for normal data exchange is in SNA, the Request/Response Unit.
- Quarantine service. A service that is similar to the quarantine service is the *Chaining* protocol in SNA. This is, however, not a quarantine service in the full sense, since it is not possible to specify that the Request Units making up the chain should not be released until the end of the chain. If a chain has to be recovered, this has to be done in cooperation with the Presentation Service. From this point of view, the Chaining protocol may be looked at as a session-connection synchronization protocol (see below) rather than a quarantine service.
- Expedited data exchange. No expedited flow is defined for session-service-data-units in SNA.
- Interaction management. The interaction management service is provided in SNA through the Send/Receive Mode protocol:

- Two-Way-Simultaneous. This mode is called Full-Duplex in SNA.
- Two-Way-Alternate. For this mode, there are two possibilities in SNA: the Half-Duplex Flip/Flop or the Half-Duplex Contention protocol. In both protocols, the direction of active transmission can be changed through the Change Direction Indicator.
- One-Way. The one-way mode is not explicitly defined in SNA, but a sender can enforce it by not sending Change Direction.

● Session-connection synchronization. The session-connection is synchronized in SNA using the Request/Response Control Mode protocols. In summary, these are:

a Request Control Mode
  i Immediate Request Mode. Several Request Units may be sent, but only one—the last one—will require a Definite Response.
  ii Delayed Request Mode. Any number of Request Units can be sent, independent of the response type requested.
b Response Control Mode
  i Immediate Response Mode. Responses must be returned in the order in which the requests were received.
  ii Delayed Response Mode. Responses may be returned in any order, except for the response to the CHASE Request, which must stay behind all responses to previous requests.

● Exception reporting. Exceptions are reported through the Exception Response Indicator (ERI) in the Request Header. The cause of the exception is specified in a 4-byte sense code that immediately follows the Request Header.

● Additional. In the Reference Model, several functions are listed as potential additions to the services in the Session Layer. They are listed here, although not yet part of the Reference Model, because some of these functions are defined already in SNA.

a Session-service-data-unit sequence numbering. Basic Information Units in SNA can be sequence numbered when they are sent on the *normal flow*, which is always the case for the services provided by Data Flow Control to the presentation entities.
b Brackets. This service is defined in Data Flow Control as the Bracket protocol. It is used by the session partners to synchronize the initiation and termination of transactions.
c Stop–go. This service is provided in Data Flow Control through the Quiesce (QEC) and Release Quiesce (RELQ) Request Units.
d Security. SNA allows session-level encryption of data through the services of the Connection Point Manager (in the Transmission Control Layer), although the encryption can also be done by the end-user.

Functions in the Session Layer
- Mapping of session-connection onto transport-connection. In SNA, there is implicitly a one-to-one mapping of sessions onto a transport-connection, i.e. (SNA) session.
- Session-connection flow control. The Reference Model specifies that there is no session-connection flow control and that the presentation-entities will apply back pressure across the transport-connection using transport flow control. Data Flow Control can apply this back pressure by not accepting incoming Request Units from Transmission Control.
- Expedited data transfer
- Session-connection recovery
- Session-connection release. A session-connection is released via the SHUTDOWN Request.
- Session Layer Management

7.9.4 Transport Layer

The SNA equivalent of the Transport Layer is the Transmission Control Layer. Below, a summary of equivalent services and functions is given.

Services provided by the Transport Layer
- Identification
  - Transport-addresses. The equivalent of the transport-address is the (SNA) network address of the Network Addressable Unit.
  - Transport-connections. The equivalent of the transport-connection is the (SNA) session.
  - Transport-connection-endpoint-identifiers. The transport-connection-endpoint-identifier is the Session Identification, the (SNA) network address of the Network Addressable Unit, suffixed with the (SNA) network address of the correspondent NAU.
- Establishment services
  - Transport-connection establishment. The transport-connection establishment service is not directly provided to the Data Flow Control Layer. Instead, the NAU Services Manager sends the request to the SSCP, which in turn directs the Transmission Control Layer to send a BIND Request Unit to the intended correspondent.
  - Class of service selection. Class of Service (COS) is not defined in SNA for the Transmission Control Layer, but for Virtual Route Control. This is a sub-layer of Path Control and it is mapped against the Network Layer. However, when a transport-connection is established, a certain Virtual Route Class of Service can be selected.
- Data transfer services
  - Transport-service-data-unit. The transport-service-data-unit is the

Request/Response Unit (RU) that is received from the Data Flow Control Layer, together with DFC protocol-control-information. (No separate name is defined for a protocol-data-unit in the Data Flow Control Layer.)
- Expedited transport-service-data-unit. Data Flow Control may request certain Request Units to be transmitted on an expedited flow. These Request Units are called Expedited RUs.
- Transport-connection release. Data Flow Control can request release of the transport-connection only indirectly via the services managers.

Functions in the Transport Layer
- Addressing. The transport address associated with a (SNA) half-session is the network address of the NAU, followed by the network address of the correspondent NAU.
- Connection multiplexing and splitting. Only multiplexing is defined; several transport-connections, i.e. (SNA) sessions, can be multiplexed on one network-connection (i.e. Virtual Route).
- Phases of operation
  - Establishment phase. In the establishment phase, the correspondent NAU agrees on the parameters for the (SNA) session via the BIND Request Unit. This does not only concern the parameters for the transport-connection, but also those for the higher layers. In certain cases (i.e. LU-types), the BIND can be negotiable.
  - Data transfer phase
    - Sequencing. The Connection Point Manager checks the sequence of the Request Units using the RU sequence number generated by Data Flow Control.
    - Blocking
    - Concatenation
    - Segmenting
    - Multiplexing or splitting. The Transmission Control Layer can offer multiple (SNA) sessions to the same Virtual Route in Path Control.
    - Flow control. Transmission Control uses a pacing mechanism with a fixed window to regulate the flow on the transport-connection (SNA session pacing).
    - Error detection. The Connection Point Manager in Transmission Control is responsible for checking the sequence numbers of service-data-units and for detecting loss, duplication or misordering.
    - Error recovery. Recovery from sequence errors can be achieved by the Session Control component of Transmission Control with the Set and Test Sequence Numbers (STSN) and Start Data Traffic (SDT) Request Units.

○ Expedited data transfer. The Connection Point Manager will make sure that Expedited RUs are not queued, both on the sending and the receiving side.
○ Transport-service-data-unit delimiting. Not explicitly defined in SNA. The length of the Transport Layer protocol-control-information (Request Header—RH) is fixed. The length of the total Transport Layer protocol-data-unit is passed in the Network Layer interface-control-information (Path Control parameter).
○ Transport-connection identification. Through the ordered pair (*nai, naj*), where *nai* is the address of the primary NAU and *naj* the address of the secondary NAU.
— Release phase. In the release phase, the Session Control component sends the UNBIND Request Unit to the correspondent transport-entity (SNA half-session).
● Transport Layer Management. Layer management functions are provided partly by the Session Control component, partly by Network Services outside the Transmission Control Layer.

7.9.5 Network Layer

The SNA equivalent of the Network Layer is mainly the Path Control Layer. Path Control is composed of three sub-layers: Virtual Route Control, Explicit Route Control and Transmission Group Control. Only the first two sub-layers together can be compared to the Network Layer. The services provided by Transmission Group Control (i.e. control of multiple physical connections in parallel) are part of the Data Link Layer in the Reference Model.

The services provided to the Transport Layer are mainly those provided by the Virtual Route Control, while the Explicit Route Control can be considered an internal function of the Network Layer.

Services provided by the Network Layer
● Network addresses. The addresses by which the transport-entities are known are the SNA network addresses, consisting of a subarea address and an element address. In SNA, there can be several transport-entities that are served by one network-entity. The subarea address can therefore be considered as the (OSI) network-address and the element address as the connection-endpoint-suffix.
● Network-connections. Path Control gives its users access to its network-connections, the Virtual Routes.
● Network-connection-endpoint-identifiers. The Virtual Route is fully defined by the Origin Subarea Address, the Destination Subarea Address, the Virtual Route Number and the Transmission Priority. In any node, i.e. end-system, the combination of Destination Subarea

Address, Virtual Route Number and Transmission Priority may be considered the network-connection-endpoint-identifier.

- Network-service-data-unit transfer. The network-service-data-unit is the Basic Information Unit (BIU).
- Quality of service parameters. The Class of Service allows selection of these parameters.
- Error notification. Unrecoverable errors in the Path Control Layer (i.e. failure of an Explicit Route, which results in the failure of a Virtual Route) are reported to the Transmission Control Layer and result in the termination of the transport-connection (the SNA session).
- Sequencing. The sequence of Basic Information Units is guaranteed on the Virtual Route.
- Flow control. A transport-entity may cause the Virtual Route flow control to be enforced by not receiving incoming BIUs.
- Expedited network-service-data-unit transfer. A high-priority transfer is defined as a service of the Virtual Route Control Layer.
- Reset
- Release services. No explicit release services are available to the Transmission Control Layer. When Virtual Route Control detects that the last (SNA) session that uses the Virtual Route has been terminated, the Virtual Route itself is terminated.

Functions in the Network Layer
- Routing and relaying. Virtual Routes are mapped onto Explicit Routes. Routing along Explicit Routes is based on the concept of source-independent explicit routing. A pre-defined routing table contains an entry for each Destination Subarea–Explicit Route Number (DSA–ERN) pair. The outgoing Transmission Group (link or group of links) is selected on the basis of this table. A BIU may be relayed by several subarea nodes before reaching the Destination Subarea.
- Network-connections. Network connections are provided as the end-system to end-system Virtual Routes, based upon Explicit Routes. No tandem sub-network connections are defined.
- Network-connection multiplexing. Several Virtual Routes may be multiplexed on an Explicit Route, while several Explicit Routes may be multiplexed onto the same Transmission Group.
- Segmenting and blocking. Segmenting can be performed in the Virtual Route Control sub-layer. Blocking is not performed in the Virtual or Explicit Route Control sub-layers, but Transmission Group Control provides for the blocking of several PIUs into one BTU if they must be transmitted on the same Transmission Group.
- Error detection. The quality of the service is not monitored in Path Control. Error notification from the Data Link Control Layer may result in failure of the routes involved.

- Error recovery
- Sequencing. This is performed in Transmission Group Control in the Data Link Layer. The Virtual and Explicit Routes guarantee that this sequence is left unchanged.
- Flow control. The flow control mechanism in the Virtual Route Control sub-layer is not mainly a service to the transport-entities, but a means of congestion control inside the network. Congestion conditions are reported by Transmission Group Control to the Virtual Route Control sub-layer, which enforces flow control based on a variable window pacing mechanism (Virtual Route Pacing).
- Expedited data transfer. There is a special network priority defined, which can be used by the Path Control Layers themselves. It is not available as a service to the Transport Layer.
- Reset
- Service selection
- Network Layer Management. This is performed by the Virtual Route and Explicit Route managers that are part of the Physical Unit.

7.9.6 Data Link Layer

The Data Link Layer is provided in SNA by the Transmission Group Control sub-layer of Path Control and the SDLC layer (or the Channel Interface). For the following comparison, we base ourselves on the HDLC comparison (Section 4.6). It should be noted that, at the time of writing, SDLC uses only the HDLC Unbalanced-Normal Response Mode Class of Procedures. Any comments below identify either an HDLC function not present in SDLC or an additional service provided by Transmission Group Control.

Services provided by the Data Link Layer
- Data-link-connections. The data-link-connection in SNA is the Transmission Group, rather than the individual SDLC link.
- Data-link-service-data-units
- Data-link-connection-endpoint-identifiers
- Sequencing. Within a priority class, Transmission Group Control guarantees sequential delivery.
- Error notification
- Flow control
- Quality of service parameters

Functions in the Data Link Layer
- Data-link-connection establishment and release
- Data-link-service-data-units mapping
- Data-link-connection splitting. Transmission Group Control may use several SDLC links in parallel to provide the data-link-connecton.

- Delimiting and synchronization
- Sequence control. Transmission Group Control assures sequential delivery of data-link-service-data-units within a priority class. Whenever a frame is taken from one of the queues, it is assigned a unique Transmission Group Sequence Number. Frames are delivered according to this sequence number (and resequenced if necessary).
- Error detection
- Error recovery
- Flow control
- Identification and parameter exchange
- Control of data circuit interconnection
- Data Link Layer Management

7.9.7 Physical Layer

The Physical Layer is not explicitly defined in SNA. Reference is made to existing international standards and recommendations, such as V.24, X.21, etc.

References

1 Schultz, G. D. and Sundstrom, R. J., SNA's first six years: 1974–1980, *Proc. 5th Int. Conf. Computer Commun.*, Atlanta, 1980, pp. 578–585
2 Atkins, J. D., Path Control: the Transport Network of SNA, *IEEE Trans. Commun.*, vol. Com-28, no. 4, pp. 527–538
3 Ahuja, V., Routing and flow control in Systems Network Architecture, *IBM Syst. J.*, vol. 18, no. 2, 1979, pp. 298–314
4 IBM Corporation, *Systems Network Architecture—concepts and products*, GC30-3072
5 IBM Corporation, *Systems Network Architecture format and protocol reference manual: architectural logic*, SC30-3112
6 IBM Corporation, *IBM Synchronous Data Link Control General Information*, GA27-3093
7 Jueneman, R. R. and Kerr, G. S., Explicit path routing in communication networks, *Proc. 3rd Int. Conf. Computer Commun.*, Toronto, 1976, pp. 340–342
8 Maruyama, K., On the generation of explicit routing tables, *Proc. 5th Int. Conf. Computer Commun.*, Atlanta, 1980
9 Deaton, G. A. Jr., Flow control in packet-switched networks with explicit path routing, *Proc. Flow Control in Computer Networks Conf.*, Paris, 1979
10 IBM Corporation, *Systems Network Architecture—sessions between Logical Units*, GC20-1868
11 IBM Corporation, *Systems Network Architecture—introduction to sessions between Logical Units*, GC20-1869
12 Corr, F. P. and Neal, D. H., SNA and emerging international standards, *IBM Syst. J.*, vol. 18, no. 2, 1979, pp. 244–262

8 DEC's Distributed Network Architecture

8.1 DECNET

DEC announced its Distributed Network Architecture (DNA) in 1975. It was implemented in a first series of software and hardware products under the name DECNET.

From the start, DNA contained, as an architecture, a very high level of network sophistication. The elements were meshed network, distributed network control and management, application level protocols (DAP), dynamic routing, etc.

The first DECNET implementation included only a very small subset of the global architecture. Experiences with the first release of DECNET resulted in a review of the specification. A new version of DNA was defined in 1978 and a new implementation DECNET PHASE 2 was announced at the same time.

During 1980, DECNET PHASE 3 was announced. At the same time, a completely revised set of DNA descriptions was published. The changes integrated the experiences of previous releases and the relaxation of network configuration restrictions.

References [1–3] illustrate the evolution of DNA. A good general overview of the DNA version that is discussed in this chapter can be found in [4]. For more detailed information on the specific layer protocols, references [5–8] are suggested reading.

8.2 Architecture overview

DNA features eight 'layers', which are shown in Fig. 8.1. When compared to the Reference Model, it seems that some of the layers contain network control functions, such as configuration services, logical connection services, etc. These are more than typical layer functions that assist communication between users under steady-state conditions. One can re-arrange the layers in a way that they follow more closely the Reference Model. The Network Management Layer, for example, could be extracted and be put as an application. It is a privileged application that has hooks in the different layers. Figure 8.1 represents DNA in this way [3]. Several of the defined layers do not necessarily have to get involved in this communication process. For example, a user of DECNET does not have to use the Network Application Layer. This layer assists in the access of data files and allows the manipulation of those files. Some of the functions are, for example, to create or update information in a file or to move a file to

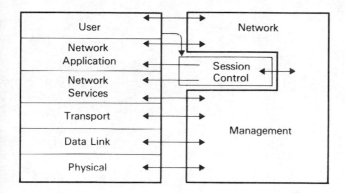

Fig. 8.1 DNA: the layers

another destination. Other layers are a prerequisite and mandatory for user communication. The Physical Layer connects the physical nodes where the user processes reside. Another required layer is the Data Link Layer, which controls the orderly exchange of data between nodes. The same applies to the Transport Layer, which routes messages through the network, and the Network Services Layer, which gives a logical channel appearance to the communicating user programs or processes. If communication is required between two processes in the same physical node, then only the two lowest layers will not be used. A node can contain multiple users of DECNET services. Some of the layers will be unique to a user process while other layers will be shared or execute services for all user processes in that particular node.

Figure 8.2 shows a simple network consisting of two end nodes and an intermediate node. Let us consider that two processes want to communicate with each other. The user in system A will request, from Session Control, a connection with a process in system B. It will make this request by using symbolic names to indicate the process that it wants to reach, and the node where the process resides. As shown in the figure, the process is called *FINANCEA* in the node *SYSTEMB*. The Session Control Layer maps the node name to a Node Address. It will also verify if the particular end-user exists, in this case FINANCEA, and if it is related to the physical destination, in this case SYSTEMB. Next, the Session Control Layer formats a connection request to the Network Services Layer for the establishment of a logical channel between the Source User Process and the Destination User Process. It will also start a timer to monitor that connection process. The Network Services Layers in both end nodes create a logical link allowing the two user processes to exchange data. The logical link will appear to the users as a Full-Duplex logical channel between

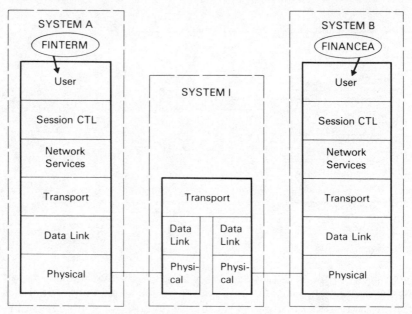

Fig. 8.2 DNA: network example

them. The Network Services Layer will have passed a Connect Initiate Message to the Transport Layer before this is complete. This layer selects, on the basis of the Destination address, which link to use. Next, it puts the Connect Initiate Message on the Data Link Control Layer of the link, making the first hop towards the destination node, in our example SYSTEMI. SYSTEMI is a node with an intermediate node function. This type of node is called an *Intercept node* in DECNET. It contains at least the three lowest layers because they are required for the principal intermediate node function, i.e. the routing of the data further towards the destination. In our example, it will select the link that connects it to SYSTEMB, the destination node. The only layers involved are the Transport Layer for selection of the link, and the Data Link Control Layer for the transmission to the end node over the physical connection. Finally, the Data Link Layer in the node SYSTEMB will receive the Connect Initiate Message and pass it to the Transport Layer. Here, it is recognized that the destination node is the one it resides in and the control message is passed to the Session

Control Layer. The Session Control Layer now validates the request. It checks the control information for passwords and determines the source node address. Eventually, the layer activates the requested end-user process and passes the connection request to that process. Again, a timer is started to monitor the end-user's process response. The acceptance by the, in our case, FINANCEA process in SYSTEMB is passed to Session Control, which formats it and adds the source node address, SYSTEMA, which now becomes the destination address of the acceptance message. Then, it requests a confirmation message to be sent to the Network Services Protocol Layer. This layer sends a Connect Confirm message through its Transport, Data Link and Physical Layers towards SYSTEMA. The message passes, in our example, through SYSTEMI and will be delivered through the different layers in SYSTEMA to the requesting user process. Now, the user processes can communicate over a Full-Duplex logical channel with each other. The function of the Session Control Layer is now reduced to simple pass-through, i.e. the layer becomes a null layer after the logical channel has been established. The Network Services Layer controls the data exchanges and makes sure that the data is transferred in an orderly way, in sequence and with guaranteed delivery, through the network. The Transport Layer assures the selection of an optimal path through the network.

The user process can access data stores in data files in a remote system. It has the option to code its own programs to get to the data, or it can use the services of the Data Access Protocol (DAP). These protocols are situated in the Network Application Layer. The layer theoretically also exists in the previous example but was not mentioned because FINAN-CEA did not use DAP. Then, the Network Application Layer becomes a null layer, i.e. a defined layer but with an empty protocol set. The user process does its own thing to get the data.

DNA is an architecture which allows several nodes, for example minicomputers, to be interconnected and to have user processes to exchange data with each other. As seen before, the Network Services Protocol Layer gives these processes a Full-Duplex logical channel. The layers under the Network Services Protocol Layer allow the physical transport of the message through the network. The transport network (Transport Layer and below) uses the principle of *datagrams* for the transmission of the messages through the network. This means that messages, exchanged over a logical link, will possibly physically follow different paths through the network. The path will be optimized depending on the algorithms implemented in the Transport Layer. It also means that message delivery is on a best-effort basis. Hence, the delivery guarantee to the user process and the resequencing have to be performed in the Network Services Protocol Layer. If this were not the case, then the user would have to include these functions in its application code or accept this kind of a service.

Descriptions of the different layers will now follow. At the end of the chapter, a comparison can be found with the Reference Model. An effort is made to equate the layers in the Model with the layers in DNA.

DEC's DNA documentation is very complete and therefore some of the protocols are given as an example of a particular layer function. The reader interested in detailed functions and/or protocols will find DEC's literature cited in the reference list at the end of this chapter.

8.3 Physical Layer

DNA does not explicitly define a Physical Layer. This does not mean that there is no Physical Layer but simply that there is no explicit description. The main function is the management of the physical transmission of data over a channel. It includes monitoring channel signals, clocking on the channel and interrupts over the channel. It uses for the specifications of this layer the standards that are available in the communications world, such as CCITT and ISO, and the specifications of DEC computer link interfaces.

8.4 Data Link Layer (DDCMP)

DEC defined Digital Data Communications Message Protocol (DDCMP) as their implementation of a Data Link Layer protocol [5]. Unlike most other manufacturers, DEC did not choose HDLC as its data-link control. DDCMP is not the only defined protocol on this layer; there is also the *Maintenance Operations Protocol* (MOP), which usually operates within DDCMP. Basically, MOP is a protocol which assists configuration services and the maintenance services within DNA. It allows, for instance, the loading of a remote node through DDCMP. Also, the dumping of a remote node in the case of a systems failure and loop-back testing of the link are possible. MOP assists network operations because of its ability to restart a remote, unattended system.

In general, DDCMP is responsible for the creation and management of a communication path between two adjacent nodes. It will assure the sequentiality and the integrity of data messages over that communications path. Recovery in the case of detected errors is an integral part of the protocol. DDCMP is a byte-oriented protocol against the bit-oriented HDLC protocol. This means that messages have to be a multiple of bytes and that the count of the number of bytes in the message has to be carried in the message in order to ensure transparency. The operation of the communications path is independent of the channel bit-width and the transmission characteristics. The physical link can be serial, like a telephone line, or a parallel path, like a channel between computers and other devices. Also, the transmission technique can be synchronous or asynchronous. Other characteristics are

a Full-Duplex or Half-Duplex.

b Pipelining (*n* number of messages outstanding without having to receive an ACK).

c Piggybacking (ACKs are carried by a data message received by the original sender).

d Point-to-point and multipoint link configurations.

From the organizational point of view, DDCMP has three functional components: Framing, Link Management and Message Exchange. The next sections review the protocols of the three functions.

8.4.1 Framing

A receiving station on a link should be able to extract, from a bit stream, a message destined for it. Framing is concerned with locating the start and the end of such a message and will allow that receiver to extract it. Synchronization, on the other hand, is an integral part of the protocol. It requires the detection of a bit or byte pattern (byte in the case of DDCMP) that indicates to the receiver from which point the receiver can keep in step with the transmitter. DDCMP provides synchronization on two levels: byte level and message level. Bit synchronization, the operation of locating a bit on a link, is done by the modems or the physical interfaces of the link and is a part of the Physical Layer. Byte synchronization, i.e. the matter of detecting a particular byte configuration in an 8-bit window, depends on the transmission technique used. On 8-bit parallel links or a multiple of 8-bit parallel links, the operation is inherent. On serial links, the synchronization will depend on the transmission technique used. On asynchronous links, the receiver is actuated by the start bit in front of the byte, allowing it to extract the following 8 bits, whereas the stop bits on the other side terminate the synchronization. Synchronous links have to operate using 8-bit bytes and a bit timing signal provided by the modem or superimposed on the data signal.

Byte framing is done in DDCMP by looking for a unique 8-bit pattern in the bit stream. The receiver should at least locate one sequence of two consecutive SYN bytes to achieve synchronization. Message framing is done in DDCMP by means of any one of three particular byte configurations: *SOH*, *ENQ* or *DLE*. ASCII is used for the character code.

The end of the message is detected through combining the message type and the data count of the message. Figure 8.3 shows the message lay-out of the three types. Following the starting byte are 5 bytes completing the Message Header followed by a 2-byte header block check (CRC). In the case of an ENQ message or control message, this is the total message. For data messages (SOH) and the maintenance messages (DLE), the header is followed by a number of bytes equal to the 14-bit data-count in the header and 2 bytes of data block check (CRC).

Message type	Bytes in message										
	0	1	2	3	4	5	6 7	8	n	n+1	n+2
Data message	SOH	COUNT	FLAGS	RESP	NUM	ADDR	BLKCHK	DATA		BLKCHK	
Control message	ENQ	TYPE *1	FLAGS	*2	FILL	ADDR	BLKCHK				
Maintenance message	DLE	COUNT	FLAGS	FILL		ADDR	BLKCHK	DATA		BLKCHK	

*1   Control message type

*2   Response number for certain types of command

RESP   Response number
NUM   Transmit number
ADDR   Station Address
BLKCHK   Block check
FILL   Fill byte (X '00')

Fig. 8.3 DDCMP: message types and their layout

8.4.2 Link Management

The Link Management component controls the transmission and the reception of the stations on the link. Depending on the link configurations, Half-Duplex or Full-Duplex, point-to-point or multipoint, stations can transmit or receive at a certain point in time. For example, a selected station on a Half-Duplex multipoint link, will be receiving until the 'controlling station' allows it to send.

The vehicle for this control is one bit of the two flag bits in the header, namely the Select flag (see Fig. 8.4). The control station will allow a tributary station to start transmitting by setting the Select flag bit to 1 in a data message (SOH), or in a control message (ENQ) to that tributary station if there is no data ready for transmission. The control station then stops transmitting and the tributary station starts its transmission. When all the data messages have been transmitted, it returns control to the control station by putting the Select flag bit to 1 in a data or a control message.

The moment a control station selects a tributary station, it starts a selection timer. This timer allows the control station to detect the loss of a message carrying the Select flag. Its expiration returns control to the control station. The addressing of a particular tributary station, i.e. to select a station for transmitting data messages to it, is done by putting the

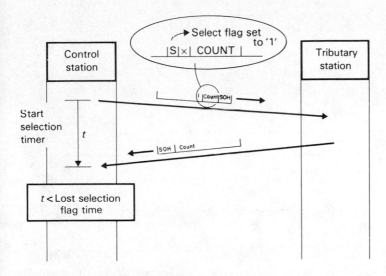

Fig. 8.4 DDCMP: selection mechanism

address of the tributary station in the ADDR field of the Message Header, see Fig. 8.3. The management of the link, i.e. selection and addressing, is based on an implementation-defined selection or polling algorithm, within the control station. The selection interval can be based on a maximum number of messages that a selected station can transmit and will be a function of the DDCMP user's implementation requirements and the total performance requirements of the link.

The above is only an example of the protocol for a specific link configuration. Similar operations are described for other link configurations.

8.4.3 Message Exchange

This component creates a sequential error-free link. It ensures that data is transmitted in sequence over a physical communications path that is in itself not error free. The protocol used by DDCMP is called a *positive acknowledgment retransmission* protocol. Correctly received data messages are acknowledged through a positive acknowledgment transmitted from the receiver to the transmitter. Acknowledgments can be carried with data messages (this is called piggybacking) or they can be given through separate control messages.

Type	Function
ACK	Acknowledges one or more messages; contains an acknowledgement number
NAK	Negative Acknowledgement
REP	Reply to message number
STRT	Start message
STACK	Start Acknowledge Message

Fig. 8.5 DDCMP: control messages

Figure 8.5 gives the different control messages that are defined in DDCMP.

The main ingredients of the protocol are a message number, n, given to each data message and contained in the Message Header, a positive ACK control message, or piggybacking, and a timer. This timer is connected with the timer of the selection process in as far as the other station has to be selected and will transmit before it will try to determine if the message or the ACK itself was not properly received.

The operation works as follows (see also Fig. 8.6). The transmitter builds a data message with count n in the header and adds a CRC block check to the header and the data. The CRC block check is computed using the CRC-16 polynomial. When the data message is sent, the timer is started. The receiver gets the message and checks the block check. If the data message is received without an error, the message number is checked against the expected message number. If correct, the data message is passed onto the higher level. Next, the station sends, if selected, an ACK control message with the number of the data messages received and it increments its expected message number, n, by one to $n+1$. The transmitter receives the ACK and compares the number with its own expected number and, if they are in agreement, the transmitter releases the messages which it kept for recovery reasons. It then informs the higher layer of the successful operation and increases its expected number to $n+1$.

If the transmitter does not receive the ACK before the timer expires, it will start an error recovery procedure, which is shown in Fig. 8.6b,c. One possibility is for the station to send a *Reply to Message Number* (REP) control message carrying the previously sent data message number, n.

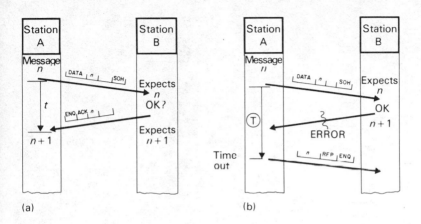

(a)   (b)

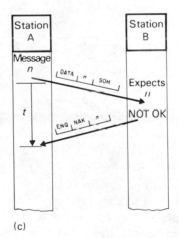

(c)

Fig. 8.6 DDCMP: basic acknowledgement schemes

It is possible that the receiver discovers that the message has been received in error, for example, because of a transmission error. In that case, the data part would result in a wrong CRC check at the end of the data. Instead of waiting for the time-out to expire, which could give a bad performance, the receiver can send a *Negative Acknowledgment* (NAK) control message carrying n, the message number of the data message received in error. If the transmission error occurred in the header, and was detected by the header-CRC, then the station would do nothing because it cannot even be sure that the message was meant for its station. For example, it is conceivable that the error happened to be in the Address Field, changing it into its own address.

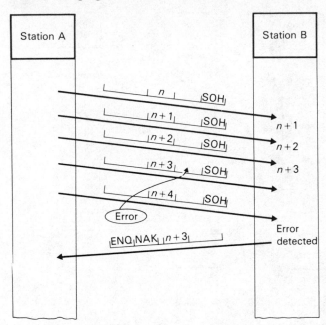

Fig. 8.7 DDCMP: error while pipelining

The NAKs are not sent when sequence errors are detected. In that case, the transmitting station waits for the timer to expire and then starts the error recovery.

The above-described data exchange protocol is expanded according to the capacity of the message number in the Message Header, namely, 8 bits wide or 256 messages. The numbering starts from 0 to 255 and is cyclic, modulo 256. It means that multiple data messages can be transmitted and that the ACK sent by the receiver not only acknowledges the data message whose number is carried in the ACK control message, but also all the previous not yet acknowledged data messages (pipelining). Also, an eventual NAK control message would acknowledge all the data messages up to the number in the NAK header minus one and indicate that the data message carrying the number was in error.

In Fig. 8.7, data messages with numbers n, $n+1$, $n+2$ are acknowledged while the transmitter is informed that data message $n+3$ was in error. The transmitter can now recover by resending $n+3$, $n+4$, etc.

DDCMP has also a feature called *Piggybacking*. Here, the received data message contains a number (RESP in Fig. 8.3) which acknowledges the data messages received by the transmitter. This technique saves a number of separate ACK control messages.

Before any data message exchange can start, an initialization protocol must be executed. This protocol establishes initial contact and station synchronization on a DDCMP link. It is only used by the user of DDCMP,

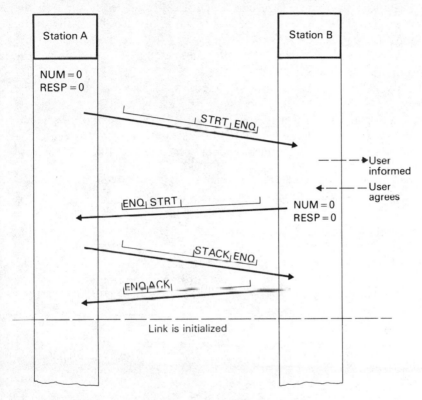

Fig. 8.8 DDCMP: initialization of the link

the higher layer, for link start-up or for a re-initialization after a link failure, usually a persistent error. A *Start* (STRT) control message is transmitted which makes the receiver notify its user. Now, if this user agrees, the receiver side will send an STRT control message. This STRT control message is then acknowledged by a *Start Acknowledge* (STACK) control message (see Fig. 8.8). This initial four-way sequence allows for both stations on the link to reset their sequence numbers for the data messages and the STACK control message tells its receiver that the other side is properly initialized. The station in its turn does the same by sending an ACK control message.

DDCMP contains also error recording and error reporting features. The specifications include suggestions as to how detected errors should be recorded in counters, and how to set the threshold for error notification and background counters. The mechanisms are not described and will be left to the implementer.

8.5 Transport Layer

The Transport Layer in DNA has functions that are equivalent to the Network layer in the Reference Model (Section 8.10). One of the prime functions is to ensure delivery of messages to the node where the destination process resides. The messages are called *packets* in the Transport Layer context [1,2,6].

The packet delivery system is defined as a Datagram service. The principle consists in delivering messages, or packets in this case, on a best possible effort basis. Delivery, however, is not guaranteed and the packets can very well arrive out of order at the destination. For this reason, a mechanism should be introduced which resequences the packets and checks for possible missing messages. Two possibilities exist: the resequencing and missing packet detection is passed to the user as a user responsibility or the next higher layer provides the mechanism. In the first case, the task of communication through the network will be very cumbersome for the user. It is, in the case of DNA, the NSP Layer that takes care of these functions.

Packets will move through the network from node to node, following the best possible path. The path is chosen according to the available links, the lowest number of hops, i.e. the lowest number of nodes that the packet has to pass through, and for the lowest cost. The routing function will be responsible for this.

Other functions are also defined. They are basically four:

a Routing

b Congestion control

c Packet lifetime control

d Transport initialization.

Let us now review these functions in more detail.

8.5.1 Routing

The routing function routes the packets through the network on the basis of the available paths and an operator assigned facility cost. The choice of path depends on an algorithm for the minimization of cost and number of hops. The routing algorithm uses databases that are defined as a part of the Transport Layer (Fig. 8.9).

One of these is the *Forwarding Database*, which contains information as

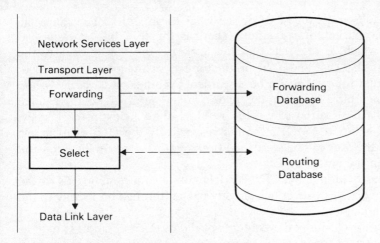

Fig. 8.9 Transport Layer: databases for routing

to which node-link combination the packet has to be routed through in order to get it to its destination. Another is the *Routing Database* containing information on the number of hops and the cost to route a packet to a particular destination. The routing of a packet, given to the Transport Layer for transmission, is handled by two processes called *Forward Process* and *Select Process*. The forward process verifies whether the necessary resources are available and passes the packet to the Select Process. The latter examines the Packet Header and determines over which link the packet should be sent. Control information concerning the operation of the Transport Layer is contained in a Transport Header. That header is featured in Fig. 8.10.

The header field labelled RTFLG contains the routing flag bits. These

DDCMP Header	Transport Header			
	RTFLG	DSTNODE	SRCNODE	FORWARD
Byte	0	1 2	3 4	5

RTFLG   Routing Flags

DSTNODE   Destination Node Address

SRCNODE   Source Node Address

Fig. 8.10 Transport Layer: header information

bits allow the Select Process to define what to do with, for instance, an undeliverable packet. For example, there is the *RTS* bit, or *Return to Sender* bit, which, if set, tells that the packet is on its way back to the originator. In that case and if the originator cannot any longer be reached, it instructs that the packet can be discarded. Another bit is the *Return to Sender request* bit asking for the packet to be returned to the Source Process if the destination cannot be reached. Two fields in the header, DSTNODE and SRCNODE, contain respectively the Destination node address and the Source node address. Both addresses are 16 bits long and are unique in the network.

The header field labelled FORWARD contains information as to the number of nodes this packet has already passed through on its way to the destination node.

The Select Process uses the contents of the destination address field as an index argument for a search in the Forwarding Database in order to select an output link. Next, the packet is put in the queue for that link.

The Select Process will also drop packets that cannot be delivered, for example, a packet that does not carry the Return to Sender request flag and that cannot be delivered. Another example is a packet being returned to the sender but where the source node is no longer reachable.

Another process is the *Receiver Process*. It receives packets from the Data Link Layer. The Transport Header is examined and the packet is passed to the Forwarding Process if the destination node is another node. If the Destination Process is residing in the node itself, the packet is passed to the user process through the NSP Layer after the Transport Header has been stripped off.

The packet could also be a control message that is exchanged between Transport Layers. The information carried will most probably contain changes in routing. The different messages are shown in Fig. 8.11.

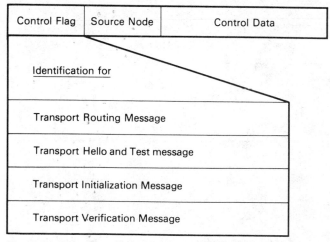

Fig. 8.11 Transport Layer: control messages

The control messages or packets are processed by the *Decision Process* in the case of a *routing message*. Whenever the network configuration changes, for example, a line goes down, a Routing Message is received. Another reason could be that an operator intervention changes a line cost, or reduces the maximum number of hops or the total cost. The Decision Process will update the Transport Layer databases with the information of the routing message. Routing messages can be propagated or initiated at the Transport Layer in a particular node by means of a process called the Update Process. Significant is that the Routing Messages—and this is true for all Transport Layer control messages—are only sent to adjacent nodes and have, as such, no Transport Header. The other control messages assure the synchronization of the Transport Layers in adjacent nodes and the availability and reachability of these nodes.

8.5.2 Congestion control

The congestion control function monitors the buffer occupancy by packets. It will reduce the queue size for a link to acceptable limits. Transit packets are protected from performance degradation through the rejection of packets that are originated by processes residing in the node itself. As such, the existing communications are favored over new services.

8.5.3 Packet lifetime control

A loop detector limits the number of nodes a packet can pass through. Once the limit is reached, the packet will be rejected. The number of nodes a packet has already visited is contained in the Forward field of the Transport Header (see Fig. 8.10). The loop detector adds one to that field and checks it against the Packet Lifetime Control Database, which contains the maximum number of nodes a packet may visit. If the limit is not reached, the packet is passed to the Select Process for further transmission.

8.5.4 Transport initialization control

This function contains procedures that are used for synchronization of the Transport Layers in adjacent nodes. The *Initialization and Verification Message* makes sure both nodes use the same level of Transport Layer protocols. It also checks whether their Data-Link Controls use the same block sizes.

8.5.5 Physical line monitor

In absence of data to be transmitted, this function checks or allows one to check whether the link is still there. The *Hello and Test Message* performs an echo test with adjacent nodes. It tests the physical link between two nodes and the status of the node itself.

8.6 Network Services Protocol (NSP) Layer*

The NSP Layer's basic function is to connect two user processes together. Once the connection is made, the two processes communicate with each other over a Full-Duplex logical channel One of the other functions, but inherently connected with the logical channel concept, is to move the data from origin to destination with guaranteed delivery and in the same sequence as originally sent. This layer will correct the possible disturbance of the packet sequence caused by the datagram transmission principle of the transport-network (see Transport Layer). Further, flow control protocols are defined on this level together with segmentation of the messages. The available functions are

a Creation of Logical Links
b Transmission and reception of data over Logical Links
c Transmission and reception of interrupt data over Logical Links
d Destruction of Logical Links
e Provision for Logical Link flow control
f Error control
g Assurance of guaranteed delivery and guaranteed sequentiality
h Segmentation

NSP provides *Logical Link services* so that session-control modules can exchange information regardless of their physical locations in the network. It requires, on the other hand, transmission services from the Transport Layer. The major NSP functions were briefly reviewed in the beginning of this section. A more detailed discussion of some of these functions and of some of their most important protocols now follows.

8.6.1 Establishing and destroying Logical Links

The establishment of a Logical Link is shown in Fig. 8.12.

The Session Control Layer will request from the NSP Layer the creation of Logical Links and the destruction of them after the processes involved decide to close their communications. The node containing the process that wants to initiate communication triggers, in the Session Control Layer, the transmission of a *CONNECT XMT* command to the NSP Layer. This layer then sends a *Connect Initiate Message* to its counterpart within the destination node. The transport-network will deliver that initiation message. This message contains a *Destination Logical Link Address*

* The NSP described is Version 3.2.0 [7].

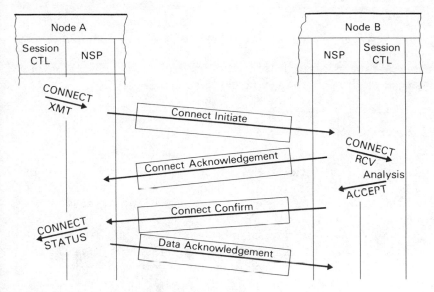

Fig. 8.12 DNA: logical link set-up sequence

(DSTADDR) and the *Source Logical Link Address* (SRCADDR). The DSTADDR is set at zero in the Connect Initiate Message because the receiving NSP has still to assign a valid *Logical Link Number* on its side. The SRCADDR, on the other hand, is the number of the Logical Link chosen by the sending NSP. The Connect Initiate Message also carries information describing the transmitting NSP Layer:

- Source and sink
- NSP Version
- Segmentation parameters
- Flow control options

The receiving NSP then transmits a *Connect Acknowledgment* telling the other party that it received the message with the Connection request and that it passed it to the Session Control Layer. The Session Control Layer analyzes the information in the message and, if it can agree with it, indicates this with an *ACCEPT* primitive to the NSP. The NSP now sends a *Connect Confirm Message* which contains about the same kind of information as that in the Connect Initiate Message, i.e. DSTADDR and SRCADDR, requested services, version number of the NSP, etc. The receiving NSP acknowledges the receipt through the transmission of a Data Acknowledgment.

The result is a Full-Duplex Logical Link that can now be used for data transfer. The Logical Link has two sub-channels. The first, called the *Data sub-channel*, carries the information exchanged by the user processes. Segmentation is allowed on this sub-channel. The second, called the

Other-Data sub-channel, will be used for the transmission of *Interrupt Messages* and *Link Service Messages*. No segmentation is allowed on this sub-channel.

The user process can request the NSP services on a message or on a segment level. Flow control can be executed on both levels.

8.6.2 Error control

Error control is done through a basic acknowledgment scheme. It is based on the sequential numbering of the messages. The number is found in the NSP Header. Figure 8.13 shows an exchange of messages and acknowledgments. The acknowledgment is done in a separate *Data Acknowledgment Message* or it is piggybacked on a data message, i.e. the NSP Header contains an ACKNUM field which indicates if it is a positive or a negative acknowledgment and the number of the message that is acknowledged. Also, the acknowledgment can act for multiple messages at the same time.

The NSP Layer also uses a timer to detect non-delivery of a message. The sending NSP starts the timer the moment the message is handed over to the Transport Layer. If the timer expires without receiving an acknowledgment, then the NSP will resend the message.

8.6.3 Flow control

The data stream over a logical channel could overflow the process resources. Hence, there is a need for end-to-end flow control over the Logical Link.

The principle of the flow control on the NSP level is that no data messages can be transmitted unless the receiving NSP has committed buffer space. The sending side will request buffer allocation with the *Data Request Message* (DRM). The receiving side signals the allocation with a *Link Status Message* (LSM). The message indicates to the transmitter the number of data messages that can be received. The number is contained in a field called FCVAL. Figure 8.14 shows such an operation. Three messages have to be sent to BETA. ALPHA cannot send until BETA has sent a Link Status Message telling ALPHA it can send two more data messages (FCVAL +2). The Link Status Message does not flow over the Data sub-channel but over the Other-Data sub-channel.

ALPHA sends two messages, numbers 24 and 25, while acknowledging an earlier data message 15 that was sent from BETA. Now ALPHA has to allow BETA to send one Data or Data ACK message in order to get an acknowledgment for the two data messages it has just transmitted. BETA acknowledges and allows ALPHA to send two more data messages. ALPHA sends one, number 26, because it has no more data to send and will now allow BETA to send an ACK, and so on.

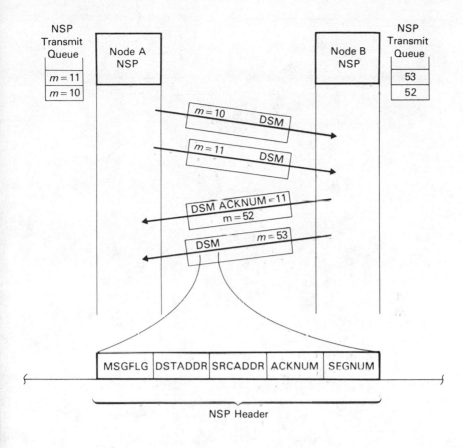

| MSGFLG | DSTADDR | SRCADDR | ACKNUM | SEGNUM |

NSP Header

ACKNUM	Number of last NSP data segment number that was correctly received.
SEGNUM	Number of this NSP data segment message
DSM	Data Segment Message
m	Segment message number

Fig. 8.13 NSP: error control

There are three kinds of flow control available:

a Segment flow control.
b No flow control.
c Session control message flow control.

Case (*b*), no flow control, is self explanatory. Case (*c*) is a flow control on a

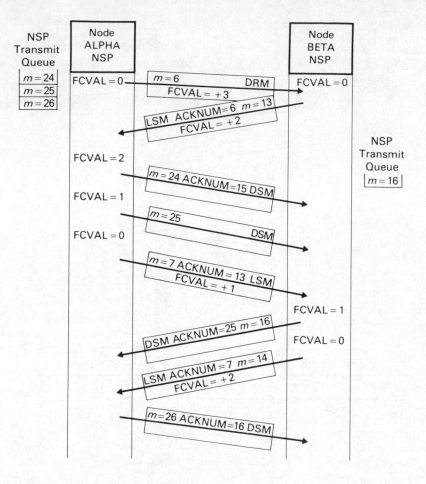

DRM	Data Request Message	
LSM	Link Status Message	
DSM	Data Segment Message	
m	Segment message number or Control message number	
FCVAL	Forward Count Value indicates the number of segments a receiving NSP can accomodate	

Fig. 8.14 DNA: flow control

selected number of complete session control messages. Normally, the messages received from the Session Control Layer are divided into segments of a size suitable to comply with the constraints of the underlying transport-network.

The Other-Data sub-channel has also a flow control mechanism that will control the Interrupt messages flow.

8.6.4 Segmentation and reassembly

As described above, it is sometimes required to cut the original message, passed down by the Session Control Layer, into pieces that can be handled by the transport-network. This function is performed by the NSP Layer and is called *Segmentation*. The NSP receiving the different pieces or segments has the task of reassembling the segments into the original data message. Each of the segments, since they are transmitted as individual packets through a datagram service, carries a sequence number in the NSP Header. The receiving NSP can then ascertain that the segments are put together in the correct sequence.

8.7 Session Control Layer

An end-user process that wants to communicate with another end-user over DNA will request the establishment of a Logical Link from the Session Control Layer. The Session Control Layer has a database which allows it to translate node names into node addresses. The Layer puts Connect XMT to the NSP in order to create a Logical Link. Next, it will receive from the NSP a Connect Confirm Message sent by the receiving NSP. The layer examines the contents and, if acceptable, instructs the NSP to acknowledge the connection process.

If a Connect request is passed to the Session Control Layer, then the Layer will analyze the information and will, if in agreement, pass an ACCEPT to the NSP together with some data. The analysis consists of a verification that the destination user process is active. If this is not the case, then the Session Control Layer can activate the particular process.

Once the Logical Link is established, data will be exchanged. The Session Control Layer intervention is minimal and merely consists of passing the data directly to the NSP from the user's process and vice versa.

Finally, when the processes no longer need the connection, the Session Control Layer will request the disconnection of the Logical Link to the NSP.

8.8 Network Application Layer

This layer can be used by the user process for the manipulation of data in a remote node. The user process can, however, decide not to use these modules and to interface immediately to the Session Control Layer all by itself. If file manipulation is required, then it is all handled under the control of the user process.

If the user chooses to use these commonly available modules, then his task is greatly simplified. For example, the mere mention of a remote node

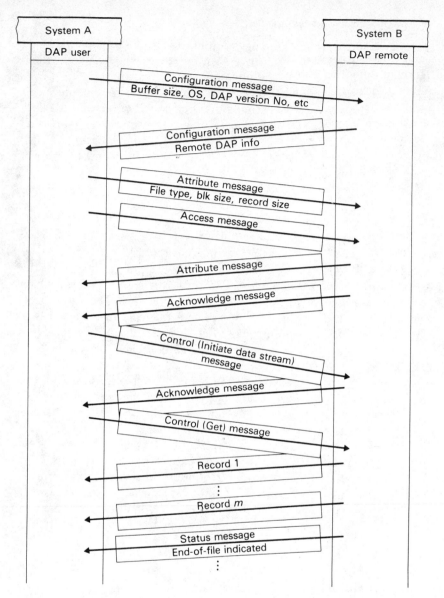

Fig. 8.15 DNA: DAP protocol

name in an access to a database will automatically execute whatever function is requested at the remote side through protocols in this Network Application Layer. In fact, the 'roll your own' version means that the user writes in his processes and application programs, the equivalent of pre-designed Network Application Protocols. These protocols are implemented in common modules that are available to the user.

An example of such modules is the *Data Access Protocol* (DAP) [8] which allows remote file access and manipulation. A series of protocols and functions are provided. Examples are file transfer, file updating, deletion or renaming, directory manipulation and so on. A series of special DAP messages are defined. Figure 8.15 shows such a flow of messages.

First, a configuration message is exchanged defining which types of operating system run in both nodes. Other information pertains to files, DAP versions and so on. The next is the information exchange concerning the type of file, its organization, block size, etc. Then a control message is sent by the originating process in order to define the kind of function that is requested and the necessary data stream is set up. In our example, it is the transfer of a file from the remote node. The file is transmitted record by record until the end of the file is reached. The remote DAP informs the requester of the end of file situation in a Status message. The originating DAP assumes the Access Complete messages are exchanged.

A user process that does not take advantage of the DAP modules has to define similar protocols and control messages. The use of DAP modules will greatly reduce the development effort of applications. Also, it will allow a standardization of the data file manipulation process.

8.9 Network management

In DNA, the network management functions are specified as a separate layer. During a normal communication between two user processes, this layer will not be used. The user process will then immediately go to the Session Control Layer or if required will use the Network Application Layer if some Data Access Protocol (DAP) services are required.

Figure 8.16 shows the exact relation between the layers and the Network Management Layer. The functions can be accessed by user processes which are user-written or by system processes such as the Network Control Program (NCP). On the other side, interfaces exist with the underlying layers of DNA. Hooks were designed in the Data Link Layer to allow the loading and dumping of down-stream nodes and link tests. Other hooks allow the collection of the events that were recorded in a particular layer and are logged in an event file.

The NICE Protocol, Network Information and Control Exchange Protocol, allows the exchange of commands between Network Control Management Layers of different nodes. As such, the total network control can be organized in a centralized manner or completely decentralized. Also, events can be passed from node to node using the Event Logger Protocol.

The Network Management Layer allows the status of network parameters to be checked. Examples of such parameters are line status, line cost or node. Then the systems manager can change the characteristics by

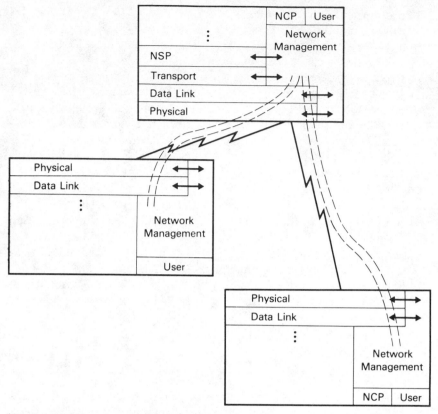

Fig. 8.16 DNA: Network Management Layer

changing certain of the parameters. For example, a systems manager finds that too many messages are thrown away because of congestion. He can modify some of the routing parameters in order to correct the situation by changing the route taken by the messages.

The network management can be expanded by user processes that analyze information on events stored in log-files. They also can access that kind of information in other nodes. The process can initiate testing so that a network supervisor can take decisions and reconfigure the network in a certain way.

8.10 Comparison with the Reference Model

In the previous sections, we have shown that DNA as an architecture exhibits a layered structure similar to the Reference Model. Figure 8.17 shows a representation of both OSI and DNA in such a way that equivalent layers are shown side by side. The interpretation of DNA in terms of the

Reference Model is a view of DNA by the authors. Not everybody necessarily agrees with this view for reasons that are explained several times in this book.

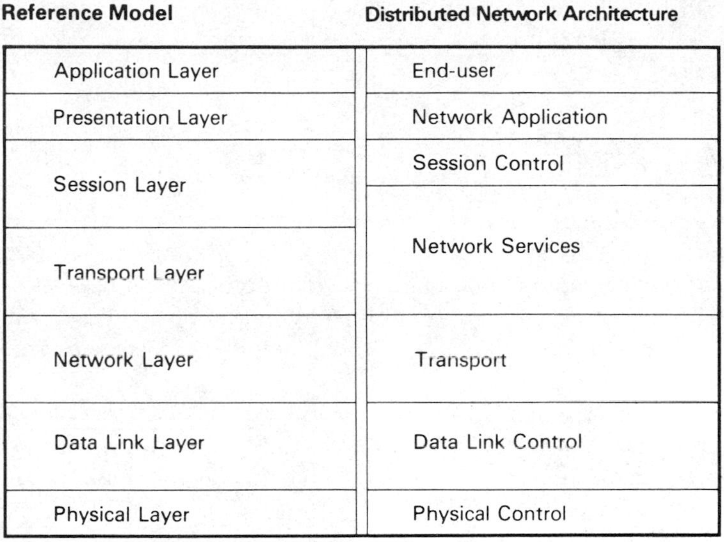

Reference Model   **Distributed Network Architecture**

Reference Model	Distributed Network Architecture
Application Layer	End-user
Presentation Layer	Network Application
Session Layer	Session Control
	Network Services
Transport Layer	
Network Layer	Transport
Data Link Layer	Data Link Control
Physical Layer	Physical Control

Fig. 8.17 DNA: comparison with the Reference Model

The representation includes a Network Application Layer that can, for instance, contain the modules for the Data Access Protocol. It is, however, very well possible to implement a system where these modules do not exist and where the user process takes care or, rather, has to take care of the equivalent of Presentation Control.

A more detailed analysis of the layer equivalence between DNA and the Reference Model is given below. For each of the layers of the Reference Model, the equivalent in DNA is sought. Functions that are missing in a particular layer or can be found in another layer are also indicated. When no comment is given with respect to a certain service or function, it means that we could not identify an equivalent service or function in DNA.

8.10.1 Presentation Layer

The Network Application Layer in DNA is functionally equivalent to the Presentation Layer. An example of the protocols in DNA for this layer are the DAP. They allow for the exchange of data between two systems. The functions provided by DAP are only a part of the potential functions of the Presentation Layer in the Reference Model. They are only concerned with data manipulation.

Services provided by the Presentation Layer
- Data transformation. No data transformation is done by DAP. It is a user responsibility to perform this function. Available data codes are ASCII, EBCDIC and Image, which means any bit stream.
- Data formatting. The only data formatting available is record formats, for example, fixed length formats or variable length formats.
- Syntax selection.
- Presentation-connections.

Functions in the Presentation Layer
- General.
  - Session establishment request. A DAP system requests a connection with another DAP system by means of a Configuration message.
  - Presentation image negotiation and renegotiation. The configuration message does not actually negotiate the configuration required, but allows one side to show or to get to know the other side's configuration.
  - Data transformation and formatting.
  - Special-purpose transformations.
  - Session termination request. This is done through a Disconnect request issued by either DAP.
- Addressing and multiplexing.
- Presentation Layer Management.

8.10.2 Session Layer

As Fig. 8.17 shows, the Session Control Layer only partially overlaps the Session Layer in the Reference Model.

Services provided by the Session Layer
- Session-connection establishment. This function is executed for a DAP module or for a User Process. The Session Control Layer passes a Connect XMT to the Network Services Layer.
- Session-connection release. Disconnection of a Logical Link is requested with a Disconnect Data Message.
- Normal data exchange. The unit of data is called a session control message. It carries the data for the higher layer.
- Quarantine service.
- Expedited data exchange. The Other-Data sub-channel of the NSP Layer gives the possibility of a kind of expedited data exchange.
- Interaction management.
  - Two-Way-Simultaneous. A Logical Link has a Full-Duplex capability.
  - Two-Way-Alternate. The flow over a Logical Link can be forced in Half-Duplex through NSP flow control.
  - One-Way. Through NSP flow control.

- Session-connection synchronization. This function consists of the analysis of the Connect request and the Connect Confirm message exchange.
- Exception reporting. This is available in the NSP Layer by means of a positive acknowledgement scheme. Exceptions reported are the loss of messages, messages out of sequence and mutilation of messages.
- Additional. In the Reference Model, several functions are listed as potential additions to the services in the Session Layer. They are listed here, although not yet part of the Reference Model, because some of these functions are defined already in existing architectures.

  a Session-service-data-unit sequence numbering. In the NSP layer as part of positive acknowledgement scheme.
  b Brackets.
  c Stop–go. Can be performed with the flow control mechanism. There is no special protocol.
  d Security.

Functions in the Session Layer
- Mapping of session-connection onto transport-connection. There is a one-to-one mapping of sessions onto transport-connections called Logical Links.
- Session-connection flow control.
- Expedited data transfer.
- Session-connection recovery.
- Session-connection release.
- Session Layer Management. A Session Control Layer and NSP Layer management function is available which manages the databases used in both layers.

8.10.3 Transport Layer

The equivalent functions of this layer can be found in DNA in the Network Services Protocol Layer.

Services provided by the Transport Layer
- Identification.
  - Transport-addresses. The transport-addresses are called logical link identifications and consist of port addresses on each side of the link.
  - Transport-connections. The transport-connections are called Logical Channels.
  - Transport-connection-endpoint-identifiers. The identifiers are composed of the port addresses of both sides.
- Establishment services.
  - Transport-connection establishment. The transport-connection

establishment is done by the exchanging of Connect Initiate, Connect Acknowledgment, Connect Confirm and Data Acknowledgment messages between NSPs.
- Class of service selection.
- Data transfer services.
  - Transport-service-data-unit. This unit is called an NSP message.
  - Expedited transport-service-data-unit. Assuming that the expedited service is approximately equivalent to the Other-Data sub-channel, the messages flowing are Interrupt messages, Data Request messages and Interrupt Request messages.
- Transport-connection release. Exchange of Disconnect Request messages.

Functions in the Transport Layer
- Addressing. Done in the NSP Layer by assigning 16-bit port addresses.
- Connection multiplexing and splitting. Done in the NSP Layer with different port assignments.
- Phases of operation.
  - Establishment phase. Consists of the allocation of a port and the definition of the functions to be performed. For instance, a decision is made whether segmentation will be used or not. Also a decision will be taken whether flow control will be used. The port address is mapped onto a network node address.
  - Data transfer phase.
    o Sequencing. The sequence numbers in the data messages are checked.
    o Blocking.
    o Concatenation.
    o Segmenting. The NSP Layer provides for segmentation on the Data channel of the Logical Link. The receiving NSP performs reassembly using the sequence number of the data message.
    o Multiplexing or splitting.
    o Flow control. On the NSP level, through the exchange of Data Request Messages flowing over the Other-Data sub-channel.
    o Error detection. Done in the NSP Layer by means of a positive acknowledgement scheme using sequence numbers in the Data messages.
    o Error recovery.
    o Expedited data transfer.
    o Transport-service-data-unit delimiting.
    o Transport-connection identification. The NSP data messages carry the addresses of the ports of both NSPs of the logical link.
  - Release phase. Deallocation of a port.
- Transport Layer Management.

8.10.4 Network Layer

The Transport Layer in DNA is equivalent to the Network Layer in the Reference Model.

Services provided by the Network Layer
- Network addresses. Each network node has a Node address. The Transport Header carries the Source Node Address and the Destination Node Address.
- Network-connections. Network-connections are on a node-to-node basis. The Transport Service is a Datagram service.
- Network-connection-endpoint-identifiers.
- Network-service-data-unit transfer. The network-service-data-unit is called a Packet.
- Quality of service parameters.
- Error notification.
- Sequencing. None, Datagram service.
- Flow control.
- Expedited network-service-data-unit transfer.
- Reset.
- Release services.

Functions in the Network Layer
- Routing and relaying. The routing of packets is done by the Transport Layer based on the Destination Node Address. This serves as a pointer in a routing database. Algorithms allow the choice of an optimal path through the network. Packet-life control prevents the looping of packets in the Transport network.
- Network-connections.
- Network-connection multiplexing. Not applicable in a Datagram service.
- Segmenting and blocking.
- Error detection.
- Error recovery.
- Sequencing.
- Flow control.
- Expedited data transfer.
- Reset.
- Service selection.
- Network Layer Management. The functions provided are buffer management, node verification, updating of the routing database in its own node or adjacent nodes and the management of packet path characteristics.

8.10.5 Link Layer

The Data Link Control Layer in DNA is equivalent to the Data Link Layer in the Reference Model. The protocol used is called DDCMP.

Services provided by the Data Link Layer
- Data-link-connections. Provides data-link-connections between two network nodes for the Transport Layer.
- Data-link-service-data-units. These are called DDCMP messages.
- Data-link-connection-endpoint-identifiers. These are called Station Addresses.
- Sequencing. Done by means of a Transmit number in the DDCMP Message Header.
- Error notification. Loss of a message, detected by the receiving DDCMP module, can be notified with a Negative Acknowledgement in a separate DDCMP control message or piggybacked on a DDCMP data message. Error counters are maintained and there is an automatic error notification to the user.
- Flow control.
- Quality of service parameters.

Functions in the Data Link Layer
- Data-link-connection establishment and release. The initialization protocol between DDCMP modules with the exchange of STRT and STACK DDCMP control messages.
- Data-link-service-data-units mapping.
- Data-link-connection splitting. Even though *Bit-parallel* links, such as channels, are supported no parallel bit serial links (such as telephone lines) support is defined.
- Delimiting and synchronization. Transmission and reception is synchronized on byte and message level. DDCMP messages start with a specific ASCII control character.
- Sequence control. A state variable that is compared with the transmit number in the DDCMP Data Message Header.
- Error detection. Transmission errors are detected by means of a CRC check on the DDCMP Data Message Header and on the data part of the Data Message. Lost messages are detected by checking the transmit sequence number.
- Error recovery. Retransmission to correct errors.
- Flow control.
- Identification and parameter exchange.
- Control of data circuit interconnection.
- Data Link Layer Management. Supports point-to-point and multipoint data link configurations.

8.10.6 Physical Layer

The Physical Layer is not explicitly defined in DNA. Its existence is merely acknowledged and a whole series of standards are enumerated which are supported in DNA.

References

1 Loveland, R. A., Putting DECNET into perspective, *Datamation*, Mar. 1979, pp. 109–114.
2 Conant, G. E., Extending Digital's Network Architecture to use X.25, *Proc. 4th Int. Conf. Computer Commun.*, Kyoto, 1978
3 Wecker, S., DNA: The Digital Network Architecture, *IEEE Trans. Commun.*, vol. COM-28, no. 4, Apr. 1980, pp. 510–526
4 Digital Equipment Corporation, *DECNET general description*, Order no. AA-K179A-TK, 1980
5 Digital Equipment Corporation, *DNA Digital Data Communications Message Protocol (DDCMP) functional specifications, Version 4.1.0*, Order no. AA-K175A-TK, 1980
6 Digital Equipment Corporation, *DECNET Transport functional specifications, Version 1.3.0*, Order no. AA-K180A-TK, 1980
7 Digital Equipment Corporation, *DECNET Network Services Protocol (NSP) functional specifications, Version 3.2.0*, Order no. AA-K176A-TK, 1980
8 Digital Equipment Corporation, *DECNET Data Access Protocol (DAP) functional specifications, Version 5.6.0*, Order no. AA-K177A-TK, 1980

9 Univac's Distributed Communication Architecture

9.1 Architecture overview

Data Communications Architecture was defined by Sperry-Univac [1,2]. The architecture comprises a homogeneous network with a layered structure (Fig. 9.1). There are two layers at the base:

a The Applications Environment (AE).
b The Communications System (CS).

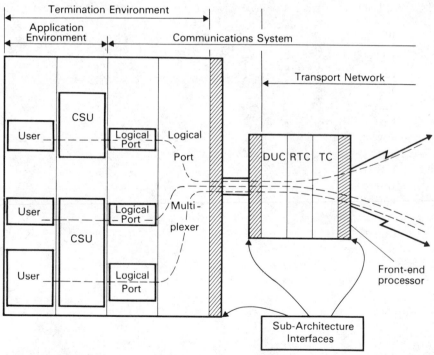

CSU	Communications System User
DUC	Data Unit Control
RTC	Routing Control
TC	Trunk Control

Fig. 9.1 Univac's DCA structure

The Applications Environment contains the *end-users*. The Communications System consists of the Termination System (TS) and the Transport Network. The end-users are connected with the network through a Communications System User (CSU). The CSU contains the Interface between the Applications Environment and the Communications System. In the network are a number of CSUs that together with the Termination System form the Termination Environment.

The Termination System contains a number of Logical Ports and a Logical Port Multiplexer (LPM). The Logical Ports connect two CSUs in the network. They, in fact, constitute a session between CSUs through a Logical Port Session.

The LPM attributes to each active Logical Port a *Logical Sub-Channel Number* within a *Logical Channel* that connects the Termination System to the Transport Network. The Logical Port has two important functions:

a Port Presentation Services, for the translation of data, addresses and control information from a CSU format to a format acceptable by the Transport Network.
b Port Flow Control for the end-to-end flow control in the session.

Three architecture layers are defined in the Transport Network:

a Data Unit Control (DUC). This layer is responsible for:
   i   Adaptation of data length (possibly the segmentation of the data in 'packets' from Port Data Units to Network Data Units).
   ii Transformation of a Logical Port Multiplexer Sub-Channel Number to a route number and vice versa.
   iii Flow control within the Transport Network. This layer has the responsibility of delivering the data in sequence and acknowledging its receipt.
b Routing Control (RTC). This layer is responsible for the routing of the messages based on the session number. This number is generated at the session establishment time. The architecture allows dynamic or adaptive routing through the Transport Network.
c Trunk Control (TC). This layer is responsible for the communication facilities. It controls, for example, the input and output queues for these facilities. The transmission facilities themselves (UDLC or channel) are not a part of Trunk Control, but are viewed as a Sub-Architecture Interface.

Network management is a Hierarchical Network Management distributed through the network (Fig. 9.5). Every Termination Environment has an 'Application Management Service' (a special CSU) for the local control of, for example, the Logical Unit Ports. Global Network Control is done through an hierarchy of Network Management Services (Local, Area and Global NMS). If an NMS cannot handle a situation, it will notify the next higher level of NMS.

This brief overview of DCA shows that the architecture was defined with a distributed system in mind. The definition of major groupings of layers and their functions, which can be related with a particular hardware unit, undoubtedly shows that. Also, the network management is built in an hierarchical way with distribution in each unit taking part in the communications network.

The next section discusses in some detail the interesting concept of a Sub-Architecture Interface. We will see that it can be used to connect different layers or to connect different physical boxes or to do both at the same time. Then, each of the layers will be reviewed in more detail.

9.2 The Sub-Architecture Interface (SAI)

The Sub-Architecture Interface (SAI) in DCA represents an interesting concept. The architects of DCA consider that the layers in the model have logical functions rather than physically moving the data through the network. The physical moving of data, naturally within the context of a DCA communications system, happens through protocols that are said to be outside the architecture and that are called SAIs. What is meant is that the protocols are not actually operating on the data but are merely moving it between physical boxes.

So, SAIs control physical environments rather than logical connections through or within the communications network. Examples of such physical connections are computer channels, connecting CPUs to communication controllers or cluster controllers, telephone lines, X.21 circuits or X.25 Virtual Circuit services, and so on. Examples of an SAI are the channel programs implemented in the CPU and control units to control the transfer of data between the two. Another example is the line control used to transfer data over a telephone line. In this case, Univac uses Universal Data Link Control (UDLC), which is a subset of HDLC.

The next interesting aspect of the SAI is the two ways it is used in DCA. First, there is the transfer of data between layers of the architecture, and secondly, the transfer of data in the sense of the Reference Model, i.e. between two physical units or nodes of the network.

Let us look into these two possibilities. Figure 9.2a,b shows the case where the SAI is used for the transfer of data between two layers within the architecture. In terms of DCA, this means, for example, that the layer $N+1$, which represents the Port Multiplexer and multiplexes the different port sessions for one physical unit such as a CPU, is connected to layer N, which represents the Data Unit Control (DUC) located in a communications controller, through an SAI—which, in this case, is most likely to be Sperry–Univac's parallel channel interface. The interface between N and $N+1$ contains the same primitives and parameters as that between any two other layers within the same hardware box, but the communications

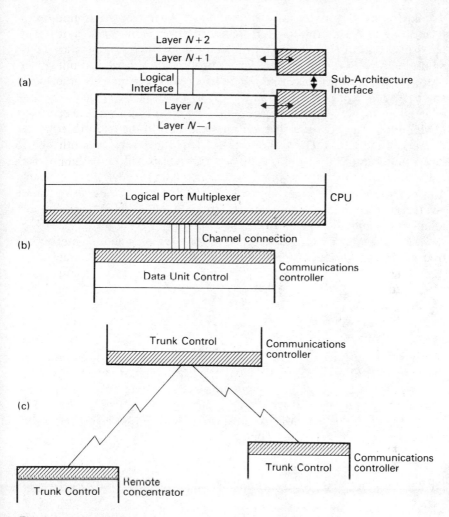

Fig. 9.2 DCA SAI example

happen to go through the SAI instead of over a classical program interface. Within a cluster controller which participates in the Transport Network, the connection between the Port Multiplexer and DUC will not be made through an SAI but through a program interface. On the other hand, a terminal could be connected to a remote concentrator. In this case, the Termination System with the Port Multiplexer will be located in the terminal and the DUC will be in a remote concentrator. The connection between the two will be a telephone link and the SAI will be UDLC.

The second way to use the SAI is concerned with the physical transfer of data between two units participating in the Transport Network (see Fig. 9.2c). Here, the two architecture layers involved are both the same—the

Trunk Control Layers. In this case, we do not have a connection of layers N and $N+1$, but a peer-to-peer connection between two N layers. The physical-connection is normally a telephone line or an equivalent communication facility. The SAI that most probably will be used is UDLC.

So, the interesting aspect of the SAI is that it enables DCA to offer another approach to the distribution of functions in the network to that adopted normally. Where most architectures, including the Reference Model definition, consider that the physical units at the end of a network contain all the layers, DCA allows the distribution of the total end-set of layers in different boxes in the network. In other words, only the physical units taking part in the Transport Network contain the lowest three layers. This is not the case in other network architectures where the lower three layers are also found in the end nodes. In DCA, these three layers are not found in the end nodes—hardware units such as CPUs or terminals. All in all, there is a much higher adherence to the idea of function distribution over all possible nodes in the network.

9.3 DCA's layers

9.3.1 The user

A user communicates through DCA with another user. DCA provides the two with an end-to-end controlled communications environment. The user is located in what is called a Termination Environment. What is meant is that the collection of users within a physical box or node is at one end of the communications network. An example of such a user is an application program or a terminal with its operator.

9.3.2 Communications System User (CSU)

The user connects to the communications network through another layer in the Termination Environment, of which it is a part. As said before, the Termination Environment can be equated with one hardware unit or node. It can contain several CSUs, each accommodating several users and providing them with services. An example of a CSU is a transaction-handling control system. It would in that case provide services to transaction application programs, the latter being the end-users.

At the other side of the network, there needs to be a corresponding CSU which has the same characteristics. In other words, it has to speak the same language. It is conceivable that the corresponding CSU will be physically located in a terminal.

The basic functions of this layer are to give the communication capability for the typical user application. It will control the communication part for a particular user.

9.3.3 Logical Port (LP)

From the CSU, data will be transmitted over the communication network through a *Logical Port* (LP). A Logical Port is the CSU's entry point in the Communications System. It is the door, so to speak, through which a user can communicate with another user.

On the other side of the network, next to the corresponding user–CSU combination, will be another LP. These two LPs will be connected by means of a unique session called a *Logical Port Session*. The session is by definition a Full-Duplex Logical Channel and gives a bidirectional logical path through the communication network. The number of LPs that is available to a particular CSU is dependent on that CSU's data-handling requirements and the access requirements of the other CSUs.

Within a Logical Port, two sub-layers are identified. The first sub-layer provides presentation type services and is called the *Port Presentation Services* (PPS). The second sub-layer is concerned with data flow control and is called *Port Flow Control* (PFC).

Let us look in more detail at the Port Presentation Services. The functions provided by the PPS are heavily dependent on the user and the application. The sub-layer will transform data, address and control information that the CSU presents to the Logical Port. In fact, the PPS transforms the data into a format that is acceptable to the Transport Network and also in such a way that it remains understandable to the paired CSU.

The place where these transformations take place is not defined. If one of the CSUs resides in a large mainframe computer and the other in a simple terminal, then it is rather obvious that the PPS functions will be placed in the large mainframe and not in the much less powerful terminal. It is also clear that the PPS should transform the data in such a way that it relieves the terminal of processing power. If the two corresponding CSUs each reside in powerful CPUs, then each side's Logical Port will take care of its own translation requirements.

The communication between paired PPSs is achieved through higher level protocols. The protocols are dependent on the kind of function that is required by the user. For example, it could consist of the interface rules to an operating system. Another set of protocols could be the job control for a remote job-entry system. Still another set of protocols could meet the requirements for a particular transaction system that interactively accesses a database system. In fact, the protocols could be the virtual terminal protocols that are studied by the standards organizations of different countries.

The moment a port session is requested by the CSU, a proper set of PPS protocols will be selected. This assumes that a variety of PPS higher level protocols is available to the users, ultimately the CSU, to choose from. This type of dynamic allocation of PPS protocols requires a complex implementation. Smaller systems can have predefined PPS protocol sets for a particular CSU or group of CSUs having the same PPS demands. The pre-definition could be done through a generation process.

In summary, the PPS can be viewed as a complete set of data and control transformation functions to be applied to the data. During the Logical Port Session establishment, negotiation can take place to define the subset to be used by the paired LPs.

The second sub-layer has to see to the control of the data flow between the paired LPs. The goal of this function is to protect LPs from overflow conditions. The protocols that are defined will limit the flow of data, called *Port Data Unit* (PDU), so that the receiving LP has enough resources to handle the incoming data. For example, is there enough memory available for the buffers and is there enough processing power left to handle the data? The protocol that is defined is based on an end-to-end acknowledgment. Figure 9.3 shows how the protocol works in general terms.

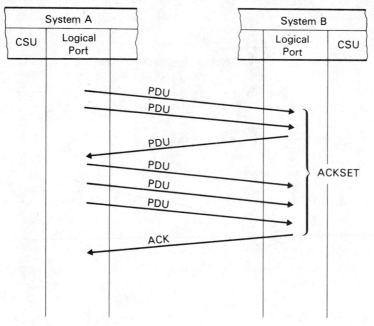

PDU	Port Data Unit
CSU	Communications System User
ACK	Acknowledgement

Fig. 9.3 DCA: control of the data flow

A number of Port Data Units is put together in what is called an *Acknowledgment Set* (ACKSET). This ACKSET is the smallest recoverable entity that is exchanged between two LPs. An ACKSET is composed of a number of PDUs. The size of the PDU and the ACKSET is application-dependent. If we are controlling the data flow for an interactive application, such as a database update, then a small PDU size will be chosen. The ACKSET in this case will be set to the number of messages—or transactions, as they are called in DCA—required to complete the database operation. For example, if it takes six messages going back and forth, then the ACKSET size will be six PDUs. If the application is a file transfer, then the PDU length will be chosen close to the record size in the file. The ACKSET will be the size of a file segment giving then a recoverable entity of 10 000 characters or more.

All the Port Data Units have now to be injected into the Transport Network. This is done through a layer which serves the total set of LPs in a node. This layer is called the Logical Port Multiplexer.

9.3.4 The Logical Post Multiplexer (LPM)

The Logical Port Multiplexer (LPM) transfers the data or PDUs to the Data Unit Control Layer, which is a part of the Transport Network. PDUs flowing over one Logical Port Session will do so over a particular logical sub-channel into the DUC. In fact, the LPM multiplexes the LP session together in one logical channel into the Transport Network (see Fig. 9.4).

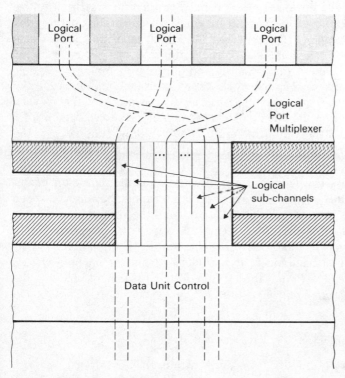

Fig. 9.4 DCA: Logical Port Multiplexer

The moment an LP session is set up, the LPM assigns a logical sub-channel to the session. On the other side of the network, the LPM there will assign a sub-channel to the session. The sub-channel number does not have to be the same at both sides. Some of the sub-channels are reserved for network control applications which will be discussed later.

Now, the data is entering the Transport Network through a layer which is called the Data Unit Control (DUC).

9.3.5 Data Unit Control (DUC)

As Fig. 9.1 shows, Data Unit Control (DUC) constitutes the outer layer of the Transport Network. As such, it is responsible for the relative address translation between the Transport Network and the Termination System. It will translate the Logical Sub-channel Number into the address that is suitable for delivery of data to the Termination System on the other side.

The DUC is also responsible for the assembly and disassembly of *Network Data Units* (NDUs). The Port Data Units (PDUs) that are sent in the network by the Port Multiplexer are transformed into NDUs by adapting their size to the network data size. This process is also called segmentation. The paired DUC will then assemble NDUs into a PDU or PDUs, which are then passed to the proper Termination System. The size of the data unit in the network is a function of the constraints imposed by the physical appearance of the network. The limitation could be because of the bad quality of a telephone line or the buffer size of a particular node.

Immediately related to the assembly and disassembly function is a flow regulation mechanism. The network flow control should prevent the Transport Network from becoming saturated. The protocol that is used consists of numbering the NDUs. That permits the acknowledgment of a batch of NDUs at a time, allowing more NDUs to flow. It allows also the resequencing of NDUs in the case where the Transport Network would allow them to get out of sequence. This would be the case when the Transport Network configuration would contain parallel links, for example. Data uniformly distributed over the links would, because of speed differences or because of intermittent errors and the consequent retransmissions, get out of order. The DUC would repair this situation before reconstructing the PDUs and delivering them to the Termination System.

The paths going through the Transport Network and ending on each side with a DUC are called *Routes* through the TN. The element selecting the path is called *Routing Control*.

9.3.6 Routing Control

The Routing Control (RTC), located within the Transport Network Control (TNC), selects a Route or path through the Transport Network over which NDUs will travel. Depending on the network configuration, a pre-established number of routes will be defined.

The way a particular route will be selected is left to the discretion of the implementer. Two methods are proposed for the DCA architecture level. The first one is static. It assigns a route to a particular port session. To increase availability, it is possible to define alternative routes which are dynamically assigned in case a route fails.

The second method binds a session dynamically to a route depending on the network load. This method is commonly known as adaptive routing. It requires a frequent update of the routing tables in the RTCs. This will cause increased traffic in the Transport Network because of the NDUs carrying the change information to the RTCs.

The RTC has one additional function which allows the blocking of traffic over a route. This requires that messages of different sources, but following the same route, are available for transmission at the same time. A special mechanism is available to allow high-priority traffic to pass ahead of the normal traffic.

9.3.7 Trunk Control

Trunk Control (TC) is the last layer before the SAI that connects two Transport Network Control (TNC) elements with each other. This layer manages the communication resources. It will control the queues to and from the SAI. Initialization and recovery of the communications resources are also its responsibility. If the trunk consists of several physical, parallel links, it is the TC's task to feed each of the links. The Data Link Control itself is not a function of the TC. As seen before, this is done by a Sub-Architecture Interface. In this case, the SAI will use the HDLC-like protocol called Universal Data Link Control (UDLC).

9.3.8 Network Management

It is very well to define all these layers and SAIs; however, all these elements need to be activated, or deactivated, controlled and maintained. DCA defines a whole series of Network Management functions which are distributed hierarchically through the system. The communications between the distributed management functions use the previously defined communications services.

Figure 9.5 shows the different network elements. There is the *Global Network Management Services* (NMS), constituting the highest level of control in DCA. The next level is the *Area NMS*, which controls, for example, a grouping of Termination Systems. These TSs need not be in the same physical environment. A criterion to put a TS in a specific Area NMS could be frequent interactions with that NMS.

The lowest level of NMS is called the *Local NMS*. It supports only the

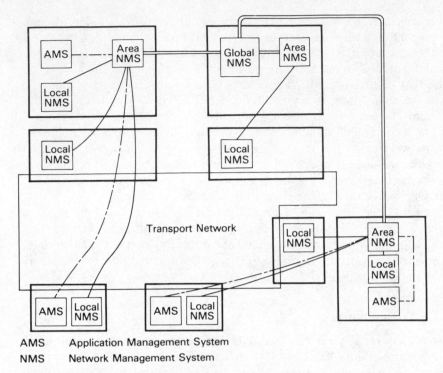

AMS   Application Management System
NMS   Network Management System

Fig. 9.5 DCA: Network Management

set of Termination Systems that is physically associated with it. This means, for instance, all the TSs within a host computer.

Different functions are performed by the NMS. There are session-oriented services that are involved with the setting up of session paths between Termination Systems, their maintenance and their disconnection. For the establishment, they get requests for sessions from the Application Management Services, which they validate. Then they set up session paths through the Transport Network and allocate session identifiers. Also accounting information is provided as a part of these services.

The next big functional area of the NMS is concerned with Physical Resource Services. It manages and allocates physical network components such as network processors, communication facilities and terminals. A physical resource directory, kept up to date, contains all processors, channels, peripherals, lines and terminals. Dynamic reconfiguration is another function allowing the circumvention of problem areas in the network. There is also performance monitoring of every component. Statistics are compiled and passed to the maintenance service function or to the Network Administrator Services.

The next area is the Maintenance Services of the NMS. It provides information to the network administrator function and to the people maintaining the network and those measuring the network's performance. Control of the ARM (Availability Reliability Maintainability) factors are monitored and the required actions to maintain levels of ARM are transmitted to the required functions, such as the customer engineers. These can then, through the Maintenance Services, initialize diagnostic and confidence tests.

The Security Services in the NMS protect the Transport Network from misuse and malicious interventions. It will prohibit a user from accessing the system if it has not been cleared in its security files.

The last but not least functional area is the NMS Network Administrator Services. Starting, stopping and monitoring the network are typical base functions of these services. It will allow reconfiguration through activation or deactivation of lines and network components. All these services are made accessible to a network controller via a network console. The network console can be assigned to any terminal in the network as long as it falls under its control.

9.3.9 Establishing a session between two end-users

Figure 9.6 shows an activated DCA network. Two end-users INTERACT and TERM are shown with their CSUs and their AMSs. Also shown is the

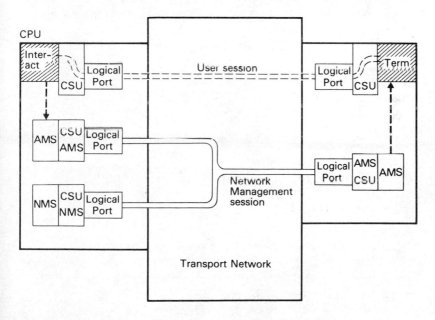

CSU   Communications System User

AMS   Application Management System

Fig. 9.6 DCA: session establishment

NMS which has a session going with both the AMSs of our end-users that want to communicate.

End-user TERM will make a request to its AMS for a connection with end-user INTERACT. The AMS functions will validate the request. They will assure that INTERACT is an allowed address and the TERM is capable of connecting to it.

The AMS will now select a Logical Port and it prepares the port for presentation services and flow control mechanisms. In more sophisticated implementations, these functions can be negotiated while establishing the session, i.e. later on.

Next, the AMS will, through its session with its area NMS, request the next level of processing needed to establish the session between TERM and INTERACT. The NMS will now, with the aid of other NMSs, hand the request to the end-user's INTERACT AMS. Validation of the request from a network point of view will be done by the NMS. The NMS will also set the Transport Network linkages in the network databases to create the route that the session path has to take.

The receiving AMS will once again validate the request, allocate resources and make the linkages. A session-accepted message is returned through the NMS, and end-user INTERACT and end-user TERM are linked through a series of relative address transformations. Data will keep on flowing, unless malfunction occurs, without AMS/NMS intervention.

9.4 Summary

In this chapter, we have given an overview of Univac's Distributed Communications Architecture. The major functions of each of the layers in this architecture have been discussed and from that discussion it can be concluded that DCA has a structure that is very similar to the structure of the Reference Model. The only notable exception, which also sets DCA apart from other architectures, is the formal concept of the Sub-Architecture Interface. This concept makes it possible to package actual systems along other division lines than the vertical cross-section of the architecture.

In Fig. 9.7, the equivalence of the DCA layers with the Reference Model is illustrated. Since the information that was available for the preparation of this chapter was less detailed than that for others, we do not give a detailed analysis here. Briefly, the equivalence is as follows.

The Logical Port provides some Presentation Layer services, and also some Session Layer services. The Session Layer services are completed by the Logical Port Multiplexer. Some of the Logical Port Multiplexer Services are in the Transport Layer. Most Transport Layer services are, however, provided by Data Unit Control.

Reference Model	Distributed Communication Architecture DCA
Application Layer	End-user
Presentation Layer	Communications Systems User
	Logical Port
Session Layer	Logical Port Multiplexer
Transport Layer	Data Unit Ctl
Network Layer	Routing Control
Data Link Layer	Trunk Control
	Data Link Control
Physical Layer	N/A

Fig. 9.7 DCA's layers compared with the Reference Model

Routing Control is the equivalent of the Network Layer, while the Data Link Layer services are provided by both Trunk Control and Data Link Control. The latter is, however, not considered part of DCA proper, but a Sub-Architecture Interface.

References

1 Sperry–Univac Corporation, *Distributed Communications Architecture: system description*, UP-8469, 1976.
2 Timmons, M. L., Distributed Architecture forms framework for network design, *Computer Design*, Feb. 1981, pp. 121–125.

10 Burroughs' Network Architecture

10.1 Architecture overview

Burroughs' Network Architecture [1, 2, 3] is an extension of Burroughs' previously available products for telecommunications. These products, part of a package called Environmental Software, provide for transparent support of terminals connected to a host computer. To the application programmer, these terminals look just like a 'file'; the interface is at the Read/Write level without any concern for the physical connections.

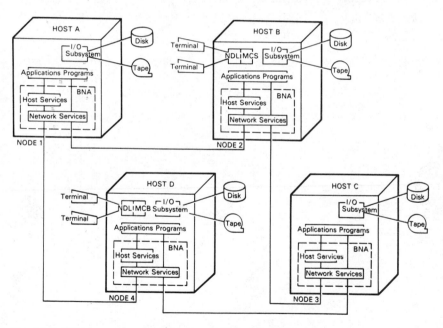

Fig. 10.1 BNA network. (By courtesy of the Burroughs Corporation)

BNA is defined to interconnect these centralized networks and to provide transparent host-to-host communication for distributed processing. In a sense, BNA is thus an 'interconnection' architecture. The physical interconnection can be through leased or switched telecommunication lines or via a Public Data Network supporting X.25.

A BNA network is homogeneous—all participating systems must be Burroughs' (host) systems. BNA is entirely embodied by the aggregate of interconnected hosts. The terminals attached to these host systems are supported by the Environmental Software in each host. There is no single controlling or coordinating agent; all hosts in the BNA network are cooperating 'peers' to each other, with individual responsibility for the performance and integrity of the BNA functions. It is possible, however, to control each host through a remote terminal using a special protocol. This could be used to centralize the control of a network into one host if one wants it that way. Figure 10.1 shows such a BNA network.

BNA is divided in two main levels: the *Network Services* and the *Host Services*.

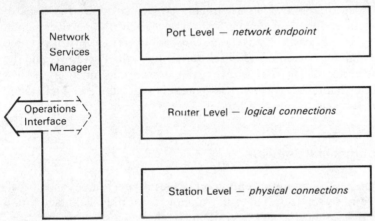

Fig. 10.2 Levels in Network Services. (By courtesy of the Burroughs Corporation)

The Network Services provide the communication protocols required to support the BNA networking environment. It consists of three (sub-) levels and the Network Services Manager (Fig. 10.2). The lowest level is the *Station Level*. This level is responsible for the transfer of messages across physical links between neighboring nodes. Instead of physical links, this level can also use Virtual Circuits in a Public Data Network. The next level is the *Router Level*, which provides logical connections between nodes that are not necessarily neighboring nodes, i.e. this level provides full connectivity from one node to all other nodes in the BNA network. In this level, the transit routing of messages takes place. The *Port Level*, which is the next higher level, provides the using processes with reliable end-to-end message transfer. At this level, communicating processes are associated with *dialogs* between *ports* and *subports*.

The Network Services Manager is responsible for the management functions across the three Network Services Levels that are local to the node. It also provides an operations interface for Network Services, i.e. it interfaces between the operator of the node and the BNA levels in the node.

Host Services provide functions associated with distributed processing in such a way that, to the user, distributed processing is as simple as accessing a local resource. The functions that have been defined are

a Job transfer for execution at a remote host.
b Task initiation and control at remote hosts.
c Logical I/O, i.e. access to remote files, but also transfer of files between hosts.
d Terminal transfer, i.e. a terminal attached to one host accessing an application program at a remote host.
e Operator communication across systems.

The remainder of this chapter is roughly structured along the lines of BNA's structure. First, we devote a short section to the Environmental Software, and then we discuss the Network Services, with detailed information on the Station Level, the Router Level, the Port Level and the Network Services Manager. Then, we review the various functions in Host Services. The chapter is concluded, like the other chapters, with a detailed comparison with the Reference Model.

10.2 Environmental Software

In this chapter we focus our attention on BNA proper. Sometimes, it will, however, be necessary to refer to the support for terminals attached to a host, since that support is an integral part of Burroughs' communications products and it contains functions that are not found in BNA. An example is the functions in the Presentation Layer in the Reference Model. Most of those functions are in the Environmental Software and not in BNA itself. We give, therefore, a brief overview of the Environmental Software in this section.

Actually, Burroughs' Environmental Software not only applies to tele-communications, but it insulates in general the application programs from any concern about such physical problems as database organization, terminal network configuration and management, etc. In the context of this book, we will limit ourselves to the aspects of terminals attached to host computers.

The Environmental Software consists of two elements: a *Network Control Program* and a *Message Control System*.

The Network Control Program is concerned with the control and operation of the physical network. It performs all the functions that are directly related to this control in order to make the network transparent to the applications programmer. First of all, it manages the configuration, i.e.

which lines, concentrators and terminals are attached. For this purpose, a special language, the Network Definition Language, is used to describe the configuration which is always star- or tree-shaped. In addition, the Network Control Program supports the various line-control protocols that can be used in the communication with terminals. Thus, the specific attachment, the configuration and changes to it are not of concern to the application programmer.

The Message Control System (MCS), on the other hand, is concerned with the logical relationship between terminals and application programs. This comes down to the problem of relaying messages from those terminals to the appropriate application. That routing can be performed on the basis of a transaction code in each message. MCS also performs a formatting service for display terminals, thus removing the dependency on physical screen characteristics from the programmer. Finally, MCS provides for the authorization of operators to use a specific terminal and/or terminals to use certain applications.

10.3 Network Services

Network Services is the true communications part of BNA. It consists of three levels, which perform

a Adjacent node communication—the Station Level.
b Routing of messages along several nodes—the Router Level.
c End-to-end controls—the Port Level.

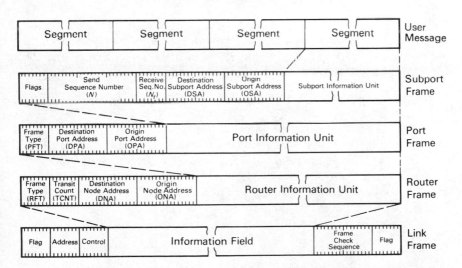

Fig. 10.3 Frame Format Relationships. (By courtesy of the Burroughs Corporation)

The three levels communicate with each other through *frames*, where each level may add its own information to a frame that it receives from a higher level. This information is added in the form of a header and, in the case of the Station Level, also a trailer. Normally, the frame at each level consists of a Header (e.g. the Router Header) and an Information Unit (e.g. the Router Information Unit). The Header contains the control information relevant to the peer entity in the layer. The Information Unit contains the next higher level's frame. For example, the Router Frame consists of the Router Header and the Router Information Unit, which contains the Port Frame (refer to Fig. 10.3). The total structure in the figure applies only when a message originates from a user process and is passed down through all the levels for further transportation. It is, however, also possible that a message originates *inside* a level and is destined for the peer entity. The body of the frame is then not called an Information Unit, but a Control Unit. When, for example, the Router Manager sends a message to its neighboring Router Manager, the Router Frame consists of the Router Header and a Router Control Unit. Lower levels are unable to see the difference between an Information Unit and a Control Unit since the difference is indicated in the Header that belongs to the same level as the Control Unit.

The total structure has been discussed very briefly here to introduce the concept—which is not different from any other architecture—and the specific nomenclature. The usage of these frames, the contents of the various headers, etc., will be discussed in more detail in the following sections, whenever it is relevant.

10.3.1 Station Level

The Station Level is responsible for the transfer of messages between two adjacent BNA nodes. The interconnection between these nodes can be one of the following possibilities:

a Global Memory.* This is a procedure to link two local Hosts as loosely coupled systems, using a memory-to-memory interface. We will not discuss this method in the context of this book.

b A telephone line. Either a switched or a leased telephone line can be used. The control discipline is Burroughs Data Link Control (BDLC), which is compatible with HDLC.

c A Virtual Circuit through a Public Data Network. In this case, BDLC is used for X.25 Level 2, while an extra sub-level is then used in the Station Level to correspond with X.25 Level 3.

Structurally, the Station Level consists of a Station Level Manager (SLM) and a number of Station Groups. These Station Groups are either BDLC

---

* Global Memory is a trademark of Burroughs Corporation.

stations, in which case the group contains one BDLC station, or an X.25 Station Group for the DTE (the BNA node)—DCE connection, and which contains one X.25 station for each X.25 logical channel across the DTE–DCE interface. In the following sections, the BDLC stations, the X.25 stations and the Station Level Manager are described in more detail. The Station Groups together provide the next higher layer (the Router Level) with a reliable communication path to the neighboring nodes. The interface between the Router Level and the Station Level is a set of queues. Outbound there are two queues for each neighboring node, one for priority and one for routine traffic. Inbound there is only one queue, in which all stations place their traffic to the Router on a first come first serve basis.

BDLC stations

For each physical link to an adjacent node, a BDLC station exists that controls the data transfer and the operation of the link. A BDLC Station Group uses only point-to-point links between the BNA nodes. When these links are leased, the Two-Way Simultaneous (Full-Duplex) mode of operation is used. When the links are switched (dialed), the Two-Way Alternate mode (Half-Duplex) is used. The operation is equivalent with the HDLC procedure class for balanced operation in Asynchronous Response Mode.

Since BDLC is compatible with HDLC, we will not discuss it in detail. HDLC was discussed in Chapter 4. In Fig. 10.4, the HDLC frames that are

```
Commands            Responses

     I                   I

    RR                  RR
    RNR                 RNR
    REJ                 REJ

    SABM
    DISC
    TEST
                        UA
                        DM
                        FRMR
```

Fig. 10.4 BDLC Commands and Responses

supported in BDLC are listed. When a BDLC station supports LAP-B in an X.25 Station Group, the addressing used in the frame is the standard HDLC addressing. The BNA node, being the DTE, uses the 'A'-address (X'C0'), the DCE in the X.25 network the 'B'-address (X'80'). The relation between commands and responses is as discussed for HDLC, i.e. a received frame carrying the station's own address is a command, when it carries the other address it is a response.

This is different on BNA node-to-node links. There, the 'A'-address is used in both directions to indicate a command, the 'B'-address to indicate a response.

X.25 stations

BNA nodes can be interconnected via a Public Data Network (PDN) supporting the X.25 interface, which was described in Chapter 5. In such an interconnection, an *X.25 Station Group* represents the connection of the node with the X.25 network. In this group, there is one X.25 station for each Logical Channel on this connection.

The three levels defined in Recommendation X.25 are supported as follows. Levels 1 and 2, which represent the physical-connection and the link control required across it, use the same procedures as a BDLC node-to-node link, except for the minor addressing difference in BDLC. Level 3 is provided via an extra layer of protocol in between the BDLC station and the Router Level, through the X.25 station. This Packet Level is completely compatible with Recommendation X.25. The result is that the frame transmitted on the link not only contains the BDLC header and trailer, but also the X.25 Packet Header. Router Frames or Station Level Control Frames are carried in the packet as 'X.25 User Data'. The packet length used by BNA X.25 stations conforms to the packet length used in each Public Data Network and is therefore user-selectable. The packet sequence numbering operates modulo 8.

A number of optional features that Public Data Networks may offer are not relevant to the user of BNA, since the BNA network already performs these functions. The features that are relevant are the *Closed User Group* and the *Bilateral Closed User Group*. When two BNA nodes through their X.25 Station Groups (DTEs) form a Bilateral Closed User Group, it means that they can set up a Virtual Call with each other but with no other DTE. With the Closed User Group facility, it is possible, for instance, to form a fully connected BNA network using a Public Data Network and shield it from all other users of the PDN. BNA nodes can, however, also belong to different Closed User Groups, depending on the arrangements made with the PDN administration. It is up to the network designer to decide how this can be used to advantage in the particular BNA network.

The Station Level Manager

The operation of the Station Level is controlled and coordinated by the Station Level Manager (SLM), which is present in each node. The SLM has the required tables with information about attached or potential neighbors, and it can thus be instructed to set up connections. This can be done by activating a permanent connection, by performing a dial-out operation or by accepting incoming calls. The communication between neighbor SLMs uses Station Level Control Frames. These frames are transmitted as normal BDLC frames in the Information Transfer format or as X.25 packets, like the Router Frames. They are differentiated from the Router Frames through the use of the frame-type field. For Station Level Control Frames, the frame-type field also indicates which of the seven possible commands is contained in the frame. The various frames are given below.

Station Level Greetings (0, 1 and 2)   The greeting frames are used in the mutual validation of two neighbor nodes. When a Station Dialog is opened, the two Station Level Managers exchange Greeting-0 messages via the dialog to identify themselves to the other Station Level Manager (SLM). The Network Address of the node in which they reside is carried in this frame, so each SLM can check in its local database (called the 'neighbor table') whether this node is acceptable. After that, the Greeting-1 messages are exchanged to verify the passwords of the two nodes. In this message, the maximum segment size to be used on the link is also established. This size can be the same as the maximum size for the network, which is verified in the Greeting-1 or it can be smaller for the particular link. Once established, it can be used by the Port Level to decide whether segmenting of messages is necessary. Once the Greeting-1 messages are successfully exchanged, the validation process is completed with the exchange of Greeting-2 messages, each of which grants permission to the receiver to send traffic.

Initialization Complete   This control frame is sent to indicate to the receiver that the sending node has completed its Station Level initiation. At the receiving node, the Router Level is then informed that the link is operational.

Send X Text

X Test Response   These control frames are used only on X.25 links. They are the equivalent of the BDLC Unnumbered frame 'Test'. The receiving station will return a response with the same Information Field.

The Station Level Manager is also responsible for the management of parallel links, if they exist between two nodes. By allocating the same set of queues to the stations for these links, they appear as one link to the Router. Since the operation of the Station Dialogs is mutually asynchronous, frames may get out of sequence in such a configuration. The Station Level will not attempt any resequencing, but leave that to the Port Level.

10.3.2 Router Level

The Router Level provides Logical Connections among all communicating Hosts. The main function of the Router Level is to forward messages along the next step in their route from a source node to a destination node. What this actually involves depends on how the frame got into the node. There are three possibilities:

a Frames that originated in the node are routed to the appropriate Station Level queues, after a Router Header has been appended.
b Frames for which the node is the destination node are either handled internally by the Router if they are Router Control Frames, or they are queued for the Port Level if they are Router Information Units. The Router Header is stripped off after the frame type has been decided.
c Frames that enter the node via the Station Level and do not terminate in the node—transit frames—are queued for the appropriate Station Level for the next node.

Apart from the creation of the Router Header, the routing of locally originating frames and of transit frames is the same. This routing is based on routing tables that are dynamically updated to reflect changes in the configuration. No adaptation is made for the load on the various links and nodes or the cost factors involved. In the following section, we describe the algorithm used in more detail.

The BIAS algorithm

The routing algorithm used in BNA is called the BIAS† algorithm. It is based on the concept of a *link resistance factor* and a *node resistance factor*. This resistance factor can be seen as a measure of the time it takes to transmit a frame on a link or to transmit it through a node. For a particular route through the network, a total resistance factor is calculated by summing up the resistance factors of the links and nodes in the path. The origin and destination nodes are excluded from this calculation. In each node, a table is built which contains, for each destination, the total resistance factor for the routes through each of the neighbor nodes. In Fig. 10.5, an example of such a table is given for all nodes in a simple network configuration. In each node, the minimum resistance factor for each destination is calculated and the associated route used is the 'best' route towards that destination. The minimum value is also communicated to the neighbor nodes, which can then use it for their calculations.

When the configuration changes, i.e. when nodes are activated or deactivated or when the status of links changes, the nodes exchange messages to communicate the change. These messages are

- LINKCHANGE, which is sent between two neighbor nodes when the status of the link connecting the two nodes changes (e.g. when one line in a multiple parallel line is going down).
- NETCHANGE, which is used to communicate to neighbor nodes that resistance factors and/or hop counts in the routing tables were changed.

† BIAS is a trademark of the Burroughs Corporation.

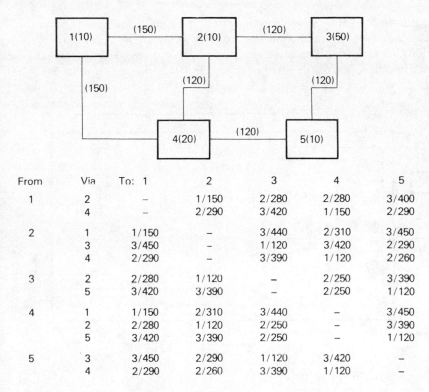

From	Via	To: 1	2	3	4	5
1	2	–	1/150	2/280	2/280	3/400
	4	–	2/290	3/420	1/150	2/290
2	1	1/150	–	3/440	2/310	3/450
	3	3/450	–	1/120	3/420	2/290
	4	2/290	–	3/390	1/120	2/260
3	2	2/280	1/120	–	2/250	3/390
	5	3/420	3/390	–	2/250	1/120
4	1	1/150	2/310	3/440	–	3/450
	2	2/280	1/120	2/250	–	3/390
	5	3/420	3/390	2/250	–	1/120
5	3	3/450	2/290	1/120	3/420	–
	4	2/290	2/260	3/390	1/120	–

Fig. 10.5 Example of BNA network and routing tables. In the table, the value
x/yyy means: number of hops (x) and total resistance factor (yyy) from the origin
node to the destination node

Then they go through the route calculation to find out whether the
configuration change affects the routing tables, and whether the resistance
factors to one or more destinations have changed. If so, this is again
communicated to the neighbor nodes, etc. If no more changes are made to
the configuration, the update process will quickly settle at new stable
routing tables. Otherwise, the process continues as long as changes are
being made.

The effect of this update algorithm is that, during the update process, the
routing is unstable and frames may temporarily bounce between two nodes
or follow a loop. To detect this, the Routing Header carries a *Hop Count*
field, which is incremented by one in each node that is visited. When the
Hop Count exceeds a certain (network) maximum, the frame is discarded.

10.3.3 Port Level

The communication between end-user processes in BNA is established
through the concept of a dialog between *ports*. A port appears to a

programmer writing a program that uses communication as a file, like any other file. The communication is achieved basically by reading from and writing to that file. The interface that is given to the user in this way is described in terms of file attributes. In Fig. 10.6, the structure of the Port

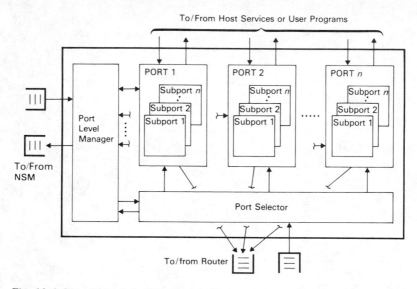

Fig. 10.6 Structure of the Port Level. (By courtesy of the Burroughs Corporation)

Level is illustrated. Each port has one or more *subports*, each of which can have a dialog with a subport in the same or another host. To the user process, each subport manifests itself as a subfile that can be individually addressed in the READ and WRITE operations. The dialog connections are bidirectional (Full-Duplex), although they can be used in a uni-directional way. When a subport transmits a frame, it puts it in the input queue for the Router Level, which will take care of the proper routing through the network. When the Router Level receives a message from the network—via the Station Level—it will place it in the input queue for the Port Selector. This Port Selector will route each message in its queue to the input queue of the addressed port, after checking that the port exists and that other items in the Port Headers are valid. Inside the port, further de-multiplexing is performed in the selection of the proper subport that should receive the message. The subports actually manage the protocols for the dialogs between them, including segmenting and reassembly of messages (see below). When a message must be passed to the user process, it is placed in a *message forwarder* queue. There is one message forwarder for the port and it will pass a message to the user process for each READ operation performed for the port or subport.

In the following sections, we describe first the protocols that are defined in BNA for the subport dialog. We then describe in more detail how such a dialog is established via the 'matching' procedure.

Subport dialogs

When a user process wants to communicate with another user process, a subport dialog is established, as will be described below. Once such a dialog exists, the user process has to worry only about the exchange of messages with its counterpart, the *endpoint* user process, but not about the details of the message exchange. These details are handled by the port and its associated subports. The port is the interface to the user process, with one subport for each endpoint user process. Those functions that are related to the interface with the local end-user are handled by the port; those that are related to each dialog separately, such as the status of the endpoint user processes, are handled by the subports. In this way, all endpoint user processes are represented to the user process as subfiles in the port file, which can be accessed using a subfile index.

The primary operations on the port file that the user process can use are the WRITE and the READ. The functions that are provided by the Port Level are

a Sequence numbering of frames
b Acknowledgement of frames
c Flow control between subports
d Segmenting of messages
e Segment retransmission
f Data compression

Except for the last one, these functions are closely related. Although some cross-reference is unavoidable, we will, however, discuss them separately.

Sequence numbering of frames   Each frame that a subport hands over to the Router Level is assigned a unique sequence number. The Send Sequence Number occupies a 3-byte field in the Subport Header. This allows for over 16 million frames to be sent before a wrap around of the sequence number occurs. Since the Router Level discards all messages that have exceeded the maximum number of hops, the probability for messages to be one wrap-around behind is practically zero. It is even more unlikely because of the maximum window of 60—see later under Flow control. The only way in which 'stale' messages could still occur would be through a node holding transit messages for a long time. Because of the segment retransmission scheme, duplicates would be created and when the originals would eventually be released they might be 'stale', if and only if they would happen to fall right inside the current window. This situation, which is very unlikely indeed, cannot be detected with the defined mechanisms.

When a frame arrives at the destination subport, its sequence number is checked first. If it is lower than the last number acknowledged or higher than the last frame acknowledged plus the window size, it can be discarded as a duplicate. If it is inside the current window but not equal to the next expected sequence number, it is queued until the preceding frames have arrived.

Acknowledgement of frames   A subport can acknowledge the frames it receives in three ways:

a Whenever a frame is sent to the other subport, the low-order byte of the sequence number of the last frame received in sequence is copied in the Subport Header as the Receive Sequence Number. The 1-byte value is sufficient, since the flow control mechanism (see later) never allows more than 60 frames for a subport dialog to be in the network at any time.
b When it is detected that the receive window is half full and no frame is ready in the reverse direction that can carry the acknowledgement, a subport control frame is sent, called the *Unnumbered Ack*. The frame is called unnumbered since it only carries the (full 3 byte) sequence number of the subport frame it acknowledges, but it is not sequence-numbered itself.
c A subport may request from the other subport an acknowledgement as soon as possible. This acknowledgement may be sent in a subport frame if it is available—in which case it would have contained the acknowledgement anyway—or otherwise an Unnumbered Ack must be sent.

Flow control   The flow control mechanism in BNA is based completely on the subport-to-subport flow. It allows a receiving subport to slow down the sender if it cannot accept the incoming frames at the rate they are being sent. The mechanism is the basic window mechanism, meaning that the sender may continue to send as long as the send sequence number has not exceeded the last acknowledged sequence number plus the window size. In this way, the window 'slides' with every acknowledgement received. This automatic window adjustment may be temporarily halted if the receiver wants the sender to stop completely. In that case, a subport control frame *Receive Not Ready* is sent. Permission to resume sending is granted with the *Receive Ready* subport control frame.

The size of the window is chosen when the dialog between the subports is established via the *Offer* and *Match Found* control frames (see below). Each Port Level Manager has a value for the window size that is acceptable for its node. This value is compared in the matching process with the size for the other Port Level Manager. The smaller of the two is used for the dialog between the subports.

The value kept by the Port Level Manager can be changed through the Operations Interface, but the change will only be effective for dialogs created after the change.

Segmenting of messages   When a BNA network is configured, an overall network maximum segment size is established, which can only be changed through the Operations Interface (refer to Section 10.3.4). The segment size information is kept in the routing tables at the Router Level, and passed to the Port Level Manager. When a subport transmits a message, this value is used to decide whether the message must be segmented or not. If it has to be segmented, each segment will be sent as an independent frame. The Subport Header of the last segment contains an indication that this is the last segment of a message. An unsegmented message is thus transmitted with the 'last segment' indicator on. Segments are re-ordered and re-assembled in the receiving subport using the frame sequence numbers.

Segment retransmission   Since the Router Level may route various segments of one message along different paths in the network, the arrival sequence is not guaranteed and, moreover, the arrival itself is not guaranteed. The Router Level may discard a frame when the maximum Hop Count is exceeded. It is therefore necessary to define a time-out after which an acknowledgement for a segment should be received. If it is not received after this time-out, the segment is retransmitted on the assumption that the original was lost. This may create duplicates, which can easily be detected through the sequence number and then discarded.

The time-out value is something that must be carefully chosen. It should be based on the normal average length of the route through the network and the segment size. In addition, delays due to normal load should be taken into account. In BNA, default values for these parameters are used, but they can be set explicitly through the Operations Interface.

Data compression   Data compression is defined in BNA to achieve information transfer with the smallest number of data bytes, so as to utilize the data links in the most efficient way. Although it is handled completely by the Port Level, it must be enabled by the user process. During the set-up of the subport dialog, the capability for compression is also negotiated. If compression can be used, this is made known to the user process via a file attribute. When the user requests compression in the course of the dialog, the subport first sends a subport control frame, *Change Compression*, to the endpoint subport to indicate the beginning of compressed data. From there on, all data will be sent in compressed form, until another Change Compression control frame is sent.

The compression defined in BNA compresses a string of identical characters of length 4 to 255 by replacing it with a 3-byte field: the *escape* character; one byte containing the length of the string; and the character to be repeated. When the escape character itself is present in the data, it is always sent in compressed form, to avoid misinterpretation. Example:

The string Y A A A A A B is replaced by Y 'ESC' 5 A B.
The string Y 'ESC' A B is replaced by Y 'ESC' 1 'ESC' A B.

Subport dialog establishment

A subport dialog is established when a user process issues an OPEN to a subport file. A temporary subport is then created in the port and the Port Level Manager is invoked to perform the matching process. Although there are several possibilities, we start the discussion with the case where the user process has requested that an *offer* be made to the remote subport.

It is now a proper moment to review the addressing mechanism in BNA. As we have seen before, each host, i.e. each node, in the BNA network is identified through a *node name* and a *node address*. The node names are for use by the users, the node addresses are used in the Router Level and carried in the Router Header as the Destination Node Address and the Origin Node Address. These node addresses are 2 bytes long and each is unique in the network. Inside a node, user processes may request the opening of a port. At that time, they will identify it with a *port name*. The Port Level Manager will assign a *port address* to it, if this port has not yet been allocated. In addition, a *subport address* is allocated for each open subport. To the user process, this subport address is the same as the subfile index.

Now back to the subport dialog establishment (see Fig. 10.7). We assume that the Port Level Managers in the involved Hosts are aware of each other and have their own subport dialog already established. When a user process in HOST-A issues an *OPEN*, this is interpreted by the Network Services Manager, which passes it on to the Port Level Manager. The parameters that must be supplied by the user process are

a The port name it wants to use locally, i.e. the file that must be opened, for example AA.
b The host name where the port is located with which the dialog is to be established, for example HOST-B.
c The port name of that remote port, say BB.

The Port Level Manager maps the remote host name onto the node address, using a table in which all remote hosts of which it is aware are listed. If we assume that this is the first reference to port AA, a port address is now allocated and the port added to the Ports Allocated table. Next, a subport address is allocated and this subport is added to a *Candidates for Match* list, since it is now able to accept a dialog.

For the example, we assume that the user process has specified in the OPEN options that an *offer* should be made to the remote port (BB). The Port Level Manager in HOST-A now creates a Port Level Manager

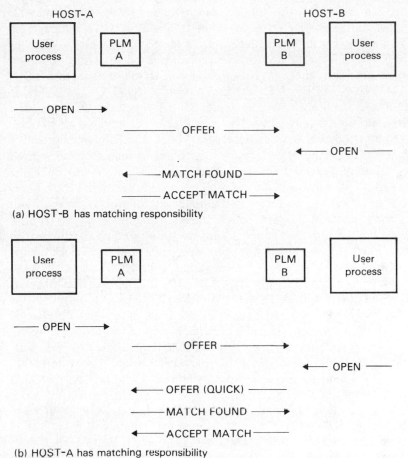

(a) HOST-B has matching responsibility

(b) HOST-A has matching responsibility

Fig. 10.7 Subport dialog establishment

message that is sent to the Port Level Manager in HOST-B, using the PLM-to-PLM subport dialog. The message is called the *OFFER* message and it specifies the characteristics of the offering port and subport. Among other things, this message specifies

a The names of the initiating host and port (MYHOSTNAME=HOSTA, MYNAME=AA).
b The addresses of initiating host, port and subport.
c The name of the host and port to which the offer is sent (YOUR-HOSTNAME=HOSTB, YOURNAME=BB).
d Proposals for window size, message size, etc.

Further, the required response for the OFFER is specified. In this case it is: *BE PATIENT*, which means that if no matching candidate exists already at the destination host, i.e. no matching OPEN has been issued for a port BB at HOST-B, this subport can be added to the Candidates for Match list until such an OPEN is issued. The Port Level Manager in HOST-A will now wait until a reaction from HOST-B is received. Whether control is returned to the user process depends upon the OPEN options.

Now let us assume that next a user process in HOST-B issues an OPEN, with MYNAME=BB, YOURHOSTNAME=HOSTA and YOUR-NAME=AA. The Port Level Manager in HOST-B gets the OPEN request and first allocates a port address to port BB. A subport address is also allocated and added to the Candidates for Match list. The same list is then searched and now the offer from AA is found as matching the current OPEN. Assuming that HOST-B's Port Level Manager has matching responsibility, it sends a *MATCH FOUND* message to the Port Level Manager in HOST-A, indicating that a matching subport has been found. This message contains the same set of addresses and names as the OFFER message plus the port and subport addresses allocated to the subport in port BB. Furthermore, it contains the accepted or modified values for the window size, etc. If the Port Level Manager in HOST-A accepts the MATCH, it confirms it with *ACCEPT MATCH*; otherwise it sends *REFUSE MATCH*, indicating the reason for the refusal.

In the foregoing example, we assumed that HOST-B's Port Level Manager had matching responsibility. This is one of the few instances in BNA where the architecture is asymmetric. Only one of the two participating Port Level Managers can have this responsibility and it is by definition the one with the smaller node address. If HOST-A had had the matching responsibility in our example, then the Port Level Manager in HOST-B would have sent an *OFFER* message with the option JUDGE QUICKLY set. This means that HOST-A should respond immediately with a MATCH FOUND, since there should be a matching subport already in its Candidates for Matching list. The rest of the sequence is then as before. Both cases are illustrated in Fig. 10.7.

10.3.4 Network Services Manager (NSM)

In Fig. 10.2 the structure of the Network Services Level is illustrated. From that figure, it can be seen that, in addition to the management functions at each level—the Port Level Manager, the Router Level Manager and the Station Level Manager—there is also an overall management function in the Network Services Level.

This management function is called the Network Services Manager and it is responsible for those management functions that are global to the three levels. These functions are

a Host and node initialization.
b Control communication between the three functional levels.
c Logging and monitoring of the Network Services.

d Providing a control interface to the next higher level—either Host Services or the user.

e Providing an interface to the network operator, the Network Services Operations Interface.

We will take a closer look at two of these functions, the initialization and the Operations Interface, in the remainder of this section.

Host and node initialization

In BNA, a distinction is made between Network Services Host initialization and Network Services Node initialization. A host system can be operating in stand-alone mode without being connected to the network. Even in that case, some of the BNA functions are required since local Inter-Process Communication (IPC) is performed the same way as remote process communication. Only the Port Level is needed in that case, since the processes communicate through their ports and subports.

Network Services Host initialization performs the required initialization of the Network Services Manager and the Port Level to enable these local operations. The initialization process itself is much the same as the initialization of any operating system. Once this initialization is complete, the Network Services Manager and the Port Level are in a mode—the *Isolated Mode*—that supports the local subport dialogs. Any requests that require the network, such as an OPEN for a remote port, are rejected with an error message: NOT IN NETWORK MODE.

When the host is operational and the Network Services are initialized for local operation, then the next step can be performed, the node initialization. This is done either automatically or at the request of the operator.

A BNA network does not have any form of centralized control. It is therefore necessary for each node that wants to initialize itself in the network, to contact its neighbors and find out how much of the network is already active. The node should then make itself known to all active nodes.

The first step in the initialization procedure is to start the Router and the Station Levels and to prepare all three levels for network initialization. The Network Services Manager then obtains from its local files or through operator commands the potential configuration of the network and the characteristics that must be known.

Once the levels are initialized with the proper attributes, the Network Services Manager enables the Station Level to initiate Station Dialogs with its neighbors. This initialization is local to the Station Level. It is performed by the Station Level Manager using the Greeting control frames. The procedure was discussed in Section 10.3.1. When the Station Dialogs have been set up with all neighbor nodes that are currently active, completion of the initialization phase is signaled to the Network Services Manager.

Each time the Station Level Manager has set up a Station Dialog with a neighbor node, it signals this to the Router Level. The Router Level can then exchange LINKCHANGE messages with that neighbor node. The next step would be to send a NETCHANGE message to the active neighbors, but there is reason to wait a while. The initializing node itself has little knowledge of the network yet, so it would make no sense to send out this limited knowledge right away. It waits, therefore, for all its neighbors to send in their NETCHANGE messages, from which it can build a more useful picture of the network. When no LINKCHANGE and/or NETCHANGE messages have been received during some fixed time-out, the node starts sending out its NETCHANGE messages to its neighbors. This can happen at the earliest when the Station Level has completed its initialization.

The sending of NETCHANGE messages by the initializing node may result in the reception of new NETCHANGE messages from the neighbors, until the tables in all nodes stabilize. Then, the Router Level can report to the Network Services Manager which nodes are reachable. This information is subsequently used by the Port Level. Completion of the Router Level initialization also means the completion of Node initialization.

Node shutdown

Each node in a BNA network can be taken down independently. It may, however, have an impact on the rest of the network. If nodes were only reachable through the one that is shut down, they are no longer part of the network. It is a matter of careful planning when a node can be taken down and when not.

There are two ways in which a node may shut down: fast and slow. The difference between the two modes is only visible at the Port Level. Fast shutdown means that all existing non-local subport dialogs are deactivated and no requests for new ones are accepted. In slow shutdown, new requests for non-local subport dialogs are not accepted, but existing dialogs may continue until they complete. Slow shutdown can, therefore, not proceed beyond the Port Level until all non-local dialogs have terminated.

In both fast and slow shutdown, completion of the Port Level shutdown is reported to the Network Services Manager, which informs the Router Level that it should shutdown. All the Router Level has to do for that is to tell its neighbors that it can no longer be reached. It does that by sending a NETCHANGE message in which the resistance factor is set to maximum.

Control communication between the functional levels

In a way, the control communication between the Port, Router and Station Levels has already been introduced in the previous section. The Network Services Manager gets control information from each level and passes it on to whichever levels it feels should have the information.

The Operations Interface

Although Network Services performs the management functions in the node, it must have an interface with some outside controlling agent such as a node operator. Through this interface, it can receive commands and send responses about the management function.

In BNA, this interface is called the Operations Interface, for which a repertoire of Operations Interface messages has been defined. These Operations Interface messages can be

a commands, which request a certain function to be performed;
b responses, which report the result of a command; or
c reports, which are not the result of a specific command, but indicate that some event has occurred.

Agents send commands through the interface and they receive responses and reports.

The commands can be used to control completely the operation of the node in its network environment. Through them, the node can be initialized, attributes can be changed, the configuration of the network can be changed, calls with neighbor nodes can be initiated, inquiries can be made, etc. Three different types of agent have been defined that may control the Network Services Manager.

The first type is the *Operator Agent*, who uses an Operator Display Terminal (ODT). This ODT can be the system console, but it can also be any other terminal designated as an ODT or it can be a remote terminal. The fact that it can be remote implies that, although each node in a BNA network is independent in its management, the control of the network can be exercised from a central operator terminal if the user wants it organized that way. These terminals use the normal BNA procedures to communicate with the Operations Interface. Local terminals use the Operator Display Terminal subsystem. Remote ODTs use the local ODT subsystem via a subport dialog. The Host Services ODT protocol is used on this dialog to control the exchange of Operator Interface (OIM) messages.

The second type of agent is a *File agent*—a disk file with Operations Interface messages, or a printer file that receives responses and reports. This file can also be local or remote. In the local case, the messages are retrieved from the file through the normal I/O subsystem of the Host and passed to the Operations Interface. In the remote case, the procedure is the same as for any other remote file. The local I/O sybsystem sets up a communication with the remote I/O subsystem using the Host Services Logical I/O protocol.

The third type of agent can be a user program that generates and accepts Operations Interface messages. As for the other two agents, this program can also be local or remote. In either case, the user program communicates with the Operations Interface through a subport dialog.

10.4 Host Services

So far, we have only discussed the Network Services in BNA, i.e. the services that make the communication between remote processes possible. As part of BNA, a number of Host Services have been defined that make use of the communications services of the network and allow user operations to be the same for local and for remote hosts. The services are defined in three areas, in the handling of

a Files: the Logical I/O protocol that can be used by programs to read, write or update remote files and the File Transfer Utility, a file copy program that uses the Logical I/O protocol.
b Terminals: the Operator Display Terminal protocol that allows a terminal operator to issue a request to a remote host and to receive responses from that host, and the Station Transfer protocol that allows a terminal physically attached to one host to be logically attached to another host. Essentially, it is a pass-through program that is attached to the local terminal using the standard Burroughs' Network Definition Language and Message Control System—the Environmental Software. The protocol defined is unidirectional under the control of the thing which initiated the dialog, which can be either the terminal or the remote process.
c Jobs and tasks: the Job Transfer protocol and the Remote Tasking protocol. The Job Transfer protocol allows a terminal operator to transfer a job to a remote host and execute it there by only adding the name of the remote host to the START command for the job. Similarly, the Remote Tasking protocol allows a program task to initiate another task or subtask at a remote host and to control its status.

In all cases, the definition is such that a user program or terminal operator can use the same procedures to access a local resource and a remote resource. In those protocols where commands are transferred to the remote host, no syntax checking is done in the local host. The syntax used, as for example in a job stream, must be the syntax of the remote host.

10.5 Comparison with the Reference Model

In the preceding sections, we have discussed Burroughs' Network Architecture in quite some detail. Armed with this information, we can now try to map the structure of BNA onto the structure of the Reference Model.
A first impression would be to map the Port Level against the Session Layer and the Router Level against the Network Layer, leaving the Transport Layer somewhere in between. However, a closer look does

reveal that most of the services defined for the Session Layer are not provided by the Port Level. The services that are provided have more to do with the Transport Layer of the Model. Some services on the other hand are related in the Reference Model to the Presentation Layer. Therefore, we map the Port Level onto (part of) the Presentation Layer, the Session Layer and the Transport Layer with the comment that the emphasis is on the Transport Layer.

In the following comparison, we use the list of services and functions as compiled in Appendix B. For each service and function, we indicate the equivalent in the relevant level of BNA. Where no comment is given for a specific service or function, this indicates that we could not identify an equivalent service or function in that layer of BNA. Particularly in the case of the Presentation and Session Layers, such services may be provided by the Environmental Software or by user processes. This is, however, outside the scope of our book.

10.5.1 Presentation Layer

In the following list, services and functions in the Port Level that are equivalent to Presentation Layer services and functions are indicated. As stated earlier, the main thrust of the Port Level is equivalent to the Transport Layer in the Reference Model.

Services provided by the Presentation Layer
- Data transformation. A data compression service is available to the user process. The compression itself is transparent to the user, but the service must be requested explicitly.
- Data formatting.
- Syntax selection.
- Presentation-connections. There is a one-to-one relationship with the transport-connection, i.e. the support dialog.

Functions in the Presentation Layer
- General.
  - Session establishment request.
  - Presentation image negotiation and renegotiation.
  - Data transformation and formatting.
  - Special-purpose transformations. The user process may request compression to be performed. If this is enabled, any string of from four up to 255 identical characters is represented as a three-character string.
  - Session termination request.
- Addressing and multiplexing.
- Presentation Layer Management.

10.5.2 Session Layer

In the terminology of the Reference Model, no separate session-entities exist in BNA and thus no explicit session-connections. There are no services defined in the Port Level that are the equivalent of the Session Layer services in the Model. We therefore skip the list of services and functions for this level.

10.5.3 Transport Layer

The equivalent layer of the Transport Layer is the Port Level in BNA.

Services provided by the Transport Layer
- Identification.
  - Transport-addresses. User processes request association with a certain port when they request a connection. The Port address, which is also the equivalent of the network-address, maps therefore one-to-one in the transport-address.
  - Transport-connections. The subport dialog is the equivalent of the transport-connection. This subport dialog is a Two-Way Simultaneous data path between two subports. A port may have multiple dialogs with other ports, one for each subport.
  - Transport-connection-endpoint-identifiers. The Port file name and the Subport index serve as the transport-connection-endpoint-identifiers.
- Establishment services.
  - Transport-connection establishment. When a user process issues an OPEN request for a Port file, indicating a remote Port file, a transport-connection is established.
  - Class of service selection.
- Data transfer services.
  - Transport-service-data-unit. The message passed to the subport by the user process is the transport-service-data-unit.
  - Expedited transport-service-data-unit.
- Transport-connection release. A user process may request the release of a transport-connection withe CLOSE request.

Functions in the Transport Layer
- Addressing. The Port Level Manager performs mapping functions to set up the addressing. It assigns Port and Subport addresses to the local port and subport. The name of the destination Host is also translated into the Host address.
- Connection multiplexing and splitting. Several transport-connections

can be multiplexed onto one network-connection (i.e. a route through the network).

- Phases of operation.
  - Establishment phase. In the establishment phase, an OFFER frame is sent to the Port Level Manager in the destination Host. This frame indicates the requested port and the parameters proposed for the transport-connection (window size, etc.). The phase is terminated when a match is accepted or refused.
  - Data transfer phase.
    - Sequencing. Segments of user messages are resequenced on the basis of the Port Level sequence number.
    - Blocking.
    - Concatenation.
    - Segmenting. User messages can be segmented into multiple subport information units that are combined with subport and port control information into Port Level frames (i.e. transport-protocol-data-units).
    - Multiplexing or splitting.
    - Flow control. This is performed on the subport dialog using an acknowledgement scheme with a sliding window. In addition to this scheme, the flow can temporarily be halted with the Receive Ready/Receive Not Ready control frames.
    - Error detection. The loss, misordering or duplication of transport-protocol-data-units can be detected with the Send and Receive sequence counters that are transmitted with the frames.
    - Error recovery. Port frames that arrive out of sequence will be re-ordered. Lost Port frames (i.e. no acknowledgement is received within a time-out period) are retransmitted by the sender. When this results in duplicate frames, the duplicates are discarded. If repeated retransmission is unsuccessful, the transport-connection is terminated.
    - Expedited data transfer.
    - Transport-service-data-unit delimiting. The length of the Transport Layer protocol-control-information is fixed (Subport and Port Headers). The total length of the Port frame is passed to/from the Router Level.
    - Transport-connection identification. The transport-connection is uniquely identified through the Host, Port and Subport addresses on both sides of the connection.
  - Release phase. The release phase is entered when a REQUEST CLOSE is sent to the correspondent subport. This phase is terminated when the CLOSE is acknowledged.
- Transport Layer Management. The Port Level Manager performs all management functions related to the operation of the Port Level.

10.5.4 Network Layer

The equivalent of the Network Layer is the Router Level in BNA.

Services provided by the Network Layer
- Network addresses. The transport-entities (Ports) are known through Port addresses to the Router Level.
- Network-connections. A route between BNA Hosts is the equivalent of a network-connection. Several routes can be defined between any two Hosts, but only one will be active, as indicated by the BIAS algorithm.
- Network-connection-endpoint-identifiers. The node address of the destination Host is the network-connection-endpoint-identifier.
- Network-service-data-unit transfer. The Port frame is the network-service-data-unit. In the Router Level, it is called the Router Information Unit. Unlike the specification of the Reference Model, a network-wide maximum segment size is defined, which implies a maximum length for the Router Information Unit (maximum segment size plus the various headers).
- Quality of service parameters.
- Error notification.
- Sequencing. The Router Level does not guarantee sequential delivery of network-service-data-units.
- Flow control.
- Expedited network-service-data-unit transfer.
- Reset.
- Release services. Release of a network-connection cannot be specifically requested by the Port Level. A specific route is only terminated if one of the intermediate Hosts is taken down (Node Shutdown). As long as other routes are available, this is transparent to the Port Level. If the endpoint Hosts are taken down, the existing subport dialogs (transport-connections) are terminated as part of the shutdown procedure.

Functions in the Network Layer
- Routing and relaying. The nodes perform routing functions based on destination routing tables. The best route among alternatives is selected with the BIAS algorithm.
- Network-connections. The active route can be viewed as the network-connection.
- Network-connection multiplexing. Several network-connections may be (and normally will be) multiplexed on the same data-link-connection (i.e. Host-to-Host link).
- Segmenting and blocking.
- Error detection.
- Error recovery.
- Sequencing.

- Flow control.
- Expedited data transfer.
- Reset.
- Service selection.
- Network Layer Management. The Router Manager manages the BIAS algorithm and the updating of configuration information (i.e. LINK-CHANGE and NETCHANGE).

10.5.5 Data Link Layer

The Data Link Layer in BNA is the Station Level. This level uses BDLC, which is compatible with HDLC. The reader is referred to Section 4.6 for a comparison with the Reference Model. BNA stations can also support X.25 Virtual Circuits. Once the Virtual Circuit is set up, it is used as a data link only and the services provided are the same as those for a BDLC station.

10.5.6 Physical Layer

No Physical Layer is explicitly defined in BNA. The Station Level supports the usual standards for this level (e.g. CCITT V.24 and EIA RS-232-C). For X.25 stations, CCITT Recommendation X.21bis is also supported.

References

1 Burroughs Corporation, *Introduction to Burroughs Network Architecture (BNA)*, no. 11222421, 1979
2 Burroughs Corporation, *Burroughs Network Architecture (BNA). Architectural description, Reference Manual Vol. 1*, no. 1132172, 1981
3 Burroughs Corporation, *Burroughs Network Architecture (BNA): Network Control, Reference Manual Vol. 2*, no. 1132180, 1981

11 Other network architectures

11.1 Introduction

In the previous chapters of Part 2, we reviewed in some detail the network architectures of some major computer manufacturers. DEC, one of the largest minicomputer manufacturers, and Burroughs, Univac and IBM, representing the larger system manufacturers, were discussed. Other manufacturers had to follow the trend set by those four companies in order to keep a competitive position in the marketplace. However, this is not the only reason. Another incentive is the work of the international standards organizations which has led to ISO's Reference Model and CCITT's X-series recommendations. To be prepared in advance would be nice. A way to do that is to develop a home-grown, similar architecture which will facilitate the implementation of the standard, when available, in the products. The major advantage would be the experience gathered with one's own development and the network management aspects.

All the architectures that are defined show a layered structure. Hence, a structure similar to the Reference Model will already be in place. Theoretically, the support of the Reference Model could be achieved by the replacement of existing layers by the ISO-defined layers. Practically, however, another solution looks to be more suitable. It is still based on a proprietary architecture, but it implements the Reference Model through Gateways. These Gateways map the original architecture onto the Reference Model definitions of layers and protocols and vice-versa. It is clear that, for both solutions, having a network architecture and its implementations in existence constitutes a considerable advantage.

It is also interesting to analyze briefly why some of the early architectures arrived a long time before work on the Reference Model started.

Several different reasons are at the root of the answer. At IBM, it was partly because of the fast-growing teleprocessing business at the end of the 1960s. Teleprocessing was the name for the remote access to a CPU through terminals, connected over a telephone line in most cases. The terminals were what we call today 'dumb' terminals, which means that a terminal is not intelligent or, rather, not programmable. All terminal functions are hard-wired or, in other words, implemented in circuitry.

With circuitry, dynamic modifications are practically impossible. Consequently, to change the behavior of a terminal is a lengthy process. The terminal, for its proper operation, relied heavily on the programming in the CPU. These control programs are very complex and have to run at the highest priority because of the memory-less properties of a telephone line. Different applications required different terminals with specific features. These specific features in circuitry required specific programming in the host and so on. Thus, IBM stood before an enormous proliferation of terminals and programming, all slightly different. This made design, implementation and use of such systems very difficult and the maintenance practically impossible. The result was that, in 1973 IBM defined a common interface and the network to go with it, with which terminals wanting to communicate with the CPUs had to comply. The architecture at the base was called SNA. IBM solved in this way the proliferation of specific features by putting them in layers which were easier to contain and replace, or into programs which could be distributed throughout the network. The first releases of SNA supported terminal-to-CPU communications only, but the architecture contained already the base for the extensions to allow computer-to-computer communications. This was then implemented in later releases.

The reason for DEC to develop DNA, with DECNET implementations, was different. DEC was, at the time, selling minicomputers. These minicomputers are self-contained systems but much smaller than the so-called mainframe CPUs. They have their own peripheral devices and some teleprocessing capacity, i.e. the possibility to connect a number of terminals. Typically, a DEC minicomputer would be sold to a department of a company. That company would have different systems in house and would like very much to have them talking to each other. To solve this particular requirement, DEC developed in 1975 DNA and implemented it in products which were called DECNET components. The terminal-control is not a part of DNA. DNA only defines the way minicomputers can talk to each other.

Univac had the problem of different terminals, minis and communication controllers. Consequently, Univac's DCA gives a solution to the communication problem that includes terminals communicating with CPUs and with each other. Burroughs, on the other side, manages teleprocessing, i.e. terminal-to-computer communication, the way it already did in the 1960s. Their so-called 'No-Name' architecture takes care of controlling that kind of an environment. For their major node or CPU interconnection, they developed BNA, which allows interconnection of CPUs into a complex computer network.

The other manufacturers followed. In 1978, Siemens announced TRANSDATA, a combined terminal and computer network. At the end of 1978, CII–Honeywell–Bull announced DSA, again a terminal and computer network. Then, NCR announced DNA and ITT–Comten announced CNA, all computer communications networks. ICL, the largest UK computer manufacturer, announced its architecture, IPA, in 1980. The Japanese manufacturers also developed proprietary architectures. An example is Fujitsu's FNA.

Reviewing all these architectures on a structural and layer-functional basis shows that newer architectures differ from the previously defined ones. This is normal and to be expected. Newer architectures learn from the mistakes made in older architectures and from the results published on these networks and on experimental networks, such as, for example, ARPANET. It is also very clear that the later architectural definitions show more resemblance to the Reference Model. Examples of the latter case are Honeywell's DSA, ICL's IPA and Fujitsu's FNA.

The mini- and microcomputer manufacturers also developed proprietary network architectures for interconnecting their machines. We have already mentioned DEC with DNA, which is described in Chapter 8. To name some others, there are architectures defined by Data General, Texas Instruments and Hewlett-Packard. This list is not exhaustive. This book has, on purpose, limited its scope to the large mainframe manufacturers' architectures, and even in this group not all of them have been covered. That limitation is mostly due to the non-availability of external documentation on the architectures.

In the following sections are some general descriptions of a few of the not yet fully described network architectures. The difference in treatment is simply because of the amount of documentation available. This does not mean, though, that these architectures are not properly documented or defined by the manufacturers, but simply that not much external documentation is available. Specifically reviewed are Siemens' TRANSDATA, Honeywell's DSA, ICL's IPA and ITT–Comten's CNA. All these architectures have a layered structure, but in some cases a different number of layers, allowing for similar functions—as we have seen before. It will be shown that they are all technically prepared to adopt a standard if and when this standard becomes available.

11.2 TRANSDATA (Siemens)

TRANSDATA [1, 2] is the name of Siemens' communication network architecture. As in all the previously described architectures, it has a homogeneous network approach. The layering technique is again the key and provisions are made to support Public Data Networks for basic communications means.

The architecture allows for centralized network configurations with one processor, i.e. a terminal network as well as complex computer networks. The implementation of TRANSDATA matches Siemens' hardware and software components in one homogenous communication network.

As a basic conceptual definition, TRANSDATA accepts as equal users of its communication system all agencies of the teleprocessing network that cooperate in the solution of a problem—that is, computer programs and people together with the terminals at which they work. Each user, independent of whether he is a terminal operator or a program operator, is uniformly and uniquely addressable within the entire network. In principle, he may—as far as he is authorized to do so—enter into a communication relation with any other user and exchange messages with him.

Thus, communication relations are possible between programs in the same or different computers, between a program and a terminal user, or between terminal users. The communication system connects the 'real' communication partners and not just their physical components, such as computers and terminals. As far as the communication partners are concerned, the exchange of messages can take place without knowledge of the technical means for that.

The computer network can be configured in a star, in a mesh or in a combination of these structures. The functional units implemented in the computer through communication software are called *Processor Nodes*. The sum of these nodes forms the *Communication System* as far as the software is concerned. The end-users connected to the Processor Nodes are represented by software elements called *Stations*.

The Processor Nodes have two basic tasks:

a To connect the end-users to the network.
b To transport messages between the end-users according to the communication relation between them.

11.2.1 TRANSDATA: network architecture

The network architecture of TRANSDATA is based on a structural organization of a teleprocessing system into different levels. Each node will contain the different levels or layers that are defined in the architecture. Common layers on both sides of the communication talk to each other through the use of protocols, and between adjacent layers through well-defined interfaces. The following is a short description of the functions performed in each of these layers (see Fig. 11.1).

Port Services to the User couple the user to the node. In the case of a program being the user, the coupling will be done through a program interface. When the user happens to be a combination of an operator and a terminal, the coupling will be done by means of a line-control procedure. The users exchange data between each other through these port-to-user services.

The next layer that is defined is called *Station Services*. The Station Services, located again on both ends of the communication, exchange

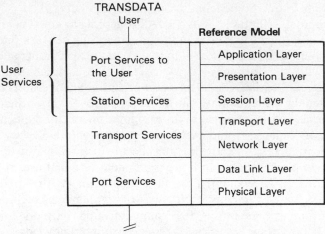

Fig. 11.1 TRANSDATA: the network layers

Station Services protocols. The control information concerning these protocols is contained in a Station Services Header, which is analyzed by the peer layer. The functions provided by this layer are basically those that are defined for the Presentation Layer in the Reference Model. They include message handling related to individual terminals, virtual terminal support, text editing, data formatting and other services. These port and station services are oriented towards the characteristics and requirements of the connected users. The combination of Port Services to the User and Station Services is called User Services.

The User Services are connected to each other through functions in the underlying layers called *Transport Services*. This layer will build a *Virtual Connection* between the two communicating users. The connection is established by so called Connection Managers, which also supervise the communication afterwards. In this way, the two users are shielded from the underlying complexity of the network and of the particular physical communication means that are used. Next, Transport Services route the messages processed by the User Services, from the sender node to the receiver node. In order to determine the destination, a destination address is used. It is included in the Transport Services Header that the Transport Layer builds. The address is processed in two stages. First, the message is transferred to the Processor Node of the receiving station on the basis of a node address. Next, the message is distributed locally in this node on the basis of a station number. Larger networks that contain multiple, large processors are organized in regions and a more elaborate three-stage addressing scheme is employed. Another function of the Transport Services Layer is to control the data flows in the network in order to ensure that the stores of the individual computers do not overflow and are not monopolized by one user. An optional function of the Transport Services consists of delivering to the sender of a message an acknowledgement of the arrival of that message at the receiver. The Transport Services also allow the structuring of a data stream and optional high-priority transmission.

Finally, the data exchange between each pair of users has to be physically transferred between them. The Port Services control the transfer of data on the transmission lines between Processor Nodes. The Port Services communicate by means of link protocols. When the nodes are interconnected by telephone lines, HDLC is used as Data Link Control. If the nodes are interconnected by means of a computer channel, a parallel link protocol will be used.

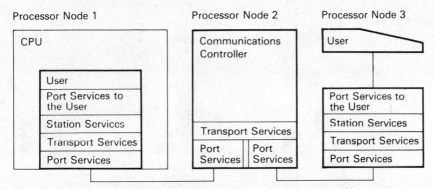

Fig. 11.2 TRANSDATA: message flow

As shown in Fig. 11.2, the path of a message leads successively through the different functional layers and through the elements of a simple network: a CPU, an intermediate node and a terminal node. Obviously, Processor Node 2 behaves for the virtual connection as an intermediate node function. The Port Services between Processor Nodes 1 and 2 will probably be a computer channel and the link protocol a channel program. The Transport Service in the intermediate node, Processor 2, selects an outgoing Port Service. The selection will be based on the node address part of the destination address in the Transport Services Header. The message will then pass through the layers in Processor Node 3. While doing so, the header information will be stripped off and the protocol information duly analyzed. Finally, the Port Services to the User deliver the data in a format suitable to that user.

11.2.2 TRANSDATA: network management

Besides the above described layers of the communication network, TRANSDATA also defines communication network management functions [3, 4]. It is called *Network Administration*. It contains a well defined concept, with, for instance, a Network Administration Language definition, which enables the complete control of the TRANSDATA computer communications network. For control purposes, the network will be divided into areas. Each area has an *Administration Center*. These centers can have a discrete, but contiguous, or overlapping control span. An Administration Center gets directives from an *Administrator*. The Administrator can be a physical person that uses a TRANSDATA terminal, or a user-written program, the so-called programmed administrator, or a combination of both.

In general, the task of the Administration Center is the coordination of the network start-up, control and supervision of the network components, user-analysis and registration of network operational information. TRANSDATA administration contains, for instance, software management. The control programs in the processor nodes have to be coordinated before start-up. An example of such a coordination is the definition of the transport routes through the network. The Transport Services will use the resulting routing tables for routing the messages to their proper destination. These routing tables are contained in the software of each of the Processor Nodes.

The next function of an Administration Center is one of supervision. There are automatic supervisory functions defined that materialize in modules in the software of each processor node. They supervise the working of hardware and software components associated with a processor node. An example here is the monitoring of a transmission line, or a terminal or even an application program. Errors are communicated, recovery is tried and statistics are kept. Secondly, there are supervisory functions that are not automatic and that must be activated. These functions allow the Administrator to inquire into the status of the various components. The Administrator can define which components are active, which are temporarily out of order, and so on.

Control functions of the Administration Center are functions which allow the Administrator to change network configurations in order to compensate for failures. A possible input in the decision-making process for reconfiguration can come from the supervision process. The control functions allow the substitution of components and alternate-route activation, such as switched network back-up. It also comprises the loading and dumping of nodes.

The last important function concerns the registration and statistical evaluation of operational data collected by the supervising functions. It allows the accumulation of statistics in each node. This provides input to the preventive maintenance team. It also provides input for the redesign of the network if a need arises to do so.

The network administration of TRANSDATA is based on one or more centralized controls of the network. Information about the network is sent to these points from distributed administration managers contained in each node of the network. The homogeneity of this administration is the prerequisite for the possibility of realizing the administration either as a completely centralized function or as a decentralized function, while coordinating this administration system-wide.

The above description of TRANSDATA shows that the network is structured in line with the other proprietary networks and the Reference Model. Even though only four layers are defined in TRANSDATA when the Reference Model becomes a standard, TRANSDATA will be adaptable to support the standard in one way or another. Also important is the elaborated network management structure that allows complete control of the network. This control can be chosen to be centralized or distributed.

11.3 Honeywell's Distributed Systems Architecture (DSA)

CII–Honeywell–Bull announced their network architecture, called Distributed Systems Architecture (DSA), at the end of 1978 [5]. DSA is a part of

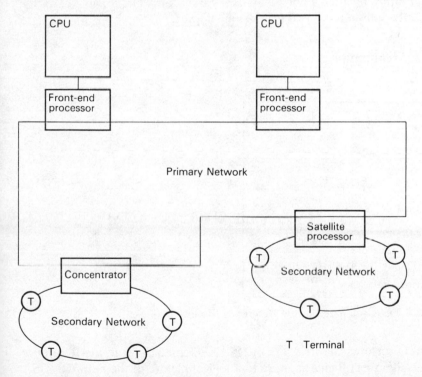

Fig. 11.3 DSA: network structure

a larger concept called DSE (Distributed Systems Environment) which is their master plan for the design and implementation of distributed data processing systems.

DSA is one of the more recently announced proprietary architectures and it follows closely the Reference Model. It also takes, as an integral part of the architecture definition, advantage of the new Public Data Networks (X.21/X.25).

A DSA-based network is divided in two parts (see Fig. 11.3). There is first the Primary Network which follows entirely the DSA rules. Next, the so-called Secondary Networks are defined, which can use protocols other than the DSA protocols. An example is the loop or the electronic interface between cluster controllers or concentrators and the terminals attached to them.

The architecture allows the implementation of different types of network: an hierarchical network is one possible configuration. This is typically a terminal network with CPUs in control of the terminals. Another configuration is the horizontal network. This is a network where hosts are interconnected, each possibly with its own terminal network. There is no particular hierarchical relationship between the CPUs. Yet another configuration includes Public Data Networks, for example, an X.25 PSN. The PDN will be used as transmission support.

11.3.1 Architecture

DSA Layers   **Reference Model**

DSA Layers	Reference Model
ACTIVITY	Application Layer
Presentation Control	Presentation Layer
Session Control	Session Layer
Transport Control	Transport Layer
Path Control	Network Layer
Link Control	Data Link Layer
Physical Link	Physical Layer

Fig. 11.4 DSA compared to the Reference Model

Figure 11.4 shows the structure of DSA and compares it to the Reference Model. Figure 11.3 gives a more topological picture of the network. DSA talks in terms of *Activities* that constitute the end-users of the communcation system. There are two kinds of Activities: an Automatic Activity that is handled entirely within the data processing system and is computer-program driven; and a Manual Activity where people are involved. It will typically be an operator using a terminal. All Activities are network-addressable *Endpoints*. The endpoint can be seen as a borderline between the activity and the network and it has a unique name in the global network. Endpoints are connected to each other through *Logical Connections*. Logical Connections are mapped onto a *Path*, the name for the route that data physically will take from one end-user to the other.

A collection of endpoints that share hardware and software resources is called a *Site*. An example of a site is a CPU, the secondary network of a concentrator, or a terminal itself.

As can be seen in Fig. 11.4, DSA has a structure of hierarchical layers conforming reasonably well with the structure described by the Reference Model. The layers of DSA are divided into two functional groups. The first group of layers relates to Message Management. It defines conventions for the control of the data exchange between endpoints. It contains Presentation Control and Session Control Layers. The second group handles Communications Management. It provides basically a data transport service. The layers included in this group are Transport Control, Path Control, Link Control and the Physical Link.

These layers have essentially the same functions as those in the other architectures. For example, in Presentation Control, we find *Standard Device Protocol*, which seems to be equivalent to ISO's Virtual Terminal protocols. In Transport Control, logical connections are multiplexed if they use the same path. Also a 'fragmentation function' is placed on this level. It requires, of course, a reassembly function at the other endpoint Transport Control Layer.

Path Control routes the data between the Transport Control Layers of two sites. There are four techniques for implementing Path Control, depending on whether the communication service is public or private.

a Datagram service
b Virtual Circuit packet switching (X.25)
c Circuit switching (X.21)
d Dedicated lines

The Link Control Layer uses the ISO–CCITT High-level Data Link Control (HDLC)

Figure 11.4 shows a comparison between the DSA layers and the Reference Model layers.

11.3.2 Network management

DSA also defines network management functions, which they call *Network Administration*. The following functions are found:

a Network configuration control
b Initialization of network elements
c Status monitoring of network elements
d Collection of statistics
e Network testing

This 'Administration' runs at two levels. The Node Administration controls the elements connected to a node. It is included in the control programs of the node. All hardware and software connected with the node are monitored and operational statistics are gathered. This information is then passed to the second administration, the Network Administration. It controls and coordinates the operations of the global network. The Network Administration is in communication with the different Node Administrations. It can activate nodes, links and other resources. The Network Administration will also analyze the information gathered by the node administrations. Any node in the network with the necessary resources can handle global network administration, but it will normally be located in a CPU.

DSA shows a lot of resemblance to the Reference Model. Functions equivalent to the Reference Model functions are easily identified. The network management follows a philosophy of hierarchical control for a terminal network and peer-to-peer control between different CPUs in a multi-system network environment.

11.4 CNA (ITT–Comten)

CNA stands for Communication Network Architecture [6]. It is implemented in CNS (Communication Network Support). It allows the interconnection of different types of system which have their own networks eventually. CNA, with its implementation CNS, is again based on a layered concept.

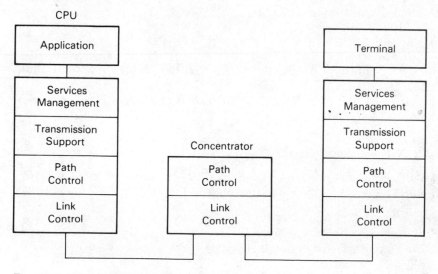

Fig. 11.5 CNA layered concept

Figure 11.5 shows the layer organization. We find an Application Layer as the end-user of the network. Next, the Services Management Layer which handles presentation services selection and connection set-up. As transmission support, we find Communication Support (CS), Path Control function and, finally, Link Control (LC). Again, this is a structure which allows for technical support of ISO standards for the Reference Model when and if available.

11.5 ICL's Information Processing Architecture (IPA)

ICL's Information Processing Architecture was announced in July 1980 as that Company's concept to support information processing in its widest sense [7]. This means that the emphasis is on what type of job must be done and not so much on how it should be done: distributed, centralized or any form in between. The idea is a range of building blocks that perform selected functions but that all fit in the Information Processing Architecture. For that reason, ICL has chosen as a basis for its architecture the Reference Model as it stands, with the intent to follow the standardization in the higher layers as they develop (Fig. 11.6).

IPA supports all possible network configurations, from highly centralized mainframe dominated environments to totally distributed systems.

From IPA's point of view, the layers of the Reference Model can be grouped into three main categories. First, there are the Application-Specific Functions that are completely defined between two communicating entities such as applications or terminals. Secondly, there are the Dialog-Oriented Functions which control the dialog but which are of no direct concern to the communicating parties. Thirdly, there are the Telecommunications Functions which are required whenever the two parties are not resident in the same computer.

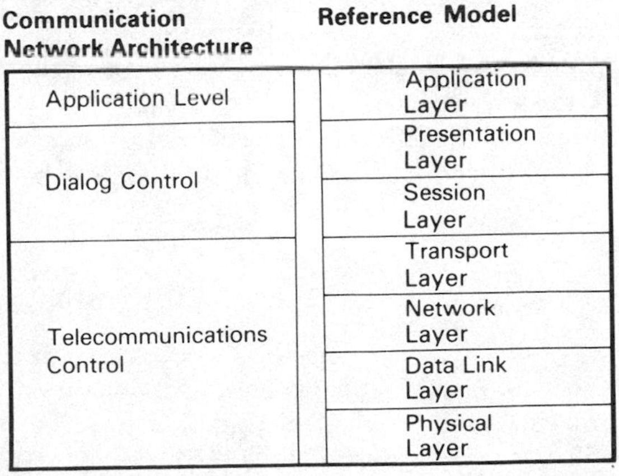

Communication Network Architecture	Reference Model
Application Level	Application Layer
Dialog Control	Presentation Layer
	Session Layer
Telecommunications Control	Transport Layer
	Network Layer
	Data Link Layer
	Physical Layer

Fig. 11.6 IPA layers compared to the Reference Model

Until now, two sets of protocols have been defined for use in an IPA environment: CCITT Recommendation X.25 and ICL's Full XBM (Extended Basic Mode). Full XBM is an already existing ICL protocol to support both bulk and interactive data traffic across a single link between hosts or between a host and a terminal or terminal cluster. Full XBM can be viewed as having a number of levels that correspond to the IPA levels:

a Application Level, where the user- or system-supplied application functions run. Therefore, no protocols are defined for this level.
b Access Levels, which are concerned with how devices are controlled and how the operating system in the host can be accessed.
c Group Level, where the handling of terminal clusters and their addressing rules are defined.
d Link Level, to control the format of the data on the link, actually the character-oriented ISO Basic Mode link-control procedure.
e Physical Level, to control the electrical interface.

The second set of protocols is concerned with Public Data Networks. X.25 protocols can be used to connect ICL machines to Public Data Networks, thus taking advantage of the services offered in these networks. The same protocols can also be used for point-to-point connections of ICL machines in the IPA environment. Since the X.25 protocols cover only the lower three layers of the Reference Model, ICL uses the Full XBM protocols for the higher layers.

Within this framework, a number of application building blocks have been defined, to achieve such functions as remote file access, file transfer, etc.

Network management functions are also defined. It is in itself a distributed system. It uses systems components to achieve functions such as network directory, network control and so on. The way the network is controlled is at the user's choice. It may be a centrally or a distributedly controlled network. For example, a central network control point would handle automatic back-up centers as well as configuration control, statistics, maintenance, diagnostics, etc. The communication between the distributed elements uses IPA facilities itself.

Again, ICL is using the Reference Model structure (Fig. 11.6) and is preparing the way to use the ISO protocols if and when the standard will be available.

11.6 Summary

In this chapter, we have reviewed briefly some proprietary computer network architectures. A lack of publicly available architecture-level documentation is the reason for the short descriptions. However, they allow us to see that these architectures are also similar to the Reference

Model. Adaptation for the support of a standard, when available, can consequently be expected. Most of them also allow the use of Public Data Networks as a substitution for the lower layers defined in the proprietary architecture.

References

1 Feldman J. et al, Siemens' Teleprocessing system TRANSDATA, *Telcom Report*, vol. 1, no. 2, 1978
2 Siemens, Sales literature
3 Jilek, P., The concept of administration in TRANSDATA. Part 1: Principles and practices of administration, *Telcom Report*, vol. 1, no. 3, pp. 136–141
4 Jilek, P., The concept of administration in TRANSDATA. Part 2: Administration structure and language and user aspects, *Telcom Report*, vol. 1, no. 4, 1978, pp. 223–228
5 CII–Honeywell–Bull, *DSA Distributed Systems Architecture*, 1979
6 ITT–Comten, CNA sales literature, 1979
7 International Computers Limited, *Guide to IPA*, 1981

Part 3 Public Data Networks

12 CCITT X-series recommendations

12.1 Introduction

Before we discuss the Public Data Networks (PDN) in more detail, it will be interesting to review briefly the evolution from teleprocessing to PDN.

During the 1960s, terminals started to be connected to computer systems. Initially, a terminal configuration was, most of the time, a simple printer keyboard configuration. If the terminal location is close to the CPU, then the connection consists of a channel attachment. If the terminal is remote, the connection will normally be made over a telephone line. A basic characteristic of the telephone network is that it is very well suited to telephone service, i.e. an analog service with a feedback on the status of the call or the connection through audible signaling.

Computers and terminals are digital engines. Therefore, conversion equipment has to be inserted between the CPU, or its communications control unit, and the telephone line at one end and the terminal and the telephone line at the other end. The signal converters, analog-to-digital and vice versa, are called *Modem*, a short name for Modulator/Demodulator equipment.

The user can rent from the telephone network administration or PTT, or common carrier, a permanent telephone link between the computer and the terminal. This is commonly known as a *leased line facility*. A facility of this kind is easy to control with a computer program. However, the service is very expensive because the administration of the network uses selected high-quality telephone lines. Invoicing is done on a global monthly charge basis.

Terminal-to-computer communication will, most of the time, not completely utilize the capacity of the leased line. The charge, however, will anyway be the complete monthly charge. Hence, it would be a more economic solution to make the connection when it is needed, for example, at the moment that data has to be transmitted. This is exactly the way we use the telephone. We dial the party we want to talk to the moment we want to talk to him. This is known as *Calling* on the Public Switched Telephone Network (PSTN). The charge paid for the call will be related to the distance and the duration of the call.

For computer communication, the same switched telephone network can be used. The control of this environment becomes much more difficult though. The dial information has to be provided and the dialing must be performed under computer program control. This is called *Auto Dial*. During this process, problems can arise and they should be handled by the computer. For example, the called number can be out of order or can be disconnected by the administration because the subscriber did not pay the telephone bill, etc. In these cases, most of the telephone networks provide the caller with messages, which unfortunately for the computer are spoken. Consequently, the computer program will have difficulties analyzing the reason for the call set-up failure. Normally, the computer or terminal will re-try the call set-up a number of times, using the *same* telephone number. In the case of a wrong number, this could give repeated bad experiences to people answering a phone which was wrongly dialed by a computer! The computer program will stop after unsuccessful re-tries and notify an operator, who can take alternative action.

In short, a complete automatic solution for the use of public switched telephone facilities is difficult to implement. Certain PTTs therefore prohibit Auto Dial on their Public Switched Telephone Network.

An alternative solution is a procedure called *Hooky Dial*. It consists in having an operator call the other operator and when the connection exists, they both push a 'data button' on the modem and the data transmission can start. Obviously, this is a complex procedure which could require a sizable operator staff for reasonably large networks.

It is clear that data transmission and the telephone network are not the ideal combination for computer communications. On the other hand, *Teleprocessing*, as it is called, was booming at the end of the 1960s. This large market coupled with the technological advances pushed the PTTs towards considering the implementation of specific networks exclusively reserved for the transmission of data. This requirement was recognized and the CCITT started studying this type of network through their Study Group VII. The result was a series of recommendations on Public Data Networks (PDN).

12.2 The Recommendations

The CCITT (International Telegraph and Telephone Consultative Committee) issues recommendations with which its members agree to comply. CCITT members are nations, which very often delegate as representatives their PTT administrations. A Public Data Network (PDN) is a network established and operated by a Network Administration (PTT in Europe) for the specific purpose of providing data transmission services to the public. Because of this the CCITT concluded that:

> The establishment in various countries of Public Networks for data transmission creates a need to standardize user data signaling rates,

terminal operating modes, address selection and call progress signals to facilitate *international interworking*.

Data transmission over PDNs is the concern of the *X-series recommendations* [1, 2]. The discussion of the recommendations in this book is based on the 1980 level. A list of the recommendations defined in the November 1980 Plenary meeting of the CCITT is given in Appendix D.

The following sections describe some of the recommendations. We have selected those that are mostly encountered in the literature and discussions on computer networks. We start with the user service classes offered on the PDNs, Recommendation X.1. Next two recommendations describing the terminal interfaces to Public Data Networks are reviewed. One is concerned with the attachment of a DTE to a circuit-switching network, X.21, the other with the attachment of a DTE to a packet-switching network, namely, X.25. The attachment of asynchronous character-oriented terminals to a Public Packet Switched Network is very important and Recommendations X.3, X.28 and X.29 describe how this is done. Finally, the interconnection of networks is a crucial element in international communications. X.75 is the recommendation which describes the interconnection of packet-switched networks.

The reader should keep in mind that this chapter reviews the PDNs. As such, only a brief overview of the most important recommendations is given. The text is at the level of the definition of functions in order to review the place of PDNs in computer communication networks. If more detail is required, one should consult the appropriate chapters in this book, such as Chapter 3 on Recommendation X.21 and Chapter 5 on Recommendation X.25.

12.3 X.1 International User Classes of Service in PDNs

This recommendation specifies the different user classes in PDNs and their services offered. Table 12.1 gives the characteristics of the service classes.

As a terminal operating mode, we find the classical start–stop and synchronous terminals. Further, a new class of terminals appears, the packet-mode terminals. The interface of this new class of terminals is described in Section 12.5.3, which covers X.25.

Table 12.1 Classes of Service in Public Data Networks

Classes	Speed, bit/s	Terminal Operating Mode
1–2	50–200, 300	Start–stop
3–7	600/2400/4800 9600/48 000	Synchronous
8–11	2400/4800/9600 48 000	Packet

12.4 Recommendations X.21 and X.21bis

A detailed discussion of Recommendation X.21 can be found in Chapter 3.

The recommendation describes how a terminal should be implemented in order to communicate through an X.21 network. This network will mostly be based on digital technology. Modems, as we know them for analog services, are not needed any longer. Feedback about the progress in the call establishment will be provided by the network to the terminal or computer, where it can be analyzed and where appropriate action can be taken.

X.21bis describes a DTE–DCE interface that allows old-technology terminals, which have V.24 interfaces and modems, to work with an X.21 network (Fig. 12.1).

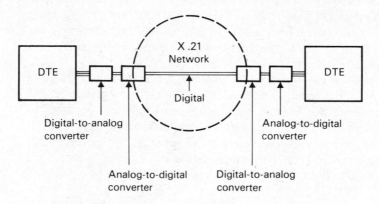

Fig. 12.1 X.21bis

12.4.1 Projected networks using X.21 and X.21bis

Table 12.2 lists a number of circuit-switched networks using X.21 and X.21bis which are operational or being planned for the 1980s. (The dates in the table were current at the end of January 1982.)

12.4.2 X.21 support in proprietary network architectures

Several manufacturers which offer computer networks also offer support for X.21-based circuit-switched networks.

This support includes both new hardware and software—new hardware because the attachment is now X.24 interchange circuitry (see Chapter 3) instead of the more complicated V.24. The software in the DTE has to control this new interface. These changes are not too extensive in the area

Table 12.2

Country	Year of installation	Network type
Austria	1982–1983	X.21
France	1980s	X.21 (Hermes)
West Germany	1981–1982	X.21 (Hfd)
	2nd half 1980 (operational)	X.21 (Datex-l)
Italy	1984–1985	X.21
Japan	1979 (operational)	X.21 (DDX)
Netherlands	1985	X.21
Nordic	2nd half 1981 (operational)	X.21/X.21bis
Switzerland	1985	X.21/X.21bis
UK	1982–1985	X.21/X.21bis (DDS)

of the leased-line support but become major in the switched-line support. The switched-line support impacts, for instance, the distributed network node management programming. An example is the analysis of the call progress signal feedback, which has to be processed in these programs.

It is to be noted that the X.21 circuit-switched networks are what we could call 'slow starters'. The basic reasons are the rapid evolution of communications technology and the relatively minor share of the data communications revenue in the total revenue of the PTTs. Big investments in X.21 networks become, therefore, a questionable undertaking. At the end of the 1970s, several PPTs decided to delay the implementations of their X.21 networks.

12.5 Recommendation X.25

A general overview of X.25 is given here. A more detailed discussion of the different levels can be found for the *Physical Level* in Chapter 3, the *Link Level* in Chapter 4 and the *Packet Level* in Chapter 5.

12.5.1 History of X.25

The *Public Packet Switched Network* (PPSN), as a proposal for a PDN, and Recommendation X.25 have not been under study for very long. The approval of the CCITT Plenary Meeting in 1976 came after a very short study period.

The history of X.25 starts in the fourth quarter of 1974, when Bell Canada announced its decision to install and offer the services of a data network using the packet-switching technique. This network was called *DATAPAC*. At the same time, they announced a *Standard Network Access Protocol* (SNAP) to provide the user with a standard access method to all the features of the DATAPAC network. This SNAP is the basis of Recommendation X.25.

Next, Bell Canada approached the European PTTs for the use of DATAPAC-like networks in Europe. France and the UK submitted an X.25 proposal to the CCITT during the fourth quarter of 1975. The proposal was the result of a joint study between DATAPAC, TELENET (USA) and TRANSPAC (France). The CCITT approved the proposal prepared by Study Group VII in the first quarter of 1976. During the third quarter of 1976, the Sixth Plenary Meeting of the CCITT approved X.25 as a recommendation. It is obvious that the time spent studying X.25 was much less than that for X.21, while Recommendation X.25 is at least an order of magnitude more complex. It contained a lot of interpretable points which are at the origin of significantly differing implementations of networks based on X.25 [3].

After 1976, Study Group VII of the CCITT kept working on the improvement of Recommendation X.25. By 1978, a Grey Book [4] had come out with provisional recommendations for X.25. It contained a new link-level procedure, called LAPB, which was added to the old LAP. The document described also the attachment of simple start–stop terminals to a X.25-based Public Packet Switched Network (PPSN). These recommendations are designated X.3, X.28 and X.29.

It was not the end of Study Group VII's work because it was at that time agreed that most of the 'lack of commonality' was concentrated in the Packet Level. In February 1980, an agreement was reached on a new completely revised recommendation, which came up for voting during the CCITT Plenary Meeting of November 1980. This new version does away with some of the incompleteness and unresolved issues.

By mid-1980, all the PTTs and PPSN operating carriers verbally agreed to align their existing networks, or the specifications of their planned networks, to the new revision. This will, of course, ease the task of DTE manufacturers since there will be a kind of consistent, universal or common X.25 DTE which would operate with the different networks.

Table 12.3 gives an overview of the changes that were studied and the suggestions that were made.

Why X.25 PDNs?

Most of the compatibility problems between the networks is due to the complexity of X.25-based networks. In fact, it complicates things for both the network administration and the DTE manufacturers. Why, then, X.25 over X.21, or, more precisely, why packet switching over circuit switching for common carrier transport services?

It is a fact that most of the European PTTs opted for the implementation of a data network that uses the packet-switching technique. Many of them plan also to have a circuit-switching data network. The technical reasons why the PTTs chose this type of network are not always clear. Increased reliability for the user and optimization of the communication resources of the PTTs are valid claims. A major consideration is the much lower

Table 12.3

1977	End-to-end diagnostic fields
1978	National Facility Marker
	Formatting extension policy
	New Call progress signals
1979	Incoming call time-out
	Diagnostic codes
	Diagnostic packet
	Delivery confirmation bit (D-bit)
	Packet and window size negotiation
	Throughput class negotiation
	Logical Channel assignment rules
	Byte-oriented data field
	Universal parameter defaults

investments that are required for a packet-switching network. However, circuit switching has definite advantages over packet switching and also offers more freedom to the DTE manufacturers.

In general, the advantages of packet switching over circuit switching are considered by the PTTs to be

a More effective use of the communications bandwidth of a physical connection through statistical multiplexing of the logical channels over that connection.

b Asymmetric connection. The network will do speed conversion. For example, one end will transmit at 48 000 bit/s, e.g. the CPU, while at the other end the data is transmitted, for example, to the terminal at 2400 bit/s.

c Wide range of transmission speeds. The bandwidth will be shared by different users, allowing the use of different speeds or throughputs depending on the user's requirements of the moment.

d Cost by volume, independent of distance.

e Very low connection set-up times (<1 s).

f Quality of service:
  i Low error rate. The undetected packet error rate is esimated at 10^{-12}, due to out-of-sequence packets, mutilated packets, etc.
  ii Increased availability through rerouting of the connection in the case of failure.

g Other facilities are code conversion and protection against unauthorized access.

Even when, technically speaking, most of the listed advantages can be reversed in favor of circuit switching, we should not forget that these PPSNs can be made successful. The PTTs are semi-government bodies and could easily outprice today's communications facilities in favor of a Public Packet Switched Network.

Some of the advantages just listed can be advanced in favor of circuit switching. For example, rerouting and code conversion are not part of the advantages of Recommendation X.25 because they are not a part of the recommendation. They are value-added services to the communication services, due to the technology used in this type of network.

Circuit switching has improved error rates. Digital techniques bring bit error rates down to 10^{-9}. The error rate mentioned as an advantage of packet switching is, in fact, an error rate for the transmission of packets through the network from DSE to DSE. The packet error rate is a measure of the undetected errors in the network because of packet mutilation, lost packets and packets out of sequence. The packets must then still be transmitted from the network to the DTE, for which, in the case of X.21bis, normal telephone lines are used. Automatic error recovery is featured because of the use of HDLC on the link level. So, in fact, the error rate will be the error rate of the weakest link, which, in the case of X.21bis, will be the telephone line or at best, where X.21 is used at the physical layer, it will be the error rate of the X.21 connection. So, for HDLC over a X.21 link, we have the same reliability of service as in the packet-switched case, but for an easier and less costly implementation of the DTE.

Shorter connection times could also be argued in favor of circuit switching. For a PPSN, they are in the order of 1.5 to 3 s. In a digital circuit-switched network, connection times are an order of magnitude smaller, 100–200 ms.

Cost by volume independent of the distance is not a packet-switching characteristic but a tariffing policy. The computation of the charges is easier since well-defined packets are transmitted and the network nodes can contain charge programs based on the number of packets and packet sizes. Digital technology that also uses computerized switching centers could also make charges distant-independent. The effort is, however, greater because bits have to be counted.

Why, then, packet switching? The prime reason for the preference of packet switching over circuit switching seems to be a commercial one. The requirements for data communication facilities are rising very fast. There are not enough analog telephone network based services. Digitization of the telephone network, the biggest source of revenue for the PTTs, is planned for the end of the 1980s. The X.25 packet-switching networks represent a solution to the shortage of the data communication facilities, because they allow the PTTs to optimize the use of their trunk lines, and their high-speed and high-quality facilities, through sharing amongst different customers. Also, the PTTs see a business opportunity in expanding their transport services with value-added services. Examples are Viewdata, electronic mail and others that are planned on top or around PPSNs.

12.5.2 What is a X.25 Packet Switched Network (PSN)?

An X.25 PPSN is a communication network offered by a PTT, where the user rents communication facilities which allow him to transmit data to remote locations.

Figure 12.2 shows a PSN. An example of a PTT PSN, or PPSN, is TRANSPAC in France, operational since the end of 1978. Another example is the Canadian DATAPAC network, operational since 1976. The PPSN consists, as the figure shows, of a series of computers, usually *minicomputers*, which are interconnected with each other. The user subscribes to the network administration for the use of X.25 communication facilities. Thus, his DTE will be physically attached, through a DCE, to the nearest *Data Switching Equipment* (DSE) in the PPSN using a *leased link*, X.21 or X.21bis. In the case of X.21bis, this connection will use base-band modems at the user's premises and at the network administration location. The user will request a specific line speed and a number of *Permanent Virtual Circuits* (PVCs) and *Virtual Calls* (VCs). He will also subscribe to a number of *operational facilities* on a DTE basis or on a per call basis. The subscription will also define the maximum user packet length and the window size.

On the outside, i.e. the DTE–DCE interface, the PPSN follows Recommendation X.25. The inside of the network, i.e. how it gets packets from one DSE to the other, is not described in the recommendation. Each implementation can have its own inner network, with its own flow control, transmission control, link controls and network management. The internal routing can be static, fixed alternate or dynamic. In the implementations, one talks of TELENET technology, DATAPAC technology, etc. Each of these technologies is based on specific communication processor nodes, for example TELENET's TP4000 network node. All these networks behave to

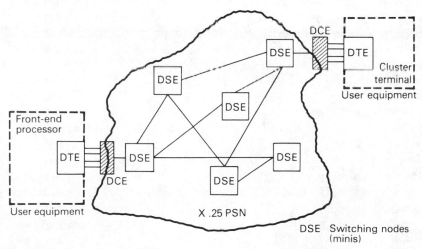

Fig. 12.2 Example of a PSN

the outside as X.25 networks and should therefore be interconnectable. A user of a US-based X.25 network could make a Virtual Call to a user connected to TRANSPAC in France, if both networks are interconnected, for example through X.75, and, of course, only if both networks use a common subset of X.25 protocols and facilities.

12.5.3 X.25 structure

Figure 12.3 illustrates how X.25 is structured. The following layers are defined:

Level 1: the Physical Level.
Level 2: the Link Level.
Level 3: the Packet Level.

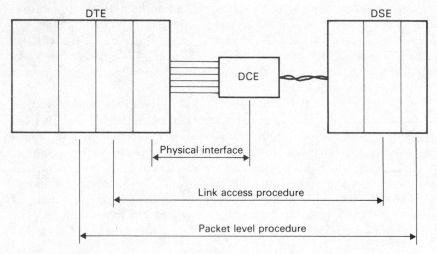

Fig. 12.3 X.25 structure

A more detailed discussion of the levels can be found in Chapters 3 through 5.

The Physical Level
The physical interface for the X.25 PSN is X.21. But because most of the countries will not have an X.21 network, a second standard was adopted: the X.21bis interface.

Figure 3.6 shows the X.21bis interface. It is a simplification of the V.24 interface. Only the leads necessary for leased-line point-to-point Full-Duplex are used. The PTTs will provide the customer with PTT modems to connect to the PSN.

The Link Level
The Link Level is the layer that is responsible for the transfer of data from

the DTE, e.g. a Communications Controller or another unit, to the DCE or vice versa.

Asynchronous Response Mode The CCITT decided to use the ISO HDLC standard (for more detail, see Chapter 4). In the 1976 Recommendation, there is only mention of the Asynchronous Response Mode of HDLC, called LAP (Link Access Procedure), which is depicted in Fig. 12.4. LAP never became an ISO standard.

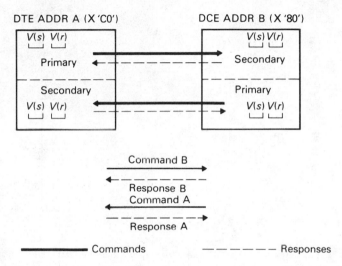

Fig. 12.4 HDLC Asynchronous Response Mode

Basically, both sides have to implement two stations: a secondary and a primary. The DTE will be primary for all the data that will be transmitted into the network, and the DCE will be primary for all the data coming from the network to the user. The CCITT included LAP originally in the recommendation based on the assumption that ISO would accept LAP as an HDLC mode of operation. This did not happen, however. The first PPSN implementations all have LAP at the Link Level. In 1977, CCITT [4] and ISO decided that the Asynchronous Balanced Mode of operation, called *LAPB*, would be the preferred one.

Asynchronous Balanced Mode LAPB is depicted in Fig. 12.5. It is compatible with the ISO balanced Class of Procedures, class BAC with options 2 and 8.
   The LAPB does not require two separate station implementations but only one combined station on each side of the link. Each station has one address and only one set of counters, a Receive counter and a Send counter (for details, see Chapter 4).

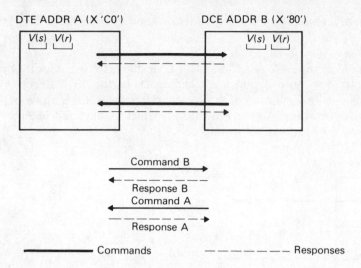

DTE ADDR A (X 'C0')   DCE ADDR B (X '80')

$V(s)$ $V(r)$ $V(s)$ $V(r)$

Command B

Response B
Command A

Response A

————————— Commands   — — — — — — Responses

Fig. 12.5 HDLC LAPB link configuration

The commands transmitted contain always the address of the remote station, and the responses transmitted carry the local address.

One of the advantages is that once communication has been established, anomalies between primary and secondary behavior will not occur since the stations are combined stations. Either station can establish communication but it will preferably be the DTE. Each station has recovery responsibilities. This LAPB is also known as the *Asymmetric* LAPB version. It simplifies considerably the implementation of DTEs.

There also exists a *Symmetric version* which allows all commands to be sent to the DTE by the DCE. The important advantage, then, is the possibility to back-up the X.25 PDN with a leased line. For example, the West German PTT will use the symmetric LAPB for its X.25 network.

LAPB is now the preferred mode of operation and will be available in all networks.

The Packet Level

For a detailed discussion, see Chapter 5.

The basic services offered at the X.25 Packet Level interface are *Virtual Call* (VC) and *Permanent Virtual Circuit* (PVC). A VC is a switched Virtual Circuit service that needs to be set up (Fig. 12.6). A PVC is a permanent association between two DTEs. On both the PVC and the VC, packets are delivered in the same sequence as they were submitted to the network.

The Packet Level allows the multiplexing of VCs and PVCs over one physical connection between a DTE and DCE. The multiplexing is done through Logical Channels in the DTE. There are 16 groups of 256 Logical Channels giving a maximum of 4095 communications with other DTEs.

There are two packet types defined, Data packets and Control packets. Control packets are used for establishing and terminating VCs, for data flow control, for the resetting of connections, etc.

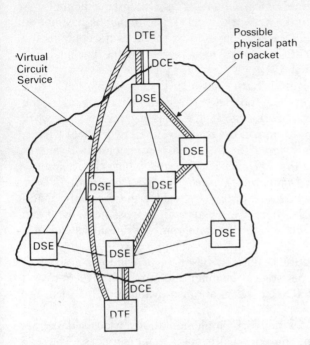

Fig. 12.6 A Virtual Circuit service

The recommendation contains a series of procedures. There is a procedure for call set-up and termination. Data flow control between DTE–DCE and interrupt procedures are defined. Also, feedback on the behavior of the network during call set-up or data transfer is described.

Most of the procedures have only local significance. An exception is the D-bit, Delivery confirmation bit, procedure. When the D-bit is set in the Packet Header, an end-to-end or DTE-to-DTE significance is given to some of the control information in the Packet Header.

Flow control is based on a windowing scheme which allows data to be sent between DTE and DCE, or vice versa, for as long as the window allows it. A window is reset by acknowledgment control information in the Packet Header of a received packet.

A series of optional facilities are defined. They can be taken at subscription time or at call set-up time.

Datagram   Datagram services [1, 5] are also a part of Recommendation X.25. These services do not have a preferred status, i.e. certain networks can have a Datagram service but such services will not be internationally available.

The Datagram service consists of an exchange of *Datagram packets* between the DTE and the DCE over a Logical Channel. A user can subscribe to one or more Logical Channels as Datagram channels. A Datagram packet sent into the network by a DTE contains the destination DTE address. A Datagram packet delivered by the network contains the address of the source DTE. The user data carried in the packet has a maximum length of 128 bytes.

Datagrams will be delivered by the network to the destination with a high probability of success but no delivery guarantee is given. If the network loses a packet, or rejects it for reasons such as network congestion, it will attempt to inform the source. The network uses what is called a *Datagram Service Signal* for this. The recommendation defines three specific signals. The first is *Datagram Rejected*, which carries a sense code. The other two are *Datagram Non-delivery* and *Datagram Delivery Confirmation*, facilities which are optional. Besides these specific Datagram packet related signals, there are signals with more general meaning. They carry information relative to the Datagram operation instead of a particular Datagram packet.

A flow control procedure is defined based on a windowing scheme. There is a flow control per logical channel and for each direction in a logical channel. RR and RNR packets are also available to assist in the flow control.

Internally the first X.25 network implementations used a datagram technique instead of one based on Virtual Circuit services. They all changed to Virtual Circuit services because of the lesser overhead, 3 bytes versus 16 bytes for the Datagram Header, which allows, for example, better line utilization. The Datagram services were reviewed in the 1980 revision of X.25 but are not contained in the preferred set of services.

12.5.4 Alternatives to X.25?

Louis Pouzin argues [6] that X.25 is not necessarily the right solution.

When one looks at a simple DTE, it is obvious that the X.25 interface is too complex. An example of a simple DTE is a teletypewriter. In order to cope with these complexities, a supplementary box is needed, called a PAD (Packet Assembler and Disassembler). In fact, even for more complex DTEs, such as one that uses multiple virtual circuits, there is no real justification for X.25. Figure 12.7 shows the duplicated basic functions of the different layers as defined by X.25. It is obvious that all of the Level 3 functions are already represented in the recommendations for Levels 1 and 2.

	X.21 Level 1	HDLC Level 2	Packet Level 3
Connection set-up	X		X
Data Transfer set-up		X	X
Error Control		X	X
Flow Control		X	X
Connection Clearing	X		X

Fig. 12.7 Functions of X.25 layers

One could, because of this overlap, very well consider using a simpler solution. It is conceivable, for instance, to use only HDLC with some additions in order to perform some of the control protocols of the X.25 Packet Level (Fig. 12.8). The addressing scheme of HDLC leaves 255

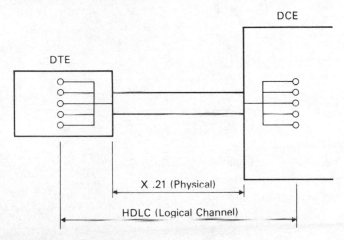

Fig. 12.8 Alternative solution

distinct addresses which could represent up to 127 Logical Circuits. The concept of a Data Link in HDLC is defined logically as a set of one Primary and one or several Secondaries.

Of course, some of the Packet Level protocols have to be defined so that the connection or the clearing of a logical connection can be done. For this, the HDLC Unnumbered Information frame could be used, carrying the required information. The Data Transfer Phase itself would use straight HDLC.

This interface is also called *Frame Mode DTE*. Some contributions on it have been made to the CCITT, but it does not seem that it will become a recommendation.

12.5.5 X.25 support in proprietary networks

Most proprietary computer communication networks are based on architectures with the same layered structure as the Reference Model. Examples are DEC's DNA, Univac's DCA, IBM's SNA, etc. Theoretically, it would be appropriate to replace the layers corresponding to the three X.25 layers with the X.25 levels in these network implementations, i.e. in the units which constitute the DTEs connected to the PPSN.

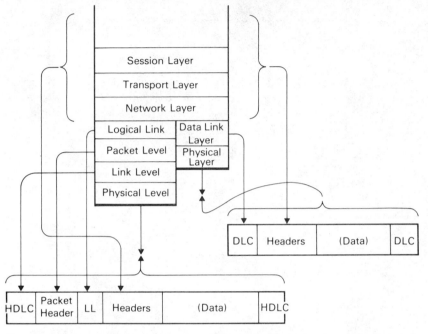

Fig. 12.9 X.25 support in proprietary networks: physical link replacement

However, this assumes that all X.25-based networks would show the same DTE–DCE interface. Brethes et al. [3] show that this is not the case. Network administration and PTTs, in an effort to rectify the situation, decided that from 1982 all networks would be aligned on the latest recommendation [7, 8].

However, the replacement of layers alone does not solve completely all the problems. For instance, a major problem is the support of X.25 connectivity with, as prime element, the addressability of the total network. Before the introduction of PPSN, the connections within a commercial network were based on links from circuit-switched networks. Most of these links used to be leased. X.25 transport services, certainly when they go international, favor switched support (VCs). Depending on who provides the network address resolution and the switched-network telephone numbers, the integration of X.25 PPSNs into the commercial networks will not be trivial. It could mean more complex higher-level transport protocols in the minor nodes, such as terminals or terminal clusters.

Corr and Neal [9] describe a series of approaches that can be taken for X.25 support integration. Their conclusion, at that time, was to replace a physical link with a PVC or VC for connections between DTEs belonging to the same network architecture implementation—in their example IBM's

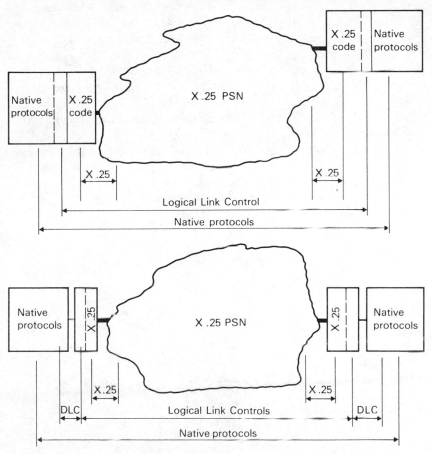

Fig. 12.10 X.25 support in proprietary networks: the Black Box approach

SNA. They suggest that the data-link control used with physical links is partly kept for end-to-end control over the Virtual Circuit service: not all protocols of data-link control, of course, but only those that are concerned with error detection, the essence of end-to-end control. For further discussion on this topic, refer to Chapter 13.

Replacing a physical link with a virtual link and keeping data-link control mean a minimal impact in the DTE implementations of proprietary networks. The three X.25 levels replace the original Physical Layer.

Data-link control is modified and all other layers of the native architecture stay intact. There is also a disadvantage.

Figure 12.9 shows the accumulation of layers, which means more control added to the data to be transmitted. Apparently, this solution is not the most efficient and carries more control information than it already does for the native network.

Alternatively, the X.25 support can be put in a *Black Box* which looks like an X.25 DTE on one side and a native network link station on the other (Fig. 12.10). This solution is expensive and has performance problems because of extra transfers between the Black Box and the native network node.

Another drawback of the link-level support with end-to-end control through native Data Link Level protocols is the required homogeneity of this solution. Basically, all nodes in the network have to implement that same protocol, which normally means using equipment from the same manufacturer.

The discussions in Chapter 13 inspire another solution, which is illustrated in Figure 12.11. All participating networks, not necessarily with all levels and functions, are put in cascade with a wrapping layer around them to ensure end-to-end control for data integrity and recovery.

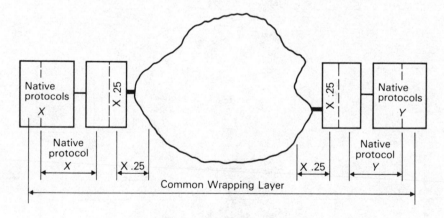

Fig. 12.11 X.25 support in proprietary networks: serialization

The best solution, though, is to replace equivalent functional layers in the native network with, for example, an implementation of the 'common DTE'. Here, 1982 is the crucial date, since that is the date that the PTTs will align their networks and from that point in time a common DTE can be implemented. Manufacturers will then have the necessary economic justification for the implementation of an X.25 DTE that will attach to most of the X.25-based PPSN network implementations. This at least for the basic services and the optional facilities described in Recommendation X.2.

12.5.6 Planned X.25 networks in Europe

Table 12.4 gives a number of operational or planned PSNs based on X.25. Most of them are PTT-owned and some are international. (The table represents the situation at the end of February 1982.)

Table 12.4

Country (network)	Date	Type
Canada (DATAPAC)	6/1977	X.25–X.21bis
US (TELENET)	9/1979	X.25–X.21bis
France (TRANSPAC)	12/1978	X.25–X.21bis
Japan (DDX)	6/1979	X.25–X.21bis
EEG (EURONET)	1979	
West Germany (DATEX-P)	1981	
UK (NPSS)	1980	
Netherlands (Datanet 1)	1981	
Belgium	2nd half 1982	
Israel	1982–1983	
Italy (NRD-P)	1982–1984	
Luxembourg	1982	
Nordic	1983	
South Africa	1982	
Spain (RETD)*	1982	
Switzerland	1982	

* Spain has had a packet-switched network since 1976. This network does not contain X.25 interface support.

12.5.7 Tariffing of X.25 PDN

The structure of X.25 tariffs has three basic parts. First, the tariffs tend to be distance-independent in most countries. Secondly, all of them are volume dependent and thirdly, there are charges for the attachment to the network, the services and the optional facilities. Figure 12.12 shows this basic structure.

When one attaches to an X.25 PDN, there is first of all a one-time attachment charge. It covers the cost of physically connecting the DTE to the network. The monthly charges are composed of the elements shown in the figure. First, there is the attachment charge which is a function of the speed of the connection. Also included are modem and line costs. Optional facilities defined on a DTE basis are also a part of this monthly attachment charge.

Charges for usage of the Virtual Circuit services are the second part. There is a monthly usage charge per PVC. For a VC, the charge is computed as a function of the duration of the connection with, very often, a fixed minimum charge. Optional facilities requested for a PVC or the use of optional facilities at the moment of call establishment are added to the monthly bill.

The last part is the volume-dependent cost. It is computed as a function of the number of 64-octet or byte segments that are sent. Depending on the

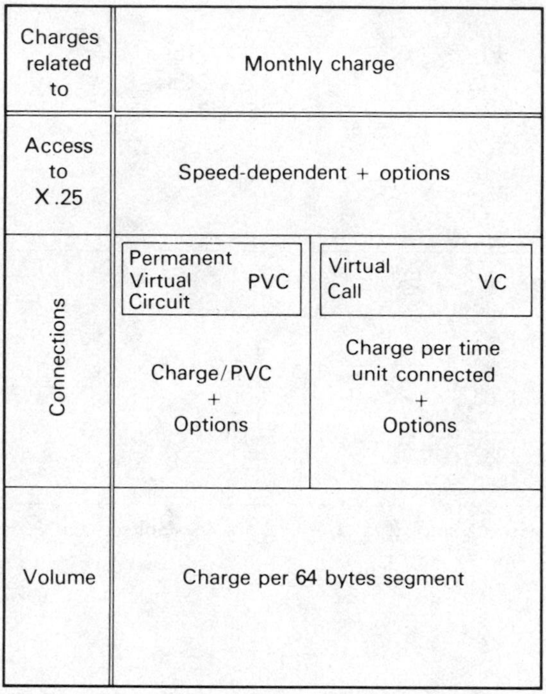

Charges related to	Monthly charge	
Access to X.25	Speed-dependent + options	
Connections	Permanent Virtual Circuit PVC Charge/PVC + Options	Virtual Call VC Charge per time unit connected + Options
Volume	Charge per 64 bytes segment	

Fig. 12.12 PDN X.25 tariff structure

network, the segment-cost will vary with the time of day. Overnight transmissions will be less expensive than daytime ones.

X.25 Virtual Circuit services can globally be less expensive than the use of leased lines or the switched telephone network. However, for certain networks, the tariffs are more advantageous for low-load connections, for example, 10 to 30 per cent load of an equivalent leased-line connection. A network administration can change such a pattern by changing the cost per segment or the connection charges. In the beginning, low-load situations seemed to be favored, which can be explained by the lack of experience of the administrations with computer-communication based networks of the X.25 type.

A potential user should analyze the X.25 connection by looking at the distance between DTEs and the traffic. That, together with the possible cost of the manufacturer's attachments, will show if it is economically justified to replace leased lines with X.25 Virtual Circuit services.

12.5.8 Common or universal DTE

Brethes et al. [3] give the situation at the beginning of 1979 of the implementation of Recommendation X.25. They showed that the four existing networks, TELENET (US), TRANSPAC (France), DDX (Japan) and DATAPAC (Canada) were practically incompatible with each other. The only common service available in the four networks was a Permanent Virtual Circuit carrying packets 128 bytes long. Since PVC is not going to be an international service, there would be no possibility of connecting two DTEs belonging to different networks. For manufacturers of DTEs, this is a serious problem because of the requirement of different DTE implementations for each specific network implementation.

As we have seen already, more work had to be done by the CCITT. It resulted in the new recommendations voted in November 1980. Commitments were given by the PTTs that the networks would comply with these new recommendations by 1982.

In the literature [7, 8, 10], we find an answer to Brethes et al., in view of the updated recommendations. At the same time, attempts are being made to define a *common* or *universal DTE*. The common DTE would allow DTE implementations to work with most of the networks.

Knightson [8] defines the conditions for the universality of the implementations, i.e. definition of universally available defaults and upgrading of facilities in the past and the future. The default values for the DTE parameters should be applied and all precautions should be taken in the DTE implementation not to prevent the future upgrading of the network facilities. Knightson and also Rybczynski et al. [7] define a *simple* and a *sophisticated* DTE. A simple DTE supports only one VC for instance, and should only implement default values. Also, requests for optional facilities, for example in Call packets, should be accepted but ignored so that no error conditions will be generated. The DTE on the other side should carefully reset all optional facilities requests to defaults, because the DCE will always analyze all possible control information. The sophisticated DTE should try to take advantage of the full range of options provided. Again, care should be taken to allow future upgrades of the networks, i.e. imply no dependencies on fields in packet headers or control packets that are momentarily not used.

The common DTE concept defines universal options on all three levels. The number of options increases as one climbs up the different levels. The

Physical Level is rather straightforward with the Link Level only having a few options. It is the Packet Level where the complexity starts, because of the different procedures and options.

Physical Level

The DTE should be engineered as a function of the DTE's performance requirements, for example, response time and number of packets transmitted. The only variable here is the speed of the physical connection. This requirement is local to the connection. Most PDNs will offer data access rates of 2.4, 4.8 and 9.6 kbit/s.

Link Level

The Link Level implements HDLC. The use of LAPB is suggested because this mode of operation is approved by both the CCITT and the ISO. An option could be the implementation of the *symmetric version* of LAPB. This would allow a compatibility between DTE–DCE and DTE–DTE operation. The symmetric version will automatically include support for the asymmetric version. Timer values for time-outs, re-try counts and maximum number of unacknowledged frames should be set to universal default values.

Packet Level

Simple DTE   As said before, default parameters should be used and no error conditions generated if DTE non-supported optional facilities are requested. Also, the use of Logical Channel 1 is mandatory. DTE-produced packets should only contain network-supported functions because of detailed DCE error analysis. After the clearing of a VC by the network, a simple DTE may not try to re-establish the VC.

Sophisticated DTE   The sophisticated DTE should support as large a subset as possible and required. The negotiation of facilities should be supported. It should be kept in mind that negotiations are local to the DTE–DCE and that on the other side the negotiation could be different.

Packets should be transmitted in sequence in the network and retransmission should not occur. The DTE should return the $P(r)$ as fast as possible or, if it wants to control the flow of packets from the remote DTE, it should do it as soon as possible in an RNR packet. The data should be a multiple of 8 bits.

The packet-level error handling should be consistent with the level of sophistication. A sophisticated DTE could attempt to re-establish a cleared VC. Error information should be logged and analysed afterwards.

Elements of a common DTE   The essential features of the common or universal DTE are

- X.21bis on the Physical Level
- HDLC LAPB symmetrical on the Link Level
- On the Packet Level:
  - Permanent Virtual Circuit
  - Virtual Call
  - *D*-bit
  - *M*-bit
  - *Q*-bit
  - Window size = 2
  - Maximum data packet size = 128
  - Standard logical channel assignment rules.

The essential facilities in Recommendation X.2 should also be available [11]. Table 12.5 shows these facilities. Default values should be specified for these facilities. The parameter negotiations should start from, or attempt to get to, the default values.

Table 12.5

Facility	Description
Closed User Group (CUG)	Used to restrict operation of a DTE within a group of other DTEs. A DTE can be a member of multiple CUGs
Flow Control Parameter Negotiation	Selection of window sizes and packet sizes. Values can be negotiated by DTE or DCE
Throughput Class Negotiation	Throughput class can be negotiated by DTE and DCE
Incoming calls barred	DTE cannot accept incoming calls
Outgoing calls barred	DTE cannot make outgoing calls
One-way LGN outgoing	Logical Channel is only used for Call-out

12.5.9 Recommendations X.3, X.28 and X.29 or the 'PAD'

CCITT Recommendations X.3, X.28 and X.29 [1] define the necessary interface and protocols for the support of non-intelligent asynchronous start–stop terminals (Fig. 12.13).

In order to access a Packet-mode terminal from a character oriented terminal, and vice versa, some supplementary functions should be executed elsewhere. For example, the character stream from the terminal should be assembled in packets and packets should be disassembled in a character stream. In other words, a converter or Protocol Mapper is needed. Recommendation X.3, *Packet Assembler/Dissassembler* (PAD) facility in a PDN, describes such a mapper. The recommendation suggests that the mapping is done in software located in the DCE of the packet-switched network. Recommendation X.28 defines the interface between a Character-mode terminal and a DCE containing the PAD. These two recommendations allow the exchange of data between the terminal and the PAD. Seen from the packet-switched network point of view, the PAD is, in fact, another Packet-mode terminal or behaves like it at least. Both are involved in a peer-to-peer communication through the PSN. Recommendation X.29 describes protocols which allow the setting of parameters in the PAD from a Packet-mode DTE.

In the following discussion, we will call the Character mode terminal, C-DTE, and the Packet-mode DTE, P-DTE.

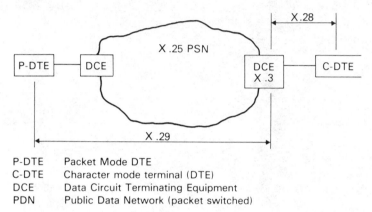

P-DTE   Packet Mode DTE
C-DTE   Character mode terminal (DTE)
DCE   Data Circuit Terminating Equipment
PDN   Public Data Network (packet switched)

Fig. 12.13 X.3, X.28 and X.29

Recommendation X.3—the PAD

The PAD is a protocol converter between the packet-switching network and an asynchronous terminal. The PAD will assemble characters from the C-DTE in packets and transmit them to the P-DTE. Similarly, it will receive packets from the P-DTE and transmit characters to or execute functions on the C-DTE. It will perform all X.25 protocols, such as Call establishment, Call clearing, and, for example, flow control with the P-DTE. The PAD on the other side also acts as a driver for the C-DTE and performs a number of functions, based on control characters and, for example, the BREAK signal.

Recommendation X.3 defines a series of parameters which allow the selection of functions offered by the PAD. These functions are concerned with procedure management between PAD and C-DTE, the assembly and disassembly of packets, and some operational characteristics of the start–stop terminal.

Some of the parameters are listed below:

Escape from data transfer
Echo
Recognition of data forwarding signal
Selection of idle timer delay
Ancillary device control (e.g. flow control between PAD and C-DTE)
Suppression of PAD service signals
PAD procedure when receiving a BREAK signal
Discard output
Padding after Carriage Return
Line folding
Terminal speed
Flow control of the PAD by the terminal
Line-feed insertion
Line-feed padding

Recommendation X.28

Recommendation X.28 describes the interface between the C-DTE and the PAD, the data exchange and the control exchanges between them. The physical attachment can be achieved in four ways:

a Access via public switched telephone network or leased lines with V-series interfaces (Recommendation V.21).
b Access via public switched data network or leased lines with X-series interfaces (Recommendation X.20).
c Access via telephone-type network (Recommendation X.20bis).
d Access via the TELEX network.

The procedures for service initialization and character exchange define the way the terminal will be controlled by the PAD. The control characters used have to be in accordance with International Alphabet No. 5 and Recommendation X.4.

There are two phases: the *control phase* and the *data transfer phase*. Control procedures for establishing and terminating the PAD to C-DTE connection are defined. During the control phase, the PAD does not send the control data it exchanges with the C-DTE to the P-DTE. A series of terminal control commands are defined which should be recognized and processed in the start–stop terminal or C-DTE.

Some of the commands available to a user are given below. These commands allow, for example, a VC to be set up and to be reset or cleared when it is no longer needed. In addition, the X.3 parameters can be examined (read) and changed (set). In most cases, the only command initiated by the C-DTE is the command for call set-up. After that, the P-DTE controls the X.3 parameters via X.29 and determines when the call is cleared. The commands are

Call Request
Profile Selection (sets of PAD parameters)

Reset
Interrupt
· Interrupt and Discard Data
Call Status Request
Read PAD Parameters
Set PAD Parameters
Set and Read PAD Parameters
Clear Request

Whenever a command is sent from the terminal to the PAD, the PAD returns a response in the form of a service signal. An example of a response is 'Call Successfully Set Up (COM)'. If the call is not set up or prematurely cleared, the PAD outputs a 'Clearing Service Signal (CLR)' with the reason for the clear—such as X.25 DTE busy, X.25 DTE not operating, wrong address or Closed User Group violation. Some examples of X.28 PAD Service Signals are

Command Acknowledgement
Indication of Call Connected (COM)
Error
Reset and reason why
Call Status
Clear and reason why

Recommendation X.28 describes the procedures between the PAD and the terminal. The PAD will be responsible for the Call set-up with the remote X.25 DTE (P-DTE). Once the VC is active, the P-DTE will exchange control information with the PAD. This exchange of control information is described in Recommendation X.29.

Recommendation X.29

The exchange of control information, or *PAD messages*, between the P-DTE and the PAD is done through the User Data Field in the Data Packets. The distinction between real user data and that control information is indicated through the setting of the *Qualifier-bit* (*Q*-bit) in the Data Packet Header. Control information will have the *Q*-bit set to *one* and user data will have the *Q*-bit set to *zero*.

The procedures for PAD messages include, for example, the reading and setting of PAD parameters, by the P-DTE, inviting the PAD to clear the connection, interrupt procedures, resets and error handling.

With the use of X.29, we have not really introduced another protocol level into the hierarchy. Just as packets were embedded in the Information Field of Information frames, X.29 is embedded in the Data Field of Data Packets. When an X.25 DTE sends a Data Packet, it must indicate whether the data is to be interpreted by the PAD or sent directly to the terminal. As mentioned earlier, the indication is the *Q*-bit. The user data should also contain start–stop terminal-oriented data, i.e. control characters, in order to control the I/O operations of the terminal.

12.6 Recommendation X.75

International X.25 services require the interconnection of adjacent X.25 networks. This interconnection concatenates two national Virtual Circuit services into one while maintaining the X.25 characteristics that the DTEs experience on the national networks.

The CCITT decided to use at the base the X.25 protocols and improve them according to the network interconnection requirements. As in Recommendation X.25, Recommendation X.75 contains three levels, the Physical Level, the Link Level and the Packet Level.

The Physical Level accommodates higher-speed links than that in the case of Recommendation X.25.

The Link Level is LAPB with an extension of the numbering scheme to modulo 128. This allows the use of high propagation delay links, such as satellite links. Also, a *multi-link* protocol is defined which allows higher reliability of the inter-network links. This is important since all Virtual Calls are multiplexed over that interconnection and when it breaks, all Virtual Calls will be broken.

The Packet Level differs in two ways. First, only Virtual Calls are supported, no PVCs. Secondly, the call set-up packets contain an extra utility field with inter-network Virtual Call parameter information. Clearing and reset causes or diagnostics are transparently passed from network to network.

The interconnection is also called an X.75 gateway.

12.7 Summary

Public Data Networks, X.21 or X.25 based, have been or are being implemented or planned in several countries around the world. Circuit-switched networks are few because of the considerable financial investments that are required. As digitization of the telephone network progresses, the PDNs will be re-integrated with the voice services. The PDN-interfaces are expected to be available on these new Integrated Services Data Networks (ISDNs). Public Data Networks, as described in this chapter, will satisfy the fast-growing demand for communication services with the implementations available in the first half of the 1980s.

References

1 CCITT, *Data communication networks. Services and facilities. Terminal equipment and interfaces. Recommendations X.1–X.29*, Yellow Book, Vol VII—Facicle VIII.2, CCITT VIIth Plenary Assembly, Geneva, 10–21 Nov. 1980, ITU, Geneva, 1981

2 CCITT, *Data communication networks. Transmission, signalling . . . Recommendations X.40–X.180*, Yellow Book, Vol. VII—Facicle VIII.3, CCITT VIIth Plenary Assembly, Geneva, 10–21 Nov. 1980, ITU, Geneva, 1981

3 Brethes, M., Hess, M. and Saito, A., A comparison of four X.25 Public Network interfaces, *ICC '79 Boston Conference Record*, vol. 3, pp. 38.6.1–8

4 CCITT, *Provisional Recommendations X.25, X.3, X.28 and X.29*, Grey Book, ITU, Geneva, 1978

5 Folts, H. C., X.25 transaction-oriented features—Datagram and Fast Select, *IEEE Trans. Commun.*, vol. Com-28, no. 4, Apr. 1980, pp. 496–500

6 Pouzin, L., *A restructuring of X.25 in HDLC*, IRIA Report, TRA 526.2, Dec. 1976

7 Rybczynski, A. M. and Palframan, J. D., A common X.25 interface, *Computer Networks*, vol. 4, no. 3, 1980, pp. 97–110

8 Knightson, K. G., A universal X.25 interface, *Data Networks: developments and uses*, Online 80 Conference, London, June 1980, pp. 405–417

9 Corr, F. P. and Neal, D. H., SNA and emerging international standards, *IBM Syst. J.*, vol. 18, no. 2, 1979, pp. 244–262

10 Drukarch, C. Z., Karp, P. M., Knightson, K. G., Lavandera, L., Rybczynski, A. M. and Sone, N., X.25: the universal packet network, *Proc. 5th Int. Conf. Computer Commun.*, Atlanta, 27–30 Oct. 1980, pp. 649–657

11 CCITT, *COM VII No. 414-E revised, proposed revisions on X.2*, ITU, Geneva, Feb. 1980

13 Proprietary architectures and X.25

13.1 Introduction

Public Data Networks and networks based on architectures defined by computer manufacturers (the proprietary networks) have something in common, but they also have their differences. As a general observation, we could say that Public Data Networks transport data on behalf of their users, whereas proprietary networks not only transport the data but also have to support meaningful communication. Public networks use only the lower layers of the Reference Model. Proprietary architectures, on the other hand, usually cover all layers.

In such an environment, interconnection is not a trivial task. Gien and Zimmermann [1] have discussed this problem and classified the various aspects of interconnection. When two or more layers of a certain architecture are replaced by another architecture with slightly different interfaces (and/or services), it is necessary to augment the new architecture to bridge the gap between the expected and the offered service. This can also happen in a negative sense, when the new service is richer than the old one. In that situation, services of the new architecture cannot be used in that environment.

If the differences are many, it is also possible, instead of replacing the layers, to cascade (part of) one architecture with the other architecture. For this cascading, a 'gateway' is used, a mapping machine which moves data from one architectural environment into another while making the necessary conversions in protocols, etc. The gap between the two architectures can then be bridged at a level where they offer equivalent service.

Where the aim of the Reference Model is to make network interconnection easier, we will study in this chapter whether that is indeed the case. In a research environment, several interconnections have successfully been made. As a matter of fact, many ideas behind the Reference Model come from this environment. Not much experience is available, however, in the direct interconnection of two different proprietary architectures.

Interconnections that have been made and that do involve proprietary architectures, usually involve also a Public Data Network. As we discussed in our description of the individual architectures, several of them can attach to a public network. A closer look reveals, however, that in many cases the interconnection is made in a special way: the X.25 Virtual Circuit is used as a physical-connection. Because of this, no use is made of the Network Layer (the X.25 Packet Level) functions in the context of the proprietary architecture.

In the remainder of this chapter we describe first in more detail how such usage of the Virtual Circuit is made in the case of SNA. Our reason for discussing this in more detail is that the ideas are used in an example of interconnection that we want to describe next. In that case, a network in West Germany, various data processing centers, each with their own systems and networks of different architectures, are interconnected via a private X.25 PSN.

We discuss the overall network definition and how one particular proprietary architecture, in this case SNA, is connected to that network.

13.2 SNA and X.25

In Chapter 7, Systems Network Architecture was discussed, and in Chapter 5, the CCITT Recommendation X.25. With respect to X.25, it must be emphasized that the highest level in X.25, Level 3, which is the equivalent of the Network Layer in the Reference Model, has node-to-node significance only: it applies to the DTE–DCE interface, the interface of the X.25 network with its attached users, even though some implementations of X.25 do attach end-to-end significance to some of the X.25 Level 3 protocols.

13.2.1 X.25 as a data link in an SNA network

The use of X.25 as a transport mechanism in an SNA network has been described in detail in [2, 3, 4]. In the first paper, an overview is also given of the design options available for the interconnection, and the reason why the Link Level connection was chosen.

In summary, the options were:

a Complete protocol insulation, which means that each SNA frame, including the headers for all layers, is treated as data in the X.25 sense and thus included in the data portion of the X.25 packet. This leads to a significant overhead in terms of the headers (duplication). This approach would also result in SDLC polling to go across the Public Network, thus causing the generation of an excessive number of X.25 packets without useful data.

b Link Level mapping, which means that an X.25 Virtual Circuit is handled by SNA as if it were a physical (real) circuit.

c Session Level mapping, which means that the (SNA) session-connections are replaced by X.25 Virtual Circuits. This approach has the advantage of a lower overhead due to the duplication of function, but it can only be done if the X.25 Virtual Circuit provides the same level of end-to-end service as the SNA session (refer to Section 7.9.4, the Transport Layer).

The option chosen by IBM (and others as well, e.g. Section 10.3.1) is the second one, mapping to the Link Level. This approach solves also the additional problem, that there are implementation differences between the various Public Networks. Such differences can be taken care of more easily in the Link Level than at the level of individual sessions (proliferation).

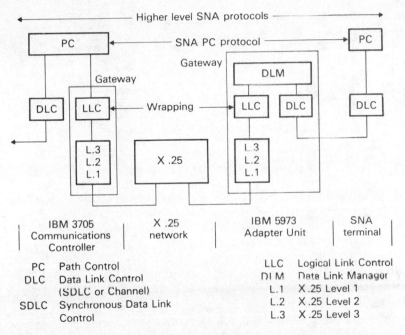

Fig. 13.1 Use of X.25 in an SNA environment

The X.25 Virtual Circuit is given the appearance of a single data link with end-to-end control. To achieve this, a wrapping technique [1] is used, giving the additional function to the wrapped network. The wrapping is done in a special layer, called *Logical Link Control*. The two gateways involved (one in the IBM 3705 Communications Controller and the other at the other side of the 'link' in the IBM 5973 Network Interface Adapter Unit) contain this wrapping function (Fig. 13.1). As discussed in [2] other solutions were less attractive, basically because Level 3 in X.25 and the SNA Path Control Layer do not map one to one.

Since the total Data Link Control function is replaced by the (wrapped) X.25 Virtual Circuit, there is no end-to-end polling across the X.25 network, as was suggested elsewhere [5]. Polling for the attached SNA terminal is performed in the remote gateway (the IBM 5973 unit).

13.2.2 SNA interconnection with X.25 native equipment

An extension of the X.25 support in an SNA network allows a non-SNA terminal (Fig. 13.2), which is native to the X.25 network (i.e. not through the PAD) to communicate with an SNA host [3]. This support is called Protocol Converter for Non-SNA Equipment in [3] and hereafter will be called *Protocol Mapper*.

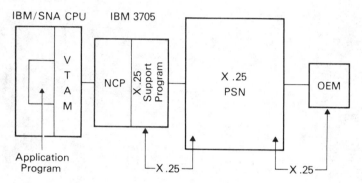

Fig. 13.2 Protocol Mapper for X.25 PSN natively attached terminals: (OEM = other equipment manufacturer—in this case, non-IBM equipment)

The necessary end-user commands and messages are transparently transmitted through the SNA layers to the terminal. It is the responsibility of the application program to perform the controls and the data stream mapping required by the native X.25 terminal. The X.25 support extension relates all message or command exchanges to a simulated SNA Physical Unit/Logical Unit–Application represented in Fig. 13.3 by the heavy-lined box called Protocol Mapper.

The simulated SNA Physical Unit (PU) is a PU type 1 (see Section 7.2.1). The mapping of the protocols of one network (SNA) into protocols of the X.25 network is performed in the simulated LU–Application.

Protocol Mapper: an overview

The Protocol Mapper allows communication between an Application using an SNA access method, such as VTAM, and X.25 native equipment such as terminals, clusters and hosts or X.25 Network Services. SNA protocols are converted into X.25 protocols and vice versa.

The conversion is made between

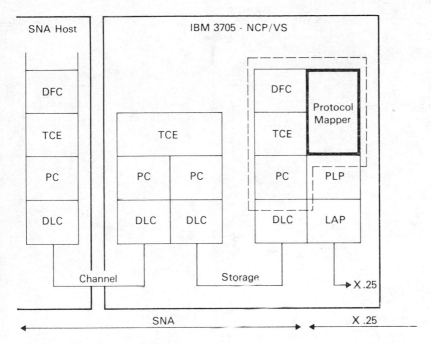

Fig. 13.3 Protocol Mapper

a The Packet Header of some X.25 control packets and the Transmission
Header (TH)/Request Header (RH) of the SNA Path Information Unit
(PIU).
b Commands of various layers.

The data contained within the SNA Request Unit (RU) or in the X.25 data
packets is not processed by the Protocol Mapper but transferred without
conversion.

The handling of the SNA headers by the Protocol Mapper is like the
IBM 3767 secondary LU. Only one LU can be associated with one PU,
which means that on the X.25 side only one PU–LU combination can be
associated with an X.25 Virtual Call.

13.2.3 Mapped functions and protocols

Below is a list of the different functions and protocols that the Protocol
Mapper maps from SNA to X.25 and vice versa.

- Address mapping: one LU–PU pair is mapped onto one X.25 Virtual
  Call

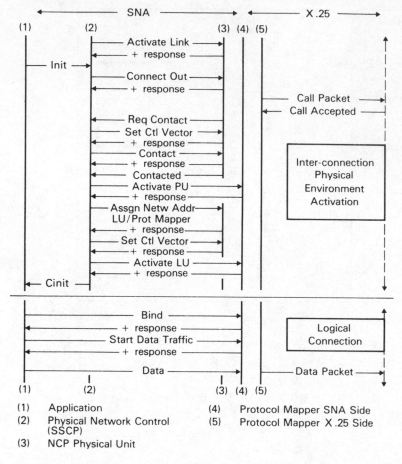

Fig. 13.4 Physical environment initialization (1)

- Data transfer protocols:
  - The SNA session uses the HDX Contention Mode for data transfer and it is mapped into a FDX Virtual Circuit.
  - Outboard RUs, i.e. data transmitted into the X.25 network, are converted into independent X.25 packets. Any SNA protocols for the logical chaining of successive RUs are ignored.
  - Inboard Packets with the More-data bit set are sent to the Host as a single RU in multiple segments, reassembled by Path Control at the destination.
  - The data part of the SNA RUs sent within the session is not processed by the Protocol Mapper. This means that the application program must understand the data format and requirements of the X.25 native equipment with which it communicates.

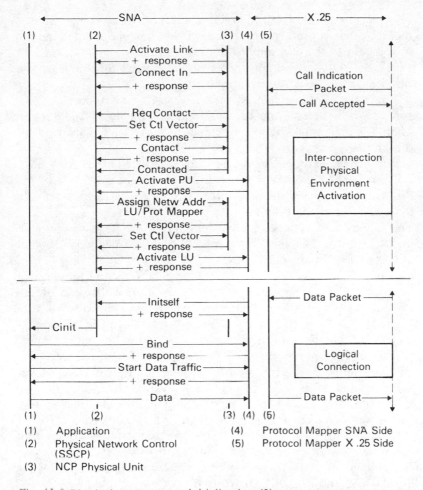

SNA ⟶ ⟵ X.25 ⟶

(1)   (2)   (3) (4) (5)

⟵————— Activate Link ————⟶
⟵——— + response
————— Connect In ———⟶
⟵——— + response ———   Call Indication
                                       ⟵————Packet ————
                                       ———— Call Accepted ——⟶
⟵——— Req Contact ———
————— Set Ctl Vector ———⟶
⟵——— + response ———
————— Contact ———⟶   ┌─────────────┐
⟵——— + response ———   │ Inter-connection │
⟵——— Contacted ———   │ Physical   │
————— Activate PU ——————⟶   │ Environment │
⟵——— + response ———   │ Activation │
————— Assign Netw Addr ———⟶   └─────────────┘
————— LU/Prot Mapper
⟵——— + response ———
————— Set Ctl Vector ———⟶
⟵——— + response ———
————— Activate LU ——————⟶
⟵——— + response

⟵————— Initself —————   ⟵——— Data Packet ———
⟵——— + response
⟵— Cinit —| ┌─────────────┐
————————— Bind —————⟶   │ Logical   │
⟵——— + response ——   │ Connection │
————— Start Data Traffic ——⟶   └─────────────┘
⟵——— + response ——
————————— Data —————⟶   ———— Data Packet ——⟶

(1)   (2)   (3) (4) (5)

(1) Application   (4) Protocol Mapper SNA Side
(2) Physical Network Control   (5) Protocol Mapper X.25 Side
     (SSCP)
(3) NCP Physical Unit

Fig. 13.5 Physical environment initialization (2)

● Communication set-up and clearing.
  — Physical SNA network control protocols [6, 7] are used to create the physical environment of the interconnection (Figs 13.4 and 13.5).

  When the interconnection request originates in the SNA host (Connect Out, Fig. 13.4), the Call procedure is started from the X.25 side of the Protocol Mapper. Then the SNA protocols are executed to activate the SNA part of the Protocol Mapper. These protocols are the same as the SNA dial-out protocols used for switched telephone lines and are transparent to the user application program.

  When the Interconnection request comes from outside the SNA host (Connect In, Fig. 13.5), a Call Accepted is sent to the originator of the call. Next, the SNA protocols are executed to activate the

SNA part of the Protocol Mapper. These protocols are the same as the SNA dial-in protocols used for switched telephone lines and are transparent to the user application program.

— Physical SNA network protocols are also used to deactivate the physical interconnection environment.

When the Clearing request originates in the SNA host, a Clear protocol is initiated from the X.25 side of the Protocol Mapper. Then, the SNA protocols are executed to deactivate the SNA side of the Protocol Mapper.

When the Clearing request originates from outside the SNA host, a Clear Confirmation Packet is transmitted by the X.25 side of the Protocol Mapper and the SNA protocols are executed to deactivate the SNA side of the Protocol Mapper.

— The Logical connection is a concatenation of the SNA session with the X.25 Virtual Circuit. The protocol mapping depends on what initiated the Connection request (Fig. 13.4 and Fig. 13.5).

When the application in the SNA host initiates the request, an SNA protocol will establish a session with the SNA side of the Protocol Mapper and concatenates as such the session with the X.25 Virtual Circuit. The first data will be transmitted as a Data Packet on the Virtual Circuit and will not be changed by the Protocol Mapper. It will, for example, be an *OPEN* record of a *Wrapping protocol*.

When the request is initiated from outside, the first Data Packet will be mapped into a SNA request for session establishment.

— Logical clearing depends also on what initiated the clearing request for the interconnection. When the SNA host is the origin, the SNA deactivation protocol is used. When the request has come from outside the host, then disconnection of the physical environment, e.g. Clear Indication Packet Received, will trigger the deactivation of the SNA session and the SNA environment.

Note An alternative is given for the establishment and clearing of logical connections, by means of session service protocols being mapped into Interrupt Packets with one octet of information indicating the SNA protocol commands. This supposes that the other user can identify the Interrupt Packet codes as an indication of the SNA protocols.

References

1 Gien, M. and Zimmermann, H., Network interconnection, *Proc. 6th Data Commun. Symp.*, Pacific Grove, Nov. 1979
2 Corr, F. P. and Neal, D. H., SNA and emerging international standards, *IBM Syst. J.*, vol. 18, no. 2, 1979, pp. 244–262

3 IBM Corporation, *The X.25 Interface for attaching IBM SNA nodes to Packet-Switched Data Networks*, GA27-3345

4 IBM Corporation, *IBM 5873–L02 Network Interface Adapter (NIA): product description manual*, GA11-8632

5 Scantlebury, R., SNA, X.25 and Transpac—can they co-exist?, *Proc. Online Conf. IBM Teleprocessing*, Online Conferences Ltd, Uxbridge, England, 1979

6 Cypser, R. J., *Communications architecture for distributed systems*, Addison-Wesley, 1978

7 IBM Corporation, *Systems Network Architecture format and protocol reference manual: architectural logic*, SC30-3112

14 LDS Germany

14.1 Introduction

In this chapter we review an application of the interconnection of proprietary networks of different manufacturers and an X.25 packet-switched network into one global, heterogeneous network. This network implements the principles discussed in the previous chapter. A part of the network went operational at the end of 1981.

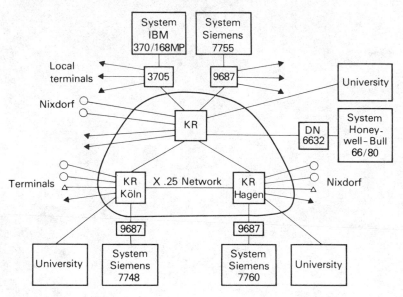

Fig. 14.1 LDS network

The LDS network is a private network owned by the Landesamt für Datenverarbeitung und Statistik (LDS), Nordrhein-Westfalen (State Institute for Data Processing and Statistics) [1, 2, 3]. This network will be called DVS in the remainder of the chapter.

In 1974, a bill was passed by the North Rhine-Westphalia Parliament which outlined the basic concept for the organization of electronic data processing in the public administration sector. It requires the integration of the various computing centers into a statewide network. The heterogeneous nature of this network should be noted since it is composed of different computer systems and their local networks. Together with the attached computer centers, this telecommunication network will form the base for the administration's DP-communication system. The services provided will be remote job processing, file transfer, transaction processing and interactive processing.

At the base, Layers 1 to 3, is an X.25-based packet-switched network (Fig. 14.1). At the start, it was a private X.25 network. Now it also uses DATEX-P, the German Bundespost X.25 network, since that became operational. During the development of the concept, special consideration was given to the separation of the different system functions e.g. the transport function from the processing function.

14.2 Overview of the DVS network architecture

At the start of the DVS design, there was no generally accepted architecture of networks. The actual design specifications of the LDS network differ therefore at certain points from the ISO proposal. Up to Level 3, the design follows the CCITT–ISO recommendation.

Figure 14.2 shows the different layers or levels in the network. Level 4 is the end-to-end transport protocol and the Host access protocol. It is named

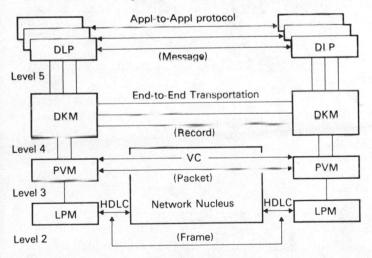

DLP   Application program e.g. RJE, Interactive, etc.
DKM   Communications monitor for end-to-end transmission
PVM   Packet Level (X.25).
LPM   Data Link Control (HDLC)

Fig. 14.2 LDS network layers

the *DV-Strom Kontroll-Modul* (DKM). The DV-Strom includes the Reference Model Transport Layer functions and some basic Session Layer functions.

Level 5 contains the user facilities of the network, which are called *Dienstleistungsprozesse* (DLP). This level combines the functions of the Presentation Layer and the Application Layer.

Figure 14.3 shows a table that gives the different layers and the elements involved. DST and BST in the table refer respectively to a header constructed by the DKM, implementing the end-to-end transport protocol, and by the DLP or application program implementing the DLP-to-DLP or Application-to-Application program protocol.

IBM 3705 NCP/PCNE

Protocol Level	Level 2	Level 3	Level 4	Level 5
Protocol	Link Control	Packet Level	End-to-End	Appl to Appl
Logical partners	DTE Network	DTE—DCE	DKM's	Appls or DLPs
Data Unit	Frame	Packet	Record	Message
Header	HDLC	Packet Header	DST	BST
Logical connection	Physical connection	VC	Session	Message stream

IBM VTAM Program

PCNE   Protocol Converter for non-SNA Equipment

Fig. 14.3 LDS layer characteristics

The DKM became the base for the German Interim Layer 4 standard called EHKP4, an Interim Transport Layer. EHKP4 is reviewed in detail in Chapter 6. Below is a discussion of the IBM solution through the SNA X.25 packet-switched interface support.

14.3 IBM/SNA–X.25 Protocol Mapper application at LDS

Figure 14.4 represents the connection of an IBM SNA system to the LDS network [4]. This is based on the extension of the X.25 support described earlier.

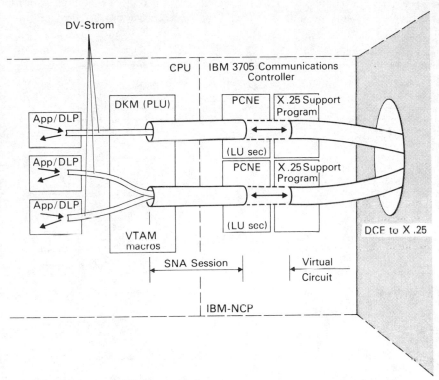

Fig. 14.4 LDS–SNA–CPU connection

The CPU will contain Levels 4 and 5. At Level 5 are the user application programs. Level 4, the DKM, is the end-to-end transport layer. DKM will be an application program of Virtual Telecommunication Access Method (VTAM), an implementation of IBM's SNA for a CPU. It transmits data to the Protocol Mapper (PCNE) and receives data from it.

The VTAM program (DKM) uses the SNA session as an extension of the Virtual Circuit. Each Protocol Mapper/'simulated LU' converts the SNA protocol into X.25 protocol and passes the data to the X.25 Packet Support and vice versa (Fig. 14.4). Also, data from the X.25 network is passed to the Protocol Mapper by the Packet Support and is converted by the Protocol Mapper into an SNA format and transmitted to the host.

14.3.1 Protocol mapping

The Protocol Mapper in the Network Control Program allows for the mapping of several SNA protocols. In the LDS case, only a subset of these is used (Fig. 14.5).

Figure 14.6 shows the protocol mapping. At the user level, there is the DLP-to-DLP with its protocol, which is supported by the end-to-end transport protocol implemented in DKM. Because of the use of that

Protocols	IBM SNA Protocols	X .25 Protocols
Call set-up	Switched Node	Call Packet
	Session establishment	First Data Packet if originated inbound
Data flow	HDX contention	FDX
	Inbound segmentation	More-data bit
Recovery	Switched Node	Clear Call sequence
Call clearing	Switched Node	Clear Packet

Fig. 14.5 LDS subset of mapped protocols

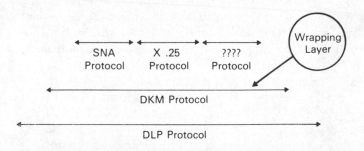

DLP   LDS user application program
DKM   LDS end-to-end transport

Fig. 14.6 LDS protocol mapping

274 Computer network architectures

version of IBM X.25 support that does not allow access to the X.25 level, the DKM running in an SNA host cannot use the X.25 Level 3 of the DVS network. DKM has to access the packet network by means of SNA and its protocol. SNA ends in the IBM NCP/VS in the Protocol Mapper. This shows again that, when networks are cascaded, the interconnection takes place at the lowest equivalent level, thus degrading the capabilities of some of the networks. The SNA network capabilities are reduced to a transport function in this case.

At the other end of the DVS is an SNA host or another (non-SNA) host. If it is an SNA host, the Protocol Mapper in that NCP/VS will convert the X.25 protocol back into an SNA protocol which will send data to the DKM VTAM application program or receive data from it. If it is another (non-SNA) host, then the X.25 protocol will be converted to that particular system's network protocol and the data passed to its DKM implementation in that host.

Interconnection rules

The interconnection of the transport networks is done through 'Gateways', called Protocol Mappers. The Protocol Mappers select levels of equivalent services which, for example, will cause the degradation of the SNA network to a transport network. The wrapping in the DKM layer gives the required end-to-end control over the global network.

14.4 Conclusion

The interconnection of networks is a difficult subject, and it is important to understand all aspects of such an interconnection. Our discussion of the interconnection of SNA networks with X.25 networks and devices, and, in particular, the example of LDS, shows that a formal treatment of the interconnection principles as set forth by Gien and Zimmermann (Chapter 13, reference [1]) is not only of theoretical interest, but has definite practical value. When these principles are used in the actual interconnection, the gateway design, they will lead to a better understanding of the overall operation of the global network.

References

1 *Aufgabenstellung und Konzept Datenvermittlungssystem NW (DVS)*, Landesamt für Datenverarbeitung und Statistik Nordrhein-Westfalen, Düsseldorf (Status 15 Oct. 1979)
2 *Schnittstellenfestlegung für das Datenvermittlungssystem NW (DVS): Prozeduren zur Datenübermittlung*, Landesamt für Datenverarbeitung und Statistik, Nordrhein-Westfalen, Düsseldorf (Status 1 Feb. 1979)

3 Dropman, E., *Datenvermittlungssystem Nordrhein-Westfalen*, Landesamt für Datenverarbeitung und Statistik, Nordrhein-Westfalen, Düsseldorf (Status Aug. 1980)

4 Kuhn, W., Anschlusz eines IBM-Groszrechners an ein Paketvermittlungs-Netz, *Online-ADI-Nachrichten*, Nov. 1979, pp. 952–955

15 Future of computer networks

15.1 Introduction

Right now in the communications area, we are experiencing an exciting period. The 1980s look definitely like becoming the decennium of communications. Digitization of the telephone networks, Videotex that brings the terminal and the computer into the home, Teletex (the super-telex), satellites, local networks, OSI, and so on, are only the beginning.

Reality or science-fiction? Some of them are certainly realities, others are not altogether science-fiction but still very distant in the future, at least as full-scale operational services. Most standards associated with the Reference Model are still in the future, at least at the time of writing this book. Sometimes, the communications community is convinced that within five or ten years we will be using a particular technology or concept, but the outcome is often different. An example of such an expectation is the X.21-based digital circuit-switching networks. At the end of the 1960s, the PTTs and common-carrier organizations forecasted that, within the next five to ten years, a major part of data communications would be done on a digital basis. The standard or, rather, the recommendation they had in mind was Recommendation X.21. Some 15 years later, the status of the X.21 network implementations and plans in Europe shows that only two European PTTs have implemented a network and that the others have deferred installation plans to the second half of the 1980s. If we analyze why it evolved this way, we find that the underlying reason seems to point to a money problem. It is a fact that, at the beginning of the 1980s, over 95 per cent of the revenue of the PTTs consisted of telephone service revenue. The revenue from communications services only started to grow considerably at the end of the 1970s. It is true that the increase in data transmission revenue is steeper than that in the telephone service revenue but the main thrust is still the telephone. The only place where digital technology is economically justified for the PTTs is in their internal transmission services, such as trunk lines between switching centers. Recommendation X.21 only handles the data transmission part and hence is no commercial justification to the PTTs for its implementation. Today, technology exists to replace the basic element of the telephone network, the telephone. ISDN recommendations that are under study in the CCITT discuss such telephone networks where digital data communications become a reality because of their merging with the new digital voice services.

Other reasons are that new technologies keep on being developed, such as fiber optics. Optical fiber products carry a potential of very large bandwidths with transmission speeds of hundreds of Mbit/s.

Advances in microelectronics are at the base of the digitization of the telephone network. Digits are digits and resemble each other whether they come from a voice source and are coded in binary form, or are generated by a computer. Hence, it is natural that the CCITT study groups decided to study the new digital telephone network in the light of merging voice and data back together again—in other words, *Integrated Services Digital Networks* (ISDN). At the same time, in September 1979, the PTTs and common carriers decided to define some added-value services such as Telefax, a facsimile system, Videotex, electronic mail, etc. At that point, they also decided to delay their X.21 networks to coincide more or less with the ISDN implementations planned from 1985 on.

Because of what happened with X.21, the future of networks should be analyzed first of all in terms of the near future where, in the area of networks, the Reference Model will be the key. Secondly, in the more distant future, the new basic transmission services, such as ISDN, will be most important. In between these two time periods, the integration of Local Area Networks (LAN) in the computer networks will become important. They will bring a new type of basic communications technology on a restricted geographical basis—within the site of a company, for instance.

After discussing these new technologies and services, we will review, as a summary, their impact on the Reference Model layers. So, this chapter about the future will be an extrapolation of technological advances in the context of the Reference Model.

15.2 The Reference Model and proprietary networks

Standards for the Reference Model have, at the time of writing, still a long way to go. We can expect them to be available in the second half of the 1980s. These standards will then include standards for *each* of the layers. Throughout this book, it has been shown that, in general, all proprietary architectures follow the same structural pattern. The grouping of services into layers, however, is different for most of them. The boundaries between the layers tend not to match exactly as architectures are put next to each other. This is an illustration of a statement that was cited previously: '. . . it may be difficult to prove that any particular layering selected is the best possible solution.'

The moment the Reference Model becomes a standard and the standards for the layer protocols become available, the computer manufacturers can work towards supporting these standards. It seems very likely that all of the described architectures have the possibility of using the Model as an interface definition between them. They all have the structural appearance and the functional layer definition that allows the implementation of the Reference Model in one way or the other.

For one architecture, mappers and gateways will be built which will map the proprietary architectures into the OSI layers and protocols. Sometimes, a one-to-one mapping will not be possible. In these cases, services of one network will be used to a certain degree or at a different level in another architecture. Techniques for implementing these kinds of solution were reviewed in Chapter 13.

Mappers and gateways look like the most interesting solution for the older types of proprietary network. These networks are implemented in products and would require an enormous investment if they had to be based on the Reference Model. The second generation networks are younger and their basic initial development coincided with the OSI study period. Consequently, these networks show a closer resemblance to the Reference Model and will have fewer problems in replacing layer protocols with the OSI ones.

Manufacturers will most likely implement the Reference Model if there is a market for products based on it. Already, during the study period for the ISO standards, some customers of the computer manufacturers needed heterogeneous network solutions, i.e., the interconnection of computer products of different manufacturers. These customers developed their own *interim standards*. These interim standards represent their view of the Session, Presentation and Application Layer protocols. They designed, developed and implemented them to interconnect their computer systems. It allowed a Nixdorf terminal to access data in an IBM or a Siemens CPU. Most of the development of the interim protocols is based on the use of Recommendation X.25 for the lowest three layers of the Reference Model. Their Level 4 private protocol would assume very often the use of a private or public packet-switched X.25 network for the basic communication function. Different manufacturers have implemented the support for these interim protocols. It turns out that the ones that had a layered structure in place had less problems in implementing the higher levels and X.25.

The conclusion seems to be clear: once standards become available and the market demands them, computer manufacturers will implement them. They are absolutely interested in standards. It allows them to economize on their product development, and on the manufacturing and maintenance of their systems. They have already complied with recommendations such as the CCITT's V-series recommendations and more recently the X-series recommendations. In the case of the Reference Model, the situation will most likely not be different. But, unlike the CCITT recommendations, the manufacturers would like to see standardized protocols instead of rigid service interface recommendations (i.e. between layers), so that they have the choice of implementation of the standard.

15.3 Technological advances in basic transmission facilities

Technological advances in basic transmission facilities can be divided into two major classes. The first is *microelectronics*, and in fact this class influences considerably the other one or is even at the base of it. The second is *fiberoptics*.

Microelectronics allow the digitization of voice, images and so on. Fiberoptics allow the transmission over a terrestrial link, of the huge amounts of data that result from the digitization process. We emphasize terrestrial links because there are also satellite links which have very large bandwidths. However, two main problems are associated with satellite links. First, there is the large propagation delay which presents difficulties for the support of interactive or conversational traffic. Secondly, there is the inescapable influence of politics on satellite communications. Not only are there local regulations governing the transmission of information, for example, the European PTT regulations, but most of all the effects of world politics. But without satellites, world-wide communications would be difficult. Indeed, satellite connections are used in computer communications networks today. This chapter is therefore not the place to discuss how they affect the Reference Model.

Terrestrial links using fiberoptics technology open new horizons with a service quality equivalent to satellite links and with transmission speeds difficult to imagine. The first contact with the implementations of these new technologies is in the area of *Local Area Networks*.

15.3.1 Local Area Networks

Local Area Networks are a natural answer to a requirement which has its origin in the recent explosion of the number of terminals, in addition to the number of telephone sets. Work without a telephone is difficult to imagine and now many businesses additionally use terminals. Secretaries have terminals to help them in their job with text-processing applications. Clerks need the information they can access through the terminal in order to do their job. Before the end of the first half of the 1980s, most companies are expected to have one terminal for every two employees. Reorganizations cause employees to move around taking with them their basic tools, the telephone and the terminal. This causes in turn an enormous problem of cabling. Buildings, at least those built in recent years, have a certain capacity of coaxial cables already installed but this will be insufficient in the next few years.

Therefore, the idea was born to lay *one* cable through a building. To this cable, terminals, printers, CPUs, peripherals and telephones can attach by means of a uniform plug and circuitry. The cable in its first implementation will be a coaxial cable, with speeds from 5 to 100 Mbit/s, and later would be based on fiberoptics allowing transmission speeds from one to hundreds of gigabits per second. The ultimate goal of the Local Area Network is to provide all in-house communications over one cable system. It will include transmission facilities for voice, image, facsimile, text and data to be exchanged within a building or site and to and from the outside world. In fact, we could call it a local or user ISDN. This is what Local Area Networks are all about.

There are two basic cable-configurations, although other configurations are possible. The first one is a *Bus configuration* and the other one a *Ring configuration* (see Fig. 15.1).

Configuration	Communication management	Transmission media	
Bus 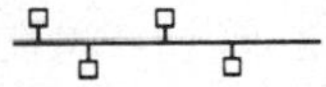	Collision Detect	Base-band	• Coaxial cable
Ring	Token	Base-band	• Coaxial cable
			• Optical fibre
		Broad-band	• Coaxial cable
			• Optical fibre
			• Waveguide

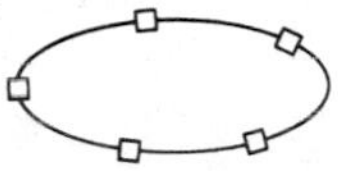

Fig. 15.1 LAN configurations and their characteristics

The communications management is different for each configuration. The bus uses a collision detect mechanism and the ring a token technique. A well-known bus configuration is Ethernet. An example of the ring configuration is the Cambridge ring. Only these two configurations were kept by the IEEE in their 1981 standardization work. From Fig. 15.1 it appears that the token ring approach has the widest choice of media. Therefore, it is this technique that, from a cost point of view, will be in a favourable position.

In the following section, we briefly describe these basic communication services and discuss how they can fit in the Reference Model.

15.3.2 Ethernet

Ethernet was initially developed as a research project in the early 1970s at the Xerox Palo Alto Research Center [1]. It was described under the name

'Experimental Ethernet'. After publication of the original Ethernet paper, many different but similar systems emerged from other research groups, universities and corporations. In the late 1970s, a 10-Mbit/s system was developed in a joint venture between Xerox, DEC and Intel. The result was Ethernet, which is described in a specification that shows how equipment can attach to the Ethernet bus and how it can transmit and receive data over it.

Ethernet uses a simple passive environment, usually a coaxial cable. There is no need for a central controller of any kind because of the fully distributed link access mechanism, known as a Carrier Sense Multiple Access with Collision Detection (CSMA/CD), that is used. A station connected to Ethernet that wants to transmit will first listen on the cable to see if the channel is free. If the station finds the channel in use or if a collision with another transmitting station is detected, it will back-off and wait for a certain amount of time and then try again. The time for which it will wait is the result of a truncated binary exponential back-off computation with a random initial value.

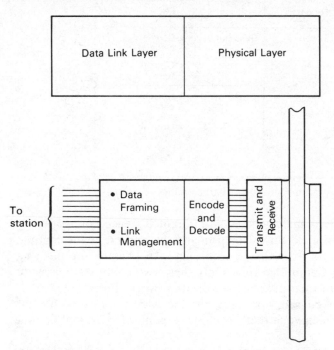

Fig. 15.2 Ethernet connection

The Ethernet specification [2] contains the description of the connection to the cable and explains how to transmit data. So, in fact, it describes functions which we find back on the Physical Layer and on the Data Link Layer (see Fig. 15.2).

The Physical Layer describes the electronic circuitry and timings needed to attach equipment to the cable. The Data Link Layer, implemented in the Ethernet controller board, contains Data Link Layer functions. It defines frames composed of 6-byte destination and source addresses, a 2-byte frame type, data and a 32-bit frame check sequence. The error checking is done through a 32-bit cyclic redundancy check. The specification contains also link management functions. It describes how collision can be avoided and what should be done if collision occurs. It is, however, not a Level 2 that contains all possible Data Link Layer functions. There is, for instance, no acknowledgement scheme, nor are functions such as piggybacking or pipelining defined.

15.3.3 Cambridge ring

The second Local Area Network configuration is a ring configuration. The ring is physically a coaxial or an optical-fiber cable that is strung through a building, for example. Instead of being open-ended as a bus configuration, the two ends are connected together. An example of a ring-structure local network is the Cambridge ring.

A station on the ring contains circuitry that allows it physically to connect to the cable and to transmit bits on the ring in a well-defined way. First, a token is sent on the ring. Stations are monitoring the ring for the token. When the token arrives at a station that wants to transmit, it takes it off the ring and transmits the data, with address and checking information, on the ring. Other stations are monitoring the ring for the token or for data, in which case they will be monitoring for their own address. In any case, a station propagates the bits over the ring towards the next station. The transmitting station will read its own data back and will take it off the ring. When it has finished transmitting, it replaces the token on the ring so that another station can take it in order to start its own transmission. The biggest problem in the Cambridge ring is the so-called 'lost token' problem. In the case of such an event, communication would cease completely over the ring. The circuitry used to attach to the ring includes the Physical Layer function and some functions of the Data Link Layer.

15.3.4 LANs and computer network architectures

Both configurations, ring as well as bus, offer a basic transmission facility that includes Physical Layer functions and apparently some Data Link Layer functions. These are addressing, framing and basic bit error checking. The other functions of the Data Link Layer, such as acknowledgment schemes, error recovery and all link set-up functions, are not handled.

To fit the Local Area Network to the Reference Model, or, for that matter, onto a proprietary network scheme, certain things have to be done.

First, the Physical Layer and the Data Link Layer have to be enhanced with the LAN layers standards when available. The Physical Layer will contain all the functions defined on the LAN Layer 1. The new physical medium will provide two stations with a temporary simplex point-to-point connection. Inherently, a broadcast function will be available at this level.

The LAN Layer 2 does not contain all functions of the Reference Model Data Link Layer. But Layer 2 of the LAN could be supplemented, for instance, with the missing Data Link Layer functions. It could be equivalent to HDLC or otherwise HDLC would have to be extended to support LAN-type functions. An example of such an extension is the provision of a priority scheme that is needed to provide real-time functions, which are an essential service for voice or moving images, for example. On the other side, Layer 2 could be left as it is defined in the LAN and the missing function could be taken care of by the higher layers of the network architecture, for example, a Level 3 or 4 protocol.

Two stations, communicating with each other over an LAN, see the physical-connection as a point-to-point configuration. From this point of view, only end-to-end control functions of a layer are required. They would compensate for the missing functions on Layer 2. The Transport Layer could provide multiplexing facilities for different processes using the same network-connection. The functions of the other layers would absolutely not be affected by the use of an LAN in the global network implementation. The LAN represents only another communication facility within the total network, exactly like telephone lines or packet-switching services.

One has the possibility of connecting to an LAN a piece of equipment that is a gateway to another LAN or to the outside part of a global network. Figure 15.3 shows such a configuration.

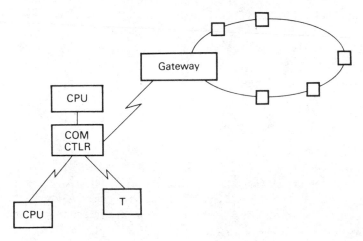

Fig. 15.3 LAN in a computer network

An LAN can also be a part of two or more networks. Stations connected to the LAN could be elements of network A and other stations could be part of network B. Both networks, A and B, do not even have to be the same as long as they accept the LAN on their Levels 1 and 2.

Local Area Networks of all configurations and types will become available in the near future. They will be used in most enterprises because they allow for efficient in-house communication. As we saw above, their inclusion in the Reference Model or in a layered proprietary architecture will not be a great problem. Sometimes, a simple replacement will be possible, in other cases an extension of some of the layers would be required. These implementations will give us the necessary experience to cope with the next important technology-driven evolution called ISDN.

15.3.5 Integrated Services Data Networks

In the early 1980s, telephone services will remain the main business of the PTTs and the common carriers. The recent technological advances permit the digitization of the telephone network. The switching centers will be digital and the most common terminal in the world, the telephone, will be digital too. The CCITT recommendations describing this digitization process are called Integrated Services Digital Network (ISDN). PTTs and common carriers plan to instal ISDN equipment from 1985 on. The expectations are that, by the end of the decennium, the greater part of the telephone network will be replaced.

In the first stage of ISDN, a private home will get a wire, coaxial cable or fiber-optics cable with a communications capacity of 64 kbit/s. In the following stages, this speed will increase to 2 Mbit/s and higher. This opens a completely new perspective. Data communication suddenly becomes within the reach of a private person. It is no longer the privilege of companies or government organizations. A connection box will be attached at the end of the high-speed link that enters the private home. To this box can be connected a digital telephone, videophone and/or other added services that will be offered by the PTT. An example of such services is Videotex, also called Viewdata. This service has for some time been available on analog telephone connections. Pictures have been composed of primitive lettering and graphics because of the low-speed connections, 75 bit/s in and 1200 bit/s out. With ISDN, a far better resolution of the picture will be possible. Because of the bandwidth available, the TV picture will be at least 40 to 50 times better than today's Videotex services. The ISDN speeds will allow electronic newspapers, books, records or films to be requested from 'mediatheques' by touching a keyboard. Electronic mail and facsimile services will be standard services available in one's home. Telemetering will allow power distribution companies to measure consumption automatically and either invoice or directly debit their customers' bank accounts. Personal computers will be attached to databases and could be connected to larger computers for the execution of certain jobs. People will be able to work with terminals from their homes instead of commuting to their work.

For the traditional users of data communications facilities, the industrial users, ISDN will mean higher bandwidths, more reliability of the services and better-quality connections. At the beginning of the 1980s, their base communications facilities consist of 9600 bit/s connection. Higher speeds, from 19.2 up to 64 kbit/s are available but rare and expensive. With ISDN, 64 kbit/s will be the low-speed connection for the communication services user. ISDN will be a circuit-switched system with circuit set-up times in the order of microseconds. All connections will be point-to-point. Because of the set-up times, connections will only be made when they are needed and for the duration for which they are needed. LAN-type connections are suitable for that type of a connectivity. The X-series recommendations are expected to be available. As a migration path, the common carriers will still offer X.21 types of attachment possibilities and X.25 packet-switched interfaces. Other value-added services will be expanded. Today's facsimile services will be improved. Videotex, electronic mail, Teletex, teleconferencing will all be a part of the normal ISDN services. Leased connections will still be available for high-speed dedicated trunks for speeds of 100 Mbit/s and up.

ISDN is an expensive undertaking for the PTTs, equipment-wise and because it is labor-intensive. The user, too, will have to make big investments in new equipment. To ease this, it is to be expected that the PTTs and common carriers will offer analog adapters that allow the connection of analog interface-based devices.

15.3.6 ISDN and the Reference Model

What will the effect be of ISDN on the Reference Model and related standards? ISDN will provide new basic communications facilities. As such, it will represent a new service on Level 1 and possibly on Level 2. Because the circuit switching will result in point-to-point connections, some of the functions on Level 3, such as routing, will become increasingly unnecessary. Value-added services will be based on the Reference Model standards. The S-series recommendations of the CCITT are concerned with Teletex services and constitute an example of a candidate for some of the Reference Model protocols. Here, the PTTs defined seven layers—not the Reference Model but similar to it—in order to get Teletex by 1981. For the first three layers, Teletex uses V-series or X.21 interfaces with HDLC or X.25 levels. The Layer 4 that the PTTs defined is nearly empty. Layers 5, 6 and 7 are considerably elaborate to allow document handling. The S-series recommendations are kinds of interim standards that have been defined by the CCITT because, like manufacturers had to do for their own requirements, they needed to implement Teletex by 1981. All other added services will be developed in the same direction.

If anything brings a change in the Reference Model as it stands today, it will be the very short time it takes to set-up a circuit. This effect was first noticed at the beginning of the 1980s with the Nordix X.21 network. This network has a call set-up time in the order of 150 ms. This, together with the tariffing of the service by the Nordic PTTs, gave birth to what is called the *Short Hold*. When Short Hold is used, the connection is only made when data has to be transmitted. For example, a terminal sends a request to a CPU and the connection is suspended until the CPU has the response to the terminal request. At this time, the connection is built up again by means of the X.21 protocol. Since the tariffing is connection-time based, this can result in considerable savings against the analog circuit-switched facilities. In analog circuit-switching, the connection is held for the duration of a transaction or a session.

Short Hold, however, requires special care by the upper layers, for example HDLC. HDLC itself has a link set-up phase and a data phase. During the latter, it assumes that the physical-connection exists and is permanently there between the two data link control stations. This is not the case with Short Hold. Special arrangements have to be made, at the link level, to control in an orderly way the disconnection and reconnection of the link. This is needed to ensure correct operation of the HDLC link control.

ISDN will generalize this aspect of circuit-switching. Very fast connection times (microseconds) and point-to-point connections will result in circuits only when they are needed. In the Reference Model, all protocols on all levels have characteristically a connection set-up phase, a data transfer phase and a disconnection phase between equivalent layers. Connectivity is here a prime requirement. Each layer expects the underlying layers to be connected. A Short Hold type of function on the Physical Layer will create problems It is therefore to be expected that the protocols on the different layers of the Reference Model will evolve towards non-connected protocols. Each time a service is required, some of the layers will set up connections temporarily without the big overhead of connection set-up and disconnection protocols.

Layers 3 and 4 seem to be affected by the new services because their functions tend to be required for more complex network-oriented configurations than a point-to-point connection of the ISDN network. It is apparent that what functions would be left on these levels, would have to be connection-less protocols of the type discussed before. The higher layers, 5 and up, do not seem to be affected by the change of service on the Physical Layer.

15.4 Conclusions

The evolution of technology in data communications is driven by micro-electronics technology. Satellite systems, fiber optics, digitization of telephone networks, Local Area Networks take advantage of very large-scale integration (VLSI). During the 1980s, the implementation of these new communications facilities will forge ahead. The 1980s will also see the realization of the ISO effort to standardize the interconnection of systems through the Reference Model and related standards. Once the standards are available, it is to be expected that manufacturers of computer equipment will implement the standards if a market exists.

The next important point is the influence of the new communications facilities, existing or coming in the near future, within the framework of the Reference Model. The new facilities will impact some of the thinking put forward in the protocols on the different layers. Therefore, we now offer a short overview of the possible impacts per layer.

The ISDN recommendations as well as the LAN type of facilities and related standards (when they become available) must be added to the Physical Layer.

The Data Link Layer functions could end up being reduced, for example, to the level of the Ethernet Level 2 functions. On the other hand, it is also possible that protocols, such as HDLC, have to be expanded in order to be able to cope with a connection-less environment of an LAN type of service. The same can be argued for the ISDN type of fast circuit-switching.

The Network Layer functions will have a tendency to be reduced because of the simplicity of the network configurations. The new services will be point-to-point links between end-users.

The Transport Layer functions seem to evolve the same way as the Network Layer functions and protocols, and, for the same reason, the simplicity of the underlying network configurations.

The Session Layer functions look as though they are not going to be affected by the new communications facilities. The logical connections will require all the different protocols that are found on this level. They are completely shielded from the underlying physical network and are based on a logical Full-Duplex point-to-point connection between two end-users.

The Presentation Layer will subsist in all of its complexity and will not at all be affected by the new services.

The Application Layer is not going to be affected, other than in that the greater communications bandwidths will open up new application areas.

The emerging technologies will provide more efficient, more reliable, faster and cheaper communications facilities. They will induce change to some of the Reference Model's original work but will not make obsolete the work done in the ISO TC97 committees. On the contrary, it will focus attention more on the higher-layer protocols where most of the work still has to be done at the time of writing this book.

References

1 Shoch, J. F., An Introduction to the Ethernet specification, *ACM Computer Commun. Rev.*, vol. 11, no. 3, July 1981, pp. 17–19
2 Digital, Intel and Xerox (30 Sep. 1980), The Ethernet—A Local Area Network. Data Link Layer and Physical Layer specifications. Version 1, *ACM Computer Commun. Rev.*, vol. 11, no. 3, July 1981, pp. 20–66

Appendix A Draft International Standard ISO/DIS 7498: Information Processing Systems–Open Systems Interconnection–Basic Reference Model (April 1982)

This draft is reproduced with the permission of ISO. Being a working document, it is therefore subject to change and may not be referred to as an International Standard. Information can be obtained at the ISO Central Secretariat, Case Postale 56, 1211 Geneva 20, Switzerland.

Information processing systems - Open Systems Interconnection - Basic Reference Model

CONTENTS

1

0 INTRODUCTION

0.1 About this standard

The purpose of this International Standard Reference Model of Open Systems Interconnection is to provide a common basis for the coordination of standards development for the purpose of systems interconnection, while allowing existing standards to be placed into perspective within the overall Reference Model.

The term Open Systems Interconnection (OSI) qualifies standards for the exchange of information among systems that are "open" to one another for this purpose by virtue of their mutual use of the applicable standards.

The fact that a system is open does not imply any particular systems implementation, technology or means of interconnection, but refers to the mutual recognition and support of the applicable standards.

It is also the purpose of this International Standard to identify areas for developing or improving standards, and to provide a common reference for maintaining consistency of all related standards. It is not the intent of this International Standard either to serve as an implementation specification, or to be a basis for appraising the conformance of actual implementations, or to provide a sufficient level of detail to define precisely the services and protocols of the interconnection architecture. Rather, this International Standard provides a conceptual and functional framework which allows international teams of experts to work productively and independently on the development of standards for each layer of the Reference Model of OSI.

The Reference Model has sufficient flexibility to accomodate advances in technology and expansion in user demands. This flexibility is also intended to allow the phased transition from existing implementations to OSI standards.

NOTE - The Reference Model is expected to be subject to future expansion. Some anticipated directions of expansion are indicated by notes or foot-notes in this International Standard.

While the scope of the general architectural principles required for OSI is very broad, this International Standard is primarily concerned with systems comprising terminals, computers and associated devices and the means for transferring information between such systems. Other aspects of OSI requiring attention are described briefly (see 4.2).

The justification for development of standards must follow normal administrative procedures even though such standards are identified in the Reference Model.

As standards emerge to meet the OSI requirements, a small number of practical subsets should be defined by the standards developers from optional functions, to facilitate implementation and compatibility.

2

The description of the Reference Model of OSI given in this International Standard is developed in stages:

Clause 4 establishes the reasons for Open Systems Interconnection, defines what is being connected, the scope of the interconnection and, describes the modelling principles used in OSI;

Clause 5 describes the general nature of the architecture of the Reference Model - namely that it is layered, what layering means, and the principles used to describe layers;

Clause 6 names, and introduces the specific layers of the architecture; and

Clause 7 provides the description of the specific layers.

An indication of how the layers were chosen is given in Annex A to this International Standard.

0.2 Related OSI standards

Concurrently with the preparation of this standard, work is in progress within the International Standards Organization on the development of OSI standards in the following areas:

a) virtual terminal protocols;
b) file transfer, access and management protocols;
c) job transfer and manipulation protocols;
d) Session Layer services and protocols;
e) Transport Layer services and protocols;
f) Network Layer services and protocols;
g) Data Link Layer services and protocols;
h) Physical Layer services and protocols; and
j) OSI management protocols.

The first three items in this list relate to the Application and Presentation Layers of the Reference Model and it is expected that experience gained in the development of the corresponding standards will lead to general service and protocol standards for the Presentation Layer.

1   SCOPE AND FIELD OF APPLICATION

This International Standard describes the Reference Model of Open Systems Interconnection. It establishes a framework for coordinating the development of existing and future standards for the interconnection of systems and is provided for reference by those standards.

This International Standard does not specify services and protocols for Open Systems Interconnection. It is neither an implementation specification for systems, nor a basis for appraising the conformance of actual implementations.

3

2 DEFINITIONS

Definitions of terms are included at the beginning of individual clauses and sub-clauses. An index of these terms is provided in an Annex B for easy reference.

3 NOTATION

Layers are introduced in clause 5. An (N)-, (N+1)- and (N-1)-notation is used to identify and relate adjacent layers:

(N)-layer: any specific layer;

(N+1)-layer: the next higher layer;

(N-1)-layer: the next lower layer.

This notation is also used for other concepts in the model which are related to these layers, e.g. (N)-protocol, (N+1)-service.

Clause 6 introduces names for individual layers. When referring to these layers by name, the (N)-, (N+1)- and (N-1)- prefixes are replaced by the names of the layers, e.g. transport-protocol, session-entity, and network-service.

4 INTRODUCTION TO OPEN SYSTEMS INTERCONNECTION (OSI)

NOTE - The general principles described in Clauses 4 and 5 hold for all layers of the Reference Model, unless layer specific statements to the contrary are made in Clauses 6 and 7.

4.1 Definitions

4.1.1 System: A set of one or more computers, the associated software, peripherals, terminals, human operators, physical processes, information transfer means, etc., that forms an autonomous whole capable of performing information processing and/or information transfer. In this International Standard, except in clause 4, the term system is synonymous with the term open system.

4.1.2 Open system: A system which obeys OSI standards in its communication with other systems. In this International Standard, except in clause 4, the term open system is used to refer only to those aspects of a real open system pertinent to OSI.

4.1.3 Application-process: An element within a system which performs the information processing for a particular application.

4

4.2 The Open Systems Interconnection environment

In the concept of OSI, a system is a set of one or more computers, associated software, peripherals, terminals, human operators, physical processes, information transfer means, etc., that forms an autonomous whole capable of performing information processing and/or information transfer. An application-process is an element within a system which performs the information processing for a particular application.

Application-processes can be manual processes, computerized processes or physical processes.

Some examples of application-processes that are applicable to this open system definition are the following:

a)   a person operating an automated banking terminal is a manual application-process;

b)   a FORTRAN program executing in a computer centre and accessing a remote database is a computerised application-process; the remote database management systems server is also an application-process; and

c)   a process control program executing in a dedicated computer attached to some industrial equipment and linked into a plant control system is a physical application-process.

OSI is concerned with the exchange of information between open systems (and not the internal functioning of each individual open system).

As shown in figure 1, the physical media for open systems interconnection provides the means for the transfer of information between open systems.

NOTE - At this point, only telecommunications media have been considered. The use of other interconnection media is for further study.

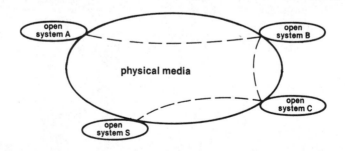

Figure 1 - Open Systems connected by physical media

5

OSI is concerned not only with the transfer of information between systems, i.e. transmission, but also with their capability to interwork to achieve a common (distributed) task. In other words, OSI is concerned with cooperation[1] between systems, which is implied by the expression "systems interconnection".

The objective of OSI is to define a set of standards to enable open systems to cooperate. A system which obeys applicable OSI standards in its cooperation with other systems is termed an open system.

---

1) Cooperation among open systems involves a broad range of activities of which the following have been identified:

  a) interprocess communication, which concerns the exchange of information and the synchronization of activity between OSI application-processes;
  b) data representation, which concerns all aspects of the creation and maintenance of data descriptions and data transformations for reformatting data exchanged between open systems;
  c) data storage, which concerns storage media, and file and database systems for managing and providing access to data stored on the media;
  d) process and resource management, which concerns the means by which OSI application-processes are declared, initiated and controlled, and the means by which they acquire OSI resources;
  e) integrity and security, which concern information processing constraints that must be preserved or assured during the operation of the open systems; and
  f) program support, which concerns the definition, compilation, linking, testing, storage, transfer, and access to the programs executed by OSI application-processes.

Some aspects of these activities may imply exchange of information between the interconnected open systems and may, therefore, be of concern to OSI.

This International Standard covers the elements of OSI aspects of these activities which are essential for early development of OSI standards.

6

4.3 Modelling the OSI environment

The development of OSI standards, i.e. standards for the interconnection of open systems, is assisted by the use of abstract models. To specify the external behaviour of interconnected open systems, each "real" open system is replaced by a functionally equivalent "abstract" open system. Only the interconnection aspects of these abstract systems would strictly need to be described. However to accomplish this, it is necessary to describe both the internal and external behaviour of these abstract systems. Only the external behaviour of abstract open systems is retained as the standard of behaviour of real open systems. The description of the internal behaviour of abstract open systems is provided in the Reference Model only to support the definition of the interconnection aspects. Any real system which behaves externally as an abstract open system can be considered to be an open system.

This abstract modelling is used in two steps.

First, basic elements of abstract open systems and some key decisions concerning their organization and functioning, are developed. This constitutes the Reference Model of Open Systems Interconnection described in this International Standard.

Then, the detailed and precise description of the functioning of the abstract open system is developed in the framework formed by the Reference Model. This constitutes the services and protocols for Open Systems Interconnection which are the subject of other International Standards.

It should be emphasized that the Reference Model does not, by itself, specify the detailed and precise functioning of the abstract open system and, therefore, it does not specify the external behaviour of open systems and does not imply the structure of the implementation of an open system.

The reader not familiar with the technique of abstract modeling is cautioned that those concepts introduced in the description of abstract open systems constitute an abstraction despite a similar appearance to concepts commonly found in real systems. Therefore real open systems need not be implemented as described by the Model.

7

Throughout the remainder of this International Standard, only the aspects of systems and application-processes which lie within the OSI environment are considered. Their interconnection is illustrated throughout this International Standard as depicted in figure 2. In this International Standard, except where noted, the terms "system" and "open system" represent abstract open systems, not real open systems, i.e. only those aspects of a system which are of concern to OSI.

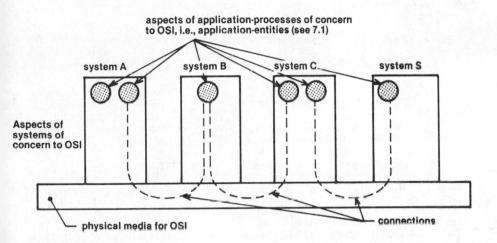

Figure 2 - Basic elements of OSI

8

5 CONCEPTS OF A LAYERED ARCHITECTURE

5.1 Introduction

Clause 5 sets forth the architectural concepts that are applied in the development of the Reference Model of Open Systems Interconnection. Firstly, the concept of a layered architecture (with layers, entities, service-access-points, protocols, connections, etc.) is described. Secondly, identifiers are introduced for entities, service-access-points, and connections. Thirdly, service-access-points and data-units are described. Fourthly, elements of layer operation are described including connections, transmission of data, and error functions. Then, routing aspects are introduced and finally, management aspects are discussed.

The concepts described in clause 5 are those required to describe the Reference Model of OSI. However, not all of the concepts described are employed in each layer of the Reference Model.

Four elements are basic to the Reference Model (see figure 2):

a) systems;

b) the application-entities which exist within the Open Systems Interconnection environment;

c) the connections (see 5.2) which join the application-entity and permit them to exchange information (see Note 1), and

d) the physical media for Open Systems Interconnection.

NOTE 1 - This Basic Reference Model for OSI is based on the assumption that a connection is required for the transfer of data. An addition to this basic model is currently being developed to extend the description to cover the connectionless forms of data transmission which may be found in a wide variety of data communications techniques (e.g. local area networks, digital radio, etc.) and applications (e.g. remote sensing and banking).

NOTE 2 - Security aspects which are also general architectural elements of protocols are not discussed in this International Standard.

5.2 Principles of layering

5.2.1 Definitions

5.2.1.1   (N)-subsystem: An element in a hierarchical division of a system which interacts directly only with elements in the next higher division and the next lower division of that system.

5.2.1.2   (N)-layer: A subdivision of the OSI architecture, constituted by subsystems of the same rank (N).

9

5.2.1.3   (N)-entity: An active element within an (N)-subsystem.

5.2.1.4   peer-entities: Entities within the same layer.

5.2.1.5   sublayer: A subdivision of a layer.

5.2.1.6   (N)-service: A capability of the (N)-layer and the layers beneath it, which is provided to (N+1)-entities at the boundary between the (N)-layer and the (N+1)-layer.

5.2.1.7   (N)-facility: A part of an (N)-service.

5.2.1.8   (N)-function: A part of the activity of (N)-entities.

5.2.1.9   (N)-service-access-point: The point at which (N)-services are provided by an (N)-entity to an (N+1)-entity.

5.2.1.10   (N)-protocol: A set of rules and formats (semantic and syntatic) which determines the communication behaviour of (N)-entities in the performance of (N)-functions.

5.2.2   Description

The basic structuring technique in the Reference Model of OSI is layering. According to this technique, each system is viewed as logically composed of an ordered set of subsystems, represented for convenience in the vertical sequence shown in figure 3. Adjacent subsystems communicate through their common boundary. Subsystems of the same rank (N) collectively form the (N)-layer of the Reference Model of OSI. An (N)-subsystem consists of one or several (N)-entities. Entities exist in each layer. Entities in the same layer are termed peer-entities. Note that the highest layer does not have an (N+1)-layer above it and the lowest layer does not have an (N-1)-layer below it.

10

NOTE - It may be necessary to further divide a layer into small sub-structures called sublayers and to extend the technique of layering to cover other dimensions of Open Systems Interconnection.
A sublayer is defined as a grouping of functions in a layer which may be bypassed. The bypassing of all the sublayers of a layer is not allowed. A sublayer uses the entities and connections of its layer. The detailed definition or additional characteristics of a sublayer are for further study.

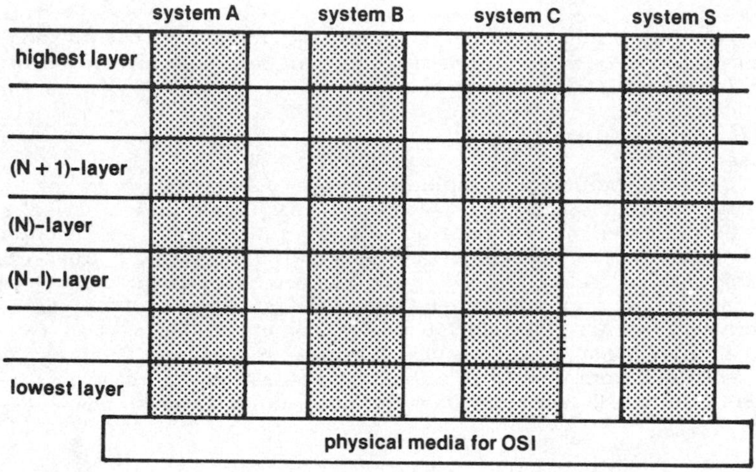

Figure 3 - Layering in co-operating open systems

11

Except for the highest layer, each (N)-layer provides (N+1)-entities in the (N+1)-layer with (N)-services. The highest layer is assumed to represent all possible uses of the services which are provided by the lower layers.

NOTE 1 - Not all systems provide the initial source or final destination of data, such systems need not contain the higher layers of the architecture.

NOTE 2 - Classes of service may be defined within the (N)-services. The precise definition of the term classes of service is for further study.

Each service provided by an (N)-layer may be tailored by the selection of one or more (N)-facilities which determine the attributes of that service. When a single (N)-entity cannot by itself fully support a service requested by an (N+1)-entity it calls upon the co-operation of other (N)-entities to help complete the service request. In order to co-operate, (N)-entities in any layer, other than those in the lowest layer, communicate by means of the set of services provided by the (N-1)-layer (see figure 4). The entities in the lowest layer are assumed to communicate directly via the physical media which connect them.

The services of an (N)-layer are provided to the (N+1)-layer, using the (N)-functions performed within the (N)-layer and as necessary the services available from the (N-1)-layer.

An (N)-entity may provide services to one or more (N+1)-entities and use the services of one or more (N-1)-entities. A (N)-service-access-point is the point at which a pair of entities in adjacent layers use or provide services (see figure 7).

Co-operation between (N)-entities is governed by one or more (N)-protocols. The entities and protocols within a layer are illustrated in figure 5.

5.3 Communication between peer entities

5.3.1 Definitions

5.3.1.1 <u>(N)-connection</u>: An association established by the (N)-layer between two or more (N+1)-entities for the transfer of data.

5.3.1.2 <u>(N)-connection-endpoint</u>: A terminator at one end of an (N)-connection within an (N)-service-access-point.

5.3.1.3 <u>Multi-endpoint-connection</u>: A connection with more than two connection-endpoints.

5.3.1.4 <u>Correspondent (N)-entities</u>: (N)-entities with an (N-1)-connection between them.

5.3.1.5 <u>(N)-relay</u>: An (N)-function by means of which an (N)-entity forwards data received from one correspondent (N)-entity to another correspondent (N)-entity.

12

5.3.1.6   (N)-data source: An (N)-entity that sends (N-1)-service-da-ta-units (see 5.6.1.7.) on an (N-1)-connection.

5.3.1.7   (N)-data sink: An (N)-entity that receives (N-1)-service-da-ta-units on an (N-1)-connection.

5.3.1.8   (N)-data transmission: An (N)-facility which conveys (N)-service-data-units from one (N+1)-entity to one or more (N+1)-entities via (N)-connections.

5.3.1.9   (N)-duplex transmission: (N)-data   transmission   in   both directions at the same time.

5.3.1.10   (N)-half-duplex transmission: (N)-data transmission in either direction one direction at a time; the choice of direction is controlled by an (N+1)-entity.

5.3.1.11   (N)-simplex transmission: (N)-data transmission in one pre-assigned direction.

5.3.1.12   (N)-data communication: An   (N)-function   which   transfers (N)-protocol data-units (see 5.6.1.3.) according to an (N)-protocol over one or more (N-1)-connections.

5.3.1.13   (N)-two-way simultaneous communication: (N)-data-communi-cation in both directions at the same time.

5.3.1.14   (N)-two-way alternate communication: (N)-data-communication in both directions, one direction at a time.

5.3.1.15   (N)-one-way communication: (N)-data communication in one pre-assigned direction.

5.3.2 Description

For information to be exchanged between two or more (N+1)-entities, an association must be established between them in the (N)-layer using an (N)-protocol.

NOTE - Classes of protocols may be defined within the (N)-protocols. The precise definition of the term classes of protocols is for futher study.

13

This association is called an (N)-connection. (N)-connections are provided by the (N)-layer between two or more (N)-service-access-points. The terminator of an (N)-connection at an (N)-service-access-point is called an (N)-connection-endpoint. A connection with more than two connection-endpoints is termed a multi-endpoint-connection. (N)-entities with a connection between them are termed correspondent (N)-entities.

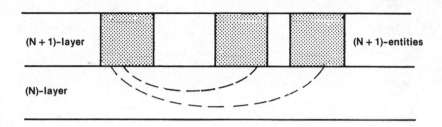

Figure 4 - (N+1)-entities in the (N+1)-layer communicate through the (N)-layer

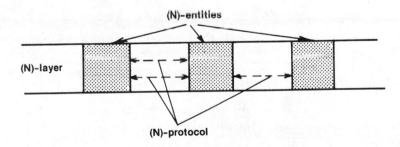

Figure 5 - (N)-protocols between (N)-entities

14

(N+1)-entities can communicate only by using the services of the (N)-layer. There are instances where services provided by the (N)-layer do not permit direct access between all of the (N+1)-entities which have to communicate. If this is the case, communication can still occur if some other (N+1)-entity can act as a relay between them (see figure 6).

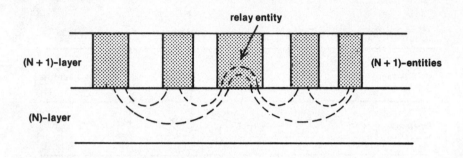

Figure 6 - Communication through a relay

The fact that communication is relayed by a chain of (N+1)-entities is known neither by the (N)-layer nor by the (N+2)-layer.

5.4 Identifiers

5.4.1 Definitions

5.4.1.1   Title: A permanent identifier for an entity.

5.4.1.2   Title-domain: A subset of the title space of the OSI environment.

5.4.1.3   Title-domain-name: An identifier which uniquely identifies a title-domain witin the OSI environment.

NOTE - Title-domains of primary importance are the layers. In this specific case, the title-domain-name identifies the (N)-layer.

5.4.1.4   Local-title: A title which is unique within a title-domain.

5.4.1.5   Global-title: A title which is unique within the OSI environment and comprises two parts, a title-domain-name and a local-title.

15

5.4.1.6 (N)-address; (N)-service-access-point-address: An identifier which tells where an (N)-service-access-point may be found.

5.4.1.7 (N)-directory: An (N)-function by which the global title of an (N)-entity is translated into the (N-1)-address of an (N-1)-service-access-point to which the (N)-entity is attached.

5.4.1.8 (N)-address-mapping: An (N)-function which provides the mapping between the (N)-addresses and the (N-1)-addresses associated with an (N)-entity.

5.4.1.9 Routing: A function within a layer which translates the title of an entity or the service-access-point-address to which the entity is attached into a path by which the entity can be reached.

5.4.1.10 (N)-connection-endpoint-identifier: An identifier of an (N)-connection-endpoint which can be used to identify the corresponding (N)-connection at an (N)-service-access-point.

5.4.1.11 (N)-connection-endpoint-suffix: A part of an (N)-connection-endpoint-identifier which is unique within the scope of an (N)-service-access-point.

5.4.1.12 Multi-connection-endpoint-identifier: An identifier which specifies the connection-endpoint of a multi-endpoint-connection which should accept the data that is being transferred.

5.4.1.13 (N)-service-connection-identifier: An identifier which uniquely specifies an (N)-connection within the environment of the correspondent (N+1)-entities.

5.4.1.14 (N)-protocol-connection-identifier: An identifier which uniquely specifies an individual (N)-connection within the environment of the multiplexed (N-1)-connection.

5.4.1.15 (N)-suffix: A part of an (N)-address which is unique within the (N)-service-access-point.

5.4.2 Description

An (N)-service-access-point-address, or (N)-address for short, identifies a particular (N)-service-access-point to which an (N+1)-entity is attached (see figure 7). When the (N+1)-entity is dettached from the (N)-service-access-point, the (N)-address no longer provides access to the (N+1)-entity. If the (N)-service-access-point is reattached to a different (N+1)-entity, then the (N)-address identifies the new (N+1)-entity and not the old one.

The use of an (N)-address to identify an (N+1)-entity is the most efficient mechanism if the permanence of attachment between the (N+1)-entity and the (N)-service-access-point can be assured. If there is a requirement to identify an (N+1)-entity regardless of its current location, then the global-title assures correct identification.

16

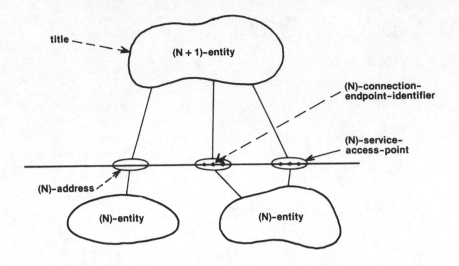

NOTE - dashed arrows refer to identifiers.

Figure 7 - Entities, service-access-points, and identifiers

An (N)-directory is an (N)-function which translates global-titles of peer (N)-entities into the (N-1)-addresses through which they coope-rate.

Interpretation of the correspondence between the (N)-addresses served by an (N)-entity and the (N-1)-addresses used for accessing (N-1)-services is performed by an (N)-address-mapping function.

Two particular kinds of (N)-address-mapping functions may, exist within a layer:

a)   hierarchical (N)-address-mapping; and
b)   (N)-address-mapping by tables.

If an (N)-address is always mapped into only one (N-1)-address then hierarchical construction of addresses can be used (see figure 8). The (N)-address-mapping function need only recognize the hierarchical structure of an (N)-address and extract the (N-1)-address it contains.

17

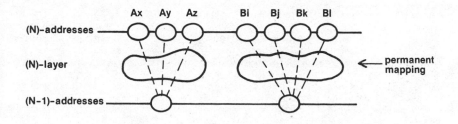

Figure 8 - Hierarchical (N)-address-mapping

In this case, an (N)-address consists of two parts:

a)   an (N-1)-address of the (N)-entity which is supporting the
     current (N)-service-access-point of the (N+1)-entity;

b)   an (N)-suffix which makes the (N)-service-access-point uni-
     quely identifiable within the scope of the (N-1)-address.

Within a given layer, a hierarchical structure of addresses simplifies
(N)-address-mapping functions because of the permanent nature of the
mapping it presupposes. It is not imposed by the model in all layers in
order to allow more flexibility in (N)-address-mappings and to cover
the case where an (N)-entity attached to more than one (N-1)-service-
access-point supports only one (N)-service-access-point.

If the previous condition is not true, i.e. either an (N)-address can
be mapped into several (N-1)-addresses, or an (N)-address is not
permanently mapped into the same (N-1)-address, then hierarchical
construction of an address is not possible and the (N)-address-mapp-
ing function may use tables to translate (N)-addresses into (N-1)-
addresses.

The structure of an (N)-address is known by the (N)-entity which is
attached to the identified (N)-service-access-point. However, the
(N+1)-entity does not know this structure.

If an (N+1)-entity has two or more (N)-service-access-points with
either the same (N)-entity or different (N)-entities, the (N)-entities
have no knowledge of this fact. Each (N)-service-access-point is considered to identify a different (N+1)-entity from the perspective of the
(N)-entities.

A routing function translates the (N)-address of an (N+1)-entity into a
path or route by which the (N+1)-entity may be reached.

18

An (N+1)-entity may establish an (N)-connection with another (N+1)-entity by using an (N)-service. When an (N+1)-entity establishes an (N)-connection with another (N+1)-entity, each (N+1)-entity is given an (N)-connection-endpoint-identifier by its supporting (N)-entity. The (N+1)-entity can then distinguish the new connection from all other (N)-connections accessible at the (N)-service-access-point it is using. This (N)-connection-endpoint-identifier must be unique within the scope of the (N+1)-entity which will use the (N)-connection.

The (N)-connection-endpoint-identifier consists of two parts:

a)   the (N)-address of the (N)-service-access-point which will be used in conjunction with the (N)-connection; and

b)   an (N)-connection-endpoint-suffix which is unique within the scope of the (N)-service-access-point.

A multi-endpoint-connection requires multi-connection-endpoint-identifiers. Each such identifier is used to specify which connection-endpoint should accept the data which is being transferred. A multi-connection -endpoint-identifier must be unique within the scope of the connection within which it is used.

The (N)-layer may provide to the (N+1)-entities an (N)-service-connection-identifier which uniquely specifies the (N)-connection within the environment of the correspondent (N+1)-entities.

5.5 Properties of service-access-points

An (N+1)-entity requests (N)-services via an (N)-service-access-point which permits the (N+1)-entity to interact with an (N)-entity.

Both the (N)- and (N+1)-entities attached to an (N)-service-access-point are in the same system.

An (N+1)-entity may concurrently be attached to one or more (N)-service-access-points attached to the same or different (N)-entities.

An (N)-entity may concurrently be attached to one or more (N+1)-entities through (N)-service-access-points.

An (N)-service-access-point is attached to only one (N+1)-entity at a time.

An (N)-service-access-point may be detached from an (N+1)-entity and reattached to the same or another (N+1)-entity.

An (N)-service-access-point is located by means of its (N)-address. An (N)-address is used by an (N+1)-entity to request an (N)-connection.

19

5.6 Data-units

5.6.1 Definitions

5.6.1.1 <u>(N)-protocol-control-information</u>: Information exchanged between (N)-entities, using an (N-1)-connection, to co-ordinate their joint operation.

5.6.1.2 <u>(N)-user-data</u>: The data transferred between (N)-entities on behalf of the (N+1)-entities for whom the (N)-entities are providing services.

5.6.1.3 <u>(N)-protocol-data-unit</u>: A unit of data specified in an (N)-protocol and consisting of (N)-protocol-control-information and possibly (N)-user-data.

5.6.1.4 <u>(N)-interface-control-information</u>: Information transferred between an (N+1)-entity and an (N)-entity to co-ordinate their joint operation.

5.6.1.5 <u>(N)-interface-data</u>: Information transferred from an (N+1)-entity to an (N)-entity for transmission to a correspondent (N+1)-entity over an (N)-connection, or conversely, information transferred from an (N)-entity to an (N+1)-entity after being received over an (N)-connection from a correspondent (N+1)-entity.

5.6.1.6 <u>(N)-interface-data-unit</u>: The unit of information transferred across the service-access-point between an (N+1)-entity and an (N)-entity in a single interaction. Each (N)-interface-data-unit contains (N)-interface-control-information and may also contain the whole or part of an (N)-service-data-unit.

5.6.1.7 <u>(N)-service-data-unit</u>: An amount of (N)-interface-data whose identity is preserved from one end of an (N)-connection to the other.

5.6.1.8 <u>Expedited (N)-service-data-unit, (N)-expedited-data-unit</u>: A small (N)-service-data-unit whose transfer is expedited. The (N)-layer ensures that an expedited-data-unit will not be delivered after any subsequent service-data-unit or expedited unit sent on that connection.

5.6.2 Description

Information is transferred in various types of data units between peer-entities and between entities attached to a specific service-access-point. The data-units are defined in clause 5.6.1. and the relationships among them are illustrated in figures 9 and 10.

20

	Control	Data	Combined
(N)–(N) peer entities	(N)-protocol- control- information	(N)-user- data	(N)-protocol data-units
(N + 1)–(N) adjacent layers	(N)-interface- control- information	(N)-interface data	(N)-interface- data-unit

Figure 9 - Relationships among data units

Except for the relative relationships defined above, there is no overall architectural limit to the size of data units. There may be other size limitations at specific layers.

The size of (N)-interface-data-units is not necessarily the same at each end of the connection.

Data may be held within a connection until a complete service-data-unit is put into the connection.

21

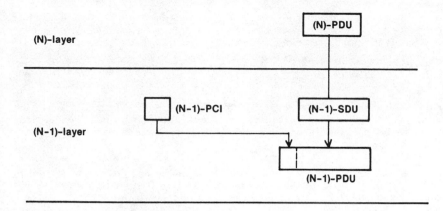

(N)-layer

(N-1)-layer

PCI = protocol-control-information
PDU = protocol-data-unit
SDU = service-data-unit

NOTE 1-   This figure assumes that neither segmenting nor blocking of (N)-service-data-units is performed (see 5.7.6.5).

NOTE 2-   This figure does not imply any positional relationship between protocol-control-information and user-data in protocol -data-units

NOTE 3-   An (N)-protocol-data-unit may be mapped one-to-one into an (N-1)-service-data-unit, but other relationships are possible (see figure 11).

Figure 10 -   An illustration of mapping between data units in adjacent layers.

5.7 Elements of layer operation

5.7.1 Definitions

5.7.1.1   (N)-protocol-identifier: An identifier used between correspondent (N)-entities to select a specific (N)-protocol to be used on a particular (N-1)-connection.

5.7.1.2   Centralized multi-endpoint-connection: A multi-endpoint-connection where data sent by the entity associated with the central connection-endpoint is received by all other entities, while data sent by one of the other entities is only received by the central entity.

22

5.7.1.3 _Decentralized multi-endpoint-connection_: A multi-endpoint-connection such that data sent by an entity associated with a connection -endpoint is received by all other entities.

5.7.1.4 _Multiplexing_: A function within the (N)-layer by which one (N-1)-connection is used to support more than one (N)-connection.

NOTE - The term multiplexing is also used in a more restricted sense to refer to the function performed by the sending (N)-entity while the term demultiplexing is used to refer to the function performed by the receiving (N)-entity.

5.7.1.5 _Demultiplexing_: The function performed by an (N)-entity which identifies (N)-protocol-data-units for more than one (N)-connection within (N-1)-service-data-units received on a single (N-1)-connection. It is the reverse function of the multiplexing function performed by the (N)-entity sending the (N-1)-service-data-units.

5.7.1.6 _Splitting_: A function within the (N)-layer by which more than one (N-1)-connection is used to support one (N)-connection.

NOTE - The term splitting is also used in a more restrictive sense to refer to the function performed by the sending (N)-entity while the term recombining is used to refer to the function performed by the receiving (N)-entity.

5.7.1.7 _Recombining_: The function performed by an (N)-entity which identifies (N)-protocol-data-units for a single (N)-connection in (N-1) -service-data-units received on more than one (N-1)-connection. It is the reverse function of the splitting function performed by the (N)-entity sending the (N-1)-service-data-units.

5.7.1.8 _Flow control_: A function which controls the flow of data within a layer or between adjacent layers.

5.7.1.9 _Segmenting_: A function performed by an (N)-entity to map one (N)-service-data-unit into multiple (N)-protocol-data-units.

5.7.1.10 _Reassembling_: A function performed by an (N)-entity to map multiple (N)-protocol-data-units into one (N)-service-data-unit. It is the reverse function of segmenting.

5.7.1.11 _Blocking_: A function performed by an (N)-entity to map multiple (N)-service-data-units into one (N)-protocol-data-unit.

5.7.1.12 _Deblocking_: A function performed by an (N)-entity to identify multiple (N)-service-data-units which are contained in one (N)-protocol-data-unit. It is the reverse function of blocking.

5.7.1.13 _Concatenation_: A function performed by an (N)-entity to map multiple (N)-protocol-data-units into one (N-1)-service-data-unit.

23

5.7.1.14 <u>Separation</u>: A funtion performed by an (N)-entity to identify multiple (N)-protocol-data-units which are contained in one (N-1)-service-data-unit. It is the reverse function of concatenation.

5.7.1.15 <u>Sequencing</u>: A function performed by the (N)-layer to preserve the order of (N)-service-data-units that were submitted to the (N)-layer.

5.7.1.16 <u>Acknowledgement</u>: A function of the (N)-layer which allows a receiving (N)-entity to inform a sending (N)-entity of the receipt of an (N)-protocol-data-unit.

5.7.1.17 <u>Reset</u>: A function which sets the correspondent (N)-entities to a predefined state with a possible loss or duplication of data.

5.7.2 Protocol selection

One or more (N)-protocols may be defined for the (N)-layer. An (N)-entity may employ one or more (N)-protocols.

Meaningful communication between (N)-entities over an (N-1)-connection requires the agreed selection of one (N)-protocol.

(N)-protocol-identifiers name the specific protocols defined.

5.7.3 Properties of connections

An (N)-connection is an association established for communication between two or more (N+1)-entities, identified by their (N)-addresses. An (N)-connection is offered as a service by the (N)-layer, so that information may be exchanged between the (N+1)-entities.

An (N+1)-entity may have, simultaneously, one or more (N)-connections with other (N+1)-entities, with any given (N+1)-entity, and with itself.

An (N)-connection is established by referencing, either explicitly or implicitly, an (N)-address for the source (N+1)-entity and an (N)-address for each of one or more destination (N+1)-entities.

The source (N)-address and one or more of the destination (N)-addresses may be the same. One or more of the destination (N)-addresses may be the same while the source (N)-address is different. All may be different.

One (N)-connection-endpoint is constructed for each (N)-address referenced explicitly or implicitly when an (N)-connection is established.

An (N+1)-entity accesses an (N)-connection via an (N)-service-access-point.

An (N)-connection has two or more (N)-connection-endpoints.

24

An (N)-connection-endpoint is not shared by (N+1)-entities or (N)-connections.

An (N)-connection-endpoint relates three elements:

a)   an (N+1)-entity;
b)   an (N)-entity; and
c)   an (N)-connection.

The (N)-entity and the (N+1)-entity related by an (N)-connection-endpoint are those implied by the (N)-address referenced when the (N)-connection is established.

An (N)-connection-endpoint has an identifier, called an (N)-connection-endpoint-identifier, which is unique within the scope of the (N+1)-entity which is bound to the (N)-connection-endpoint.

An (N)-connection-endpoint-identifier is not the same as an (N)-address.

An (N+1)-entity references an (N)-connection using its (N)-connection-endpoint-identifier.

Multi-endpoint-connections are connections which have three or more connection- endpoints. Two types of multi-endpoint-connection are defined [1]:

a)   centralized; and
b)   decentralized.

A centralized multi-endpoint-connection has a central connection-endpoint. Data sent by the entity associated with the central connection-endpoint is received by the entities associated with all other connection-endpoints. The data sent by an entity associated with any other connection-endpoint is received only by the entity associated with the central connection-endpoint.

On a decentralized multi-endpoint-connection, data sent by an entity associated with any connection-endpoint is received by the entities associated with all of the other connection-endpoints.

5.7.4 Connection establishment and release

The establishment of an (N)-connection by peer-entities of an (N)-layer requires the following:

a)   the availability of an (N-1)-connection between the supporting (N)-entities; and

b)   both (N)-entities be in a state in which they can execute the connection establishment protocol exchange.

If it is not already available, an (N-1)-connection has to be established by peer-entities of the (N-1)-layer. This requires, for the (N-1)-layer, the same conditions as described above for the (N)-layer.

_____

1) Other types of multi-endpoint-connections are for further study.

The same consideration applies downwards until either an available connection or the physical medium for Open Systems Interconnection is encountered.

Depending upon the characteristics of the (N-1)-service and of the establishment protocol exchange, the establishment of an (N)-connection may or may not be done in conjunction with the establishment of the (N-1)-connection.

The characteristics of the (N)-service with regard to the establishment of the (N)-connection vary depending upon whether or not (N)-user-data can be transferred by the connection establishment protocol exchange for each direction of the (N)-connection.

Where (N)-user-data is transferred by the (N)-connection establishment protocol exchange, the (N+1)-protocol may take advantage of this to allow an (N+1)-connection to be established in conjunction with the establishment of the (N)-connection.

The release of an (N)-connection is normally initiated by one of the (N+1)-entities associated in it.

The release of an (N)-connection may also be initiated by one of the (N)-entities supporting it as a result of an exception condition occurring in the (N)-layer or the layers below.

Depending upon the conditions, release of an (N)-connection may result in the discarding of (N)-user-data.

The orderly release of an (N)-connection requires either the availability of an (N-1)-connection, or a common reference to time (e.g. time of failure of the (N-1)-connection and common time-out). In addition, both (N)-entities must be in a state in which they can execute the connection release protocol exchange. It is important to note, however, that the release of an (N-1)-connection does not necessarily cause the release of the (N)-connection(s) which were using it; the (N-1)-connection can be reestablished, or another (N-1)-connection substituted.

The characteristics of the (N)-service with regard to the release of an (N)-connection can be of two kinds:

a)   (N)-connections are either released immediately when the release protocol exchange is initiated ((N)-user-data not yet delivered may be discarded); or

b)   release is delayed until all (N)-user-data sent previous to the initiation of the protocol exchange has been delivered (i.e. delivery confirmation has been received).

(N)-user-data may be transferred by the connection release protocol exchange.

Some (N)-protocols may provide for the combining of connection establishment and connection release protocol exchanges.

26

5.7.5 Multiplexing and splitting

Within the (N)-layer, (N)-connections are mapped onto (N-1)-connections. The mapping may be one of three kinds:

a)   one-to-one;

b)   many (N)-connections to one (N-1)-connection (multiplexing); and

c)   one (N)-connection to many (N-1)-connections (splitting).

Multiplexing may be needed in order to:

a)   make more efficient or more economic use of the (N-1)-service; and

b)   provide several (N)-connections in an environment where only a single (N-1)-connection exists.

Splitting may be needed in order to:

a)   improve reliability since more than one (N-1)-connection is available;

b)   provide the required grade of performance, through the utilization of multiple (N-1)-connections; and

c)   obtain cost benefits by the utilization of multiple low cost (N-1)-connections each with less than the required grade of performance.

Multiplexing and splitting each involve a number of associated functions which may not be needed for one-to-one connection mapping.

The functions associated with multiplexing are:

a)   identification of the (N)-connection for each (N)-protocol-data-unit transferred over the (N-1)-connection, in order to ensure that (N)-user-data from the various multiplexed (N)-connections are not mixed. This identification is distinct from that of the (N)-connection-endpoint-identifiers and is called an (N)-protocol-connection-identifier;

b)   flow control on each (N)-connection in order to share the capacity of the (N-1)-connection (see 5.7.6.4.); and

c)   scheduling the next (N)-connection to be serviced over the (N-1)-connection when more than one (N)-connection is prepared to send data.

The functions associated with splitting are:

a)   scheduling the utilization of multiple (N-1)-connections used in splitting a single (N)-connection; and

27

b)   resequencing of (N)-protocol-data-units associated with an (N)-connection since they may arrive out of sequence even when each (N-1)-connection guarantees sequence of delivery (see 5.7.6.6).

5.7.6 Transfer of data

5.7.6.1   Normal data transfer

Control information and user data are transferred between (N)-entities in (N)-protocol-data-units. An (N)-protocol-data-unit is a unit of data specified in an (N)-protocol and contains (N)-protocol-control-information and possibly (N)-user-data.

(N)-protocol-control-information is transferred between (N)-entities using the (N-1)-connection. (N)-protocol-control-information is any information that supports the joint operation of (N)-entities. (N)-user-data is passed transparently between (N)-entities over an (N-1)-connection.

An (N)-protocol-data-unit has an arbitrary, but finite, size. (N)-protocol-data-units are mapped into (N-1)-service-data-units. The interpretation of an (N)-protocol-data-unit is defined by the (N)-protocol in effect for the (N-1)-connection.

An (N)-service-data-unit is transferred between an (N+1)-entity and an (N)-entity, through an (N)-service-access-point, in the form of one or more (N)-interface-data-units. The (N)-service-data-unit is transferred as (N)-user-data in one or more (N)-protocol-data-units.

The exchange of data under the rules of an (N)-protocol can only occur if an (N-1)-connection exists. If an (N-1)-connection does not exist, it must be established before an exchange of data can occur (see 5.7.4).

5.7.6.2   Data transfer during connection establishment and release

(N)-user-data may be transferred in the (N)-connection establishment protocol exchange and in the (N)-connection release protocol exchange.

The connection release protocol exchange may be combined with the connection establishment protocol exchange (see 5.7.4) to provide means for the delivery of a single unit of (N)-user-data between correspondent (N+1)-entities with a confirmation of receipt.

5.7.6.3   Expedited transfer of data

An expedited-data-unit is a service-data-unit which is transferred and/or processed with priority over normal service-data-units. An expedited data transfer service may be used for signalling and interrupt purposes.

Expedited data flow is independent of the states and operation of the normal data flow, although the data sent on the two flows may be logically related. Conceptually, a connection that supports expedited flow

28

can be viewed as having two subchannels, one for normal data, the other for expedited data. Data sent on the expedited channel is assumed to be given priority over normal data.

The transfer guarantees that an expedited-data-unit will not be delivered after any subsequent normal service-data-unit or expedited-data-unit sent on the connection.

Because the expedited flow is assumed to be used to transfer small amounts of data infrequently, simplified flow control mechanisms may be used on this data flow.

An expedited (N)-service-data-unit is intended to be processed by the receiving (N+1)-entity with priority over normal (N)-service-data-units.

5.7.6.4 Flow control

If flow control functions are provided, they can operate only on protocol-data-units and interface-data-units.

Two types of flow control are identified:

a) peer flow control which regulates the rate at which (N)-protocol -data-units are sent to the peer (N)-entity on the (N)-connection. Peer flow control requires protocol definitions and is based on protocol-data-unit size; and

b) (N)-interface flow control which regulates the rate at which (N)-interface-data are passed between an (N+1)-entity and an (N)-entity. (N)-interface flow control is based on the (N)-interface-data-unit size.

Multiplexing in a layer may require a peer flow control function for individual flows (see 5.7.5).

Peer flow control functions require flow control information be included in the (N)-protocol-control-information of an (N)-protocol-data-unit.

If the size of service-data-units exceeds the maximum size of the (N)-user-data portion of an (N)-protocol-data-unit, then first segmentation must be performed on the (N)-service-data-unit to make it fit within the (N)-protocol-data-units. Peer flow control can then be applied on the (N)-protocol-data-units.

5.7.6.5 Segmenting, blocking and concatenation

Data units in the various layers are not necessarily of compatible size. It may be necessary to perform segmenting, i.e. to map an (N)-service-data-unit into more than one (N)-protocol-data-unit. Similarly, segmenting may occur when (N)-protocol-data-units are mapped into (N-1)-interface-data-units. Since it is necessary to preserve the identity of (N)-service-data-units on an (N)-connection, functions

29

must be available to identify the segments of an (N)-service-data-unit, and to allow the correspondent (N)-entities to reassemble the (N)-service-data unit.

Segmenting may require that information be included in the (N)-protocol-control-information of an (N)-protocol-data-unit. Within a layer, (N)-protocol-control-information is added to an (N)-service-data-unit to form an (N)-protocol-data-unit when no segmenting or blocking is performed (see figure 11a). If segmenting is performed, an (N)-service-data-unit is mapped into several (N)-protocol-data-units with added (N)-protocol-control-information (see figure 11b).

Conversely, it may be necessary to perform blocking whereby several (N)-service-data-units with added (N)-protocol-control-information form an (N)-protocol-data-unit (see figure 11c).

The Reference Model also permits concatenation whereby several (N)-protocol-data-units are concatenated into a single (N-1)-service-date-unit (see figure 11d).

30

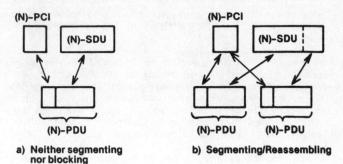

a) Neither segmenting
   nor blocking

b) Segmenting/Reassembling

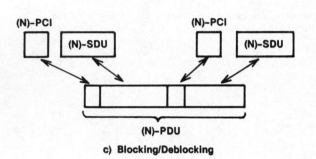

c) Blocking/Deblocking

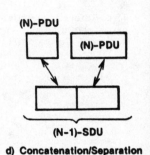

d) Concatenation/Separation

SDU   = service-data-unit
PCI = protocol-control-information
PDU   = protocol-data-unit

NOTE 1 -   This figure does not imply any positional relationship
           between protocol-control-information and user-data in proto-
           col-data-units.
NOTE 2 -   In the case of concatenation, (N)-protocol-data-unit does not
           necessarily include an (N)-service-data-unit.

Figure 11-Relationship between (N)-service-data-unit, (N)-protocol-
         data-unit and (N-1)-service-data-unit within a layer.

31

5.7.6.6 Sequencing

The (N)-services provided by the (N)-layer of the OSI architecture may not guarantee delivery of data in the same order as it was submitted by the (N+1)-layer. If the (N+1)-layer needs to preserve the order of data transferred through the (N)-layer, sequencing mechanisms must be present in the (N+1)-layer. Sequencing may require additional (N+1)-protocol-control-information.

5.7.7 Error functions

5.7.7.1 Acknowledgement

An acknowledgement function may be used by peer (N)-entities using an (N)-protocol to obtain a higher probability of detecting protocol-data-unit loss than is provided by the (N-1)-layer. Each (N)-protocol-data-unit transferred between correspondent (N)-entities is made uniquely identifiable, so that the receiver can inform the sender of the receipt of the (N)-protocol-data-unit. An acknowledgement function is also able to infer the non-receipt of (N)-protocol-data-units and take appropriate remedial action.

An acknowledgement function may require that information be included in the (N)-protocol-control-information of (N)-protocol-data-units.

The scheme for uniquely identifying (N)-protocol-data-units may also be used to support other functions such as detection of duplicate data-units, segmenting and sequencing.

NOTE - Other forms of acknowledgement such as confirmation of delivery and confirmation of performance of an action are for further study.

5.7.7.2 Error detection and notification

Error detection and notification functions may be used by an (N)-protocol to provide a higher probability of both protocol-data-unit error detection and data corruption detection than is provided by the (N-1)-service.

Error detection and notification may require that additional information be included in the (N)-protocol-control-information of the (N)-protocol-data-unit.

5.7.7.3 Reset

Some services require a reset function to recover from a loss of synchronization between correspondent (N)-entities. A reset function sets the correspondent (N)-entities to a predefined state with a possible loss or duplication of data.

NOTE - Additional functions may be required to determine at what point reliable data transfer was interrupted.

32

A quantity of (N)-user-data may be conveyed in association with the (N)-reset function.

The reset function may require that information be included in the (N)- protocol-control-information of the (N)-protocol-data-unit.

5.8 Routing

A routing function within the (N)-layer enables communication to be relayed by a chain of (N)-entities. The fact that communication is being routed by intermediate (N)-entities is known by neither the lower layers nor by the higher layers. An (N)-entity which partici-pates in a routing function may have a routing table.

5.9 Management aspects of OSI

5.9.1 Definitions

5.9.1.1 Application-management: Functions in the Application Layer (see 6.1) related to the management of OSI application-processes.

5.9.1.2 Application-management-application-entity: An application-en-tity which executes application-management functions.

5.9.1.3 OSI resources: Data processing and data communication re-sources which are of concern to OSI.

5.9.1.4 Systems-management: Functions in the Application Layer re-lated to the management of various OSI resources and their status across all layers of the OSI architecture.

5.9.1.5 Systems-management-application-entity: An application-entity which executes systems management functions.

5.9.1.6 Layer-management: Functions related to the management of the (N)-layer partly performed in the (N)-layer itself according to the (N)-protocol of the layer (activities such as activation and error con-trol) and partly performed as a subset of systems-management.

5.9.2 Introduction

Within the OSI architecture there is a need to recognize the special problems of initiating, terminating, and monitoring activities and assisting in their harmonious operations, as well as handling abnormal conditions. These have been collectively considered as the management aspects of the OSI architecture. These concepts are essential to the operation of the interconnected open systems and therefore are inclu-ded in the comprehensive description of the Reference Model described in subsequent clauses of this International Standard.

The management activities which are of concern are those which imply actual exchanges of information between systems. Only the protocols needed to conduct such exchanges are candidates for standardization within the OSI architecture.

This clause describes key concepts relevant to the management aspects, including the different categories of management activities and the positioning of such activities within the OSI architecture.

5.9.3 Categories of management activities

Only those management activities which imply actual exchanges of information between remote management entities are pertinent to the OSI architecture. Other management activities local to particular systems are outside its scope.

Similarly, not all resources are pertinent to OSI. This International Standard considers only OSI resources, i.e. those data processing and data communication resources which are of concern to OSI.

The following categories of management activities are identified:

a) application management;
b) systems-managements; and
c) layer-management.

5.9.3.1 Application-management

Application-management relates to the management of OSI application-processes. The following list is typical of activities which fall into this category but it is not exhaustive:

a) initialization of parameters representing application-processes;
b) initiation, maintenance and termination of application-processes;
c) allocation and de-allocation of OSI resources to application-processes;
d) detection and prevention of OSI resource interference and deadlock;
e) integrity and commitment control;
f) security control; and
g) checkpointing and recovery control.

The protocols for application management reside within the Application Layer, and are handled by application-management-application-entities.

5.9.3.2 Systems-management

Systems-management relates to the management of OSI resources and their status across all layers of the OSI architecture. The following list is typical of activities which fall into this category but it is not exhaustive:

34

a)   activation/deactivation management which includes:

    1)   activation, maintenance and termination of OSI resources distributed in open systems, including physical media for Open Systems Interconnection;
    2)   some program loading functions;
    3)   establishment/maintenance/release of connections between management entities; and
    4)   open systems parameter initialization/modification;

b)   monitoring which includes:

    1)   reporting status or status changes; and
    2)   reporting statistics; and

c)   error control which includes:

    1)   error detection and some of the diagnostic functions; and
    2)   reconfiguration and restart.

The protocols for systems-management reside in the Application Layer, and are handled by systems-management-application-entities.

5.9.3.3   Layer-management

There are two aspects of layer-management. One of these is concerned with layer activities such as activation and error control. This aspect is implemented by the layer protocol to which it applies.

The other aspect of layer-management is a subset of systems-management. The protocols for these activities reside within the Application Layer and are handled by system-management-application-entities.

5.9.4   Principles for positioning management functions

Several principles are important in positioning management functions in the Reference Model of OSI. They include the following [1]:

a)   both centralization and decentralization of management functions are allowed. Thus, the OSI architecture does not dictate any particular fashion or degree of centralization of such functions. This principle calls for a structure in which each system is allowed to include any (subset of) systems-management functions and each subsystem is allowed to include any (subset of) layer-management functions;

---

1)   Other principles are for further study.

35

b)   if it is necessary, connections between management entities are established when a system which has been operating in isolation from other systems, becomes part of the OSI environment.

36

6 INTRODUCTION TO THE SPECIFIC OSI LAYERS

6.1 Specific layers

The general structure of the OSI architecture described in clause 5 provides architectural concepts from which the Reference Model of OSI has been derived, making specific choices for the layers and their contents.

The Reference Model contains seven layers:

- a) the Application Layer (layer 7);
- b) the Presentation Layer (layer 6);
- c) the Session Layer (layer 5);
- d) the Transport Layer (layer 4);
- e) the Network Layer (layer 3);
- f) the Data Link Layer (layer 2); and
- g) the Physical Layer (layer 1).

These layers are illustrated in figure 13. The highest layer is the Application Layer and it consists of the application-entities that cooperate in the OSI environment. The lower layers provide the services through which the application-entities cooperate.

Layers 1-6, together with the physical media for OSI provide a step-by-step enhancement of communication services. The boundary between two layers identifies a stage in this enhancement of services at which an OSI service standard is defined, while the functioning of the layers is governed by OSI protocol standards.

37

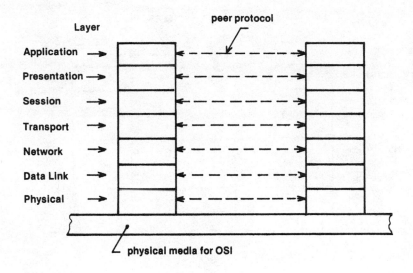

Figure 12 - Seven layer reference model and peer protocols

Not all systems provide the initial source or final destination of data. When the physical media for OSI do not link all systems directly, some systems act only as relay systems, passing data to other systems. The functions and protocols which support the forwarding of data are then provided in the lower layers. This is illustrated in figure 13.

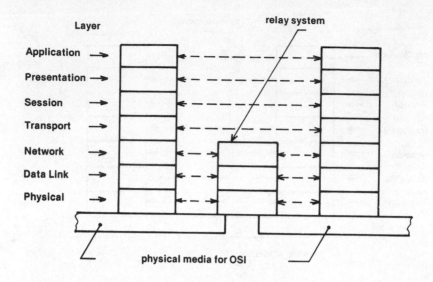

Figure 13 - Communication involving relay systems

6.2 The principles used to determine the seven layers in the Reference Model

The following principles have been used to determine the seven layers in the Reference Model and are felt to be useful for guiding further decisions in the development of OSI standards,

NOTE 1 - It may be difficult to prove that any particular layering selected is the best possible solution. However, there are general principles which can be applied to the question of where a boundary should be placed and how many boundaries should be placed.

P1: do not create so many layers as to make the system engineering task of describing and integrating the layers more difficult than necessary;

P2: create a boundary at a point where the description of services can be small and the number of interactions across the boundary are minimized;

39

P3: create separate layers to handle functions that are manifestly different in the process performed or the technology involved;

P4: collect similar functions into the same layer;

P5: select boundaries at a point which past experience has demonstrated to be successful;

P6: create a layer of easily localized functions so that the layer could be totally redesigned and its protocols changed in a major way to take advantage of new advances in architectural, hardware or software technology without changing the services expected from and provided to the adjacent layers;

P7: create a boundary where it may be useful at some point in time to have the corresponding interface standardized;

NOTE 1 - Advantages and drawbacks of standardizing internal interfaces within open systems are not considered in this International Standard. In particular, mention of, or reference to principle P7, should not be taken to imply usefulness of standards for such internal interfaces.

NOTE 2 - It is important to note that OSI per se does not require interfaces within open systems to be standardized. Moreover, whenever standards for such interfaces are defined, adherence to such internal interface standards can in no way be considered as a condition of openness.

P8: create a layer where there is a need for a different level of abstraction in the handling of data, e.g. morphology, syntax, semantics;

P9: allow changes of functions or protocols to be made within a layer without affecting other layers; and

P10:create for each layer boundaries with its upper and lower layer only.

Similar principles have been been applied to sublayering:

P11:create further subgrouping and organization of functions to form sublayers within a layer in cases where distinct communication services need it;

P12:create, where needed, two or more sublayers with a common, and therefore minimal functionality to allow interface operation with adjacent layers; and

P13:   allow by-passing of sublayers.

40

6.3 Layer descriptions

For each of the seven layers identified above, clause 7 provides:

a) an outline of the purpose of the layer;

b) a description of the services offered by the layer to the layer above; and

c) a description of the functions provided in the layer and the use made of the services provided by the layer below.

The descriptions, by themselves, do not provide a complete definition of the services and protocols for each layer. These are the subject of separate standards.

7 DETAILED DESCRIPTION OF THE RESULTING OSI ARCHITECTURE

7.1 The Application Layer

7.1.1 Definitions

7.1.1.1 <u>Application-entity</u>: The aspects of an application-process pertinent to OSI.

7.1.2 Purpose

As the highest layer in the Reference Model of Open Systems Interconnection, the Application Layer provides a means for the application-processes to access the OSI environment. Hence the Application Layer does not interface with a higher layer.

The purpose of the Application Layer is to serve as the window between correspondent application-processes which are using the OSI to exchange meaningful information.

Each application-process is represented to its peer by the application entity.

All specifiable application process parameters of each OSI environment communications instance are made known to the OSI environment (and, thus, to the mechanisms implementing the OSI environment) via the Application Layer.

7.1.3 Services provided to application-processes

Application-processes exchange information by means of application-entities, application-protocols, and presentation-services.

As the only layer in the Reference Model that directly provides services to the application-processes, the Application Layer necessarily provides <u>all</u> OSI services directly usable by application-processes.

Note - The application services differ from services provided by other layers in neither being provided to an upper layer nor being associated with a service-access-point.

In addition to information transfer, such services may include, but are not limited to the following:

NOTE - Some of the services listed below are provided by OSI management.

- a) identification of intended communications partners (e.g. by name, by address, by definite description, by generic description);
- b) determination of the current availability of the intended communication partners;

42

c) establishment of authority to communicate;
d) agreement on privacy mechanisms;
e) authentication of intended communication partners;
f) determination of cost allocation methodology;
g) determination of the adequacy of resources;
h) determination of the acceptable quality of service (e.g. response time, tolerable error rate, cost vis-a-vis the previous considerations);
i) synchronization of cooperating applications;
j) selection of the dialogue discipline including the initiation and release procedures;
k) agreement on responsibility for error recovery;
l) agreement on the procedures for control of data integrity; and
m) identification of constraints on data syntax (character sets, data structure).

7.1.4 Functions within the Application Layer

The Application Layer contains all functions which imply communication between open systems and are not already performed by the lower layers. These include functions performed by programs as well as functions performed by human beings.

7.1.4.1 Grouping of functions in the Application Layer

An application-entity can be structured internally into groups of functions. The technique used to express this structure is not constrained by this International Standard. Use of one grouping of functions may depend on use of some other functions, and the active functions may vary during the lifetime of a connection.

An application-process may determine the grouping of functions comprising the application-entity.

7.1.4.2 Systems and application management

Systems management functions and application management functions are located in the Application Layer. For details, see clause 5.9.

7.1.4.3 Application Layer management

In addition to systems and application management, there are other activities specifically related to Application Layer management (such as activation and error control). See clause 5.9 for the relationship with other management aspects.

43

7.2 The Presentation Layer

7.2.1   Definitions

7.2.1.1   Presentation-image: The OSI view of a data structure which application-entities wish to refer to in their dialogue, along with the set of actions which may be performed on this data structure.

7.2.1.2   Presentation-image-syntax: The syntactic view of a presentation-image, known by presentation-entities (thus excluding the semantic view, i.e. the meaning of the presentation-image to application-entities, which is not known by presentation-entities).

7.2.1.3   Data syntax: The syntactic view of data transferred between application-entities, known by presentation-entities, (thus excluding the semantic view, i.e. the meaning of the data to application-entities, which is not known by presentation-entities).

NOTE - The terms "internal attribute" and "external attributes" have sometimes been used outside this document to refer respectively to the syntax and to the semantics of a presentation-image. The concept of "internal attribute" is similar to the concept of presentation-image-syntax defined in this International Standard.

7.2.2   Purpose

The Presentation Layer provides for the representation of information that application-entities either communicate or refer to in their dialogue.

The Presentation Layer covers two complementary aspects of this representation of information:

a)   the data syntax which is the representation of data to be transferred between application-entities; and

b)   the presentation-image-syntax which is the representation of the data structure which application-entities refer to in their dialogue, along with the representations of the set of actions which may be performed on this data structure. A presentation-image is the OSI view of such a data structure along with the set of actions possible on it.

The Presentation Layer is concerned only with the syntactic view of the presentation image and of transferred data and not with its semantics, i.e. their meaning to the Application Layer, which is known only by the application-entities.

The Presentation Layer provides for a common representation to be used between application-entities. This relieves application-entities of any concern with the problem of "common" representation of information, i.e. it provides them with syntax independence. This syntax independence can be described in two ways:

44

a) the Presentation Layer provides common syntactical elements which are used by application-entities; and

b) the application-entities can use any syntax and the Presentation Layer provides the transformation between these syntaxes and the common syntax needed for communication between application-entities.

In this International Standard the approach outlined in b) is used.

NOTE: The approach outlined in a) is for further study.

7.2.3 Services provided to the Application Layer

The Presentation Layer provides session-services (see 7.3) and the following facilities:

a) transformation of data syntax;
b) transformation of presentation-image-syntax;
c) selection of data syntax; and
d) selection of presentation-image-syntax.

Transformation of data syntax is concerned primarily with code and character set conversions and with the modification of the layout of the data. Selection of data syntax provides the means of initially selecting a data syntax and subsequently modifying the selection.

Transformation of presentation-image-syntax is concerned with the adaptation of presentation-data-syntax including adaptation of actions on the presentation-image. Selection of the presentation-image-syntax provides the means for initially selecting and subsequently modifying the presentation-image-syntax.

7.2.4 Functions within the Presentation Layer

The Presentation Layer performs the following functions to help accomplish the presentation-services:

a) session establishment request;
b) data transfer;
c) negotiation and renegotiation of data syntax and presentation-image-syntax;
d) transformation of data syntax and presentation-image-syntax including data transformation and formatting and special purpose transformations (e.g. compression); and
e) session termination request.

7.2.4.1 Transformation of data syntax

There are three syntactic versions of the data being transferred: the data syntax used by the application-entity of the originator of the data, the data syntax used by the application-entity of the recipient of the data, and the data syntax used to transfer the data between presentation-entities ("common data syntax"). It is clearly possible that

45

any two or all three of these data syntaxes may be identical. The Presentation Layer contains the functions necessary to transform between the common data syntax and each of the other two data syntaxes as required.

There is not a single predetermined common data syntax for all OSI. The common data syntax to be used on a presentation-connection is negotiated between the correspondent presentation-entities. Thus, a presentation-entity must know the data syntax of its application-entity and the agreed common data syntax. Only the common data syntax needs to be referred to in the Presentation Layer protocols.

To meet the service requirement specified by the application-entities during the initiation phase, the Presentation Layer may utilise any common data syntax available to it. To accomplish other service objectives (e.g. data volume reduction to reduce data transfer cost), data syntax transformation may be performed either as a specific syntax-matching service provided to the application-processes, or as a function internal to the Presentation Layer.

7.2.4.2   Transformations of presentation-image-syntax

There are three versions of the presentation-image-syntax known by the Presentation Layer: the presentation-image-syntax used by the application-entity of the originator of the actions on the data structure, the presentation-image-syntax used by the application-entity of the recipient of the actions on the data structure, and the presentation-image-syntax used to propagate the actions between presentation-entities ("common presentation-image-syntax"). It is clearly possible that any two or all three of these presentation-images-syntaxes may be identical. The Presentation Layer contains the functions necessary to transform between the common presentation-image-syntax and each of the other two presentation-image-syntaxes as required.

There is not a single predetermined common presentation-image-syntax for all OSI. The common presentation-image-syntax to be used on a presentation-connection is negotiated between the correspondent presentation-entities. Thus, a presentation-entity must know the presentation-image-syntax of its local system and the agreed common presentation-image-syntax. Only the common presentation-image-syntax needs to be referred to in the Presentation Layer protocols.

To meet the service requirement specified by the application-entities during the initiation phase, the Presentation Layer may utilise any transfer presentation-image-syntax available to it.

7.2.4.3   Negotiation of data syntax and presentation-image-syntax

Negotiation of data syntax and presentation-image-syntax is carried out by a dialogue between the presentation-entities on behalf of the application-entities to determine the form that data will have while in the OSI environment. The negotiations will determine what transformations are needed (if any) and where they will be performed. Negotiations may be limited to the initiation phase or they may occur any time during a session.

46

In OSI, the data-syntaxes and presentation-image-syntaxes used by application-processes that wish to communicate may be very similar or quite dissimilar. When they are similar, the transformation functions may not be needed at all; however, when they are dissimilar, the Presentation Layer services provide the means to converse and decide where needed transformations will take place.

7.2.4.4 Addressing and multiplexing

There is a one-to-one correspondence between presentation-address and session-address. There is no multiplexing nor splitting in the Presentation Layer.

7.2.4.5 Presentation Layer management

The Presentation Layer protocols deal with some management activities of the layer (such as activation and error control). See clause 5.9 for relationship with other management aspects.

47

7.3 The Session Layer

7.3.1 Definitions

7.3.1.1 <u>Quarantine service</u>: A facility of the session-service by which an integral number of session-service-data-units sent on a session-connection are not made available to the receiving presentation-entity until explicitly released by the sending presentation-entity.

7.3.1.2 <u>Interaction management</u>: A facility of the session-service which allows correspondent presentation-entities to control explicitly whose turn it is to exercise certain control functions.

7.3.1.3 <u>Two-way-simultaneous interaction</u>: A mode of interaction where both presentation-entities may concurrently send and receive.

7.3.1.4 <u>Two-way-alternate interaction</u>: A mode of interaction where the presentation-entity with the turn may send and its correspondent is permitted only to receive.

7.3.1.5 <u>One-way interaction</u>: A form of operation of two-way-alternate interaction in which the turn can never be exchanged.

7.3.1.6 <u>Session-connection synchronization</u>: A facility of the session-service which allows presentation entities to define and identify synchronization points and to reset a session-connection to a predefined state and to agree on a resynchronization point.

7.3.2 Purpose

The purpose of the Session Layer is to provide the means necessary for cooperating presentation-entities to organize and synchronize their dialogue and to manage their data exchange. To do this, the Session Layer provides services to establish a session-connection between two presentation-entities, and to support orderly data exchange interactions.

To implement the transfer of data between the presentation-entities, the session-connection is mapped onto and uses a transport-connection (see 7.3.4.1.).

A session-connection is created when requested by a presentation-entity at a session-service-access-point. During the lifetime of the session -connection, session services are used by the presentation-entities to regulate their dialogue, and to ensure an orderly message exchange on the session-connection. The session-connection exists until it is released by either the presentation-entities or the session-entities. While the session-connection exists, session services maintain the state of the dialogue even over data loss by the Transport Layer.

A presentation-entity can access another presentation-entity only by initiating or accepting a session-connection. A presentation-entity may be associated with several session-connections simultaneously. Both concurrent and consecutive session-connections are possible between two presentation-entities.

48

The initiating presentation-entity designates the destination presentation-entity by a session-address. In many systems, a transport-address may be used as the session-address, i.e., there is a one-to-one correspondence between the session-address and the transport-address. In general, however, there is a many-to-one correspondence between session-addresses and transport-addresses. This does not imply multiplexing of session-connections onto transport-connections, but does imply that at session-connection establishment time, more than one presentation-entity is a potential target of a session-connection establishment request arriving on a given transport-connection.

7.3.3   Services provided to the Presentation Layer

The following services provided by the Session Layer are described below:

a)   session-connection establishment;
b)   session-connection release;
c)   normal data exchange;
d)   quarantine service;
e)   expedited data exchange;
f)   interaction management;
g)   session-connection synchronization; and
h)   exception reporting.

7.3.3.1   Session-connection establishment

The session-connection establishment service enables two presentation-entities to establish a session-connection between themselves. The presentation-entities are identified by session-addresses used to request the establishment of the session-connection.

The session-connection establishment service allows the presentation-entities cooperatively to determine the unique values of session-connection parameters at the time the session-connection is established.

NOTE - The provision for change of session parameters after session-connection establishment is a candidate for further extension.

Simultaneous session-connection establishment requests typically result in a corresponding number of session-connections, but a session-entity can always reject an incoming request.

The session-connection establishment service provides to the presentation-entities a session-service-connection-identifier which uniquely specifies the session-connection within the environment of the correspondent presentation-entities, with a lifetime which may be greater than the lifetime of the session-connection. This identifier may be used by the presentation-entities to refer to the session-connection during the lifetime of the session-connection, and may also be used by management-entities for administrative purposes such as accounting.

49

7.3.3.2 Session-connection release

The session-connection release service allows presentation-entities to release a session-connection in an orderly way without loss of data. It also allows either presentation-entity to request at any time that a session-connection be aborted; in this case, data may be lost.

The release of a session-connection may also be initiated by one of the session-entities supporting it.

7.3.3.3 Normal data exchange

The normal data exchange service allows a sending presentation-entity to transfer a session-service-data-unit to a receiving presentation-entity. This service allows the receiving presentation-entity to ensure that it is not overloaded with data.

7.3.3.4 Quarantine service

The quarantine service allows the sending presentation-entity to request that an integral number of session-service-data-units (one or more) sent on a session-connection should not be made available to the receiving presentation-entity until explicitly released by the sending presentation-entity. The sending presentation-entity may request that all data currently quarantined be discarded. The receiving presentation-entity receives no information that data being received has been quarantined or that some data was discarded.

7.3.3.5 Expedited data exchange

The expedited data exchange service provides expedited handling for the transfer of expedited session-service-data-units. A specific size restriction is placed on expedited session-service-data-units. This service may be used by either presentation entity at any time that a session-connection exists.

7.3.3.6 Interaction management

The interaction management service allows the presentation-entities to control explicitly whose turn it is to exercise certain control functions.

The service provides for voluntary exchange of the turn where the presentation-entity which has the turn relinquishes it voluntarily. This service also provides for forced exchange of the turn where, upon request from the presentation-entity which does not have the turn, the session-service may force the presentation-entity with the turn to relinquish it. In the case of forced exchange of the turn, data may be lost.

50

The following types of session-service-data-unit exchange interaction are defined:

a) two-way-simultaneous (TWS);
b) two-way-alternate (TWA); and
c) one-way interaction.

7.3.3.7 Session-connection synchronization

The session-connection synchronization service allows presentation-entities to:

a) define and identify synchronization points; and
b) reset the session-connection to a defined state and agree on a resynchronization point.

The Session Layer is not responsible for any associated checkpointing or commitment action associated with synchronization.

7.3.3.8 Exception reporting

The exception reporting service permits the presentation-entities to be notified of exceptional situations not covered by other services, such as unrecoverable session malfunctions.

NOTE - The following services are candidates for future extensions:

a) session-service-data-unit sequence numbering;
b) brackets;
c) stop-go; and
d) security.

7.3.4 Functions within the Session Layer

The functions within the Session Layer are those which must be performed by session-entities in order to provide the session services.

Most of the functions required are readily implied by the services provided. Additional description is given below for the following functions:

a) session-connection to transport-connection mapping;
b) session-connection flow control;
c) expedited data transfer;
d) session-connection recovery;
e) session-connection release; and
f) Session Layer management.

51

7.3.4.1 Session-connection to transport-connection mapping

There is a one-to-one mapping between a session-connection and a transport-connection at any given instant. However, the lifetime of a transport-connection and that of a related session-connection can be distinguished so that the following cases are defined:

a)   A transport-connection supports several consecutive session-connections (see figure 14); and

b)   Several consecutive transport-connections support a session-connection (see figure 15).

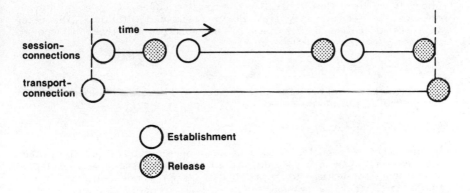

Figure 14 - Several consecutive session-connections

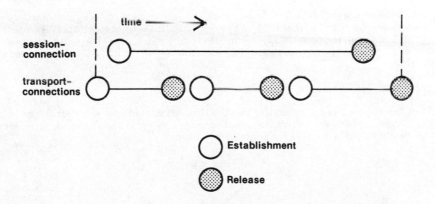

Figure 15 - Several consecutive transport-connections

52

NOTE 1 - It is also possible to consider cases in which one transport -connection is used to support several session-connections (i.e., n-to-1 mapping). In this case peer flow control would be required in the Session Layer. This case is for future development if needed.

NOTE 2 - To implement the mapping of a session-connection onto a transport-connection, the Session Layer must map session-service-data-units into session-protocol-data-units, and session-protocol-data-units into transport-service-data-units. These mappings may require the session -entities to perform functions such as segmenting. These functions are visible only in the session protocols, therefore they are transparent to the Presentation and Transport Layers.

7.3.4.2   Session-connection flow control

There is no peer flow control in the Session Layer. To prevent the receiving presentation-entity from being overloaded with data, the receiving session-entity applies back pressure across the transport-connection using the transport flow control.

7.3.4.3   Expedited data transfer

The transfer of expedited session-service-data-units is generally accomplished by use of the expedited transport service.

7.3.4.5   Session-connection recovery

In the event of reported failure of an underlying transport-connection, the Session Layer may contain the functions necessary to re-establish a transport-connection to support the session-connection, which continues to exist. The session-entities involved notify the presentation-entities via the exception reporting service that service is interrupted and restore the service only as directed by the presentation -entities. This permits the presentation-entities to resynchronize and continue from an agreed state.

7.3.4.6   Session-connection release

The Session Layer contains the functions necessary to release the session-connection in an orderly way, without loss of data, upon request by the presentation-entities. The Session Layer also contains the necessary functions to abort the session-connection with the possible loss of data.

7.3.4.7   Session Layer management

The Session Layer protocols deal with some management activities of the layer (such as activation and error control). See clause 5.9 for the relationship with other management aspects.

53

7.4 The Transport Layer

7.4.1   Definitions

No Transport Layer specific terms are identified.

7.4.2   Purpose

The transport-service provides transparent transfer of data between session-entities and relieves them from any concern with the detailed way in which reliable and cost effective transfer of data is achieved.

The Transport Layer optimizes the use of the available network-service to provide the performance required by each session-entity at minimum cost. This optimization is achieved within the constraints imposed by the overall demands of all concurrent session-entities and the overall quality and capacity of the network-service available to the Transport Layer.

All protocols defined in the Transport Layer have end-to-end significance, where the ends are defined as correspondent transport-entities. Therefore the Transport Layer is OSI end system oriented and transport-protocols operate only between OSI end systems.

The Transport Layer is relieved of any concern with routing, and rel aying since the network-service provides network-connections from any transport-entity to any other, including the case of tandem subnetworks (see 7.5.1.).

The transport functions invoked in the Transport Layer to provide a requested service quality depend on the quality of the network-service. The quality of the network-service depends on the way the network -service is achieved (see 7.5.3).

7.4.3   Services provided to the Session Layer

The Transport Layer uniquely identifies each session-entity by its transport-address. The transport-service provides the means to establish, maintain and release transport-connections. Transport-connections provide duplex transmission between a pair of transport-addresses.

More than one transport-connection can be established between the same pair of transport-addresses. A session-entity uses transport-connection-endpoint-identifiers provided by the Transport Layer to distinguish between transport-connection-endpoints.

The operation of one transport-connection is independent of the operation of all others except for the limitations imposed by the finite resources available to the Transport Layer.

The quality of service provided on a transport-connection depends on the service class requested by the session-entities when establishing the transport-connection. The selected quality of service is maintained throughout the lifetime of the transport-connection. The session-entity is notified of any failure to maintain the selected quality of service on a given transport-connection.

The following services provided by the Transport Layer are described below:

a)   transport-connection establishment;
b)   data transfer; and
c)   transport-connection release.

7.4.3.1   Transport-connection establishment

Transport-connections are established between session-entities identified by transport-addresses. The quality of service of the transport-connection is negotiated between the session-entities and the transport-service.

At the time of establishment of a transport-connection the class of transport service to be provided can be selected from a defined set of available classes of service.

These service classes are characterized by combinations of selected values of parameters such as throughput, transit delay, and connection set-up delay and by guaranteed values of parameters such as residual error rate and service availability.

These classes of service represent globally predefined combinations of parameters controlling quality of service. These classes of service are intended to cover the transport-service requirements of the various types of traffic generated by the session-entities.

7.4.3.2   Data transfer

This service provides data transfer in accordance with the agreed quality of service. When the quality of service cannot be maintained and all possible recovery attempts have failed, the transport-connection is terminated and the session-entities are notified.

a)   The transport-service-data-unit transfer-service provides the means by which transport-service-data-units of arbitrary length are delimited and transparently transfered in sequence from one sending transport-service-access-point to the receiving transport-service-access-point over a transport-connection. This service is subject to flow control.

b)   The expedited transport-service-data-unit transfer-service provides an additional means of information exchange on a transport-connection. The expedited transport-data-units are subject to their own set of transport-service and flow control characteristics. The maximum size of expedited transport-service-data-units is limited.

55

7.4.3.3 Transport-connection release

This service provides the means by which either session-entity can release a transport-connection and have the correspondent session-entity informed of the release.

7.4.4 Functions within the Transport Layer

The Transport Layer functions may include:

a) mapping transport-address onto network-address;
b) multiplexing (end-to-end) transport-connections onto network- connections;
c) Establishment and release of transport-connections;
d) end-to-end sequence control on individual connections;
e) end-to-end error detection and any necessary monitoring of the quality of service;
f) end-to-end error recovery;
g) end-to-end segmenting, blocking and concatenation;
h) end-to-end flow control on individual connections;
i) supervisory functions; and
j) expedited transport-service-data-unit transfer.

7.4.4.1 Addressing

When a session-entity requests the Transport Layer to establish a transport-connection with another session-entity identified by its transport-address, the Transport Layer determines the network-address identifying the transport-entity which serves the correspondent session-entity.

Because transport-entities support services on an end-to-end basis no intermediate transport-entity is involved as a relay between the end transport-entities. Therefore the Transport Layer maps transport-addresses to the network-addresses which identify the end transport-entities (see figure 16).

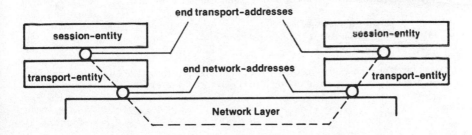

Figure 16 - Association of transport-addresses
and network-addresses

56

One transport-entity may serve more than one session-entity. Several transport-addresses may be associated with one network-address within the scope of the same transport-entity. Corresponding mapping functions are performed within the transport-entities to provide these facilities (see figure 17).

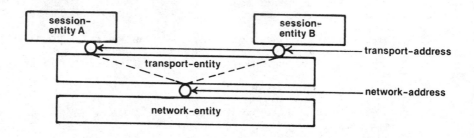

Figure 17 - Association of one network-address with several transport-addresses

7.4.4.2 Connection multiplexing and splitting

In order to optimize the use of network-connections, the mapping of transport-connections onto network-connections need not be on a one-to-one basis. Both splitting and multiplexing may be performed, namely for optimizing cost of usage of the network-service.

7.4.4.3 Phases of operation

The phases of operation within the Transport Layer are

    a)   establishment phase;
    b)   data transfer phase; and
    c)   release phase.

The transfer from one phase of operation to the other will be specified in detail within the protocol for the Transport Layer.

348 Computer network architectures

7.4.4.4   Establishment phase

During the establishment phase, the Transport Layer establishes a transport-connection between two session-entities. The functions of the Transport Layer during this phase must match the requested class of services with the services provided by the Network Layer. The following functions may be performed during this phase:

- a) Obtain a network-connection which best matches the requirements of the session-entity, taking into account cost and quality of services;
- b) decide whether multiplexing or splitting is needed to optimize the use of network-connections;
- c) establish the optimum transport-protocol-data-unit size;
- d) select the functions that will be operational upon entering the data phase;
- e) map transport-addresses onto network-addresses;
- f) provide identification of different transport-connections between the same pair of transport-service-access-points (connection identification function); and
- g) transfer of data.

7.4.4.5   Data transfer phase

The purpose of the data transfer phase is to transfer transport-service-data-units between the two session-entities connected by the transport-connection. This is achieved by the transmission of transport-protocol-data-units and by the following functions, each of which is used or not used according to the class of service selected in the establishment phase:

- a) sequencing;
- b) blocking;
- c) concatenation;
- d) segmenting;
- e) multiplexing or splitting;
- f) flow control;
- g) error detection;
- h) error recovery;
- i) expedited data transfer;
- j) transport-service-data-unit delimiting; and
- k) transport-connection identification.

7.4.4.6   Release phase

The purpose of the release phase is to release the transport-connection. It may include the following functions:

- a) notification of reason for release;
- b) identification of the transport-connection released; and
- c) transfer of data.

7.4.4.7   Transport Layer management

The Transport Layer protocols deal with some management activities of the layer (such as activation and error control). See clause 5.9 for the relationship with other management aspects.

7.5 The Network Layer

7.5.1　　Definitions

7.5.1.1　Subnetwork: A set of one or more intermediate systems which provide relaying and through which end systems may establish network-connections.

NOTE - A subnetwork is a representation within the OSI Reference Model of a real network such as a carrier network, a private network or a local area network.

7.5.1.2　Subnetwork-connection: A communication path through a sub-network which is used by entities in the Network Layer in providing a network-connection.

7.5.2　　Purpose

The Network Layer provides the means to establish, maintain and terminate network-connections between systems containing communicating application-entities and the functional and procedural means to exchange network-service-data-units between transport-entities over network connections.

It provides to the transport-entities independence from routing and relay considerations associated with the establishment and operation of a given network-connection. This includes the case where several subnetworks are used in tandem (see 7.5.4.2) or in parallel. It makes invisible to transport-entities how underlying resources such as datalink-connections are used to provide network-connections.

Any relay functions and hop-by-hop service enhancement protocols used to support the network service between the OSI end systems are operating below the Transport Layer, i.e. within the Network Layer or below.

7.5.3　　Services provided to the Transport Layer

The basic service of the Network Layer is to provide the transparent transfer of data between transport-entities. This service allows the structure and detailed content of submitted data to be determined exclusively by layers above the Network Layer.

All services are provided to the Transport Layer at a known cost.

The Network Layer contains functions necessary to provide the Transport Layer with a firm Network/Transport Layer boundary which is independent of the underlying communications media in all things other than quality of service. Thus the Network Layer contains functions necessary to mask the differences in the characteristics of different transmission and subnetwork technologies into a consistent network service.

59

The service provided at each end of a network-connection is the same even when a network-connection spans several subnetworks, each offering dissimilar services. (see 7.5.4.2).

NOTE - It is important to distinguish the specialized use of the term "service" within the OSI Reference Model from its common use by suppliers of private networks and carriers.

The quality of service is negotiated between the transport-entities and the network-service at the time of establishment of a network-connection. While this quality of service may vary from one network-connection to another it will be agreed for a given network- connection and be the same at both network-connection-endpoints.

The following services or elements of services provided by the Network Layer are described below:

a)   network-addresses;
b)   network-connections;
c)   network-connection-endpoint-identifiers;
d)   network-service-data unit transfer;
e)   quality of service parameters;
f)   error notification;
g)   sequencing;
h)   flow control;
i)   expedited network-service-data-unit transfer;
j)   reset; and
k)   release.

Some of the services described below are optional. This means that:

a)   the user has to request the service; and
b)   the network-service provider may honour the request or indicate that the service is not available.

7.5.3.1   Network-addresses

Transport entities are known to the Network Layer by means of network-addresses. Network-addresses are provided by the Network Layer and can be used by transport-entities to uniquely identify other transport-entities, i.e. network-addresses are necessary for transport-entities to communicate using the network-service. The Network Layer uniquely identifies each of the end systems (represented by transport-entities) by their network-addresses. This may be independent of the addressing needed by the underlying layers.

60

7.5.3.2 Network-connections

A network-connection provides the means of transferring data between transport-entities identified by network-addresses. The Network Layer provides the means to establish, maintain and release network-connections.

A network-connection is point-to-point.

More than one network-connection may exist between the same pair of network-addresses.

7.5.3.3 Network-connection-endpoint-identifiers

The Network Layer provides to the transport-entity a network-connection-endpoint-identifier which identifies the network-connection- endpoint uniquely with the associated network-address.

7.5.3.4 Network-service-data-unit transfer

On a network-connection, the Network Layer provides for the transmission of network-service-data-units. These units have a distinct beginning and end and the integrity of the unit content is maintained by the Network Layer.

No limit is imposed on the maximum size of network-service-data-units.

The network-service-data-units are transferred transparently between transport-entities.

7.5.3.5 Quality of service parameters

The Network Layer establishes and maintains a selected quality of service for the duration of the network-connection.

The quality of service parameters include residual error rate, service availability, reliability, throughput, transit delay (including variations), and delay for network-connection establishment.

7.5.3.6 Error notification

Unrecoverable errors detected by the Network Layer are reported to the transport-entities.

Error notification may or may not lead to the release of the network-connection, according to the specification of a particular network-service.

7.5.3.7 Sequencing

The Network Layer may provide sequenced delivery of network-service-data-units over a given network-connection when requested by the transport-entities.

352 Computer network architectures

7.5.3.8 Flow control

A transport-entity which is receiving at one end of a network-connection can cause the network-service to stop transferring network-service-data-units across the service-access-point. This flow control condition may or may not be propagated to the other end of the network-connection and thus be reflected to the transmitting transport-entity, according to the specification of a particular network-service.

7.5.3.9 Expedited network-service-data-unit transfer (optional)

The expedited network-service-data-unit transfer is optional and provides an additional means of information exchange on a network-connection. The transfer of expedited network-service-data-units is subject to a different set of network-service characteristics and to separate flow control.

The maximum size of expedited network-service-data-units is limited.

7.5.3.10 Reset (optional)

The reset service is optional and when invoked causes the Network Layer to discard all network-service-data-units in transit on the network-connection and to notify the transport-entity at the other end of the network-connection that a reset has occurred.

7.5.3.11 Release

A transport-entity may request release of a network-connection. The network-service does not guarantee the delivery of data preceding the release request and still in transit. The network-connection is released regardless of the action taken by the correspondent transport-entity.

NOTE - confirmation of receipt is a candidate for future extension.

7.5.4 Functions within the Network Layer

Network Layer functions provide for the wide variety of configurations supporting network-connections ranging from network-connections supported by point-to-point configurations, to network-connections supported by complex combinations of subnetworks with different characteristics.

NOTE - In order to cope with this wide variety of cases, network functions should be structured into sublayers.

The following are functions performed by the Network Layer:

a) routing and relaying;
b) network-connections;
c) network-connection multiplexing;
d) segmenting and blocking;
e) error detection;
f) error recovery;
g) sequencing;
h) flow control;
i) expedited data transfer;
j) reset;
k) service selection; and
l) Network Layer management.

7.5.4.1 Routing and relaying

Network-connections are provided by network-entities in end systems but may involve intermediate systems which provide relaying.
These intermediate systems may interconnect subnetwork-connections, data-link-connections, and data-circuits (see 7.7). Routing functions determine an appropriate route between network-addresses. In order to set up the resulting communication, it may be necessary for the Network Layer to use the services of the Data Link Layer to control the interconnection of data-circuits (see 7.6.4.10 and 7.7.3.1).

NOTE - When Network Layer functions are performed by combinations of several individual subnetworks, the specification of routing and relaying functions could be facilitated by using sublayers, isolating individual subnetworks routing and relaying functions from internetwork routing and relaying functions.

7.5.4.2 Network-connections

This function provides network-connections between transport-entities, making use of data-link-connections provided by the Data Link Layer.

A network-connection may also be provided as subnetwork-connections in tandem, i.e. using several individual subnetworks in series. The interconnected individual subnetworks may have the same or different service capabilities. Each end of a subnetwork-connection, may operate with a different subnetwork protocol.

The interconnection of a pair of subnetworks of differing qualities may be achieved in two ways. To illustrate these, consider a pair of subnetworks, one of high quality and the other of low quality:

63

a)   The two subnetworks are interconnected as they stand. The quality of the resulting network-connection is not higher than that of the lower quality subnetwork (figure 18).

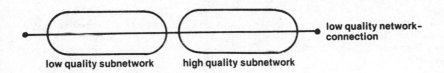

low quality subnetwork   **high quality subnetwork**   **low quality network-connection**

Figure 18 - Interconnection of a low quality subnetwork and a high quality subnetwork

b)   The lower quality subnetwork is enhanced equal to the higher quality subnetwork and the subnetworks are then interconnected. The quality of the resulting network-connection is approximately that of the higher quality subnetwork.

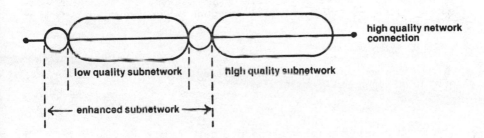

low quality subnetwork   **high quality subnetwork**   **high quality network connection**

← enhanced subnetwork →

Figure 19 - Interconnection of an enhanced low quality subnetwork and a high quality subnetwork

The choice between these two alternatives depends on the degree of difference in quality, the cost of enhancement, and other economic factors.

7.5.4.3   Network-connection multiplexing

This function may be used to multiplex network-connections onto data-link-connections in order to optimize their use.

In the case of subnetwork-connections in tandem, multiplexing onto individual subnetwork-connections may also be performed in order to optimize their use.

7.5.4.4   Segmenting and blocking

The Network Layer may segment and/or block network-service-data-units for the purpose of facilitating the transfer. However the network-service-data-unit delimiters are preserved over the network-connection.

7.5.4.5   Error detection

Error detection functions are used to check that the quality of service provided over a network-connection is maintained. Error detection in the Network Layer uses error notification from the Data Link Layer. Additional error detection capabilities may be necessary to provide the required quality of service.

7.5.4.6   Error recovery

This function provides for recovering from detected errors. These function may vary depending on the quality of the network service provided.

7.5.4.7   Sequencing

This function provides for the sequenced delivery of network-service-data-units over a given network-connection when requested by transport-entities.

7.5.4.8   Flow control

If flow control service is required (see 7.5.3.8), this function may need to be performed.

7.5.4.9   Expedited data transfer

This function provides for the expedited data transfer service.

7.5.4.10   Reset

This function provides for the reset service.

7.5.4.11   Service selection

This function allows service selection to be carried out to ensure that the service provided at each end of a network-connection is the same when a network connection spans several subnetworks of dissimilar quality.

65

7.5.4.12 Network Layer management

The Network Layer protocols deal with some management activities of the layer (such as activation and error control). See clause 5.9 for the relationship with other management aspects.

7.6 The Data Link Layer

7.6.1   Definitions

No Data Link Layer specific terms are identified.

7.6.2   Purpose

The Data Link Layer provides functional and procedural means to establish, maintain and release data-link-connections among network-entities and to transfer data-link-service-data-units. A data-link-connection is built upon one or several physical-connections.

The Data Link Layer detects and possibly corrects errors which may
occur in the Physical Layer.

In addition, the Data Link Layer enables the Network Layer to control
the interconnection of data-circuits within the Physical Layer.

7.6.3   Services provided to the Network Layer

The following services or elements of services provided by the Data
Link Layer are described below:

    a)   data-link-connection;
    b)   data-link-service-data-units;
    c)   data-link-connection-endpoint-identifiers;
    d)   sequencing;
    e)   error notification;
    f)   flow control ; and
    g)   quality of service parameters.

7.6.3.1   Data-link-connection

The Data Link Layer provides one or more data-link-connections between two network-entities. A data-link-connection is always established
and released dynamically.

7.6.3.2   Data-link-service-data-units

The Data Link Layer allows exchange of data-link-service-data-units
over a data-link-connection.

The size of the data-link-service-data-units may be limited by the relationship between the physical-connection error rate and the Data Link
Layer error detection capability.

7.6.3.3   Data-link-connection-endpoint-identifiers

If needed, the Data Link Layer provides data-link-connection-endpoint-
identifiers that can be used by a network-entity to identify a network-connection.

7.6.3.4 Sequencing

When required, the sequence integrity of data-link-service-data-units is maintained.

7.6.3.5 Error notification

Notification is provided to the network-entity when any unrecoverable error is detected by the Data Link Layer.

7.6.3.6 Flow control

Each network-entity can dynamically control (up to the agreed maximum) the rate at which it receives data-link-service-data-units from a data-link-connection. This control may be reflected in the rate at which the Data Link Layer accepts data-link-service-data-units at the correspondent data-link-connection-endpoint.

7.6.3.7 Quality of service parameters

Quality of service parameters may be optionally selectable. The Data Link Layer establishes and maintains a selected quality of service for the duration of the data-link-connection. The quality of service parameters include mean time between detected but unrecoverable errors, residual error rate (where errors may arise from alteration, loss, duplication, disordering, misdelivery of data-link-service-data-unit, and other causes), service availability, transit delay and throughput.

7.6.4 Functions within the Data Link Layer

The following functions performed by the Data Link Layer are described below:

a) data-link-connection establishment and release;
b) data-link-service-data-unit mapping;
c) data-link connection splitting;
d) delimiting and synchronization;
e) sequence control;
f) error detection;
g) error recovery;
h) flow control;
I) identification and parameter exchange;
j) control of data-circuit interconnection; and
k) Data Link Layer management.

7.6.4.1 Data-link-connection establishment and release

This function establishes and releases data-link-connections on activated physical-connections. When a physical-connection has multiple endpoints (e.g. multipoint connection), a specific function is needed within the Data Link Layer to identify the data-link-connections using such a physical-connection.

68

7.6.4.2 Data-link-service-data-unit mapping

This function maps data-link-service-data-units into data-link-protocol-data-units on a one to one basis.

NOTE - More general mappings are for further study.

7.6.4.3 Data-link-connection splitting

This function performs splitting of one data-link-connection onto several physical-connections.

7.6.4.4 Delimiting and synchronization

These functions provide recognition of a sequence of physical-service-data-units (i.e. bits, see 7.7.3.2) transmitted over the physical-connection, as a data-link-protocol-data-unit.

NOTE - These functions are sometimes referred to as framing.

7.6.4.5 Sequence control

This function maintains the sequential order of data-link-service-data-units across a data-link-connection.

7.6.4.6 Error detection

This function detects transmission, format and operational errors occurring either on the physical-connection, or as a result of a malfunction of the correspondent data-link-entity.

7.6.4.7 Error recovery

This function attempts to recover from detected transmission, format and operational errors and notifies the network-entities of errors which are unrecoverable.

7.6.4.8 Flow control

This function provides the flow control service as indicated in 7.6.3.6.

7.6.4.9 Identification and parameter exchange

This function performs data-link-entity identification and parameter exchange.

7.6.4.10 Control of data-circuit interconnection

This function conveys to network-entities the capability of controlling the interconnection of data-circuits within the Physical Layer.

7.6.4.11 Data Link Layer management

The Data Link Layer protocols deal with some management activities of the layer (such as activation and error control). See clause 5.9 for the relationship with other management aspects.

69

7.7 The Physical Layer

7.7.1   Definitions

7.7.1.1   Data-circuit: A communication path in the physical media for OSI between two physical-entities, together with the facilities necessary in the Physical Layer for the transmission of bits on it.

7.7.2   Purpose

The Physical Layer provides mechanical, electrical, functional and procedural means to activate, maintain and deactivate physical connections for bit transmission between data-link-entities. A physical-connection may involve intermediate systems, each relaying bit transmission within the Physical Layer. Physical Layer entities are interconnected by means of a physical medium.

7.7.3   Services provided to the Data Link Layer

The following services or elements of services provided by the Physical Layer are described below:

a)   physical-connections;
b)   physical-service-data-units;
c)   physical-connection-endpoints;
d)   data-circuit identification;
e)   sequencing;
f)   fault condition notification; and
g)   quality of service parameters.

7.7.3.1   Physical-connections

The Physical Layer provides for the transparent transmission of bit streams between data-link-entities across physical-connections.

A data-circuit is a communication path in the physical media for OSI between two physical-entities, together with the facilities necessary in the Physical Layer for the transmission of bits on it.

A physical-connection may be provided by the interconnection of data-circuits using relaying functions in the Physical Layer. The provision of a physical-connection by such an assembly of data-circuits is illustrated in figure 20.

70

The control of the interconnection of data-circuits is offered as a service to data-link-entities.

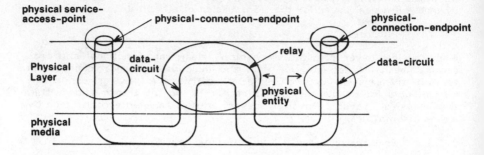

Figure 20 - Interconnection of data-circuits within the Physical Layer

7.7.3.2 Physical-service-data-units

A physical-service-data-unit consists of one bit in serial transmission and of "n" bits in parallel transmission.

A physical-connection may allow duplex or half-duplex transmission of bit streams.

7.7.3.3 Physical-connection-endpoints

The Physical Layer provides physical-connection-endpoint-identifiers which may be used by a data-link-entity to identify physical-connection-endpoints.

A physical-connection will have two (point-to-point) or more (multi-endpoint) physical-connection-endpoints (see figure 21).

7.7.3.4 Data-circuit identification

The Physical Layer provides identifiers which uniquely specifiy the data-circuits between two adjacent systems.

NOTE - This identifier is used by network-entities in adjacent systems to refer to data-circuits in their dialogue.

71

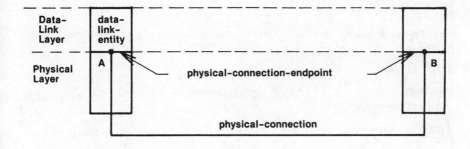

Example of a two endpoint physical connection
(connection exists between A and B)

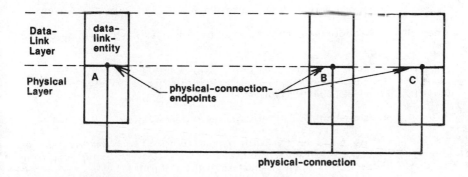

Example of a multi-endpoint physical-connection
(connection exists between A, B and C)

Figure 21 - Examples of physical-connections

72

7.7.3.5   Sequencing

The Physical Layer delivers bits in the same order in which they were submitted.

7.7.3.6   Fault condition notification

Data-link-entities are notified of fault conditions detected within the Physical Layer.

7.7.3.7   Quality of service parameters

The quality of service of a physical-connection is derived from the data circuits forming it. The quality of service can be characterized by:

a)   error rate, where errors may arise from alteration, loss, creation, and other causes;
b)   service availability;
c)   transmission rate; and
d)   transit delay.

7.7.4   Functions within the Physical Layer

The following functions performed by the Physical Layer are described below:

a)   physical-connection activation and deactivation;
b)   physical-service-data-unit transmission; and
c)   Physical Layer management.

7.7.4.1   Physical-connection activation and deactivation

These functions provide for with the activation and deactivation of physical-connections between two data-link-entities including interconnection of data-circuits upon request from the Data Link Layer.

7.7.4.2   Physical-service-data-unit transmission

The transmission of physical-service-data-units (i.e. bits) may be synchronous or asynchronous.

7.7.4.3   Physical Layer Management

The Physical Layer protocols deal with some management activities of the Layer (such as activation and error control). See clause 5.9 for the relationship with other management aspects.

73

ANNEX A - Brief explanation of how the layers were chosen

This annex provides elements giving additional information to this International Standard, which are not an integral part of it.

The following is a brief explanation of how the layers were chosen:

a)   It is essential that the architecture permit usage of a realistic variety of physical media for interconnection with different control procedures (e.g. V.24, V.25, X.21, etc...). Application of principles P3, P5 and P8 leads to identification of a Physical Layer as the lowest layer in the architecture.

b)   Some physical communication media (e.g. telephone line) require specific techniques to be used in order to transmit data between systems despite a relatively high error rate (i.e. an error rate not acceptable for the great majority of applications). These specific techniques are used in data-link control procedures which have been studied and standardized for a number of years. It must also be recognized that new physical communication media (e.g. fibre optics) will require different data-link control procedures. Application of principles P3, P5, and P8 leads to identification of a Data Link Layer on top of the Physical Layer in the architecture.

c)   In the open systems architecture, some systems will act as the final destination of data, see 4. Some systems may act only as intermediate nodes (forwarding data to other systems), see figure 13. Application of principles P3, P5 and P7 leads to identification of a Network Layer on top of the Data Link Layer. Network oriented protocols such as routing, for example, will be grouped in this layer. Thus, the Network Layer will provide a connection path (network-connection) between a pair of transport-entities, including the case where intermediate nodes are involved, see figure 13 (See also 7.5.4.1).

d)   Control of data transportation from source end-system to destination end-system (which is not performed in Intermediate nodes) is the last function to be performed in order to provide the totality of the transport-service. Thus, the upper layer in the transport-service part of the architecture is the Transport Layer, on top of the Network Layer. This Transport Layer relieves higher layer entities from any concern with the transportation of data between them.

e)   There is a need to organize and synchronize dialogue, and to manage the exchange of data. Application of principles P3 and P4 leads to the identification of a Session Layer on top of the Transport Layer.

f) The remaining set of general interest functions are those related to representation and manipulation of structured data for the benefit of application programs. Application of principles P3 and P4 leads to identification of a <u>Presentation Layer</u> on top of the Session Layer.

g) Finally, there are applications consisting of application processes which perform information processing. An aspect of these application processes and the protocols by which they communicate comprise the <u>Application Layer</u> as the highest layer of the architecture.

The resulting architecture with seven layers, illustrated in figure 12 obeys principles P1 and P2.

A more detailed definition of each of the seven layers identified above is given in clause 7 of this International Standard, starting from the top with the Application Layer described in 7.1 down to the Physical Layer described in 7.7.

75

ANNEX B - Alphabetical index to definitions

77

78

EXPLANATORY REPORT

The Open Systems Interconnection Basic Reference Model has been under
study since 1979. A first draft proposal (DP 7498) was issued for vote
in December 1980. Based on comments received, a second DP 7498
(97/16 N 719) was circulated for vote in August 1981. The results of
this vote (ref 97/16 N 806) were 12 approvals (10 with comments) and ·no
disapprovals. The Secretariat convened a small technical advisory/
editing group to review the comments and prepare a revised text for
submission as a Draft International Standard. It is this text
(97/16 N 890) that is hereby submitted for ISO Member Body vote.

Appendix B   Services and functions defined in the Reference Model

In this appendix, we list the services and functions for each of the layers of the Reference Model. This list is compiled directly from the Draft International Standard, as it is included in Appendix A. It is used in the various chapters on proprietary architectures to map them against the Reference Model.

B.1.1 Physical Layer

Services provided by the Physical Layer
- Physical-connections
- Physical-service-data-units
- Physical-connection-endpoints
- Data circuit identification
- Sequencing
- Fault condition notification
- Quality of service parameters

Functions in the Physical Layer
- Physical-connection activation and deactivation
- Physical-service-data-unit transmission
- Physical Layer Management

B.1.2 Data Link Layer

Services provided by the Data Link Layer
- Data-link-connections
- Data-link-service-data-units
- Data-link-connection-endpoint-identifiers
- Sequencing
- Error notification
- Flow control
- Quality of service parameters

Functions in the Data Link layer
- Data-link-connection establishment and release
- Data-link-service-data-units mapping
- Data-link-connection splitting
- Delimiting and synchronization
- Sequence control
- Error detection
- Error recovery
- Flow control
- Identification and parameter exchange
- Control of data circuit interconnection
- Data Link Layer Management

B.1.3 Network Layer

Services provided by the Network Layer
- Network addresses
- Network-connections
- Network-connection-endpoint-identifiers
- Network-service-data-unit transfer
- Quality of service parameters
- Error notification
- Sequencing
- Flow control
- Expedited network-service-data-unit transfer
- Reset
- Release services

Functions in the Network Layer
- Routing and relaying
- Network-connections
- Network-connection multiplexing
- Segmenting and blocking
- Error detection
- Error recovery
- Sequencing
- Flow control
- Expedited data transfer
- Reset
- Service selection
- Network Layer Management

B.1.4 Transport Layer

Services provided by the Transport Layer
- Identification
  - Transport-addresses
  - Transport-connections
  - Transport-connection-endpoint-identifiers
- Establishment services
  - Transport-connection establishment
  - Class of service selection
- Data transfer services
  - Transport-service-data-unit
  - Expedited transport-service-data-unit
- Transport-connection release

Functions in the Transport Layer
- Addressing
- Connection multiplexing and splitting
- Phases of operation
  - Establishment phase
  - Data transfer phase
    - Sequencing
    - Blocking
    - Concatenation
    - Segmenting
    - Multiplexing or splitting
    - Flow control
    - Error detection
    - Error recovery
    - Expedited data transfer
    - Transport-service-data-unit delimiting
    - Transport-connection identification
  - Release phase
- Transport Layer Management

B.1.5 Session Layer

Services provided by the Session Layer
- Session-connection establishment
- Session-connection release
- Normal Data Exchange
- Quarantine service
- Expedited data exchange
- Interaction management
  - Two-Way-Simultaneous
  - Two-Way-Alternate
  - One-Way

- Session-connection synchronization
- Exception reporting
- Additional. In the Reference Model, several functions are listed as potential additions to the services in the Session Layer. They are listed here, although not yet part of the Reference Model, because some of these functions are defined already in some proprietary architectures.

  a Session-service-data-unit sequence numbering
  b Brackets
  c Stop–go
  d Security

Functions in the Session Layer
- Mapping of session-connection onto transport-connection
- Session-connection flow control
- Expedited data transfer
- Session-connection recovery
- Session-connection release
- Session Layer Management

B.1.6 Presentation Layer

Services provided by the Presentation Layer
- Data transformation
- Data formatting
- Syntax selection
- Presentation-connections

Functions in the Presentation Layer
- General
  - Session establishment request
  - Presentation image negotiation and renegotiation
  - Data transformation and formatting
  - Special-purpose transformations
  - Session termination request
- Addressing and multiplexing
- Presentation Layer Management

Appendix C Comparison of architectures

In the figure overleaf, the major architectures that were discussed in the chapters on proprietary architectures are mapped in a pictorial way. This figure is included for easy reference. It gives, of course, only a summarized, incomplete view of the relationship between these architectures.

OSI		SNA	DNA	DCA	BNA	OSI	IPA	Full XEM
International Standards Organization		International Business Machines	Digital Equipment Corporation	Univac	Burroughs	OSI	International Computers Limited	
7	Application Layer	End-user	End-user	End-user	End-user	7	Application	Application
6	Presentation Layer	Function Management Services	Network Application	Communications System User	Host Services	6	Dialog Control	
5	Session layer	Data Flow Control	Session control / Network Services	Logical Port / Logical Port Multiplexer	Port Level	5	Dialog Control	Access Levels
4	Transport Layer	Transmission Control	Transport	Data Unit Ctl	(Network Services)	4	N/A	N/A
3	Network Layer	Virtual and Explicit Route Control	Transport	Routing Control	Router Level	3	Group Level	Group Level
2	Data Link Layer	Transmission Group Control / Data Link Control	Data Link Control	Trunk Control / Data Link Control	Station Level	2	Link Level	Link Level
1	Physical	N/A	N/A	N/A	N/A	1	Physical	Physical

BNA: Network Services

IPA: Telecommunications Control

Appendix D CCITT Recommendations

X.26	Electrical characteristics for unbalanced double-current interchange circuits for general use with integrated circuit equipment in the field of data communications
X.27	Electrical characteristics for balanced double-current interchange circuits for general use with integrated circuit equipment in the field of data communications
X.28	DTE/DCE interface for a start-stop mode data terminal equipment accessing the packet assembly/disassembly facility (PAD) in a public data network situated in the same country
X.29	Procedures for the exchange of control information and user data between a packet assembly/disassembly facility (PAD) and a packet mode DTE or another PAD

Section 3 – *Transmission, signalling and switching*

X.40	Standardization of frequency-shift modulated transmission systems for the provision of telegraph and data channels by frequency division of a group
X.50	Fundamental parameters of a multiplexing scheme for the international interface between synchronous data networks
X.50*bis*	Fundamental parameters of a 48-kbit/s user data signalling rate transmission scheme for the international interface between synchronous data networks
X.51	Fundamental parameters of a multiplexing scheme for the international interface between synchronous data networks using 10-bit envelope structure
X.51*bis*	Fundamental parameters of a 48-kbit/s user data signalling rate transmission scheme for the international interface between synchronous data networks using 10-bit envelope structure
X.52	Method of encoding anisochronous signals into a synchronous user bearer
X.53	Numbering of channels on international multiplex links at 64 kbit/s
X.54	Allocation of channels on international multiplex links at 64 kbit/s
X.60	Common channel signalling for circuit switched data applications
X.61	Signalling System No. 7 – Data user part

X.70   Terminal and transit control signalling system for start-stop services on international circuits between anisochronous data networks

X.71   Decentralized terminal and transit control signalling system on international circuits between synchronous data networks

X.75   Terminal and transit call control procedures and data transfer system on international circuits between packet-switched data networks

X.80   Interworking of interexchange signalling systems for circuit switched data services

X.87   Principles and procedures for realization of international user facilities and network utilities in public data networks

Section 4 – *Network aspects*

X.92   Hypothetical reference connections for public synchronous data networks

X.96   Call progress signals in public data networks

X.110   Routing principles for international public data services through switched public data networks of the same type

X.121   International numbering plan for public data networks

X.130   Provisional objectives for call set-up and clear-down times in public synchronous data networks (circuit switching)

X.132   Provisional objectives for grade of service in international data communications over circuit switched public data networks

Section 5 – *Maintenance*

X.150   DTE and DCE test loops for public data networks

Section 6 – *Administrative arrangements*

X.180   Administrative arrangements for international closed user groups (CUGs)

Appendix E   X.25 optional facilities

Below are listed the optional facilities which are coded as essential in Recommendation X.2: *International user services and facilities in PDN.*

Packet retransmission facility A special *DTE REJECT* packet allows the DTE to ask the DCE to retransmit packets. The DTE indicates through the $P(r)$, in the Packet Header of the REJ packet, where the DCE should restart.

Fast select facility The fast select facility allows the communication of data between DTEs while using call set-up procedures without necessarily making the connection. The Call Request Packet and its related Call Indication Packet can carry up to 128 bytes of user data. The other DTE can, depending on the subscription parameters, answer with a Clear Request (Clear Indication) Packet or a Call Accepted Packet carrying also up to 128 bytes of user data.

Extended Packet Sequence numbering The option is available, on a DTE–DCE basis, between modulo 8 and modulo 128 sequence numbers.

Non-standard Default Window sizes Window size different from 2.

Default throughput classes assignment

Incoming Calls barred Prohibits on a DTE–DCE basis incoming calls.

Outgoing Calls barred Prevents the DTE from using the VC procedure.

One way Logical Channel outgoing Logical Channel that is only available for outgoing VCs.

One way Logical Channel incoming Logical Channel that can only accept incoming VCs.

Closed User Group (CUG) Allows DTEs to be put in a group context. DTEs within the group can only communicate with other DTEs belonging to the group. A DTE can be a member of different CUGs. It precludes the DTE talking to DTEs which do not belong to the group(s).

CUG with outgoing access The DTE belongs to a group as described before but can call on DTEs in the open part of the network.

CUG with incoming access The same as above but the DTE can now receive incoming VCs from the open network part.

Incoming calls barred within the CUG Precludes the acceptance of incoming VCs from DTEs within the group.

Outgoing calls barred within the CUG Prevents the DTE from initiating VCs to DTEs within the CUG.

Bilateral CUG Two DTEs have bilaterally to agree to communicate with each other and not outside.

Bilateral CUG with outgoing access Same as above but the DTE can initiate VCs to the open part of the network.

Reverse Charging The calling DTE requests the called DTE to accept the charges.

Reverse Charging Acceptance The called DTE can accept reverse charging.

RPOA selection Request authorized Private Operating Agency.

Other optional user facilities are still under study.

Glossary

In this glossary, all abbreviations that are used in the book are listed. Where necessary, the context in which an abbreviation is used is given in parentheses. In the index, the full term is normally used instead of the abbreviation.

A-record	Answer record (EHKP4)
ACF	Advanced Communication Function (SNA)
ACK	Acknowledge
ACKNUM	Acknowledged Message Number (DNA)
ACKSET	Acknowledgement Set (DCA)
ACTCDRM	Activate Cross Domain Resource Manager (SNA)
ACTLU	Activate Logical Unit (SNA)
ACTPU	Activate Physical Unit (SNA)
ADDR	Address Field (DDCMP)
AE	Application Environment (DCA)
ANSI	American National Standards Institute
ARPA	Advanced Research Project Agency
ASCII	American National Standard for Coded Information Interchange
BB	Begin of Bracket (SNA)
BBIU	Begin (first segment) of BIU (SNA)
BC	Begin of Chain (SNA)
BCC	Block Check Code (DNA)
BDLC	Burroughs' Data Link Control (BNA)
BINDF	Bind Failure (SNA)
BIU	Basic Information Unit (SNA)
BNA	Burroughs' Network Architecture (Burroughs)
BSC	Binary Synchronous Communication (IBM)
BTU	Basic Transmission Unit (SNA)
CCITT	International Telegraph and Telephone Consultative Committee
CCW	Channel Control Word (IBM)

CDCINIT	Cross Domain Control Initiate (SNA)	**CUG**	Closed User Group (X.25)
CDINIT	Cross Domain Initiate (SNA)	**CWI**	Change Window Indicator (SNA)
CII	Compagnie Internationale d'Informatique	**CWRI**	Change Window Reply Indicator (SNA)
CINIT	Control Initiate (SNA)	***D*-bit**	Delivery bit (X.25)
CLR	Clear Service Signal (X.28)	**DAF**	Destination Address Field (SNA)
CMDR	Command Reject (HDLC)	**DAP**	Data Access Protocol (DNA)
CNA	Communication Network Architecture (ITT)	**DB**	Data Base subsystem
		DCA	Distributed Communications Architecture (Univac)
CNS	Communication Network Support (ITT)	**DCE**	Data Circuit-terminating Equipment (CCITT)
COM	Call Connected Service Signal (X.28)		
COS	Class of Service (SNA)	**DDCMP**	Digital Data Communication Message Protocol (DEC)
CPMGR	Connection Point Manager (SNA)		
CPU	Central Processing Unit	**DEC**	Digital Equipment Corporation
CRC	Cyclic Redundancy Check	**DFC**	Data Flow Control (SNA)
CS	Communications System (DCA)	**DIS**	Draft International Standard (ISO)
CS	Communication Support (CNA)	**DKM**	DV-Strom Kontroll Modull (Data Communications Control Module) (LDS)
CSI	Code Selection Indicator (SNA)		
CSMA	Carrier Sense Multiple Acess (Ethernet)		
CSMA/CD	Carrier Sense Multiple Access with Collision Detection (Ethernet)	**DLC**	Data Link Control
		DLE	Data Link Escape (ASCII)
		DLP	Dienst Leistungs Prozess (LDS)
CSU	Communications System User (DCA)	**DM**	Disconnected Mode (HDLC)

DNA	Distributed Network Architecture (DEC)	**ENQ**	Enquiry (ASCII)
DP	Draft Proposal (ISO)	**ERI**	Exception Response Indicator (SNA)
DR	Definite Response (SNA)	**ERN**	Explicit Route Number (SNA)
DSA	Distributed Systems Architecture (CII–Honeywell–Bull)	**ERP**	Error Recovery Procedure
		ESC	Escape Character (BNA)
DSA	Destination Subarea (SNA)	**EXR**	Exception Response (SNA)
DSE	Distributed Systems Environment (CII–Honeywell–Bull)	**FCS**	Frame Check Sequence (HDLC)
DSE	Data Switching Equipment (CCITT)	**FDX**	Full-Duplex
		FI	Format Indicator (SNA)
DSTADDR	Destination Address (DNA)	**FID**	Format Identifier (SNA)
DSTNODE	Destination Node (DNA)	**FIFO**	First-in/First-out
DTE	Data Terminal Equipment (CCITT)	**FM**	Function Management (SNA)
DUC	Data Unit Control (DCA)	**FMD**	Function Management Data (SNA)
DVS	Daten Vermittlungs System (Data Transport System) (LDS)	**FMH**	Function Mangement Header (SNA)
		FNA	Fujitsu Network Architecture
EBCDIC	Extended Binary Code for Digital Information Interchange	**FRMR**	Frame Reject (HDLC)
EBIU	End (last segment) of BIU	**HDX**	Half-Duplex
		HDLC	High Level Data Link Control (ISO)
EC	End of Chain (SNA)		
EDP	Electronic Data Processing	**IA**	International Alphabet (CCITT)
EFI	Expedited Flow Indicator (SNA)	**IBM**	International Business Machines Corporation
EHKP4	Unified Higher Communications Protocol for Level 4 (LDS)	**ICL**	International Computers Limited
		ID	Identifier (SNA)

IEEE	Institute of Electrical and Electronics Engineeers	**LPM**	Logical Port Multiplexer (DCA)
IFIP	International Federation for Information Processing	**LSID**	Local Session Identification (SNA)
		LSM	Link Status Message (DNA)
INITSELF	Initiate Self (SNA)	**LU**	Logical Unit (SNA)
INWG	Inter-Networking Working Group (IFIP)	***M*-bit**	More-data bit (X.25)
		M-record	Message record (EHKP4)
IPA	Information Processing Architecture (ICL)	**MCS**	Message Control System (BNA)
IPC	Inter-Process Communication (BNA)	**MOP**	Maintenance Operations Protocol (DNA)
IPR	Isolated Pacing Response (SNA)	**MPF**	Mapping Field (SNA)
ISDN	Integrated Services Digital Network (CCITT)	**NAK**	Negative Acknowledgement (ASCII)
ISO	International Standards Organization	**NAU**	Network Addressable Unit (SNA)
ITT	International Telephone and Telegraph	**NC**	Network Control (SNA)
LAN	Local Area Network	**NCP**	Network Control Program (DNA, SNA)
LAPB	Link Access Protocol Balanced (X.25)	**NCP/VS**	Network Control Program/Virtual Systems (SNA)
LC	Link Control (CNA)		
LDS	Landesamt für Daten Verarbeitung und Statistik (State Institute for Data Processing and Statistics)	**NCR**	National Cash Register Corporation
		NDU	Network Data Unit (DCA)
LGN	Logical Channel Group Number (X.25)	**NIA**	Network Interface Adapter (SNA)
		NICE	Network Information and Control Exchange protocol (DNA)
LMS	Logical Message Stream (SNA)		
LP	Logical Port (DCA)		

NMS	Network Management Services (DCA)	**PRPQ**	Program Request for Price Quotation (IBM)
NSM	Network Services Manager (BNA)	**PS**	Presentation Services (SNA)
NSP	Network Services Protocol (DNA)	**PSN**	Packet Switched Network
NSPE	Network Services Procedure Error (SNA)	**PSTN**	Public Switched Telephone Network
		PTT	Post, Telephone and Telegraph
ODT	Operator Display Terminal (BNA)	**PU**	Physical Unit (SNA)
		PUS	Physical Unit Services (SNA)
OEM	Other Equipment Manufacturers	**PVC**	Permanent Virtual Circuit (CCITT)
OIM	Operations Interface Message (BNA)		
OSI	Open Systems Interconnection (ISO)	*Q*-bit	Qualifier bit (X.25)
		QEC	Quiesce at End of Chain (SNA)
PAD	Packet Assembler/ Disassembler (CCITT)	**RD**	Request Disconnect (HDLC)
		REJ	Reject (HDLC, X.25)
PC	Path Control (SNA)	**RELQ**	Release Quiesce (SNA)
PCNE	Protocol Converter for Native X.25 Equipment (IBM)	**REP**	Reply to Message Number (DDCMP)
PDN	Public Data Network	**RERN**	Reverse Explicit Route Number (SNA)
PDU	Port Data Unit (DCA)		
PFC	Port Flow Control (DCA)	**RH**	Request/Response Header (SNA)
PIU	Path Information Unit (SNA)	**RNR**	Receive Not Ready (HDLC, X.25, EHKP4)
PLM	Port Level Manager (BNA)		
PLU	Primary Logical Unit (SNA)	**RPQ**	Request for Price Quotation (IBM)
PPSN	Public Packet Switched Network	**RQD**	Request Definite Response (SNA)
PPS	Port Presentation Services (DCA)	**RQE**	Request Exception Response only (SNA)

RQN	Request No Response (SNA)	**SHUTC**	Shutdown Complete (SNA)
RR	Receive Ready (HDLC, X.25, EHKP4)	**SHUTD**	Shutdown (SNA)
		SID	Session Identifier (SNA)
RSET	Reset (HDLC)	**SIM**	Set Initialization Mode (HDLC)
RSHUTD	Request Shutdown (SNA)		
RTC	Routing Control (DCA)	**SLM**	Station Level Manager (BNA)
		SLU	Secondary Logical Unit (SNA)
RTFLG	Routing Flag (DNA)		
RTI	Response Type Indicator (SNA)	**SNA**	Systems Network Architecture (IBM)
RTR	Ready to Receive (SNA)	**SNAP**	Standard Network Access Protocol (DATAPAC)
RTS	Return to Sender (DNA)		
RU	Request/Response Unit (SNA)	**SNRM**	Set Normal Response Mode (HDLC)
RWI	Reset Window Indicator (SNA)	**SOH**	Start of Heading (ASCII)
		SRCADDR	Source Address (DNA)
SA	Subarea Address (SNA)	**SRCNODE**	Source Node (DNA)
SABM	Set Asynchronous Balanced Mode (HDLC)	**SREJ**	Selective Reject (HDLC)
		SSCP	Systems Service Control Point (SNA)
SAI	Sub Architecture Interface (DCA)	**STRT**	Start (DDCMP)
SARM	Set Asynchronous Response Mode (HDLC)	**STSN**	Set and Test Sequence Numbers (SNA)
SC	Session Control (SNA)	**SVC**	Switched Virtual Circuit (CCITT)
SCB	String Control Byte (SNA)	**SYN**	Synchronous/Idle (ASCII)
SCS	SNA Character String (SNA)	**TA**	Turn-Around (SDLC)
SDI	Sense Data Included (SNA)	**TC**	Trunk Control (DCA)
SDLC	Synchronous Data Link Control (SNA)	**TCE**	Transmission Control Element (SNA)
SDT	Start Data Traffic (SNA)		

TG	Transmission Group (SNA)	**UDLC**	Universal Data Link Control (UNIVAC)
TH	Transmission Header (SNA)	**UI**	Unnumbered Information (HDLC)
TN	Transport Network (DCA)		
TNC	Transport Network Control (DCA)	**VC**	Virtual Call (CCITT)
TPF	Transmission Priority Field (SNA)	**VR**	Virtual Route (SNA)
		VRN	Virtual Route Number (SNA)
TS	Termination System (DCA)	**VTAM**	Virtual Telecommunication Access Method (IBM)
TS	Transmission Services (SNA)		
TSO	Time Sharing Option (IBM)		
TWA	Two-Way Alternate (ISO)		
TWS	Two-Way Simultaneous (ISO)	**XBM**	Extended Basic Mode (IPA)
		XID	Exchange Identification (HDLC)
UA	Unnumbered Acknowledgement (HDLC)	**XMT**	Transmit (DNA)

Index

Match found 206
Maximum hop count 199
Measurement services 127
Mechanical standards 20
Message 12
    control system 193
    forwarder queue 200·
    header 149
    management 225
    number 152
        expected 152
Microelectronics 280
Minicomputer 217
Modem 10, 233
More-data bit 57, 61, 266
Multi-domain network 109
Multi-link 94, 259
Multidrop 10
Multiplexing 24, 72
Multipoint 10

N-layer 16
NCR 217
Negative acknowledgement 153
Negotiable bind 130
Neighbor table 197
Netchange 198, 208
Network 3, 6
    address 22
        in BNA 22
        in SNA 91
    addressable unit 85, 91
        services 120–131
        services manager 86, 120
    administration 221
    administrator services 187
    application layer 165
    control 87
    control program
        DEC 167
        IBM 83, 273
        BNA 192
    data unit 184
    definition language 193
    information and control exchange protocol
        167
    interconnection 259, 261, 272
    management 10
        in DCA 185
        in DNA 167
        in DSA 225
        in IPA 228
        in SNA 125
        in TRANSDATA 221
        services, area/global/local 185
    services 193
        manager 191, 206–209
        procedure error 129
        protocol 160

Network-connection 22, 77
Node 3, 22, 145, 219
    address 165, 204, 220
    administration 226
    initialization 207
    name 165, 204
    shutdown 208
Node resistance factor 198
Normal flow 106
Number of hops 157
Number of logical units in a node 103

Offer 204
One-way 25
Open 204
Open system 14
    interconnection 15
Operations interface 208
Operator
    agent 209
    display terminal 209
    services 128
Optical fiber 280
Origin
    address 101
    address field 93
    node 198
    node address 204
Other-data sub-channel 162
Outgoing call 53

Pacing 98, 107
    request indicator 108
    response indicator 108
Packet
    assembler/disassembler 255
        service signals 258
    in DNA 156
    length in X.25 61
    level 52, 244
    lifetime 159
    switched network 52
    switching 8
        vs. circuit switching 239
    terminal 52
    type identifier 57
Parallel channel interface 178
Parallel link 94, 197
Parallel session 84
Path 96, 225
Path control 87, 91–104, 225, 227
Path information unit 93
Peripheral node 88, 93
Permanent virtual circuit 52, 241, 244
Personal computer 285
Physical layer 10, 19, 242
Physical level 228
Physical link 225
Physical resource services 186